WILD ABANDON

The American wilderness narrative, which divides nature from culture, has remained remarkably persistent despite the rise of ecological science, which emphasizes interconnection between these spheres. *Wild Abandon* considers how ecology's interaction with radical politics of authenticity in the twentieth century has kept that narrative alive in altered form. As ecology gained political momentum in the 1960s and 1970s, many environmentalists combined it with ideas borrowed from psychoanalysis and a variety of identity-based social movements. The result was an identity politics of ecology that framed ecology itself as an authentic identity position repressed by cultural forms, including social differences and even selfhood. Through readings of texts by Edward Abbey, Simon Ortiz, Toni Morrison, Margaret Atwood, and Jon Krakauer, among others, Alexander Menrisky argues that writers have both dramatized and critiqued this tendency, in the process undermining the concept of authenticity altogether and granting insight into alternative histories of identity and environment.

ALEXANDER MENRISKY is a Lecturer at the University of Massachusetts Dartmouth. He teaches in the Department of English & Communication and the Honors College.

CAMBRIDGE STUDIES IN AMERICAN LITERATURE AND CULTURE

Editor
Leonard Cassuto, Fordham University

Founding Editor
Albert Gelpi, Stanford University

Advisory Board
Robert Levine, University of Maryland
Ross Posnock, Columbia University
Branka Arsić, Columbia University
Wai Chee Dimock, Yale University
Tim Armstrong, Royal Holloway, University of London
Walter Benn Michaels, University of Illinois, Chicago
Kenneth Warren, University of Chicago

Recent Books in This Series

184. HEIKE SCHAEFER
American Literature and Immediacy: Literary Innovation and the Emergence of Photography, Film, and Television

183. DALE M. BAUER
Nineteenth-Century American Women's Serial Novels

182. MARIANNE NOBLE
Rethinking Sympathy and Human Contact in Nineteenth-Century American Literature

181. ROB TURNER
Counterfeit Culture

180. KATE STANLEY
Practices of Surprise in American Literature after Emerson

179. JOHANNES VOELZ
The Poetics of Insecurity

178. JOHN HAY
Postapocalyptic Fantasies in Antebellum American Literature

177. PAUL JAUSSEN
Writing in Real Time

176. CINDY WEINSTEIN
Time, Tense, and American Literature

175. CODY MARS
Nineteenth-Century American Literature and the Long Civil War

(Continued after the Index)

WILD ABANDON

American Literature and the Identity Politics of Ecology

ALEXANDER MENRISKY

University of Massachusetts Dartmouth

CAMBRIDGE
UNIVERSITY PRESS

University Printing House, Cambridge CB2 8BS, United Kingdom

One Liberty Plaza, 20th Floor, New York, NY 10006, USA

477 Williamstown Road, Port Melbourne, VIC 3207, Australia

314–321, 3rd Floor, Plot 3, Splendor Forum, Jasola District Centre,
New Delhi – 110025, India

79 Anson Road, #06–04/06, Singapore 079906

Cambridge University Press is part of the University of Cambridge.

It furthers the University's mission by disseminating knowledge in the pursuit of
education, learning, and research at the highest international levels of excellence.

www.cambridge.org
Information on this title: www.cambridge.org/9781108842563
DOI: 10.1017/9781108909952

© Alexander Menrisky, 2021

This publication is in copyright. Subject to statutory exception
and to the provisions of relevant collective licensing agreements,
no reproduction of any part may take place without the written
permission of Cambridge University Press.

First published 2021

A catalogue record for this publication is available from the British Library.

Library of Congress Cataloging-in-Publication Data
NAMES: Menrisky, Alexander, author.
TITLE: Wild abandon : American literature and the identity politics of ecology /
Alexander Menrisky.
DESCRIPTION: Cambridge, United Kingdom ; New York, NY : Cambridge University Press,
2021. | Series: Cambridge studies in American literature and culture | Includes bibliographical
references and index.
IDENTIFIERS: LCCN 2020029380 (print) | LCCN 2020029381 (ebook) | ISBN 9781108842563
(hardback) | ISBN 9781108909952 (ebook)
SUBJECTS: LCSH: American literature – 20th century – History and criticism. | Human ecology
in literature. | Identity politics in literature. | Environmentalism in literature. | Ecology in
literature. | Literature and society – United States – History – 20th century. | Psychoanalysis
and literature – United States.
CLASSIFICATION: LCC PS228.H84 M46 2021 (print) | LCC PS228.H84 (ebook) | DDC 810.9/36–
dc23
LC record available at https://lccn.loc.gov/2020029380
LC ebook record available at https://lccn.loc.gov/2020029381

ISBN 978-1-108-84256-3 Hardback

Cambridge University Press has no responsibility for the persistence or accuracy of
URLs for external or third-party internet websites referred to in this publication
and does not guarantee that any content on such websites is, or will remain,
accurate or appropriate.

Contents

Acknowledgments		*page* vii
	Introduction: Modern Environmentalism's Identity Politics	1
	Ecological Authenticity and the Wilderness Narrative	4
	The Uses of Dissolution	13
	A Literary History of Environmentalist Identity Politics	21
1	The Ecological Alternative: Civilization, Selfhood, and Environment in the 1960s	27
	Selfhood and Civilization: The New Left and Beyond	31
	The (In)Authentic Anarchist: The Self in Postwar Environmental Writing	40
	The Spontaneous Society: Ecology and the Politics of Self-Liberation	43
	"Feeling Like a River": Edward Abbey's Subjective Uncertainty	48
	Social Ecology and Psychoanalytic Vocabulary	53
	The Superficial Self	55
2	The Entheogenic Landscape: Psychedelic Primitives, Ecological Indians, and the American Counterculture	59
	The Countercultural Psyche	63
	Peter Matthiessen's Psychedelics of Water, Wind, and Stone	67
	"The Hallucinogenic Oceans of the Mind" from East to West	74
	Psychedelic Primitivism's Presymbolic Myth	81
	Simon Ortiz, Oral Tradition, and Environmental Justice	85
	Narrative, Self, and Environment	92
3	The Universal Wilderness: Race, Cultural Nationalism, and an Identity Politics for the State of Nature	95
	The New Universalism: Environmentalism Beyond Natural Rights	99
	Cultural Nationalism and Racial Authenticity	105
	Racial Particularity and Ecological Authenticity: A Reflective Stalemate	112
	Toni Morrison's Skeptical State of Nature: Race, Gender, and Wilderness	118
	An Admission of Fabrication	124
	A Brief Comment on Community and Environment	128

vi   *Contents*

4   The Essential Ecosystem: Reproduction, Network,
    and Biological Reduction   133
    Surfacing's Identity Crises: Gender and Nature in the 1970s   137
    Depth and Nature Feminism   143
    "The First True Human": Narcissistic Fantasy and Material Complexity 148
    Depth and Network   152
    New Materialisms, Old Narratives   157
    An Appeal to Obliteration   164

5   The Death of the Supertramp: Psychoanalytic Narratives
    and American Wilderness   170
    Characterizing Chris McCandless   174
    Depth and Deep Ecology   177
    The Ascetic Superhero's Boast   181
    Into the Wild's Freudian Narrative   185
    Fatal Dissolutions   190
    The Neoliberal Wilderness   195

    Conclusion: Ecological Consistency   199

Notes   210
Bibliography   228
Index   243

Acknowledgments

I planted the seed for this book in childhood, but it was the tending of many other hands alongside my own that made its completion and publication possible. Quite frankly, the book simply would not exist were it not for the stalwart kindness and investment of Michael Trask and Virginia Blum, first and foremost. Their wide-ranging knowledge, argumentative insight, constant advocacy, and ambitious motivation (not to mention the sheer extent of their time and attention) have enriched this project beyond measure. I'm forever grateful for their mentorship.

The book is also indebted to numerous other mentors and colleagues who have helped me and the project to grow over the years. Randall Roorda played a formative role in its inception, Michelle Sizemore offered gracious guidance as I began to send it into the world, and Carol Mason advised me from point A to point B, from idea to proposal. Thanks especially to my colleagues Deirdre Mikolajcik and Kadee Spencer, who always agreed (even volunteered!) to read early drafts of both this project and others. Nicole Seymour has been a reader and supporter of my work since I, as a timid graduate student, invited her to participate on a panel at the Modern Language Association (MLA). I have too many other mentors and colleagues to thank, some of whom have directly influenced the writing of this book and others whose support has been important to the broader trajectory of my career, including Jan and Thomas Hodson, Bernhard Debatin, Jeremy Webster, Katie Waddell, Cate Gooch, Elizabeth Connors-Manke, Alan Nadel, Karen Little, Hannah LeGris, Emily Handy, Brittany Sulzener, Tess Given, Jenna Goldsmith, Daniel Cockayne, Elizabeth Lehr, Jay Zysk, Chris Eisenhart, Alexis Teagarden, Eric Casero, Travis Franks, Winfried Fluck, and Cindi Katz.

Ray Ryan first saw the project's potential as a book. Leonard Cassuto and a few anonymous readers helped to iron out the kinks. Edgar Mendez made the experience easy for a first-timer. To all the copyeditors, artists, and designers: I see you. The book would not have been as engaging to

viii   *Acknowledgments*

these readers were it not for conversations at meetings of the MLA, Association for the Study of Literature and Environment, Society for the Study of the Multi-Ethnic Literature of the United States, American Literature Association, Association for the Study of Psychoanalytic Thought, and Futures of American Studies Institute. In addition to presenting work at these venues, I published versions of material in Chapters 1 and 5 in *Criticism: A Quarterly for Literature and the Arts* (vol. 61, no. 1, 2019, pp. 51–71) and *ISLE: Interdisciplinary Studies in Literature and Environment* (vol. 26, no. 1, 2019, pp. 46–64). I am grateful to the editors and to Wayne State University Press and Oxford University Press, respectively, for granting permission to republish here. Two fellowships from the University of Kentucky also proved instrumental at the moment when I turned from dissertation to book.

Of course, writing a book is as much an emotional labor as it is a professional one. I am fortunate to have an expansive family, both hereditary and found. My parents Susan and Donald Menrisky saw me from one place to another more than once, easing logistical burdens that would otherwise have made work on this project delayed at best and impossible at worst. The pedagogical commitments of my sister, Natasha Menrisky, teach me much about what it means to be a teacher every day. My grandmother, Carol Howell, can likely be blamed for putting books in my crib to begin with. Erin Newell and Alyssa Sciortino prove the best intellectual conversation might take place outside of the university. Gina Edwards, Rachel Mihuta Grimm, Stephanie Fisk, and Rachel Collins redefine what it means to have a family. Jaclyn Bakalarski and Lainie Augensen extend that meaning back in time. Justin DeCamp and Katie Irwin perfect it. Link and Lilu purr-fect it.

The process of writing a book also tends to take on the grooves and contours of one's life as it is lived outside of that work. Perhaps I'm thinking magically, but the writing of this book mirrored (almost to the day) the ups and downs, ins and outs, and infancy and maturity that came with cultivating a different, far more important sort of narrative. For that, I can only thank Vince Dominguez, to whom this book is dedicated.

INTRODUCTION

Modern Environmentalism's Identity Politics

How can the individual self maintain and increase its uniqueness while also being an inseparable aspect of the whole system wherein there are no sharp breaks between self and the other?

Bill Devall and George Sessions, *Deep Ecology*

... nature loves the idea *of the individual, if not the individual himself ...*

Annie Dillard, *Pilgrim at Tinker Creek*

Twentieth and twenty-first century literature teems with scenes of dissolution, moments at which a text appears to erase individuals' sense of self-identity in natural environs. Few such moments have gripped the popular imagination more tightly than Jon Krakauer's 1996 account of a young man's disappearance in *Into the Wild*. In his journals and letters, as well as Krakauer's own narration, Christopher McCandless dismisses his self-identity in favor of identification with the ecosystem as a whole. His personal transformation does not merely reiterate the longstanding American wilderness narrative in which typically white male subjects depart a civilizational sphere (over here) for a natural one (over there). *Into the Wild* supplements that narrative's traditional distinction between nature and culture with a psychoanalytic one. McCandless abandons his civilized ego for an ostensibly natural unconscious. *Into the Wild* is neither the first nor the last text to rewrite the wilderness script as a story of dissolution. The dissolution motif characterizes numerous literary and political texts of the past fifty years, signaling a broader shift in the representation of nature and self in the late twentieth and early twenty-first centuries. Identity, not environment, is what we talk about when we talk about wilderness today.

Wild Abandon is about the cultural narratives that emerged when political radicals of the 1960s and 1970s joined ecology with psychoanalysis. I do not mean that environmentalists took part in postwar analytic institutions. Rather, I want to suggest that psychoanalytic thought furnished one among many vocabularies with which activists and intellectuals responded to the sudden shift in subjectivity occasioned by ecology's entrance to the political scene. Ecology first reached a lay audience in 1962, when Rachel Carson published *Silent Spring* and consequently inaugurated the modern environmental movement. That same year, the Students for a Democratic Society (SDS) drafted its *Port Huron Statement*, which announced the organization of a New Left premised on "natural" libertarian alternatives to the "artificial" liberal order of the postwar United States. Movement leadership often articulated this opposition psychoanalytically, in terms of repression, elevating self-liberation to the forefront of their program. Student radicals, as well as participants in the broader counterculture and successive new social movements, sought not only to arrange authentic political institutions but also to recover authentic self-identities. At the same time, the advent of ecology – a science devoted to the myriad biophysical interrelationships that both constitute and undermine individuals – presented a challenge to selfhood's apparent sanctity. For some radicals, however, ecology merely shifted the scope of authenticity. The New Left's psychoanalytic framework made possible an enduring logic that grounded authentic identity in the whole ecosystem rather than in the limited individual.

This book will argue that an interaction between ecological science and midcentury social theory gave shape to what I term an *identity politics of ecology* (IPE). Scholars in American and environmental studies customarily view the rise of modern environmentalisms (both mainstream and radical) in the context of the new social movements, the diversity of political commitments that proliferated in the late 1960s and early 1970s, from women's liberation to Black Power. Rarely does commentary address the possibility that such causes have at times taken identity, rather than environment itself, as their principal motivation. As I will argue, the partnership writers forged between ecology and psychoanalysis resulted in a uniquely universal account of identity. In this respect, *Wild Abandon* complicates the standard narrative advanced by social historians that the rise of identity as a social heuristic in the 1970s marked the gradual demise of psychoanalysis as a structural theory and the abrupt disintegration of political universalism. Even as various identity-based movements began to critique American liberalism and its pretense to universal scope in the 1960s and 1970s, radical environmentalists mobilized rhetorical strategies employed across racial, ethnic, and gendered activisms – specifically appeals to authenticity – to reinvigorate universalism as a political value.

Modern Environmentalism's Identity Politics

A considerable body of activist and intellectual discourse approached ecology not only as a material context that shapes conditions for social, political, and economic action, but also as an exceptionally inclusive identity position defined by shared ecological circumstances. Ecology's entry into mainstream conversation in the 1960s had radicals scrambling to account for the "connections, interchanges, and transits between human bodies and nonhuman natures" whose disclosure disrupted conventional narratives of selfhood.[1] When I refer to an identity politics of ecology, I mean any response to this conundrum, from midcentury to the present, that has contended that authentic identity inheres in the matrix of one's ecological interconnections rather than in culturally mediated identity positions such as race, ethnicity, or gender (whose social construction would render them merely artificial by comparison).

The IPE holds that to be authentic is not to claim discrete selfhood or even community affiliation, but to identify holistically with the ecosystem writ large. This appeal to *ecological authenticity*, as opposed to personal or community authenticity, stemmed from Movement radicals' general anxiety regarding American culture's potentially repressive functions. Widely read social analyses such as C. Wright Mills's *White Collar* (1951), William H. Whyte's *Organization Man* (1956), and the works of Herbert Marcuse informed a political culture intent on accentuating self-expression and fulfillment to overcome the oppressive normativity of preceding decades. Unlike the New Left and counterculture's commitment to personal authenticity, however, the IPE's commitment to ecological authenticity arose from a conviction that self-identity is merely another repressive formation to dispose of. Environmentalist gestures toward self-dismissal are recurring yet critically divisive fixtures of American literary and political discourse. Even so, the historical gestation and multidisciplinary appeal of contemporary iterations of that tradition remain largely unexamined. How do we account for their appearance in such divergent contexts as, for example, materialist philosophy and Instagram? We do so by observing that the writers who deploy such claims participate in the same cultural narrative. Rather than treat the IPE as a coherent movement, I understand it as a shared rhetorical tendency uniting disparate perspectives under a common appeal to ecological authenticity.

To frame ecology in terms of the narratives told about it is to consider the consequences of those narratives today. One of the IPE's effects has been a contortion of ecology (a deeply anti-essentialist concept) into a fixed identity position of its own, one whose claim to authenticity has denied the importance of the contingent identities we experience socially. The notion of fixed identity has been passé among scholars in the humanities for some time, but it survives in both mainstream and radical sectors of environmental thought, at the expense of people of color, women, queer folks, and others. Ecological authenticity flattens sociocultural distinctions, inviting a certain political quiescence, a neglect for the standpoints that make political action – environmentalist or otherwise – intelligible and necessary to begin with. It also influences critical practice in addition to mainstream representations of wilderness. For this reason, *Wild Abandon* presents something of a cautionary tale about our cautionary tales, a reflection on the historical premises and consequent fitness of certain narratives about who we are and what we must do in the face of environmental challenges. To this end, I turn to numerous representations of ecological authenticity across a variety of political and literary texts to trace the IPE's development and contestation over the past fifty years, drawing on diverse histories of social, ecological, and psychoanalytic thought to show when, where, how, and why modern environmentalists have fashioned their work as an identity politics. I attempt to be judicious in using (and scrutinizing) terms such as *ecology, authenticity,* and *nature,* which, though exhaustively overused (or misused), remain useful critical touchstones given their contextual cachet. To be clear, I am less interested in psychoanalytic or ecological theory as bodies of knowledge than I am in the way certain writers made use of ideas borrowed from them. To examine these influences side by side is to shift our understanding of environmental politics and representation in the twentieth and twenty-first centuries.

Ecological Authenticity and the Wilderness Narrative

Modern environmentalist writing, Dana Phillips notes, has often proceeded by "troping on a vocabulary borrowed from ecology."[2] Much of it has riffed on radical psychoanalysis as well. In the years following *Silent Spring*'s publication, New Left activists and countercultural icons sought to square ecology with existing radical commentary on postindustrial America. Such analyses often viewed psychic organization as inseparable from institutional conditions of oppression. The poet Gary Snyder observed this tradition closely when he mused that "there is a problem with the . . . human ego. Is it a mirror of the wild and of nature? I think not: for civilization itself is ego gone to seed and institutionalized in the form of the State."[3] Snyder's comment aligns the ego with "civilization" and an expansive, primordial non-ego – a lack of self – with the wild aspects of "nature," drawing an opposition between artificial and natural that

Ecological Authenticity and the Wilderness Narrative 5

corresponds to an opposition between "ego" and "eco," the self and the system. Environmentalist writers like Snyder profess not (or not only) that nature and culture are spatially distinguishable, as preservationists of earlier generations had done, but that both culture and our resulting sense of selfhood construct themselves too thickly over *psychic* nature, obscuring it. This sort of statement concerns neither ostensibly pure wild spaces nor ecology so much as it does identity.

The wilderness concept – defined by Greg Garrard as "nature in a state uncontaminated by civilization" – has played an important yet powerfully malleable role in American cultural history.[4] The idea's flexibility has enabled it to crystallize numerous political, social, economic, and environmental preoccupations and anxieties over the course of centuries. Remarks such as Snyder's demonstrate the concept's continued prominence in the age of ecology, despite ecological science's disruption of the notion that nature and culture comprise cleanly divisible spheres. Like psychoanalysis, ecology came to enjoy special prominence in the 1960s as a "subversive science," despite its descriptive rather than ideological aims. "Ecology," the philosopher Paul Shepard wrote in 1967, "has become an *in* word." Rachel Carson's exposé in *Silent Spring* divulged not that pesticides threaten a distinctively separate natural world, but that "substances of incredible potential for harm" reach consumers through a variety of ecological pathways in the city, the suburb, and the home.[5] As events such as the 1969 Santa Barbara oil spill hastened awareness of environmental catastrophe, ecology's pervasive, interpenetrative scope rose to the forefront of American concern. If wilderness or the wild had conceptually cordoned nature from the civilized and industrialized for environmentalists of preceding decades, Carson made clear that such an imagined barrier had always been porous.

Nonetheless, the concept of ecology has, like wilderness, experienced a certain "discursive elasticity that allows it to be used to structure the world in any number of ways."[6] The science of ecology describes very real material networks and interactions. Even so, such processes are subject to the mediation of interpretive cultural practices. Our understanding of material reality proceeds in part as a social construction, a situated perspective no less real for its fabrication over time. One could hardly disagree with the very basic premise that human biological functions fundamentally entangle us in complex and lively networks of matter. From a political perspective, however, there is something banal about the frankly obvious statement that "everything is connected."[7] Everything will remain connected if we preserve ecosystems or pollute them beyond recognition. Our actions depend less on the fact of our interrelated condition than on what Snyder refers to as our "rhetoric of ecological relationships," the narratives we tell about our interactions with nonhuman others.[8]

Without a doubt, conventional cultural histories of postwar American environmentalism have foregrounded those ecological narratives, typically distinguishing between mainstream and progressive paradigms. That is, environmentalism exists in a variety of modes or genres, each of which subscribes to a relatively recognizable set of representational conventions that scholarship in the environmental humanities has helped to illuminate. For example, among capitalist practices of "green consumerism" and traditional approaches to wilderness preservation, ecology plays the role of a natural "balance" that humans have disrupted but might yet fix, through either purchasing power or legislative restraint. By contrast, environmental justice coalitions have demonstrated how ecological change has disproportionately impacted communities historically disadvantaged along lines of race, class, ethnicity, indigeneity, and gender, casting both place and people as victims of capitalist exploitation. Recently, the looming threats and pervasive realities of climate change have inspired important work that joins elements of preservationist and environmental justice narratives under a global banner. These conventions change over time, find inconsistent expression, and, perhaps most importantly, exist side by side with other priorities and strategies. Still, without a doubt, they represent some of the most vital environmentalist traditions of the past fifty years.

At the same time, our familiar taxonomies of environmental thought continue to treat the wilderness concept predominantly as a *spatial* narrative about natural environments that exist in opposition to civilization. An account like Snyder's appears to maintain preservationist interest in untouched environments, but its marked investment in nature's relationship to the ego reveals a deep concern with authentic identity rather than, or in addition to, authentic environs. Scholars of American environmentalism have occasionally touched on this tendency in isolated instances, but not as a deeply ingrained cultural narrative that has continually surfaced across multiple contexts. Nor have they considered the possibility that the simultaneous emergence of ecology and personal authenticity as progressive values in the 1960s influenced the direction of environmental thought. Snyder's opposition between wild nature and civilized ego reframes wilderness not as an environment but as an identity category, a condition rather than a location. The revision is no accident. Representations of wilderness shifted over the course of the 1960s and 1970s in response to identity's rise to political prominence.

Ecological Authenticity and the Wilderness Narrative   7

Such a transition was only made possible by the long arm of what Doug Rossinow calls the American New Left's "politics of authenticity," the student movement's broad commitment to the liberation, fulfillment, and singular identity of the self. *Authenticity* remains an opaque term at best, its meaning having shifted routinely over its history of use. The word is poorly defined in the *Port Huron Statement,* despite the fact that the manifesto begins with a declaration that the "goal of man and society should be ... finding a meaning in life that is personally authentic." The term never found consistent definition, but as one activist wrote in 1962, "not systems or institutions ... but the person, in his totality, in his freedom, in his originality and in his essential dignity" remained "the ultimate and most irreducible value" across the Movement.[9] According to the New Left platform, the liberal establishment subdued the self in its perpetuation of oppressive social institutions, its willingness to police behaviors, maintain class inequities, and entertain the rampant anticommunism of the previous decade. Student radicals viewed the Marxist socialism of past generations with similar suspicion. "Humanity is estranged from its authentic possibilities," the psychiatrist and social critic R. D. Laing wrote in 1967, and from the New Left's perspective both postwar liberalism and the Old Left preserved a social environment "alienated" from "a natural system." Only direct democratic governance could liberate an overly managed population from the artificiality of a rigged party system beholden to corporate interests. Laing's contention that the "experience of oneself and others as persons is primary and self-validating" resonated with the New Left as powerfully as Herbert Marcuse's call for a "great refusal" of capitalist economic and political traditions. As Rossinow puts it, a stringent "opposition between the natural, or the 'real,' and the artificial" came to constitute "a kind of preface to any discussion of specific practices and values that ought to change."[10] As the call for liberation expanded beyond exclusively economic concerns, personal matters became, for a variety of movements, political.

The New Left, for whom social liberation was only possible alongside self-liberation, largely derived its program from a coterie of intellectuals who positioned authenticity, personal fulfillment, and direct democratic governance against the artifice of postindustrial civilization. Anthropologically speaking, civilization is a pluriform concept that changes according to context. As Chapter 1 will explore in detail, however, student radicals largely came to understand the idea of "civilization" according to a Freudian narrative that collapsed this diversity into an abstract totality: civilization set against a primordial, ostensibly pure psychic nature. Under the influence

8 Modern Environmentalism's Identity Politics

of thinkers such as Marcuse, the era's politics of authenticity drew disproportionate inspiration from a loose collection of social theorists who joined psychoanalysis with libertarian socialism in the 1950s and 1960s, a "Freudian Left" that also included Wilhelm Reich and Norman O. Brown.[11] A variety of postwar conversations circled around the social dimensions of repression, playing out among a diverse cadre of thinkers who opposed institutional ego psychology's fixation on producing "normal" individuals. Despite their criticism (as well as their differences), these figures all preserved certain psychoanalytic concepts in their work. In 1974, the feminist psychoanalyst Juliet Mitchell wrote that the "generalizable" features of Laing's writing established his popularity as "one of [the] chief spokesmen ... of the preponderant 'personalism' of 1960s radicalism." Laing and other psychoanalytic revisionists introduced "the radical counter-ideology of the restoration of 'whole' ... people" in response to "oppositional stereotypes of man/woman, sane/insane, black/white and so on."[12] However, the Movement's psychoanalytic influence often replicated the "oppositional" quality of such dualisms by merely replacing them with new ones: whole/not-whole, free/repressed, and real/artificial. The New Left never succeeded in defining "authenticity" in its founding documents, but its Freudian model gave shape to a pronounced, if inchoate, interest in liberating the repressed unity of the psyche.

The Movement viewed the ecological issues Carson introduced to a wide public as largely inseparable from this broader program of self-liberation – the "restoration" of "whole" subjects. That changes acted upon environments by the corporate state impacted human health seemed yet another social limitation on individuals' quality of life.[13] However, as concepts jointly applied to liberation politics, ecology and authenticity made contentious bedfellows. Their interaction in the 1960s coincided with Movement politics' visualization of authenticity specifically as "a state of unity with the self."[14] This standard of "unity" manifested in extravagantly inconsistent ways across the countercultural landscape. Student leaders at SDS broadcast their commitment to self-fulfillment even as other figures, such as countercultural drug gurus, preached a gospel of self-deterioration. "Unity" came to signify, by turns, the harmony of a discrete individual or of a holistic system in which the self seems to lose its integrity. Nowhere did this discordance prove more salient than in radical flirtations with ecology, whose disclosure of biophysical interconnections among organisms undermined the notion that there ever *could* be a singularly unitary self. The natural unity of the ecosystem would always trump the merely apparent unity of the self.

Ecological Authenticity and the Wilderness Narrative

In the New Left framework, this dilemma presented a moral as well as an ontological quandary. Among radicals of the student left, as well as the new social movements that followed, "political potential" proceeded from "alienation." For the mostly white members of SDS, however, feelings of *existential* alienation largely came to supersede the political alienation they located in people of color, which motivated identity politics along lines of race, ethnicity, and gender that emerged in the years to come. The spiritual undertones of the New Left's search for "wholeness" imparted a distinctively moralistic flavor to the politics of authenticity that dominated the 1960s. The authentic self was *right* and the social order that would repress, alienate, and/or exploit it was *wrong*. In seeming contrast to this creed of self-fulfillment, mainstream environmentalists of the decade preached a gospel of self-renunciation, of making do with less to protect the wilderness. Despite their apparent disagreement, though, SDS and preservationism largely obeyed the same moral logic: what is *unspoiled* is *right*.[15]

How does one reconcile the rightness of the unrepressed self with the rightness of a nature defined by its ecological intricacy? For a figure like Chris McCandless, one simply equates self with ecosystem. McCandless styles himself "free from society" and therefore unconstrained by a socially mediated ego.[16] There are spiritual undertones to these proclamations as well. They evoke the "oceanic feeling" that Sigmund Freud describes in *Civilization and Its Discontents* (1930), one of the many psychoanalytic touchstones that informed the New Left and counterculture. For Freud, beatific apprehensions of "limitlessness," of subjective continuity with one's surroundings, hark back to an earlier, infantile stage of psychic development, an originary inability to "differentiate between what is internal – what belongs to the ego – and what is external – what emanates from the outer world" that predates civilization and its repressions.[17] For Freud, the ego – the part of the psyche that registers a bounded sense of self – is neither a positive nor a negative thing. It simply is. For McCandless, however, the fact that selfhood is socially constructed renders it *unnatural*, an illusion that masks the "limitlessness" of our ecological interconnection. He pursues a fantasy of subjective merger with his surroundings because this state of affairs strikes him as natural rather than artificial, unspoiled and therefore *right*. As such, he preserves a certain moral investment in authenticity even as he expands authenticity to include all of the ecosystem. This fantasy of self-erasure in nature paradoxically positions the vanished (often white and male) self as the privileged subject of both environmentalism and a seemingly anti-identitarian stance.

I use the term *identity politics of ecology* to loosely capture any environmentalism that makes this move. The IPE invokes ecological authenticity by suggesting that because selfhood is socially constructed, the ecosystem as a whole comprises our most essential identity. Posthumanist philosophers have long noted that ecology disturbs the supposed inviolability of the human subject passed down by Enlightenment thought. Because the body houses microbes, absorbs nutrients, and nourishes the soil and other creatures with waste and decomposition, one cannot easily draw clear distinctions between self and environment. This premise ordinarily troubles the very concept of identity, but the IPE mobilizes it to recapitulate identity in essentialist terms. The machinations of what Marcuse referred to in 1955 as "repressive civilization" obscure the fact that we all share the same status as matter. That matter circulates ecologically. *Ergo*, the ecosystem is all of us. An appeal to ecological authenticity is in this respect always an appeal to *universal* authenticity, in that it flattens distinctions among individuals and communities into a single, unified identity position: the ecosystem. Sociocultural forms repress this state of nature.

A writer invokes the IPE any time he or she frames ecology in terms of authenticity as the Freudian Left and its acolytes understood it – that is, as a matter of psychic alienation. If selfhood emerges from civilization's repressions, then selfhood itself is responsible for our removal from a natural condition of ecological wholeness, a "unity" both psychic and material, "a state of oneness" that the analyst Harold F. Searles described in 1960 in terms of the billions of atoms that "make up our body ... second-hand."[18] The presence of psychoanalytic concepts in environmentalist writing is not merely a matter of coincidence. As Chapter 1 will explore in more depth, many New Left voices turned to ecological politics in earnest when the Movement began to fracture late in the decade, such that Left Freudian rhetoric transferred directly to environmentalist discourse. As new generations drew inspiration from their predecessors, those narratives spread. Paul Shepard explicitly built on *Civilization and Its Discontents* in *Nature and Madness* (1982), writing that the all-embracing breadth of the infant's "maternal relationship" is more inclusive of "living plants" and "unfiltered, unpolluted air." The historian Theodore Roszak sought to access an "ecological unconscious" buried "at the core of the psyche, there to be drawn upon as a resource for restoring us to environmental harmony." Murray Bookchin, the father of Marxist social ecology, denounced the Western valuation of "intellectual experience over sensuousness, the 'reality principle' over the 'pleasure principle,'" over the course of forty years. More recently, posthumanist scholars such as Rosi Braidotti have gestured to a "vitalist

Ecological Authenticity and the Wilderness Narrative   11

notion of death ... which frees us into life" and "disintegrates the ego."[19] Such passages take their cue from the same logic as Snyder. Not every iteration of the IPE employs an explicitly psychoanalytic framework, but the concept of ecological authenticity fundamentally rests on a Freudian structure that generates a series of corresponding oppositions between nature and civilization, real and artificial, whole and fragmented, *eco* and *ego*.

By articulating ecological interconnection as the subject of repression, the IPE makes of ecology a wilderness – one premised on a *psychic* distinction between nature and culture rather than a spatial one. Just as civilization obscures the putative wholeness of nature, the ego obscures an expansive, primary, *ecological* subjectivity. The texts examined in the following chapters illuminate the extent to which representations of wilderness after the 1960s accordingly function as meditations on identity's status in relation to conditions of ecological interconnectivity, rather than as reflections on pristine natural spaces.

This is not to say that environmentalism writ large has come to map itself over the IPE's assumptions. The IPE is one among many environmentalist traditions that emerged in the postwar era. Like these others, it is also a tradition that other political practices have shaped and informed. For example, the New Left's understanding of alienation emerged largely from the student movement's engagement with civil-rights struggles in the 1960s. Its rhetoric of authenticity developed in tandem with a racial politics whose leaders also articulated relationships between identity and the liberal establishment. Chapter 3 will consider how iterations of the IPE accordingly emerged in this context. Similarly, Chapter 4 will explore how the same psychoanalytic questions that gave shape to the IPE also played a role in feminist debates in the early 1970s. What I want to emphasize, however, is that the IPE arises concurrently with the cultural movements that produced race, gender, and ethnicity as models of identity with which we are more familiar, not in reaction to them. It emerged in tandem with these others at a chaotic and diffractive political moment whose participants nonetheless – and to an unprecedented degree – organized around widespread interest in questions of identity and attitudes regarding sociopolitical alienation. As a result, even as the IPE presents ecological authenticity as a pure, unmediated psychic condition, it inevitably reflects and recycles concerns and tropes that manifested across the political landscape, in many cases even directly overlapping with or proceeding from the same antecedents.

However, the IPE is not itself a coherent movement. Sometimes appeals to ecological authenticity define an entire oeuvre. More often than not, they merely complicate (and occasionally enrich) other modes of thinking identity or environment. One does not *join* the IPE, but rather *invokes the IPE narrative.* That narrative pops up in sometimes surprising places, often augmented by other political narratives depending on the context. The very idea of interconnection "implies separateness and difference." Even so, what Timothy Morton describes as the ecological "mesh" has evidently appeared tight enough to inspire numerous activists and intellectuals to invoke the IPE narrative in multiple venues from the 1960s to the present, from social and deep ecology to organic hallucinogen circles and even social media platforms of the past five years.[20]

Much excellent criticism has already been written on these traditions and their vicissitudes, strengths, and weaknesses. Any consideration of deep ecology, for example, owes a great debt to ecofeminist writers of the 1980s and 1990s such as Val Plumwood, Karen Warren, and Carolyn Merchant, who pointed out deep ecologists' tendency to emphasize total identification with the nonhuman and overlook other systems of domination, especially along lines of race, ethnicity, and gender. Plumwood is indeed one of *Wild Abandon*'s primary theoretical influences, given her attention to the antinomies inherent in deep-ecological rhetoric of self-transcendence. However, my aim is not to merely reiterate insightful analyses of deep ecology, neoprimitivism, or even the essentialist "nature feminism" that the ecofeminist Catherine Roach (pejoratively) distinguished from ecofeminism writ large. While I draw insight from these well-established critiques, and in some cases will outline their development, my goal is to supply a broader historical narrative of the discursive antecedents and cultural consequences of deep ecology's occasionally self-pulverizing rhetoric, rather than enumerate its philosophical liabilities. Placed against the backdrop of broader political trends of the late twentieth century, such apparent idiosyncrasies (often identified with deep ecology alone) emerge not as a rhetorical eccentricity specific to a single cohort or generation of writers, but as a vital facet of North American environmentalism's agonistic and pluriform development in the postwar era, whose effects continue to influence writing and activism today. An exploration of the role played in that ongoing evolution by widespread political appeals to authenticity, as well as their underlying psychoanalytic narratives, is precisely what I hope to contribute to established commentary.

The narrative of ecological authenticity that emerges, however, certainly does neglect the conditional identities individuals experience along lines of race, class, gender, and so forth (not to mention selfhood). An earnest identity politics of ecology would view such sociocultural matters simply as artificial aspects of civilization, despite the very real material conditions and effects that

The Uses of Dissolution

generate them and they in turn generate. Complex matters of sociopolitical struggle seem to vanish, for example, when Roszak entreats readers to willfully "become the Earth and all our fellow creatures on it."[21] However, such declarations often encode certain social differences even as they purport to transcend them. The proud, self-satisfied, even aggressive tone with which McCandless insists that sociocultural phenomena merely repress the reality of our ecological interconnection would even seem to announce the IPE as an environmentalist ethics of white masculinity – though I want to again be clear that it emerges concurrently with, rather than in reaction to, other traditions. The rhetoric of heroic self-effacement that often accompanies the IPE often recalls the bombast of New Left leaders eager to combat the "emasculation" of alienation with "a strenuous sense of self."[22] Such connections drive home the IPE's continuity with other political trends, and also emphasize the extent to which the very concept of authenticity, as Chapter 2 will explore in more depth, often functions as a tool wielded to enshrine the colonial attitudes of white men.

That said, I am less interested in tracing a hermetic account of the IPE's white masculine prejudices than I am in exploring the atmosphere of contention that has built up around it over time. Ecological thinking emerged at the same chaotic moment as the cultural movements that advanced race, gender, and other social indexes as models of identity. Accordingly, the following chapters accumulate around literary and cultural scenes in which appeals to ecological authenticity experience friction not only against parallel appeals to personal authenticity, but also against complex identity negotiations undertaken by marginalized peoples. The IPE presumes to transcend or eliminate social distinctions, but remains locked in conversation with the concurrent rise of identity politics among women and people of color, as well as with alternative accounts of subjectivity in general – a conversation that plays out in the literature of the era.

The Uses of Dissolution

Wild Abandon follows two closely intertwined paths. First, it traces the development of an identity politics of ecology across a variety of postwar institutions and environmentalist traditions. Second, it examines how a number of literary texts have staged conflicts between the notion of ecological authenticity and other conceptions of identity. They do so, I argue, by dramatizing the dissolution of the ego that the IPE calls for, thereby laying bare that narrative's representational and political dilemmas. The IPE presents ecological authenticity as the "natural" state of affairs, unmediated by social practice. Identity, however, has meaning in relation to the representations that constitute it. *Dissolution* – the moment at which a text appears to erase the self in favor of identification with the ecosystem writ large – is the IPE's chief representational strategy. It is also the motif by which literary texts illuminate that tradition's limits and contradictions. Dissolution, that is, serves as a nexus of debate over the relationship between identity and ecology. *Wild Abandon* is therefore in many respects principally a study of this recurring motif, undertaken to examine how a certain conflicted history of writing about nature has taken shape and met criticism in conversation with other social, political, and cultural preoccupations of the late twentieth century.

"Proposals to do away with the self," the critic Richard Poirier once wrote, have enjoyed a rich literary history "nearly as old ... as efforts to represent it."[23] Environmentalist expressions of dissolution also participate in a long, albeit undertheorized, tradition. *Wild Abandon*'s title references the almost capricious rejection of self-identity that characterizes the "epiphanic fusions with ... natural surroundings" that Ursula K. Heise, among other critics, observes in texts authored by "white male environmentalist writers between the 1950s and the 1970s."[24] The anarchist-environmentalist Edward Abbey, for example, felt himself vanishing into the sediment of the Colorado River Valley even as Left radicals found themselves caught between contradictory imperatives to self-fulfillment and ecological sacrifice. Such moments certainly deserve scrutiny, but the historically quick dismissal of dissolution as an unsophisticated expression of privileged retreat neglects its potentially critical aspects. At the very least, such a reading fails to account for the substantial presence and function of dissolution in writing by women, people of color, and queer individuals from the postwar era to the present. What does it mean when a Black man finds himself meshing comfortably with a forest in a novel by Toni Morrison? How did Simon Ortiz's poetic exploration of the Acoma Pueblo's intimate ecological relationships contest countercultural appropriations of Native cultures in the 1970s? Why does Margaret Atwood continue to write about what it would mean to identify solely with the body's biology? To what extent have so-called new materialists – scholars who assert the liveliness or vitality of matter – refuted or upheld the notion that ecology constitutes an identity position? Though any generalization comes with its exceptions, women and writers of color have tended to pen more critical narratives about the relationship between identity and environment than their white male counterparts. These instances complicate the conventional interpretation that expressions of dissolution only ever constitute an aesthetics of naïve holism. They suggest

The Uses of Dissolution 15

that the motif might also call into question attempts to define or experience identity according to ecological authenticity.

Wild Abandon as such demonstrates how dissolution operates as a system of representation in two registers: (1) politically, as a serious appeal to ecological authenticity; and (2) literarily, as a narrative experiment that dramatizes and critiques the premises of the IPE and arranges alternative narratives about our relationships with the nonhuman world. In other words, there is a difference between the IPE and dissolution. When I refer to the IPE, I am talking specifically about a loose (often white and male) environmentalist tradition that presents the ecosystem writ large as the most authentic of identity positions. Dissolution, on the other hand, is a system of representation – one that might signal *either* an appeal to ecological authenticity *or* a critical dramatization of the limits to that sort of appeal. Dissolution's critical function proceeds from two constitutive characteristics. First, it is always rhetorical, never actual. Even if one's sense of self appears to disintegrate, an "I" always remains to testify to that apparent disintegration. To take one oft-cited example, Abbey's account of "distinctions shading off into blended amalgams of man and man, men and water, water and rock" in *Desert Solitaire* (1968) exemplifies what Morton describes as the paradoxical project of achieving "ecology without a subject." "Even if 'I' could be immersed in nature, and still exist as an *I*," Morton writes, "there would remain the *I* who is telling you this, as opposed to the *I* who is immersed."[25] It seems unlikely, however, that the remarkably self-conscious Abbey could write of his self-erasure without recognizing his own hand in describing it. The passage expresses the sort of holistic identification characteristic of the IPE, but the project wavers and falls apart even as (in fact because) Abbey puts words to it. Dissolution relies on its expression, such that its second characteristic emerges from the first: it captures an unsurpassable representational tension between self and ecosystem, individual and network. "I" cannot eliminate my own self-conscious role in articulating my self-erasure. I can only illustrate the process of trying to do so. If political expressions of dissolution take for granted that one can, in fact, wipe away the self, literary uses expand the motif, unfolding it like an accordion, enabling us to observe its contradictions, tensions, and resonances with other accounts of identity relevant to a given context.

Of course, it would be negligent to claim that some clear, convenient line exists between obtuse environmentalist and canny author. Expressions of dissolution differ in degree, not kind. Where would one draw the distinction between the ecstatic urge toward merger expressed by the plant hallucinogen guru Terence McKenna, on the one hand, and the often-tortuous theoretical rumination undertaken by the deep ecologist Arne Naess, on the other? Or the carefully considered negotiation between identity with race and identity with place explored by Bell Hooks? Dissolution first and foremost performs the work of thinking through relationships between identity and environment. The way in which one deploys the motif – one's intention, context, style, and tone, as well as degree of self-reflection and complexity of engagement – has a considerable effect on whether one's writing seems to pin down identity as a matter of ecological authenticity or approaches the matter as a sort of literary thought experiment. The distinction I have drawn between dissolution's literary and political registers is a matter of rhetorical effect rather than categorical classification – a pair of poles between which the motif oscillates.

The principal question that guides this book's analysis is: *What cultural work is dissolution performing at any given moment, and why?* Furthermore, what do different iterations of this motif tell us about the relationship between ecological thinking and the variety of identity models that emerged concurrently? These questions invite literary study and also deeply resonate with issues raised by work in the environmental humanities, an interdisciplinary field whose own attention to the relationship between ecology and representation has in turn informed my approach to literary history. In her 2008 book *Sense of Place and Sense of Planet*, Heise identifies Google Earth as an "aesthetic model" for environmental writing of the late twentieth and early twenty-first centuries, a frame that straddles the local and global "in such a way that the user can zoom from one to the other." The "zooming" Heise describes, however, also characterizes a critical practice, one that she herself mobilizes by toggling from the "whole" to the "minute" and back again.[26] It strikes me that this scalar oscillation plays out discursively as well as geographically. To "zoom" between micro and macro to observe transits between them is also to shuttle between broad, "global" cultural narratives – about environment, about identity – and the situated, "local" representations that contribute to their constitution and/or contestation over time. To my mind, it is exactly this sort of critical movement that has fostered a productive relationship between literary and environmental studies to begin with. Environment and identity take shape in part through the representations by which we comprehend them. Close attention to the aesthetic conventions and innovations that constitute those representations is central to analyzing how our ideas about environment and identity have arisen, changed, and exerted material influence over time.

The Uses of Dissolution   17

Accordingly, the chapters that follow perform an oscillation of their own, in terms of both methodology and argument. Methodologically, the chapters alternate between two primary scales of attention. On the one hand, I gather threads drawn from diverse corners of sociocultural thought and activism – ranging from ecological philosophy and New-Age psychedelia to feminist dialogue and Black nationalism – to stitch together a more or less chronological narrative about the IPE, tracing its emergence and development as a recognizable tendency in environmentalist thought. In these moments, the book favors intellectual history, presenting an argument about the significance of concepts like environment and identity, informed by patterns I observe in the way certain ideologues expressed them. On the other hand, I "zoom" in on literary representations of identity in an environmentalist mode. I turn frequently to close reading to examine how different writers have deployed the dissolution motif to wrestle with the tensions between socially discrete (though always shifting) identity positions and material conditions of ecological interconnection. These two approaches complement each other. Environmentalist intellectual history enables us to grasp the macro-level cultural frames in which literary representation participates and to which it contributes. Critical methods of close reading facilitate our understanding of the micro-level conventions that structure – and potentially undermine – certain accounts of environment and identity, as well as their material effects.

To my mind, this oscillation between intellectual history and close reading makes possible *Wild Abandon*'s central insight: that the story of the IPE is itself a story of oscillation, of a back-and-forth between writers attempting to shore up a narrative of ecological authenticity and those questioning it. It is in this back-and-forth that we might observe the extent to which the IPE has grappled with myriad cultural influences that its rhetoric has sought to efface. The IPE presents ecological authenticity as an originary state of affairs, free of social baggage or mediation, but it borrows its framing techniques from a variety of concurrent identity politics and other social movements, as well as from psychoanalysis. Reading earnest appeals to ecological authenticity in conversation with the more thoroughly narrativized dissolutions that play out in the era's literary works helps us to tease out these obscured relationships. Such scrutiny also demonstrates how such texts stage critiques of the IPE's contradictions and political weaknesses. Novelists, memoirists, and poets of the era often appear to gesture toward the same subjective expansion that characterizes the more overtly political writing of the IPE, but they also give themselves the narrative space necessary to dramatize what an attempt to access ecological authenticity might look like. Not for nothing does this book begin and end with McCandless, who represents the IPE's culmination, its crystallization as a recognizable cultural form. However, as Chapter 5 will explore in more detail, *Into the Wild* plays out not as a celebration of this emergence, but as a conversation between McCandless's self-aggrandizing self-erasure and a more critical perspective espoused by Jon Krakauer, the book's author and narrator.

Each of the following chapters plays out as a sort of dialogue, at the center of which rests the dissolution motif. I arrange them as such to reflect the fact that the history of the IPE is a history of interactions – between the IPE and its literary interlocutors, and among numerous sociocultural preoccupations surrounding the status of the human subject. Edward Abbey exchanges barbs with social theorists who joined ecology with a psychoanalytic idiom, in the process drawing attention to the political contradictions inherent in that fusion. Simon Ortiz writes back against countercultural appeals to ecological authenticity by teasing out inaccuracies in the idealizations of Native cultures that underwrote them, as well as by foregrounding matters of environmental racism they effaced. In dramatizing dissolution, Toni Morrison points to how the representational conventions of the IPE mirrored those of race- and ethnicity-based identity politics, in the process illustrating what she takes to be the limitations of *all* such positions. Margaret Atwood writes in a climate of feminist debate over essentialism, some of which the IPE narrative in fact energized. I have selected these writers not only because each has expressed dual creative interest in the ontological and political dimensions of ecology and authenticity but also because the texts in question reflect upon the kind of thinking that informs the IPE. However, I do not view these works as representative of the IPE. They do not yearn for ecological authenticity. Rather, their diverse styles of dramatizing dissolution capture the complex cultural interactions that shaped the IPE, in the process undermining its pretensions to ideological purity and political merit.

Wild Abandon therefore aspires to a twofold objective: to better theorize and historicize the dissolution motif in order to both chronicle and contest the identity politics of ecology. Perhaps such an approach to literary environmentalism seems inappropriate at a time when critics such as Rita Felski, Sharon Marcus, and Stephen Best have called for modes of critique that emphasize "making rather than unmaking." Still, it is worth keeping in mind that writers and texts themselves might be just as "paranoid," to borrow a word from Eve Kosofsky Sedgwick, as critics.[27] The texts gathered in *Wild Abandon* look skeptically on the notion of ecological

The Uses of Dissolution

authenticity. However, even as their representational strategies invite critique of the IPE, they also arrange alternative narratives of human-ecological relationships. In this respect, I hope that my readings throughout this book demonstrate how critique might be generative even as it remains suspicious. Critique emerges as the condition for advancing counternarratives.

These counternarratives are no more cohesive than the IPE against which I position them. Nor are they merely counter*examples*. They emerge in tandem with ecofeminism, environmental justice, cultural movements organized around race and indigeneity – a whole variety of traditions that have informed, shaped, and clashed with the IPE. In the process, they foreground the fact that the IPE was only one of the directions that an emerging interest in the relationship between ecology and the subject could take. Generally speaking, however, the counternarratives I identify in these texts do have one thing in common: they investigate the extent to which pragmatic action, not idealized essence, constitutes just institutions, identities, and relationships.

This distinction governs the two registers in which I've proposed we read dissolution – the literary and the political – as well as its origins. The motif is indebted to a long history of "writing off the self," to borrow a phrase from Poirier. Ralph Waldo Emerson's comments in *Nature* (1836) that "I am nothing" and "the currents of the Universal Being circulate through me" especially come to mind.[28] Poirier and other readers have noted that in the context of Emerson's nineteenth-century transcendentalism, self-erasure fulfilled a deeply critical function that came to heavily influence the school of American pragmatism cultivated by William James, Charles Sanders Peirce, John Dewey, and others. The Emersonian tradition "tends to suggest that cultural formations, no matter how imposing, can be manipulated or transformed in ways sufficient to the individual." Writing off the self became, for Emerson and his descendants, a means of testing limits – of the self, of sociopolitical life, of culture and its institutions, of writing, representation, even language itself. It is an aesthetic experiment, designed to help us "measure how much in our present circumstance can be usefully worked upon and how much is perhaps irremediable."[29]

I want to suggest that dissolution's political and literary valences proceed by fracturing this philosophical inheritance. Nineteenth-century dissatisfaction with Enlightenment principles and industrial excesses influenced numerous twentieth-century reproaches to political and commercial standardization. It would be premature, though, to understand the IPE as a mere rehash of American Romanticism, at the very least because the notion of ecological authenticity would appear to erase the sacrosanct self so venerated by Romantic writers.[30] At the same time, the IPE upholds that tradition's impulse to posit nature and authenticity as correctives or alternatives to civilization, even if for the IPE it is not the individual who is authentic but the ecosystem as a whole. The IPE's political use of dissolution primarily retains this idealistic aspect of its American lineage, even as it dresses glorification of nature in ostensibly realist clothes cut from the cloth of ecological science. Political dissolution presumes to express one's recovery of a primordial state of nature – one that does not quite or never exactly did exist.

The IPE's literary interlocutors, on the other hand, tend to preserve the pragmatic function in their uses of dissolution. What I mean is that they often view identity not as an authentic essence buried beneath a spate of repressions, but rather as a series of what Kwame Anthony Appiah refers to as workable "scripts."[31] Identity, Appiah argues, is not a nature but a narrative, an assemblage of impressions, expectations, and adaptations that accrue over time. Identities and the relationships that constitute them are subject to change. Despite their great variety, the texts I examine find common ground in their shared attention to narrative's pragmatic role in articulating meaningful relationships among selves, communities, and environments. They give their dissolutions the narrative space to run their course, teasing out the representational tension inherent in the motif – the impossibility of divorcing an "I" from the self-erasure to which it attests. In the process, they draw attention to the variety of narratives in which "I" am bound up, testing boundaries between self and world yet also positing new ones that potentially enrich relationships with the nonhuman, generating rapport between claims to discrete selfhood and impressions of continuity with one's surroundings. In imaginatively engaging the essentialist logic of ecological authenticity, these literary representations of dissolution end up undermining it. Along the way, they invite readers to look skeptically on *any* argument "for affirmed selfhood and . . . unity" in a variety of conversations surrounding identity from the 1960s to the present.[32] Dissolution becomes a tool with which writers critique the idea of authenticity altogether.

Dissolution's political and literary registers turn on the difference between declaring what immutably *is* and suggesting what sustainably *might be*. These two perspectives furnish the stakes animating the conversation *Wild Abandon* traces between the IPE and its literary resonances. Appeals to ecological authenticity seek to dissolve the social "boundaries" that Donna Haraway describes as "the result of interaction and naming."[33] Complex, intersecting positions such as *woman, man, Black, white, Indigenous,* and *settler* do indeed take shape socially and historically – too often at the expense of those they describe – but to articulate these ideas solely in terms of artificiality is to ignore, devalue, or deny the material conditions and consequences of their emergence. The postwar writers I most closely examine distrust the privilege the IPE grants to "natural" identity not only because such essentialism has historically justified racial and gendered oppression, but also because it makes of ecology an "epistemological shorthand to speak and conceive of humans as a single, unified category." Particular identities "matter," Appiah writes, because "they give you reasons for doing things," even if "there's . . . disagreement about what normative significance an identity has." One loses those "reasons" for political action when one metaphysically lumps all matter into a single, indistinguishable whole. That humans are "'tackily' made of bits and pieces of stuff," Morton writes, should signal that the most ethical act possible "is to love the other precisely in their artificiality, rather than seeking to prove their naturalness and authenticity."[34] We need those "tackily" situated yet dynamic identities to articulate how best to live in relation to both human and nonhuman others in ways that ensure our continued collective existence.

A Literary History of Environmentalist Identity Politics

Comprehensive coverage of the IPE – not to mention its literary and sociopolitical interactions – would be an impossible task for a single book. By necessity, I focus on examples I find to be most illustrative, though I also attempt to acknowledge areas of contact that otherwise escape *Wild Abandon*'s scope. Over the course of the following five chapters, intellectual history tends to cede more and more space to close reading, as the story the book tells progresses from establishing the IPE's roots in radical psychoanalysis to teasing out how a variety of writers have staged conflicts between ecological authenticity and other accounts of identity, in the process undermining the IPE. The two paths traced by the book proceed accordingly, charting the IPE from its birth in discursive interactions between ecology and psychoanalysis through its consolidation in rhetoric of ecological authenticity to its saturation of the American wilderness myth. Along the way, I argue that literary texts challenge the IPE by asserting identity's narrative rather than essential quality and insisting on that narrativity for political and physical survival.

22 Modern Environmentalism's Identity Politics

The first chapter, "The Ecological Alternative: Civilization, Selfhood, and Environment in the 1960s," begins where the IPE does: with the intersection of appeals to ecology and authenticity among the New Left's environmentalist affiliates. It also introduces how literary uses of the dissolution motif in fact critique this sort of alliance by dramatizing its contradictions. Edward Abbey illuminates how radicals unintentionally undermined their own project of self-fulfillment when they brought these two values together. New Left sympathizers increasingly dipped their toes into the rising waters of modern environmentalism as the Movement began to fracture toward the end of the 1960s. Some began to structure their plans for the alternative social formations demanded by SDS according to ideas borrowed from ecological science. For many involved with the back-to-the-land movement, Murray Bookchin's social ecology furnished an attractive philosophical framework on which to construct their alternatives. However, Bookchin's writing, like that of the New Left's primary theoretical influences, drew substantially on a psychoanalytic narrative that, when grafted to ecology, would frame the ecosystem as a wilderness divorced from civilization and dissolve the self prized so highly by student radicals. Abbey documented this subjective confusion as he outlined his own wilderness alternative in *Desert Solitaire*. Once Abbey adopts ecological principles as laws and social customs, his conception of himself as an autonomous subject begins to collapse. Far from uncritically celebrating nature's purity, Abbey and other nature writers of the decade established the representational tension between self and system that would characterize postwar literary treatment of ecology.

Chapter 2, "The Entheogenic Landscape: Psychedelic Primitives, Ecological Indians, and the American Counterculture," examines how figures across the American counterculture, and later the New Age, appealed to ecological authenticity to sustain the idea that dissolution provides access to an originary identity with the ecosystem. This notion formed the backbone of two prevalent experiments in "consciousness expansion" – psychedelic drug tests and primitivist flirtations with East Asian and Native American spiritualities – that dominated the countercultural scene. These fads dovetailed in ecological meditations such as Peter Matthiessen's *The Snow Leopard* (1978), which foregrounds the extent to which both traditions drew on the same psychoanalytic source material that informed the New Left's early appeals to ecological authenticity. At the same time, they also derived inspiration from Native valuations of environment that they nonetheless drastically oversimplified, in the process erasing the very peoples they idealized. A number of predominantly white gurus employed a shaky

A Literary History of Environmentalist Identity Politics 23

psychoanalytic vocabulary to claim that, like infants, Indigenous peoples lack the advanced symbol systems Western civilization erects as a screen against ecological authenticity. By evaporating linguistic faculties, psychedelic substances served as a threshold into an expansive psychic condition that Indigenous communities had ostensibly enjoyed for millennia. Native writers such as Simon Ortiz have long argued that colonial projections of authenticity obscure Native peoples' lived sociopolitical and environmental conditions. Ortiz's *Woven Stone* (1992) clarifies the extent to which countercultural appeals to ecological authenticity misinterpret the perspectives they appropriate, and points to how language and narrative construct and enrich ecological affiliations rather than obscure them.

Chapter 3, "The Universal Wilderness: Race, Cultural Nationalism, and an Identity Politics for the State of Nature" does not explore as many political expressions of dissolution as the previous two chapters. Rather, it asks us to think about how appeals to ecological authenticity might constitute their own form of identity politics by situating them in relation to more familiar identity movements that emerged simultaneously with modern American environmentalism. Toni Morrison's *Song of Solomon* (1977) facilitates this kind of assessment. The novel pointedly juxtaposes two characters: one who caricatures the era's Black nationalism and one who experiences dissolution in the Appalachian foothills. This arrangement effects a comparison between two accounts of authenticity: the racial and the ecological, the particular and the universal. In so doing, it enables us to consider how appeals to ecological authenticity, despite their pretense to ideological purity and universalist assumptions, rely on ideas about alienation and authenticity that mirror and often derive from the reasoning that typified movements organized along race or ethnicity. While such appeals are of a piece with the political climate, participating in broader conversations regarding identity and its social variation, the IPE denies such difference, joining the rhetoric of authenticity that characterized Red and Black Power, for example, with the sort of political universalism that such movements called into question. *Song of Solomon* also represents ecology as a universal condition that destabilizes the divisiveness of identity politics. All the same, Morrison critiques this specific state-of-nature romance for its indifference toward social realities. The IPE, like other wilderness narratives, might serve only to enshrine as universal the colonial attitudes of white men, in that it erases women and people of color – even those whose perspectives and politics inform it.

Chapter 4 flips this script and considers how the IPE itself influenced other forms of identity politics. "The Essential Ecosystem: Reproduction, Network, and Biological Reduction" begins with the debate between "nature feminists" who appeal to biology as the basis of essential woman-hood and critical ecofeminists and feminists of color who have found this appeal wanting. Nature feminists contributed one voice among many to feminist debates surrounding essentialism in the 1970s and 1980s, central to which were questions about psychoanalysis similar to those that animated the IPE. The IPE narrative became bound up in this debate as nature feminists claimed their reproductive capacity identified them with whole ecosystems. Margaret Atwood's *Surfacing* (1972) dramatizes how this logic actually undermined the woman-centric position these feminists sought to maintain. The novel's narrator attempts just such an identification with her reproductive capacity, but her identification with her bodily matter broadens her idea of reproduction to include all corporeal functions, from nutrient consumption to decomposition. This fixation on network disorients gender, just as the IPE narrative did for nature feminists. However, far from undermining identity, it also illuminates the extent to which social thought has at times rendered whole systems a matter of essentialism. Reading *Surfacing* alongside Atwood's later work, I draw out lines of rhetorical continuity between the essentialist "all women" position in nature feminism and a potential "all matter" position in contemporary new-materialist writing. *Surfacing* ends with its narrator's embrace of an ambivalent conception of subjectivity, not least because she notices a certain nihilism in her identification with the network. Total merger would require her death – her matter's dispersal.

This fate looms large in *Into the Wild*, whose subject, Chris McCandless (as well as his cult following) is the focus of Chapter 5, "The Death of the Supertramp: Psychoanalytic Narratives and American Wilderness." This chapter drives home the extent to which the IPE constitutes a certain political quiescence, in that its erasure of sociopolitical differences also eliminates reasons to care about ecological changes – including threats to our continued survival. It also suggests that the IPE narrative has largely come to redefine mainstream representations of wilderness. McCandless believes that he might access an originary yet repressed ecological authenticity, taking to an extreme a tendency among his contemporaries in the deep ecology movement to map subjectivity over the contours of the ecosystem. Ultimately, he does the most authentically ecological thing possible: he dies. Krakauer's account demonstrates how psychoanalytic narratives persist in contemporary wilderness rhetoric, despite the decline of the Freudian Left's influence in the late twentieth century. McCandless's death stems from his profound conviction that his civilized ego – the self-identity that gives him reason to stay alive – has repressed his

A Literary History of Environmentalist Identity Politics   25

natural condition. Still, this representation of wilderness has nonetheless enjoyed great commercial power. To partake of wilderness in the twenty-first century is no longer only to consume recreational or even spiritual spaces. It is to consume a certain identity that asks its consumers to disappear, defanging the IPE of whatever radicalism it once presumed.

The identity politics of ecology shaped a renewed conception of wilderness – nature not as environment but as fixed, universal identity category – that finds its apotheosis in McCandless. To the extent that *Into the Wild* serves as a cautionary tale, *Wild Abandon* ends on the contention that an IPE is not only impossible to sustain but also politically undesirable. This conclusion's stakes remain high given that the questions animating the IPE govern contemporary scholarship as well as mainstream representations of wilderness, as the last two chapters of this book demonstrate. The conversation *Wild Abandon* traces plays out over the status of the human subject, a point that situates much of the writing I study in the arena of post-humanist debate *avant la lettre*. Work in new-materialist philosophy, queer ecologies, and material ecocriticism circles around questions regarding the subject's role in vital networks, its material heft or ephemerality, and the ontological and epistemological forces that center and decenter it. These contemporary paradigms are not the focus of this book, but I do hope to shed light on some of their intellectual antecedents. The decentering of the human that such interventions undertake often proceeds from the IPE's theoretical justifications and rhetorical appeals. At the same time, many scholars working in these fields take their brief from feminist and critical race theory that seeks to *re*center the subject's political agency – projects that emerge from a number of the countertraditions that crop up in the following chapters. Chapters 2 and 3, for example, show how environmental justice emerged out of the same crucible that produced the IPE in the 1960s and 1970s, just as Chapter 4 submits the IPE to more complex and critical modes of ecofeminism and materialism that consider the same questions. *Wild Abandon* demonstrates how current engagements took shape in part as an effect of the conversation surrounding the IPE's decentering of the human – its dissolution.

That conversation also gave rise to a literary tradition whose imaginative flirtation with the IPE narrative briskly discredits authenticity altogether. Assuming an anti-essentialist stance, these texts acknowledge ecological interconnection as a universal condition, but also maintain the necessity of socially mediated identity positions from which to recognize and act on that condition. In these narratives, dissolution's power lies in its failure – in selfhood's pragmatic recoherence. Boundaries remain contingent and ever-shifting, built of action and relation rather than essence, but they grant one a position of situated identity from which to articulate a stake in how the world changes. These narratives suggest not only that dissolution always disappoints, but that such defeat is *beneficial*. If one takes too seriously one's ecological authenticity, the best one can hope for is a satisfying death, a physical means of complete dispersal throughout one's ecosystem. With that as our goal, what would be the point of either politics or literature? Keeping this question in mind, *Wild Abandon* ends with a consideration of how our current reading practices might help or hinder environmentalist goals. Rather than read our narratives suspiciously as symptoms or naïvely as affirmations of ecological authenticity, we should read them for what they are: complex cultural negotiations that have made our engagements with the nonhuman universe meaningful, effective, and worth pursuing.

CHAPTER I

The Ecological Alternative
Civilization, Selfhood, and Environment in the 1960s

What we call wildness is a civilization other than our own.
Henry David Thoreau's *Journal*

". . . civilization needs us."
"What civilization?" he says.
"You said it. That's why they need us."
Edward Abbey, *Desert Solitaire*

The United States celebrated the first Earth Day on 22 April 1970, bringing to fruition a 1969 proposal by Wisconsin senator Gaylord Nelson for a "National Teach-In on the Crisis of the Environment" at a Seattle symposium. In emulating the teach-ins of the Vietnam War protests, Earth Day looked to the New Left and associated radical movements for its program. Nelson, however, intended for this comparatively moderate curriculum to dissociate the event from the confrontational politics by which it was partially inspired.[1] The New Left in turn sought to distance itself from Earth Day and the environmentalist label attached to it. For many in the Movement, environmentalism carried associations with population control and urban-elite wilderness protection. As one student radical wrote in the January 1970 issue of *Liberation*, mainstream environmentalists, "increasingly motivated and supported by various governmental machinations," deny that "the deterioration of the natural environment all around us is . . . clearly a product of the nature of production and consumption, of cultural values and social relationships that today hold sway over industrial technological society – American or Soviet." The essay's author, Barry Weisberg, feared Earth Day especially would direct attention away from structures of domination toward individual lifestyle choices. Any successful environmentalist politics, he argued, must proceed from the New Left line that "the precondition for our survival requires the most basic transformation of the cultural, social, political and economic

27

mentalities and structures which dominate the developed nations."[2] Just as the environmental movement began to achieve some kind of national shape, the strong influence it found in the New Left started to recede amidst the ambivalent motivations of Earth Day's sponsors and participants.

Still, despite the New Left's retreat (and its concurrent collapse), much of its theoretical infrastructure – especially its psychoanalytically charged "great refusal" – remained influential to environmentally minded writers. Two states over from Earth Day's home in Washington, Edward Abbey appeared in Logan, Utah, at the event's iteration to advocate for just such a rejection of the status quo. The teach-ins marked the first nationwide organization of individuals concerned about the environment, and the moment clearly delineated an audience for Abbey's writing. If *Silent Spring* provided the movement's brain, Abbey's *Desert Solitaire* (1968) offered environmentalists an often-bleeding, anti-establishment heart.[3] Like his contemporaries in the New Left, however, Abbey viewed mainstream environmental groups as impotent at best, especially in their willingness to compromise one wilderness area to save another (the fate that befell Abbey's beloved Glen Canyon). Abbey fortified his own environmentalism with radical direct action, monkeywrenching or "ecotage," the very sort of "militant action against corporate despoilers" that Weisberg also called for in his *Liberation* article.[4] Abbey's 1975 novel *The Monkeywrench Gang* even inspired the formation of the eco-saboteur network Earth First! Abbey's life during this period of unrest, however, reads more like a record of absence than a testament to leftist revolution. Two weeks after Earth Day, Abbey rafted down the Colorado River on 4 May 1970 – the day the National Guard opened fire on and killed four students at Kent State University in Ohio.[5] He was fire spotting in a remote region of the country during the 1968 Democratic National Convention riots in Chicago, and would have been unlikely to march with student radicals even if he hadn't been. Abbey's friend and fellow environmentalist Wendell Berry notes that Abbey was "hard" on "movements": "the more solemn and sacred they are, the more they tempt his ridicule." One might read his derision as a symptom of his anarchist persuasion, which often led him to articulate what he fought against more frequently than what he fought for.[6]

This predisposition, however, also informs Abbey's gleeful capacity for contradiction, his willingness to narrate incongruities underlying leftist fantasies as he experienced them, without rejecting them wholesale. Abbey's pattern of irreverence subjected to scrutiny numerous aspects of Movement politics, in the process calling into question their implications for environmental thinking. In *Desert Solitaire* he engages two of the New Left's most consistent characteristics: its policy of direct governance and its emphasis on a politics of authenticity. The New Left never established a coherent platform, but over the course of the 1960s Students for a Democratic Society (SDS) increasingly emphasized what its National Secretary, Gregory Calvert, referred to in a 1967 speech as "the recognition of one's own unfreedom . . . in the struggle of the oppressed." What began as a movement committed to addressing the sociopolitical dispossession of the poor and especially of Black Americans, in partnership with organizations such as the Student Nonviolent Coordinating Committee (SNCC), transitioned into a campaign dedicated to voicing how its own members experienced such alienation at the level of the psyche as well as of politics. Despite the Movement's ever-shifting priorities, Herbert Marcuse's "great refusal" came to consistently assume "the significance of freedom and of human liberation . . . in a context in which both the economic system and social institutions gradually tend . . . to invade and define every aspect of citizens' lives, restricting the fundamental rights of self-realization." To liberate society's "natural system" would also be to excavate what Calvert referred to as "human potentiality" – the authentic individual.[7]

Reading Abbey in this context clarifies the extent to which SDS-adjacent environmentalists reproduced this commitment to authenticity – and along with it, the psychoanalytic narratives that underwrote the New Left's understanding of the idea. That legacy occasioned a certain subjective confusion in environmentalist writing of the period, an uncertainty as to where one should locate authenticity – in the self or in the system – that emerged alongside radical environmentalists' use of psychoanalytic thought. It also played out in narrative form in literary environmentalism by writers such as Abbey. This chapter examines both lines as they extend from the same source in New Left social thought, with particular attention to how Abbey dramatizes the contradictions that unfold at the intersection between ecology and psychoanalysis in political writing by his peers. In other words, reading Abbey alongside his political resonances illuminates the birth of appeals to ecological authenticity, as well as a literary tradition that dramatizes and undercuts them.

Abbey's own, seemingly apolitical stance serves as an interesting counterpart to the New Left treatment of every aspect of American life as political. According to his friend Jack Loeffler, Abbey had over the course of the 1960s come to believe that American culture was "lodged completely in an economically dominated paradigm" and that the American legal system functioned "to define and defend the economic system."[8] His nonfiction corpus chronicles nothing if not his own great refusal, especially given that he shared Marcuse's muted Marxist pedigree. Abbey's father observed an anticorporate communism that informed Abbey's own graduate thesis in philosophy, "Anarchism and the Morality of Violence," in which he interpreted social theorists such as Erich Fromm and C. Wright Mills as contemporary proto-anarchists. Writers such as Mills provided for Abbey – as they did for Marcuse and the student left – fresh vindication in his certainty that a state of freedom did indeed exist beneath layers of technocracy. Abbey was a *social* anarchist, one who attempted a "withdrawal from politics in an effort to ... liberate natural man" and who strongly believed such liberation is possible only in a collective fight against industry and its marriage to the state. The seemingly anomalous combination of his apparently right-wing "libertarian individualism" and left-wing "emphasis on mutual aid," however divisive by today's ideological standards, aptly characterized the New Left's intertwined commitments to individual liberation and social transformation. Abbey saw little point in "being personally whole in a dismembered society."[9] For him, as well as for his counterparts, freedom – from repression and oppression – would come about in both individual and sociocultural registers.

Desert Solitaire accordingly frames the desert as an *alternative*, in the sense in which the New Left popularly made use of the word. As early as the *Port Huron Statement*, SDS proclaimed its "initial task in establishing alternatives," later calling for "an alternative political structure of 'American democracy'" the very same year that *Desert Solitaire* hit the shelves.[10] However, though Abbey shared the New Left's intellectual lineage and commitment to social reorganization, he remained ambivalent regarding authenticity's utility as a political value. He especially troubled the idea's relevance to environmental matters, even as radicals such as Weisberg came to increasingly articulate revolution according to ecological concepts. The nascent anarcho-Marxist social ecology proposed by Murray Bookchin especially inspired radicals to approach ecology as a conceptual tool that could restore an unspoiled, ostensibly natural sociopolitical system. This chapter advances two closely intertwined arguments related to these trends. First, I contend that, when welded to an ecological paradigm, the rhetoric of authenticity deployed by utopian liberation discourse of the 1960s ultimately collapsed distinctions between individual and ecosystem, troubling its project of self-fulfillment. The rough equivalence drawn by early social ecologists between liberated society and the free "self-determination" of nature, for example, often unintentionally engendered the sort of boundary confusion that came to inform expressions of ecological authenticity. Second, I read Abbey

Selfhood and Civilization: The New Left and Beyond 31

against this backdrop to suggest that, far from uncritically celebrating nature's purity, nature writers of the era crystallized this confusion as a representational tension between self and system that results from the commingling of appeals to authenticity and ecology.

Despite Abbey's anarchic commitment to direct action fueled by individual liberty, which aligned him with New Left politics in deed if not in name, Abbey flouted the New Left's "self-assured" assumption of "the existence of an undisputed referent" – a pure state of natural selfhood and governance.[11] In his writing, he especially questions the usefulness and even desirability of authenticity politics for environmentalism. In the sections that follow, I first explore some of the ways in which New Left politics and ecological thinking began to mingle, as well as how Abbey's commitment to self-fulfillment overlapped with that of his Movement contemporaries, who relied on a psychoanalytic account of the ego's liberation from repression. I then examine how he also similarly sought to articulate a "natural" form of social organization – an ecological alternative to the postindustrial state – that would enshrine a corresponding "natural" sense of self. For Abbey, however, the scope of "natural" self-identity steadily became less clear. Over the course of *Desert Solitaire*, he oscillates between what he presents as the solidity of personal identity – his uniquely belligerent attitude, pride in self-reliance, and integrity in the face of commodity culture – and a fuzzy sense of holistic identification with the ecosystem writ large. Because of its ecological orientation, this second identification strikes Abbey as more "natural" than his socially mediated persona, an observation that implies environmentalist narratives of authenticity write off the self rather than liberate it. As a result, Abbey performs an unexpected yet compelling critique of authenticity's rhetorical usefulness to early social ecologists and New Left environmentalists, and in so doing documents the first stirrings of an embattled identity politics of ecology.

Selfhood and Civilization: The New Left and Beyond

As Abbey stepped up to the microphone to greet Logan's Earth Day assembly, Murray Bookchin addressed a similar crowd in Ann Arbor, Michigan. Bookchin's attendance concluded a decade spent proselytizing ecology's importance to New Left and counterculture leadership, partners Bookchin then found indispensable to the project he came to formulate as social ecology. The distinctive feature of the New Left lay in the stress it placed on "the *utopian* aspects of the 'American dream' as distinguished from its *economic* aspects." A properly new, homegrown left would potentially overcome the difficulties the old, "exogenous" left had in meshing with uniquely American individualistic sensibilities. For Bookchin, the *Port Huron Statement* was "the most authentically American expression of a new radicalism," one that retained the socialist foundation of the Old Left but whose participatory vision recommended a "potentially libertarian or anarchic" character. The "almost formless and erratic" counterculture, on the other hand, emphasized communal living, sexual emancipation, and "alternative diets," all of which "congealed into a distinct ... outlook, but one that was far more mystical than political." Bookchin's explicit intention during the 1960s was to bring the two together, "to infuse the counterculture with political radicalism and, in turn, to infuse the New Left with the counterculture's utopianism."[12] Ecology – and what Bookchin viewed as its utter disruption of all forms of hierarchy – would be the communalistic glue that held the union of socialism and libertarianism together.

An ardent Leninist in the 1930s, Bookchin converted to anarchism as he came increasingly to believe that capitalism generated not only economic inequalities but also other asymmetrical arrangements of domination intimately bound up with environmental issues. Narrow analyses of class violence left by the wayside other institutionalized systems of oppression, such as sexism and racism, that accrue material privileges through means beyond the ownership of property and exploitation of labor. Socialism tended to reorganize into "hierarchical bodies." Sexism, racism, and class differences "do not disappear with 'democratic centralism,' a 'revolutionary leadership,' a 'worker's state,' and a 'planned economy,'" he writes, and on the contrary "function all the more effectively if centralism appears to be 'democratic'" and "leaders appear to be 'revolutionaries.'"[13] Bookchin's condemnation voices a critique frequently leveled against the New Left. Its leadership, white and male as it mostly was, contributed to a perpetuation of the injustices it claimed to dispel. Bookchin observed a "quasi-authoritarian tone, characteristic of the Stalinist Old Left," steering SDS toward a blanket anti-Americanism, focusing the New Left's predominant anti-imperialism but abandoning its inaugural, and to Bookchin indispensable, adhesion to the "libertarian elements in the American tradition." The counterculture, on the other hand, "drifted off into the New Age and a personalism that ultimately allowed them to be absorbed by the social system."[14] The New Left and counterculture fell prey to pervasive "leninization" and commercialization, respectively, reinforcing stratifications Bookchin hoped they would transcend.

Bookchin's 1964 *Comment* article "Ecology and Revolutionary Thought" introduced his solution: a political application of ecological science based on the notion that ecology upends hierarchy and provides theoretical justification for a stateless (and therefore nonhierarchical) society, exemplified by the commune. Social ecology would place the human and its psychology "within a natural context and explore it in terms of its own natural history, so that the sharp cleavages between thought and nature, subject and object, mind and body, and the social and natural are overcome."[15] Human ingenuity or "second nature," Bookchin writes, neither fabricates nonhuman "first nature" nor papers over it – two arguments he believed respectively taken by traditional Marxism, on the one hand, and the "deep" ecology that developed in reaction to Earth Day's "shallow" commercial tendencies, on the other. As a platform, deep ecology might encompass a crowd of ecological sympathizers (including social ecologists) who share certain perspectives on the importance of biodiversity and the unsustainability of economic growth. However, as many commentators (particularly ecofeminists) have pointed out, its dominant "biocentric" theory has often tended to view *all* human activity and technology in opposition to an ostensibly balanced natural world, to the point that it has promoted "expanding one's sense of self towards a larger identification with all of nature to arrive at a denial of anthropocentrism."[16] By the 1980s, Bookchin came to actively articulate his social ecology in direct contradistinction to this position. For the social ecologist, human activity remains natural even as it mediates the natural world.

It would be impossible to overstate Bookchin's influence on the idea that radical politics might be defined in ecological terms. New Left rhetoric persisted in the granular back-to-the-land movement that established hundreds of rural communes across the country in the late 1960s and early 1970s, where communards "rediscovered ... the perfect wholeness of their own bodies, in the doing of which, it dawned on them for the first time ... just how ungodly fragmented and sealed off from themselves they had always lived before." The exodus drew inspiration from the freewheeling sort of anarchism epitomized by the hippie counterculture, but its own pilgrims, generally "a damned sight more serious about what they were leaving and what they were headed for," tempered their rebellion with an allegiance to self-sufficiency and sustainable technologies.[17] Bookchin's anarcho-communism rigorously theorized, and often inspired, the loose yet earnest community organization that serious communards envisioned, as well as the sensible application of advanced technologies that would make it possible. The New York Federation of Anarchists widely circulated

34 The Ecological Alternative

the essays that would comprise Bookchin's *Post-Scarcity Anarchism* (1970) among student radicals in an effort to revise what they considered anarchism's regrettably pervasive and "absurd" anti-technological perspective. Turned to the needs of human individuals and communities rather than of capital, "instantaneous communication networks" and "automated technologies" would "free all humanity from onerous and deadening toil."[18]

Despite student radicals' cautious and at times even hostile reception of environmentalism, these ideas asserted themselves at the forefront of prominent New Left publications. The notion of a "post-scarcity" society proved especially influential, spurring on prominent activists such as Yippie kingpin Abbie Hoffman and periodicals such as SDS's *New Left Notes* to publicize Bookchin's corpus. By the early 1970s, Bookchin's articles had attracted a loyal discipleship of young environmentalists who found the mainstream movement's agenda too tame. A manifesto published in *Rat* declared the "libertarian, ecologically oriented society" that accompanied the sort of anarchism favored by both Bookchin and Abbey a superior method of population declension to the "social controls" proposed by mainstream environmental ideologues, precisely because it appeared to maintain the critical dual emphasis on direct democracy and individual liberty.[19]

The relationship between Abbey and Bookchin, however, was unabashedly antagonistic, despite their nominal anarchic affiliation. Bookchin joined other left-leaning critics of Earth First! in the 1980s to criticize the belligerent anti-immigration program – and thinly veiled racism – of its founder, Dave Foreman, as well as its inspiration, Abbey himself. Bookchin found Foreman's biocentric position so repellent that he called him out by name when charging deep ecology with the "same kind of ecobrutalism" that "led Hitler to fashion theories of blood and soil."[20] Foreman and Bookchin share roots in anarchism, but where Foreman's deep ecology holds humanism in general accountable for environmental catastrophe, Bookchin's social ecology places emphasis on the negative effects of specific institutional and ideological apparatuses on both human and nonhuman populations. Like Foreman, Abbey contended "with his usual cantankerous flair" that illegal immigration to the United States, especially from Latin American nations, placed undue strain on the country's natural resources. Abbey's curmudgeonly approach to the argument framed it distastefully; Bookchin's response, however, also remained in keeping with his own deleterious habit of leveling attacks against those who failed to meet his own standards of revolution, as well as overstating the extent of his opponents' (including Abbey's) alleged anti-technologism. Abbey characteristically (and unhelpfully) responded by calling Bookchin a "fat old lady." Bookchin in turn spent several decades attacking Abbey and the deep ecologists' fetish for wilderness, the most "quintessential human artifice." Ironically, Abbey reckoned that wilderness spatializes the very lack of hierarchy Bookchin ascribed to ecology: "if we allow the freedom of the hills and the last of the wilderness to be taken from us, then the very idea of freedom may die with it."[21]

In their different ways, Abbey and Bookchin both articulate the idea that "freedom" – what the New Left summarized as the discretionary power to self-fulfillment – is somehow intrinsic to the idea of ecology, whether spatialized as "wilderness" or not. Despite their disagreements, both writers held the social-ecological value of "self-realization" – of human individuals, nonhuman creatures, even "the biosphere itself" – in cardinal esteem.[22] "Our individuality consists not only in the uniqueness of our behavior and character structure, but also in our *right* to act in accordance with our sovereign judgment . . . to formulate our own personal needs," Bookchin wrote in 1972.[23] Bookchin's words mesh comfortably with the New Left line on self-fulfillment he found so attractive. Abbey, on the other hand, approached ecological terminology flippantly, remarking that "I still don't know what [ecology] means. Or seriously much care." He declares himself an amateur social theorist rather than a naturalist, a distinction that suggests he is primarily interested in the human experience of the processes ecology describes rather than in ecology – the science of relationships in ecosystems – itself. The self is always at the center of *Desert Solitaire*, which Abbey insists "is not primarily a book about the desert," and instead belongs "to the category of personal history rather than natural history."[24] In this respect, *Desert Solitaire* is fundamentally concerned with exhibiting Abbey according to the ideal demanded in a 1962 issue of *New University Thought*: "in his totality, in his freedom, in his originality and in his essential dignity." As Hannes Bergthaller writes, "what is at stake" for Abbey in his "effort to confront the natural world directly is not only the essence of *nature* but just as much the essence of the *self*," an impulse at least partially symptomatic of the era's distinctively libertarian brand of radicalism.[25]

Abbey's lack of politics is deceiving, given his pursuit of the self-elevation crucial to New Left thinking, as well as his admission that he felt a "guilty envy" of "those who actually act." He did participate in Vietnam War demonstrations and was involved with the antinuclear movement in the 1970s. In *Down the River* (1982) he warns his moderate readers that "environmentalism, if taken seriously, is a greater threat" to corporate power "than labor unions or Communism." Abbey's dismissal of the efficacy of both communism and American leftism recalls the New Left's disappointment in its forebears: its contention that "the traditional base of labor's power and social influence ... is vanishing" and that "liberalism has adopted a neutral managerial role."[26] The fact that literary environmentalists such as Abbey, Wendell Berry, Annie Dillard, and Barry Lopez all concurrently advanced an "anti-ideological" position in their writing indicates, if nothing else, their generationally specific attitude toward establishment technology and entrenched biases against the natural world on both sides of the Iron Curtain.[27] Abbey rejected communists as well as capitalists for much the same reason as his revolutionary cousins: they "believe above all in technology, the ever-expanding economy ... the complete domination of nature and human beings." Bureaucratic management, authority, and technocracy *in general*, rather than technology itself, spelled the degradation of both the human individual and the natural world. The desert came to represent, for Abbey, a foundation on which to "restor[e] a higher civilization" organized around scattered anarchistic communes. This vision aligns him with utopian writers of the day (including Bookchin) and furnishes a "striking new vision" of the desert: "it lacks the damning artificiality of the other locales. It does not disguise itself." Abbey suggests that the desert is the *most* authentic of utopias, one that presents "a distinctively sixties future of ... 'absolute presence.'"[28]

Abbey recasts the New Left call to establish sociopolitical alternatives in environmentalist terms, and frames the desert wilderness – its isolation from the status quo – as the most legitimate alternative to the destructive and alienating forces of industrial and postindustrial capitalist culture. That is, he trades a civilization defined by repression for a civilization defined by wilderness itself, despite these two terms' traditional opposition. As early as his first novel *Jonathan Troy* (1954), Abbey warns readers that mere escape from civilization to wilderness is not enough to solve any perceived conflict between the two. In one of *Desert Solitaire*'s more lucid passages on the idea, Abbey writes: "A civilization which destroys what little remains of the wild, the spare, the original, is cutting itself off from its origins and betraying the principle of civilization itself" (192). Abbey never quite gets around to explaining what, exactly, the genuine "principle of civilization" is, but the passage's emphasis on "origins" suggests that Abbey understands wilderness as the original and proper mode of civilization. Twenty years later, Barry Lopez would likewise write in *Arctic Dreams* (1986) that "we need a more particularized understanding of the land itself – not a mere refined mathematical knowledge, but a deeper understanding of its nature, as if it were, itself, another sort of civilization we had

Selfhood and Civilization: The New Left and Beyond 37

to reach some agreement with." Abbey's one-time mentor Wallace Stegner also hearkened back to an older model of civilization that once existed and has since been forgotten: "I wanted to hunt up and rejoin the civilization I had been deprived of." Ours is a species, Stegner suggests, that has *repressed* its true mode of organization.[29]

The notion that "wilderness" signifies an alternative, earlier form of "civilization" appears common to a significant body of nature writing. It also recalls Herbert Marcuse's conviction that we need not live according to "repressive civilization," which informed much of the New Left's rhetoric. For Gregory Calvert, it was "no accident" that Marcuse's writings "were the most exciting . . . available." His emphasis on consciousness, self-fulfillment, and alienation both within the self and from society at large resonated with the Movement as it aimed to curb what SDS president Tom Hayden called the "psychological damage" generated by "the system's inhumanity."[30] Despite his Marxist pedigree (yet much like Bookchin), Marcuse intended for his "communistic individualism" to achieve not so much the socialization of the means of production (the traditional Marxist goal) than the repurposing of technology to support the self-realization of each individual, by each individual. Marcuse spoke of liberation in terms of pleasure and self-fulfillment, and defined "alienation" as a psychological phenomenon that the social order intensifies. "Men have unrealized potential for self-cultivation, self-direction, self-understanding, and creativity," Hayden wrote in the *Port Huron Statement*.[31] The "great refusal" of the socioeconomic status quo Marcuse called for in *One-Dimensional Man* (1964) emboldened the protest of those dissatisfied with the "coercive consumerism" of late capitalism, which would hold the self in bondage.

Marcuse's earlier *Eros and Civilization* (1955) supplied the underlying theoretical structure to *One-Dimensional Man*'s materialist critique. In it, Marcuse outlined a utopian society based on psychoanalytic principles, revising and combining Marxist analysis with the developmental narrative of Freud's *Civilization and Its Discontents*. Freud argued that the individual sacrifices the boundless pleasure and satisfaction of infantile narcissism – a sense of ambivalent union or even oneness with the world – for the realities of ego development and the protections of organized civilization. The price of civilization is diminishment, for "the feeling of happiness derived from the satisfaction of a wild instinctual impulse untamed by the ego is incomparably more intense than that derived from sating an instinct that has been tamed." The ego, Freud wrote, is "only a shrunken residue of a much more inclusive – indeed, an all-embracing – feeling which corresponds to a more intimate bond between the ego and the world about it," which diminishes as the subject progressively enters into more complex social relations.[32] Marcuse, however, revised Freud's argument that individuals, in accepting the limitations of the civilized ego, are doomed to a repressive existence. His Marxist examination of psychoanalysis led him to conclude that the ego's "reality principle" is historically, not biologically, generated. The problem is not that people are repressed but that they are repressed too much. As Theodore Roszak observed at the time, the psychic condition arranged by what Marcuse calls "repressive civilization" is only the "prevailing" reality principle.[33] A certain amount of repression is necessary for the survival of the species, but it would play a diminished role if freed from the oppressive conditions of postindustrial society. Marcuse's revolutionary mandate was to ease that repression through intertwined attention to social and self-liberation. By changing institutions, Marcuse argued, we change the structure of the psyche. "The opposition between man and nature, subject and object, is overcome," and the individual, organized by a minimally repressed ego, experiences greater satisfaction on his or her own terms: "Being is experienced as gratification, which unites man and nature."[34] Implicit in Marcuse's thesis is a suggestion that to recover a more "natural" form of civilization would also be to access a more "natural" psychic condition. It was toward this least-repressive reality principle that New Left revolutionaries aimed their sociopolitical alternatives.

However, Marcuse's theory rests on a fundamental tension that destabilizes this authentic ego even as it deifies it. Psychoanalysis, by virtue of its emphasis on an inscrutable unconscious, undermines the apparent unity of the subject. More directly, Marcuse's celebration of unrepressed psychic origins seems to suggest that we must dissolve the ego even as we satisfy it. The argument that a less repressed ego – that is, an ego that relaxes its relationship to the unconscious – exists more naturally than an ego hogtied by civilization implies that the *most* authentic ego would be no ego at all. Where should liberation politics draw the line between oceanic states of pleasure and cosmic unity on the one hand, and self-actualizing ego-fulfillment on the other? Marcuse's own environmentalist writing worries about this very question. In a 1972 lecture, "Ecology and Revolution," he declared that nature is "a dimension *beyond* labor, a symbol of beauty, of tranquility, of a non-repressive order," and that "nature is the source and locus of the life instincts which struggle against the instincts of aggression and destruction."[35] The lecture united ecology not with the cohesion of a minimally repressed, "liberated" ego, but with the illusive, expansive holism of infancy and its *lack* of ego. Marcuse grappled with the difficulty

Selfhood and Civilization: The New Left and Beyond 39

of squaring ecology with the ego within his own framework. Nevertheless, his claim that psychoanalytic prehistory is more natural than an ego repressed by civilization permeated radical discourse of the 1960s.

Perhaps unsurprisingly, environmentalists of the era seized on his contention that "nature is the source" of that repressed yet expansive origin. Roszak, for one, insisted that we must "salvage" the repressed connection between ego and world "as the raw material of a new reality principle."[36] By slight contrast, in a late chapter of *Desert Solitaire* Abbey writes that "[w]e need the possibility of escape as surely as we need hope; without it the life of the cities would drive all men into crime or drugs or psychoanalysis" (149). Elsewhere, he critiques "the Viennese quacks" who would argue that defiance of authority "was in reality no more than the rebelliousness of an adolescent rejecting his father." Abbey's words participated in the decade's fashionable trash talk against institutional analysis, and suggest that wilderness retreat negates the possibility of neurosis or psychosis, or even that retreat serves as a *form* of analysis, a "walking cure" that presumably includes Abbey's own works, which he fondly referred to as "antidotes to despair."[37] Nearly thirty years later, the ecocritic Glen Love would make a remarkably similar claim in his contribution to Cheryl Glotfelty and Harold Fromm's foundational *Ecocriticism Reader* (1996). Love notably gestures to *Civilization and Its Discontents* to contend that "society itself can be sick." The cure for civilization's ills, he writes, "cannot come from those afflicted by the neurosis." It must originate in nature itself.[38] Like Abbey, Love suggests that the natural world fulfills the function of an analyst. He also explicitly engages the source material that furnished the New Left with theoretical support for its dual commitment to personal authenticity and social revolution.

This example especially demonstrates how interactions between discourses of ecology and political psychoanalysis have enjoyed remarkable longevity, with only minor variation. Despite Abbey's repudiation, postwar environmental thought was entangled in a radical cultural context in which psychoanalysis experienced a surge in popularity beyond its institutional uses. Writers like Paul Shepard reasoned not that nature and civilization are divided, exactly, but that civilization's current mode papers over our *psychic* nature, repressing it. It is telling that in 1971, Shepard also challenged the disciplines of biology and psychology to jointly "confront the ecological function of the unconscious." His choice of the word "unconscious" frames ecology as part and parcel of the psychic content that the Freudian Left believed repressive civilization pushes to the margins, with results that mirror the tensions in Marcuse's own theory. In response to a colleague who worried that the ecosystem concept discounted the individual, Shepard mused that "individual man *has* his particular integrity," but that the "ecological thinking" we must exercise also "reveals the self ennobled and extended . . . because the beauty and complexity of nature are continuous with ourselves."[39] One byproduct of Marcuse's social theory is an uncertainty regarding where to locate "integrity." His celebration of the primary and unrepressed suggests that one must pulverize the ego even as one fulfills it. As such, the argument that a more authentic ego functions more naturally than an institutionally limited one implies that the *most* authentic ego would be no ego at all.

The (In)Authentic Anarchist: The Self in Postwar Environmental Writing

Abbey dramatizes this very tension in ecological terms in *Desert Solitaire* as he chronicles several seasons in the Utah desert, where, ideally, "the naked self merges with a nonhuman world and yet somehow survives still intact, individual, separate" (6). It would be a mistake to read such evocations of merger as romantic naïveté, or as affirmations of holism or "ecomysticism," as numerous critics have done. Abbey's apparent impulse to "identify with . . . his nonhuman surroundings" certainly speaks to a desire to investigate his ecological situation. *Desert Solitaire* perhaps even anticipates what Stacy Alaimo has labeled the "material memoir," whose subjects "undertake investigations . . . of their own materiality," such that "the self of the material memoir . . . is coextensive with the environment, trans-corporeal."[40] It is important to remember, however, the extent to which critical interventions such as Alaimo's rely not on the resolution but on the *maintenance* of paradox, irony, and friction. To either celebrate or scold Abbey for his romanticism or mysticism would be to "wrest with, but ultimately sideline what is arguably the most distinctive feature of Abbey's literary style, namely his penchant for . . . performative contradiction." *Desert Solitaire* has "posed difficulties" to ecocriticism because it "seeks to confront . . . directly" a paradox inherent to environmentalism, the circumscription of the environmentalist's desire "to speak on behalf of the whole" within "terms provided by society itself." Abbey warmly welcomes this paradox as environmentalism's "necessary and enabling condition."[41]

Abbey constantly pushed back against the romantic undertones of the nature writer brand he received throughout his life. His distrust of the categorization stemmed in part from his perception that it most often labels

The (In)Authentic Anarchist 41

"a genteel, if durable, literary occupation practiced by natural historians."[42] Apparently, Abbey's boisterousness, his belligerence and take-no-prisoners attitude, even his sexism and casual racism, proved his experiences more genuine than the pastoral hypocrisies of limp-wristed romantics who return to their cities as soon as they get their fill. Nature writing's "central dynamic," Randall Roorda writes, is retreat, the writer's "movement from human society toward a state of solitude in nature." For writers of Abbey's ilk, however, retreat does not necessarily take as its object nature as a place of solitude from which one must return to the urban center, or even of parochial distance from institutional organization. For writers such as Berry, for example, retreat is "predicated on ... a sense of community relations" between humans and nonhumans as well as among human individuals and populations.[43] Retreat, in this context, moves one out of an anthrosphere and into a biosphere – less a distinction between "nature" and "culture" or "wilderness" and "civilization" than a reconfiguration of those dualisms and the purview of each term.

Such representations of retreat, which characterize Abbey's writing as well as the work of many of his contemporaries, responded to the political climate of the day and to the idealistic promises made by both New Left thought and radical environmentalism. Abbey's intention was to examine both his place in an expanded communal sphere and the question of selfhood in general, all from a deeply personal perspective. He derived *Desert Solitaire* from his journals, sharing in a New Left commitment to personal experience that, by virtue of Abbey's combined dedication to observation and perception, expands the notion of "accuracy" by placing emphasis on "[n]ot imitation but evocation."[44] *Desert Solitaire* is not about what just anybody can see in the southeastern Utah desert. It is about what *Abbey* sees. The narrative conveys what is meaningful *to Abbey*, what is pleasurable *to Abbey*, and what is troubling *to Abbey*. He presumes to ditch universals in favor of his particular experience. This approach to nature writing adheres across countless postwar accounts of retreat, including Annie Dillard's *Pilgrim at Tinker Creek* (1974), the most distinctive feature of which, Lawrence Buell argues, is the primacy it grants to the "the process of seeing, not the objects seen."[45] Abbey and Dillard do not concern themselves with conventional mimesis. Their observance of realism responds instead to the cult of experience that circulated within and beyond the Movement. Abbey esteems the verisimilitude of his desert representation not according to how accurately he portrays each grain of sand, but against its resonance with his own personality.

The question of *Desert Solitaire*'s narrative therefore does not seem to Abbey to be a matter of fiction or nonfiction, "reality" or "artifice." Its invention instead reflects what Lopez, in his 1984 essay "Landscape and Narrative," describes as the traditional Native American valuation of story. "If the exterior landscape is limned well," Lopez writes, "the listener often feels that he has heard something pleasing and authentic."[46] That landscape might be "limned" not by excruciating scientific detail, but instead by action and reaction, a feeling and sensibility that express Abbey's particular perspective or intentions. Lopez's use of the word "authentic" lacks the essentialist tenor so pervasive in American political culture in the era of the New Left and new social movements, referring instead to the idiosyncratic way in which a writer presents, mediates, and even fabricates his or her particular emotions, sensations, and take on events. Even as Abbey sings the praises of his own personality and fulfillment, he does not necessarily affirm the idea that these values are as fundamental as some of his contemporaries believed. The raucous, littering, gun-toting rebel is "just another fictional creation."[47] His "season in the wilderness" in reality spanned many seasons in 1956 and 1957, and the rafting trip in Glen Canyon that takes up a good portion of the text's second half took place in 1959. *Desert Solitaire* is not a pure explosion of authenticity but a doubly filtered text, sifted through diary and revision, organized around a largely invented Abbey.

Despite the esteem in which Abbey holds his own sense of self, he ultimately comes to favor a creative account of identity, in contrast to the New Left-era political discourse by which he is partially inspired. "It will be objected that the book deals too much with mere appearances, with the surface of things, and fails to engage and reveal the patterns of unifying relationships which form the true underlying reality of existence," Abbey tellingly writes in his preface to *Desert Solitaire*, as if preemptively countering what he doubtless saw as a typical and tired comment on the part of critics hip to the radical mood. "For my own part I am pleased enough with surfaces – in fact they alone seem to me to be of much importance" (xiii). In light of this remark, his expressed tendency to occasionally "overlook" surfaces appears to signify less that Abbey desires to collapse himself into some material holism, as some have suggested, than his self-conscious understanding of his work as a narrative experiment on the utility of authenticity as an environmentalist virtue – one that ultimately fails. Abbey comes to understand his personality as yet another surface, a matter of style and effect rather than essence, precisely because his interest in his environment leads him to believe that essence amounts to matter,

The Spontaneous Society: Ecology and the Politics of Self-Liberation   43

and an identification with matter alone would diminish the very personality that loves and aims to care for the environment in the first place. All the same, Abbey considers his presentation of himself and the landscape no less "real" for its fabrication. Abbey is Abbey *because of* his representational manipulation, and he considers such construction necessary to his sense of self-fulfillment precisely because of the ecological context in which he articulates his alternative civilization.

The Spontaneous Society: Ecology and the Politics of Self-Liberation

In the early 1980s, Stewart Brand wrote that he intended his National Book Award-winning *Whole Earth Catalog* to "help my friends who were starting their own civilization hither and yon in the sticks" – a Jeffersonian movement of countercultural types toward an ecologically informed communalism that venerated both the individual and environment.[48] Abbey's reference in *Desert Solitaire* to the Moab desert as "my all-too-perishable republic" rhetorically participates in the back-to-the-land movement's shift toward environmentally friendly self-governance (151). He dedicates a considerable portion of *Desert Solitaire* to the decree of rules, regulations, and laws not only for wilderness habitation but also for human society in general. Elsewhere, he provides "a few tips on desert etiquette," which include, among basic survival skills, an order to monkeywrench, to "always remove and destroy survey stakes, flagging, advertising signboards." This inconsistent and frequently contradictory code nonetheless echoes the "Laws of Ecology" set forth by Barry Commoner in commandment fashion in *The Closing Circle* (1971): Everything Is Connected to Everything Else, Everything Must Go Somewhere, Nature Knows Best, There Is No Such Thing as a Free Lunch.[49]

These examples illustrate an impulse to codify what Abbey and Commoner understand as certain laws of ecology-as-society. *Desert Solitaire* is one part philosophical treatise, one part constitution, and one part declaration of independence for a new civilization, or at the very least an enclave (what one communard referred to as an "island of decency").[50] For Abbey, American civilization as we know it had reached its end. The time had come "to move on, to find another country or – in the name of Jefferson – to make another country" (185). When Abbey is accused by a park visitor of being "against civilization," he is first "flattered," but then "at the same time surprised, hurt, a little shocked." How "could I be against humanity without being against myself, whom I love ... how could I be against civilization when all which I most willingly defend and venerate – including the love of wilderness – is comprehended by the term?" (274). Ultimately, Abbey determines that it is not mankind he hates but "man-centeredness," not civilization but "culture," "the way of life of any given human society considered as a whole" (275). He distrusts, that is, the particular, momentary shape of what Marcuse described as repressive civilization.

Abbey's reflection partakes in the mandates of New Left revolution. He intimates a truer, freer alternative to contemporary mechanisms, a nature that, as Weisberg puts it, "works toward harmony, cooperation and interdependence" where "advanced industrial society works toward growth, competition and independence."[51] But if Abbey more or less clearly distinguishes between civilization and culture, his definition of wilderness – the term he uses most consistently to classify the earth in its unblemished aspects – is far opaquer. On the one hand, wilderness is a complement that "completes" civilization: "We need wilderness whether or not we ever set foot in it" (148). On the other, Abbey declares that "wilderness is a necessary part of civilization" (54). He vacillates on the question of whether wilderness is a part of civilization or exists outside of it. Lamenting the construction of a new highway through Zion National Park, he writes that the northwestern portion "has until recently been saved as almost virgin wilderness" (53). "Virgin wilderness," a longstanding rhetorical flourish on the part of settler men identifying land with woman, here seems to refer less to no human presence than to no human manufacture – no industry or major alteration. Abbey would be perfectly pleased with human presence in Zion (specifically his own). The only thing better than solitude is "society": "By society I do not mean the roar of city streets . . . or human life in general. I mean the society of a friend or friends" (110–11). Wilderness and human habitation are not mutually exclusive for Abbey, who clarifies that the destruction of wilderness fulfills "the requirements of – not man – but industry" (54). While Abbey writes at length on the dangers of industrial tourism to the natural parks, he also observes that "the chief victims of the system are the motorized tourists. They are being robbed and robbing themselves" (59). This passage perhaps surprisingly subordinates the value of the natural world to human pleasure, but it does so in a way that joins human and wilderness in common cause. Industry robs both of their natural predispositions.

Implicit in this passage is a demand for fulfillment tied to psychic wellbeing and personal freedom such that the New Left and counterculture hoped to foster through reorganized social forms. "The operation of the machine," the Berkeley free speech activist Mario Savio declared at a 1964

The Spontaneous Society: Ecology and the Politics of Self-Liberation   45

rally, "makes you so sick at heart." Abbey reiterates Savio's call for leftist radicals to "put your bodies upon the gears and upon the wheels" and "make it stop."[52] The free human, for Abbey, is a walking, experiencing creature who does not rely on technology as mediator between self and world. Even if Abbey does not consider himself a revolutionary in the strict sense of the word, he yearns to liberate these tourists: "What can I tell them? Sealed in their metallic shells like mollusks on wheels, how can I pry the people free? The auto as tin can, the park ranger as opener" (261). In one of his many diatribes against visiting parks in cars, Abbey bombastically apostrophizes his guests: "Yes sir, yes madam, I entreat you, get out of those motorized wheelchairs, get off your foam rubber backsides, stand up straight like men! like women! like human beings! and walk – *walk* – WALK upon our sweet and blessed land!" (262). The passage illustrates Abbey's troubling nonchalance toward disabled vacationers, but it also captures the unmediated sense of self he imagines possible when freed if not from technology then from technological management.

Abbey's idea of self-determination dramatizes the vision of sovereignty foreseen by radical environmentalism's New Left-influenced vanguard, which sought to incubate "politically independent communities whose boundaries and populations will be defined by a new ecological consciousness," and "whose inhabitants will determine for themselves, within the framework of this new consciousness . . . the forms taken by their social structures."[53] Solitude and needful labor breed community. Because of their isolation, and especially because of their remove from televisions, automobiles, and other technologies, the Moabites are more courteous, interesting, and generous neighbors. The supermarket and bar's "general atmosphere is free and friendly, quite unlike the sad, sour gloom of most bars I have known, where nervous men in tight collars brood over their drinks between out-of-tune TV screens and a remorseless clock" (47). Abbey's attention to collars and clocks indicts the regimented time of industry and the increasingly postindustrial workforce of the American middle class.[54] Notably, he makes no distinction between town and country. Moab itself comprises a healthy hub of wilderness while still being a site of human activity and, to a diminished and need-based extent, production. Stripped bare of undue management, wilderness furnishes genuine civilization.

Desert Solitaire even begins by intimating a sort of ecologically expanded politics of authenticity. Abbey displays a strong reflex against anthropomorphizing: a commitment – sometimes upheld, sometimes forgotten – to "confront, immediately and directly if it's possible, the bare bones of existence, the elemental and fundamental . . . I want to be able to look at and into a juniper tree, a piece of quartz, a vulture, a spider, and see it as it is in itself" (6). His fierce loyalty to his own sense of individuality translates into respect for individual freedom on a scale beyond the human. He presents as a moral imperative engagement with nonhuman others in such a way that renders them "devoid of all humanly ascribed qualities . . . even the categories of scientific description."[55] Animals, he writes, "wish nothing from us but the right to pursue happiness in their own manner." If Abbey does not attempt to speak for the natural world as to what it wants, he nonetheless suggests that it *does* want, in the process ascribing a certain human hunger to the nonhuman. Acutely aware of the difficulty of liberating nature without applying human attributes to its constituents, he determines nonetheless to commit to such egalitarian recognition "even if it means risking everything human in myself" (6).

To meet the (nonhuman) other on its own terms appears to potentially require Abbey's dismissal of his own sense of humanity – the very personality he holds in such high esteem. For this reason, it is primarily Abbey's interaction with nonhuman creatures that demonstrates a certain ambivalence at work in his reconciliation of civilization and wilderness. His confusion over the terms of his new society begins to reveal itself as he deliberates over the life of a rabbit. Abbey wonders whether he should "give the rabbit a sporting chance . . . or brain the little bastard where he is" (38). Eventually, Abbey announces that he's "a scientist not a sportsman and we've got an important experiment under way here, for which the rabbit has been volunteered." This directive both flies in the face of Abbey's earlier oath to abandon even "the categories of scientific description" and robs the rabbit of any authentic rabbit-agency Abbey earlier, one assumes, would have greeted it as possessing. For a moment Abbey is "shocked" after he bashes the rabbit over the head with a rock, but this sensation gives way to a feeling of "mild elation": "I try but cannot feel any sense of guilt." Abbey gains nothing from killing the rabbit – he uses neither its meat nor its pelt nor its bones – yet he immediately assumes an impression of kinship. "No longer do I feel isolated from the sparse and furtive life around me, a stranger from another world," he writes. "I have entered this one. We are kindred all of us, killer and victim, predator and prey. . . the foul worms that feed on our entrails, all of them, all of us. Long live diversity, long live the earth!" The importance of this passage lies not in what Abbey does or does not use of the rabbit's body, but in the sense of affinity he seems to gain from the spontaneous spirit in which he kills it.

The Spontaneous Society: Ecology and the Politics of Self-Liberation   47

Abbey's rallying cry disarms him of the vigor with which he sparred against Bookchin, for whom spontaneity – the expression of natural predisposition – formed the cornerstone of anarchist environmentalism. "Far from inviting chaos," Bookchin writes, spontaneity "involves releasing the inner forces of a development to find their authentic order and stability." When "spontaneity in social life converges with spontaneity in nature," ecological society is born. In many ways this perspective built on the New Left's aversion to bureaucratic management, grafting onto it an open-ended, equal-parts Marxist and biological evolutionary narrative. Bookchin believes spontaneity is both the foremost expression of self – a bodily verbalization of natural impulse and individual predilection – and the prime mover of what he calls ecology's "unity-in-diversity," the wellspring of the ecosystem's "fecundity" and "evolutionary potential to create newer, still more complex life-forms and biotic interrelationships." For Bookchin, spontaneity challenges hierarchical management and is "nourished" by ecology, which reveals that balance in the natural world "is achieved by organic variation and complexity, not by homogeneity and simplification."[56]

This perspective illuminates Abbey's execution of the rabbit as the moment at which he announces his new civilization as one defined by ecological interconnectivity (though he does not stoop so low as to use Bookchin's vocabulary). Abbey writes favorably of Aldo Leopold's famous dictum to "think like a mountain" – "And feel like a river, says I."[57] One wonders what "feeling like a river" adds to Leopold's original and influential appeal to a "deeper meaning, known only to the mountain itself," but at the very least the reference reinforces the fact that Abbey, in his patch of desert, replaces or overlays social mores with ecological forces – a respect not for capital or technology, but for recycled matter and energy.[58] As such, he leaves his "victim to the vultures and maggots, who will appreciate him more than I could." Abbey expresses a similarly profound connection with a snake, which he keeps in his shirt. The snake, "being a cold-blooded creature ... takes his temperature from that of the immediate environment – in this case my body. We are compatible" (22). Their interrelationship – heat for the snake, companionship for Abbey – belies a preoccupation with continuity that becomes more apparent as the narrative progresses. So powerful for Abbey is the allure of this sense of continuity that even the stones in the canyons of Arches National Park take on an interpenetrative significance: "there is method at work here . . . each groove in the rock leads to a natural channel of some kind, each channel to a ditch and gulch and ravine, each larger waterway to a canyon bottom or broad wash leading in turn to the Colorado River and the sea" (11). Where does each waterway begin and end? This is a crucially unsolvable question for Abbey, and its implications reach beyond the mutability of water. Where, too, does Abbey begin and the river end?

"Feeling Like a River": Edward Abbey's Subjective Uncertainty

Abbey originally titled the pivotal "Down the River" chapter of *Desert Solitaire* "A Last Look at Paradise." As Abbey and his companion Ralph Newcomb begin to float down the Colorado River in Glen Canyon on a leisurely expedition of twelve days and 150 miles, Abbey remarks that his initial anxieties about drifting with neither direction nor control have "vanished and I feel instead a sense of cradlelike security, of achievement and joy, a pleasure almost equivalent to that first entrance – from the outside – into the neck of the womb" (176). "Neck of the womb" presents a bizarre metaphor. It evokes first the vagina, suggesting that Abbey's pleasure is foremost sexual – he dubiously aims to screw his way to "cradlelike security" – before emphasizing the maternal. The three-word interjection, "from the outside," from beyond the canyon into it, shifts one's comprehension of the metaphor. The latter half of this sentence seems not to evoke the act of birth but to reverse its direction. Abbey maintains this contradictory imagery of severance and entrance: "Cutting the bloody cord, that's what we feel, the delirious exhilaration of independence, a rebirth backward in time and into primeval liberty" (177). This odd uterine rhetoric suggests that liberty is what happens when one is shoved back into the womb.

How one defines one's revolutionary alternative in the New Left era is an important detail, and for Abbey "paradise" apparently furnishes certain amniotic pleasures. Abbey treats wilderness as a woman to be penetrated and/or occupied, a tired patriarchal metaphor with long-standing resonance in American environmental and colonial history. His imagery updates this tradition for the politics of authenticity and marked chauvinism of New Left rhetoric, joining the revolutionary grit of his environmentalism with the era's prominent psychoanalytic narratives. The gendered landscape functions as an analogue for freedom and metaphor signifying something already known but long since repressed. "Suppose we say that wilderness invokes ... the past and the unknown, the womb of earth from which we all emerged," he muses. "It means something lost and something still present, something remote and at the

"Feeling Like a River": Edward Abbey's Subjective Uncertainty 49

same time intimate, something buried in our blood and nerves, something beyond us and without limit" (189–90). Wilderness comprises a simultaneously spatial and psychic sphere. Within its boundaries it has the capacity to include *everything*.

The notion that preconscious infancy incorporates combined qualities of liberation, nature, pleasure, and above all *ubiquity* evokes the radical applications of conventional midcentury psychoanalytic wisdom such as those with which Marcuse experimented. "Feeling like a river" might after all be an oceanic feeling – what Freud describes as a "sensation of eternity," an infantile non-detection of boundaries that persists and exists "side by side with the narrower and more sharply demarcated ego-feeling of maturity, like a kind of counterpart," a "feeling as of something limitless, unbounded."[59] The "Freudian overtones" of this scene's "erotica of sensation" have inspired numerous readings of the text's "ecoaesthetics," what Tom Lynch describes as *Desert Solitaire*'s presumed ability to help us "break through the illusion that the organism that is our self is not also part of the environment in which it dwells."[60] Abbey and Glen Canyon indeed seem increasingly indistinguishable: "we're getting accustomed to sand . . . Sand becomes a part of our existence which, like breathing, we take for granted" (186). Even if, unlike oxygen, nitrogen, and carbon dioxide, sand does not literally cycle through Abbey's body and pierce his cells, defying conventional wisdom as to where self begins and atmosphere ends, it nonetheless takes on ecological significance for its sheer presence, the role it plays for Abbey in understanding not just the canyon but himself. On the Colorado, Abbey's suddenly insignificant sense of self begins to appear far less authentic than the system in which his body participates:

> In a blue dawn under the faintest of stars we break our fast, pack our gear and launch the boats again. Farther still into the visionary world of Glen Canyon, talking somewhat less than before – for what is there to say? I think we've about said it all – we communicate less in words and more in direct denotation, the glance, the pointing hand, the subtle nuances of pipe smoke, the tilt of a wilted hat brim. Configurations are beginning to fade, distinctions shading off into blended amalgams of man and man, men and water, water and rock.
>
> > "Who is Ralph Newcomb?" I say. "Who is he?"
> > "Aye," he says. "And who is who? Which is which?"
> > "Quite," I agree.
>
> We are merging, molecules getting mixed. Talk about intersubjectivity – we are both taking on the coloration of river and canyon, our skin as mahogany as the water on the shady side, our clothing coated with silt, our bare feet

50 The Ecological Alternative

caked with mud and tough as lizard skin, our whiskers bleached as the sand – even our eyeballs, what little you can see of them between the lids, have taken on a coral-pink, the color of the dunes. And we smell, I suppose, like catfish. (209)

The most striking aspect of this passage is its rapid fall into indistinction. Abbey gets to a moment of "blended amalgams" by transitioning through nonverbal cues before symbolic communication itself becomes unnecessary (a theme that came to dominate appeals to ecological authenticity, as the next chapter explains in more detail), replaced by sensations resembling muscle twitches within the same body. The boundary-less multi-entity depicted here appears to be a work in progress, an exercise in occupying the same body and grasping the relationship between two men in terms of a confusion as to where they – and the ecosystem of the canyon – begin and end.

Such uncertainty manifests frequently throughout *Desert Solitaire*. While in the desert wrangling with an employer and another ranch hand, Abbey searches a ravine for a wayward horse. Suddenly, he pauses: "Something breathing nearby – I was in the presence of a tree. On the slope above stood a giant old juniper with massive, twisted trunk" (164). With that dash, the line draws an association between the tree and the breathing Abbey hears. The reader's impulse, like Abbey's, is to linger and consider this respiratory marvel. On closer inspection, however, Abbey sees that "[h]anging from one of the limbs was what looked at first glance like a pair of trousers that reached to the ground. Blinking the sweat out of my eyes I looked harder and saw the trousers transform themselves into the legs of a ... very tall horse." Even when the mystery of the phantom breath is solved, the beginning of this passage casts its source into some doubt. Abbey at first presents the horse and tree, as well as the hallucinated trousers, as indistinguishable. He appears confused as to where tree begins and horse ends. Even if no direct symbiotic relationship exists between horse and tree (or pants), the horse and the tree are bound by occupying the same environment.

Annie Dillard foregoes Abbey's womb imagery but professes to similar experiences in *Pilgrim at Tinker Creek*. Fowl substitute for horse and trousers: "I walked up to a tree, an Osage orange, and a hundred birds flew away. They simply materialized out of the tree. I saw a tree, then a whisk of color, then a tree again." These two passages illustrate moments of sensory confusion in which the authors perceive an indistinctness among entities within a shared environment. For Dillard, these moments provide

"Feeling Like a River": Edward Abbey's Subjective Uncertainty 51

a window into what she describes as a simultaneously ecological and spiritual transmission of both energy and matter: "The tomcat that used to wake me is dead; he was long since grist for an earthworm's casting, and is now the clear sap of a Pittsburgh sycamore, or the honeydew of aphids sucked from that sycamore's high twigs and sprayed in sticky drops on a stranger's car." Creatures – including people – that have died recycle matter by virtue of their organic composition, in a way that for Dillard renders them at once less and more than themselves.[61]

A spiritual measure of "consciousness" smooths the distressing self-destabilization at the heart of this ecological perspective. A "heightened awareness," Dillard writes, opens "the great door to the present." To attend to the processes taking place around oneself, and to the self's implication in those processes, is for Dillard a profoundly spiritual *and* pragmatic act, which allows for both ethical living on the planet and reconciliation within the self with the fragility – even illusion – of one's physical autonomy. She writes of all the creatures in the Virginia woods, "My ignoring them won't strip them of their reality, and admitting them, one by one, into my consciousness might heighten mine, might add their dim awareness to my human consciousness." The notion of consciousness functions, for Dillard, like a sort of conduit, a conception of selfhood that nonetheless welcomes the other beyond the self and imaginatively embraces its interrelation, as best it can, and is in turn enriched by it. Consciousness allows her to negotiate her interpenetration from a fixed point of selfhood, which in the process she nonetheless disrupts and revises. Tinker Creek represents this ambivalent peace as a "mediator, benevolent, impartial, subsuming my shabbiest evils and dissolving them, transforming them into live moles, and shiners, and sycamore leaves." The creek's constant movement symbolizes "the mystery of the continuous creation and all that providence implies: the uncertainty of vision, the horror of the fixed, the dissolution of the present, intricacy of beauty, the pressure of fecundity, the elusiveness of the free."[62] Dillard imbues the creek with the representational power to illustrate the boundary-shattering she perceives in matters of ecology.

Abbey shared Dillard's interest in fluvial metaphors but distrusted the spiritual angle. In a 1983 letter, he wrote to Dillard that he tried to "invoke a sense of wonder and magic in the reader without invoking the mystical, the supernatural or the transcendent." Mysticism, he wrote, irresponsibly leads its adherents to "identify their personal inner visions with universal reality." He condemned religions – *all* religions, including the then-fashionable Buddhism, Taoism, and Native American spiritualisms in addition to the Abrahamic faiths – for their tendency "to divorce men and women from the earth . . . by their mystical emphasis upon the general, the abstract, the invisible."[63] In this respect Abbey continued to resemble his would-be nemesis Bookchin, who also found the contemporary counter-cultural fashion for Eastern spiritualism unappealing. "At the risk of seeming heretical," Bookchin wrote in 1977 that the "Indian and Chinese philosophical works so much in vogue today provide no satisfactory melding of the disciplined rationalism, technical sophistication, social activism, and personalistic ethics that actually vitalize" the construction of "ecocommunities." Far more significant than Bookchin's apparent prejudice was his specific distaste for how American dissidents used Eastern spirituality to address "the widely expressed need for a sense of unity with nature" – that is, by emphasizing "the primacy this philosophy gives to 'cosmic' concerns over mundane social and individual needs."[64] Both writers' presumably heightened sense of material reality, however, did not necessarily preclude quasi-mystical accounts of "unity with nature." If anything, Abbey's fidelity to the ecosystem's complexity – coupled with his inability to precisely represent it – precipitated such accounts. Abbey's "disruption of the contained living subject via the expansion of subjectivity" might even appear to illustrate how a "process of material union was . . . central to his activism and politics," an indication that for Abbey, the authentic subject is not a self at all, but an interconnective unity – the ecosystem itself.[65]

I would like to advance a different interpretation. These scenes dramatize not Abbey's conviction but his ambivalent *mistrust* regarding the political utility of a politics of authenticity to environmentalism. It is certainly tempting to read Abbey's experience of "intersubjectivity" as a hearty embrace of the sort of "material monism" that has characterized select strains of both deep-ecological philosophy and, more recently, post-humanist criticism. But such a reading neglects his vigorous, if inconsistent, commitment to respect other creatures "as they are in themselves." Perhaps more importantly, one must consider the assumptions that animate this interpretation, which in at least one account proceeds from a conviction that "technology that disrupts or intervenes in . . . sensory experience is problematic, since it by consequence helps maintain the human alienation from the nonhuman."[66] One can't help but read traces of New Left resistance to psychic alienation – especially of the ecological variety – in the words of this critic. Technology is artificial and obscures our relationship with what is real – that is, our ecological authenticity, an apparently natural lack of subjective boundaries.

Social Ecology and Psychoanalytic Vocabulary

Abbey's flirtation with self-erasure – or, perhaps more accurately, self-expansion – draws on the psychoanalytically inflected radicalism of figures like Marcuse, who aimed to blend a minimal state of repression with institutional revolution, and Norman O. Brown, who advocated "a union with others and with the world around us based ... on narcissism and erotic exuberance." For Theodore Roszak, who helped popularize the term "counterculture," the Movement "begins where Marcuse pulls up short, and where Brown, with no apologies, goes off the deep end."[67] Marcuse's more overtly political position was less ecstatically excessive than Brown's. Roszak's preference predicted the extravagant direction of his later environmentalism, which favored the questionable (and questionably accomplished) narcissistic self-expansion that Brown recommended. The extremity of Roszak's ecological commitments directly contradicted his more conventionally countercultural platform. "We live in a time when the very private experience of having a personal identity to discover, a personal destiny to fulfill, has become a subversive political force of major proportions," he writes, echoing the New Left rally. The libertarian charisma of this passage tarnishes slightly in light of the statement, a mere nine pages prior, that "the needs of the planet and the needs of the person have become one."[68] He collapses the individual's special identity into the earth's, such that personal self-fulfillment no longer seems relevant.

My point in highlighting this example is that the introduction of ecology to the structurally psychoanalytic revolutionary discourse of the time resulted in (or, more accurately, foregrounded) potential contradictions inherent to the project's emphasis on the self. Bookchin's social ecology was not immune to these theoretical complications. "The history of 'civilization,'" Bookchin writes, "has been a steady progress of estrangement from nature that has increasingly developed into outright antagonism .... After some ten millennia of a very ambiguous social evolution, we must reenter natural evolution again."[69] One wonders how it is possible to "reenter" nature if, as Bookchin takes great pains to explain, we never left it. He criticized this kind of deviated developmental narrative among his radical contemporaries, but nonetheless seems to have taken it quite seriously himself. The conceptual bifurcation of civilization from nature, he writes, "fragmented not only the world of nature and society but the human psyche and its biological matrix." Hierarchy "is not merely a social condition; it is also a state of consciousness" that "fosters the

54 The Ecological Alternative

renunciation of the pleasures of life." His anarcho-communistic alternative, by contrast, would define community according to kinship, common interest, and "unalienated human relationships" that "transcend the traditional split between psyche and the social world."[70]

Bookchin might as well have reproduced the introductory chapters of *Eros and Civilization* in their entirety. Like Marcuse, Bookchin aims to "measure societal advances not in terms of the extent to which eroticism is sublimated into other activities but the extent to which it is released and given full expression." He also believes that "there can be no hope of liberating society without self-liberation in the fullest meaning of selfhood, of the ego and all its claims."[71] The indistinct meaning of the word "of" in the phrase "of the ego" presents difficulty in this passage. As for other writers, for Bookchin the terms of ecology tended to slide into an uncertain definition of unity that defied his own rhetoric of individual liberation. This slippage resulted from his engagement with psychoanalytic vocabulary, which inspired a shaky understanding of the implication, definition, and role of the ego in self-fulfillment. Does Bookchin mean liberation *for* the ego or *from* the ego? The addition of "and all its claims" suggests the latter. In this sentence, Bookchin allies "the ego" with an oppressive, *un*naturally imposed hierarchy. Lasting forms of social organization have obscured our natural psychic disposition, which, according to the narrative if not to Bookchin himself, comprises a lack of ego or self. Taken together, these foundational yet often glossed points of Bookchin's corpus suggest that there *is* a natural state of human organization, that civilization as it currently exists *does* obscure it, and that we *do* need to excavate its original mode. As for Brown and for Roszak, for Bookchin that ecological reality enshrines a natural subject that is egoless. His recourse to psychoanalytic terminology to describe ecological interplay between the human and nonhuman begins to collapse the dedication to fixed, autonomous, and authentic subjectivity he shared with the New Left.

Nonetheless, Bookchin is quick to contrast the "wholeness" of unity-in-diversity with the "archaic dross" of mysticism and its "static absolutes." "Ecological stability," he writes, "is a function not of simplicity and homogeneity but of complexity and variety." The idea of wholeness does not, for Bookchin, recommend "any 'totality' that leads to a terminal 'reconciliation' of all 'Being' in a complete identity of subject and object," or a sense of "cosmic 'oneness.'"[72] He vehemently contests other environmentalists' willingness to rhetorically entertain an identification with the ecosystem as a whole, such that the self seems whimsically to melt away.

At a certain point, however, Bookchin begins to split hairs with his rivals. "Wholeness," he writes, is "what integrates the particularities into a unified form, what renders the unity an operable reality and a 'being' in the literal sense of the term – an order as the actualized unity of its diversity from the flowing and emergent process that yields its self-realization."[73] This mouthful raises an especially decisive question: what, in fact, *is* "the literal sense" of being? Given Bookchin's predisposition, one is tempted to interpret these words in a biological direction, as the physical situation of life and its variable position in complex organic networks. In the context of the vague psychoanalytic narrative underwriting his theory, those networks parallel not the ego but the narcissistic origin it ostensibly covers up. The passage therefore starts to appear more a liability than an asset to Bookchin's repetitive rejection of cosmic totality. The "literal sense" of being emerges as a calcified, harmonized ecosystem that obscures the individuals and communities Bookchin tries tenuously to hold at the center of his equations. Despite his best intentions, at times Bookchin appears to commit the error he warns against, of rapturously breathing the word "ecology" in such a way that it "evaporates into a mystical" – if perhaps involuntary – "sigh."[74] In constructing the edifice of social ecology on a mildly psychoanalytic foundation, a narrative of a repressed lack of boundaries he associates with evolution, Bookchin cannot help but gravitate toward a holistic appeal of the sort he means to disparage.

The Superficial Self

Before returning to the question of the New Left's rhetorical legacy, I want to suggest that *Desert Solitaire* complicates these ideas, even as its scenes of dissolution appear to embrace an emergent, psychoanalytically charged logic of ecological authenticity. It is worth noting the final line in the long passage excerpted previously. Abbey's cursory reference to his and Newcomb's stench, and the flippant "I suppose" interjected between "we" and "catfish," signals his self-consciousness of the extent to which he imagines this exchange. The sentence expresses an admission that of course his sense of discrete selfhood – however constructed or even artificial it might seem – has not *really* dissolved. It could not have, if he later sat down to write the passage. These dissolutive moments tend to focus less on Abbey's supposedly natural identification with the ecosystem – or the metaphorical woman he enlists to represent it – than on the pride Abbey the writer takes in chronicling it. His evocation of a fetal ecosystem resonates less with the womb itself than with concurrent discourse situating the embryo as a "metaphor for 'man' in space, floating free." Obstetrical rhetoric, Karen Newman writes, has "allow[ed] for a double identificatory pleasure: identification with the immaculate, impenetrable human individual, and the power/knowledge of knowing the body as an object of study." Abbey's "'siting' of the womb as a space to be conquered" – which effaces the woman "as absent or peripheral" – "can only be had by one who stands outside it looking in . . . recalling a wildlife photographer tracking down a gazelle."[75] Abbey imagines himself as that very creature, observing himself in his ostensibly natural habitat. He simultaneously positions himself as an indeterminate object of study in a womblike wilderness yet lauds his own rugged autonomy – an oscillation between feminine and masculine metaphors.

Abbey is ambivalent, on the one hand recognizing his ecological interpenetration but on the other praising – often boastfully so – his situated apprehension of that fact. Recognizing that his own prized selfhood is subordinate to the ecological blender, he also accepts that he cannot totally dismiss his sense of self, and nor does he want to. It is because Abbey views himself as so ascetically disciplined that he believes himself worthy of a deeper relationship with the natural world (in which he nonetheless appears insignificant). For Abbey, a sense of selfhood is useful. Without it, he wouldn't be able to enjoy everything that makes him *him*. Nothing particularly solid or entirely concrete defines that personality, as his self-conscious self-representation in the process of writing *Desert Solitaire* illustrates. In fact, the only solid thing about him is precisely the ecological condition that paradoxically undercuts the individual he so much enjoys being.

It is for this reason that Abbey prefers "surfaces" over what is ostensibly "real." *Desert Solitaire* indeed supplies ample evidence that Abbey detects "no discernible difference between 'flesh' and 'essence,'" but Abbey does not consider this notion "radically progressive," mostly because he does not particularly want everything to "resolv[e] into a material monism."[76] Such a perspective, he suggests, is nominally progressive at best and downright reductive at worst, in that it not only equates individuals with their bodies but also suggests, however unintentionally, that we as persons have no real stake in remaining alive as long as our matter continues to circulate throughout the environment (a point I will revisit in Chapters 4 and 5). Abbey certainly believes that human deaths "make room for the living . . . . A ruthless, brutal process – but clean and beautiful" (242). If anything, his fascination demonstrates that he does, in fact, find such a system "real" – more tangible, perhaps, than the boisterous fiction of his authorly persona.

The Superficial Self 57

All the same, this realization does not lead Abbey to wholly, holistically identify with his body's imbrication in countless ecological interrelationships, because "human life . . . is significant . . . And this second truth we can deny only at the cost of denying our humanity" (242).

It is as if Abbey is suggesting that, for ecological radicals most concerned with the "real" or "essential," the answer to the question *What am I at my most authentic?* will always be *Nothing*. The long river passage quoted above describes not the dissolutive ecstasy of a man merging with his environment, but the bittersweet satisfaction of an environmentalist perfectly pleased with his understanding that his sense of self is something of an artifice, though not necessarily any less real for that fact. Dissolution articulates what is perhaps Abbey's most important paradox: How to reconcile the ecosystem's primary interconnectivity with the ostensible authenticity of the libertarian subject? This quandary only becomes dangerous, he suggests, when one takes ideas like "authenticity" too seriously. The only thing appeals to authenticity bring to ecology is a sense that people as such do not matter.

For this reason, Abbey's narrative draws attention to the rhetoric surrounding ecology's frequent political applications. An ecologically motivated society premised on what is "natural" or "authentic" – the hallmark values of the New Left and its environmentalist precipitates – is one in which individual lives cease to have meaning. For Bookchin, and for many subsequent social ecologists, ecology fulfilled our "desperate" need for an ethics "that will join the ideal with the real." This kind of statement gently undermines Bookchin's otherwise pragmatist interest in human civilization as an unfinished development with no particular goal, undergoing constant negotiation for the good of more individuals. It is because Bookchin dictates a vision of anarchic universalism according to what he perceives to be repressed yet insistent ecological truths that he ultimately, though unwittingly, cultivates an appeal to ecological authenticity of the sort for which he distrusted deep ecologists. Ecological society, Bookchin writes, proceeds "naturally" from human prehistory, but its utopian universalism distinguishes it from vulgar neoprimitivism. Still, the foundational value he hoped to glean from psychoanalysis was the notion that "the protoplasm of humankind retains an abiding community with the protoplasm of nature . . . in an ontological sense."[77] Despite his otherwise careful argumentation, Bookchin sustained an irreconcilable assumption that we have strayed from a natural form of society that accompanies a natural psyche, an identification with "ontological continuity" that his account could not help but prescribe.

58   The Ecological Alternative

In their different ways, Abbey and Bookchin capture an aspect of environmental writing that we are accustomed to overlook. Both come face-to-face with an uncomfortable conundrum: How does one reconcile a commitment to individual liberation with a rigorous consideration of ecology and the interconnections it implies? If Bookchin neglected this issue, Abbey embraced it for the ambiguous, unsolvable tension that it is. Despite Abbey's recognition that his sense of self is not nearly as cohesive or authentic as he would often like it to be, he nonetheless discovers that a sense of self is not only inescapable but also indispensable for a relationship with one's environment. Dillard, Lopez, and other nature writers would wrestle with the same existential and representational dilemmas over the course of the next two decades. The writing of nonfiction that considers the place of the self in relation to the ecosystem would appear to be an announcement of being caught between an almost gleeful sense of self-dismissal – a recognition that one's matter is continuous with one's environment – and the realization that a socially mediated and individually constructed sense of identity is necessary to effect that recognition in the first place.

The friction inherent in this encounter between individual and collective played out in committees and communities organized among the New Left and counterculture at large. The urgency of the 1960s fizzled in the early years of the next decade. Communards, who sought stability yet rejected even the limited authority necessary for social consistency, weathered the breakdown of their communes as "the gap between communal intention and personal experience widened" and "contradictions between individual freedom and social order turned into conflict."[78] Meanwhile, the New Left perished under its constant shift in ideological emphasis. Calvert's invocation of a white-collar "new working class" gave way to overt homegrown violence prompted by American imperial action in Vietnam and South America. As competing threads in New Left ideology vied for prominence, SDS and its affiliates strained under pressure and, following an especially brutal schism in 1969, collapsed altogether. Tom Hayden described the Weather Underground, one of the New Left's terminal scions, as "the natural final generation of SDS," their firebombs a representation of "not the conscience of their generation, but ... its id."[79] At the same time that radical politics – ecological or otherwise – demanded a rollback in repression, the New Left fractured under the weight of that mandate's apotheosis.

CHAPTER 2

The Entheogenic Landscape
Psychedelic Primitives, Ecological Indians, and the American Counterculture

. . . the child and the primitive man are satisfied with play and imitative representation . . . because they so obviously place an excessive valuation on their wishes . . . and wish-fulfillment thinking is a legacy of childhood indelible in our minds, carrying the secret project of the pure pleasure-ego.
Norman O. Brown, *Life Against Death*

We are merging, molecules getting mixed. Talk about intersubjectivity . . .
Edward Abbey, *Desert Solitaire*

One of the most conspicuous aspects of Edward Abbey's amniotic descent into the Colorado River canyon is a casual, almost flippant aside to the reader. "Talk about intersubjectivity," he remarks – and what about it? The comment provides the only mention of "intersubjectivity" in *Desert Solitaire*'s three hundred pages, but Abbey clearly finds the term indispensable to understanding his sudden inability to detect boundaries between himself and the features of his environment.[1] It expresses Abbey's sensation that his consciousness has expanded to fit the contours of the ecosystem: on the Colorado, he "merged into the Group Mind and became very psychic," as Tom Wolfe wrote of the Merry Pranksters in *The Electric Kool-Aid Acid Test*, published in 1968, the same year as *Desert Solitaire*. "Intersubjectivity!" was one of Ken Kesey's slogans for his well-publicized acid tests, communal trips hosted at festivals and in private homes during which Kesey's Pranksters freely distributed lysergic acid diethylamide (LSD) to generate "forms of expression in which there would be no separation between himself and the audience. It would be all one experience."[2] There is little doubt that Abbey was familiar with the work of Kesey and his most attentive chronicler, Wolfe. Abbey references Wolfe several times in his essays, and he overlapped with Kesey under Wallace Stegner's tutelage in Stanford University's creative writing program in the late 1950s. It was during that time that Kesey, like Allen Ginsberg and many others who "turned on" to psychedelics in the early 1960s, first ingested acid as a volunteer for a federal research program.

60   The Entheogenic Landscape

Kesey embraced the drug for the same reason the CIA wanted to weaponize it. He believed LSD, mescaline, and other mind-altering substances functioned as "truth serums." For Kesey, however, these drugs were not to be deployed against foreign agents but "ingested in company" so as to "tear apart the flimsy stupidities of life and get down to universals."[3]

Psychedelic drugs would fulfill a revelatory function, providing a glimpse of an "expanded consciousness" repressed by the civilized ego. In a 1979 interview, former SDS president Carl Oglesby reflected that LSD and leftist revolt complemented one another as "independent prongs of an over-arching transcending rebellion that took in the person and the State at the same time."[4] Oglesby's words not only reflect the New Left's general dipartite commitment to personal and communal liberation, but also hint at how psychedelic use became, among the counterculture, a method for cementing together the objects of those two goals – the individual and the collective – as a single, unified subject. For others beside Kesey, this drug-induced fusion was primarily entheogenic – spiritually as well as ontologically transformative – and often accompanied voguish engagements with East Asian and Native American iconography and ritual. Psychedelics rendered physically tangible the growing appeal of what Arthur Versluis calls "immediatism," the New Age's "assertion of spontaneous, direct, unmediated spiritual insight into reality," which arose largely from the introduction of "instant Zen" and other spiritual fads to the era's oppositional political climate by celebrity gurus such as Alan Watts. Interest in "confronting the terror of ego death . . . as a necessary prelude to an ecstatic rebirth" grew alongside the fashion for "cultures that were less sophisticated technologically but more so ecologically."[5] As the counterculture of the 1960s and 1970s bled into the resolutely apolitical New Age, gurus explored linkages among consciousness, spirituality, and ecology in a variety of contexts, from Watts's Zen Buddhism and Gary Snyder's primitivist poetics to Timothy Leary's LSD scandals and Terence McKenna's experiments with ayahuasca.

The questions raised by these intersecting countercultural interests are the central concerns of this chapter. What is the relationship between hallucinogenic revelation and the smorgasbord of nonwestern spiritual practices from which countercultural types filled their plates? How did these interests combine to contribute to a nascent identity politics of ecology? How should the vision of consciousness that resulted be represented politically and aesthetically? Chapter 1 suggested that because of its psychoanalytic framework, the New Left's politics of authenticity shifted in scale when Movement radicals articulated alternative social systems in ecological terms. In this chapter, I extend that argument by showing how countercultural types seized on the subjective uncertainty that resulted (and to which wilderness pilgrims like Abbey testified) to venerate dissolution as the consummate approach to ecological thinking. That is, countercultural experiments with drugs and alternative spiritualities inspired some figures to posit that initial subjective confusion as a glimpse at subjective *reality*, observing the same psychoanalytic narratives that earlier social theorists had grafted to ecology. This chapter, then, considers how the notion of ecological authenticity gathered spiritual, moral, and political clout as it proliferated among a pastiche of countercultural practices. As such, the chapter itself proceeds as something of a pastiche, tracing linkages among diverse encounters with psychedelia, Zen, and indigeneity that emerge at points where participants stitched these traditions together using the same psychoanalytic thread. The chapter also dives deeply into two very different texts to examine how the ecological "reality" presumptively accessed via these engagements misrepresented and thereby erased the Native cultures – and their political needs – that partly inspired that discourse to begin with.

As I will argue, the conceptual locus of these assorted countercultural interests lay in what I term *psychedelic primitivism*, a loose dogma that emerged between two intertwining cultural phenomena. First, as the political promise of the 1960s faded into the New Age of the 1970s, gurus represented psychedelics – especially organic hallucinogens such as psilocybin and ayahuasca – in terms of their erasure of the civilized ego, as well as the symbol systems that articulate it. Second, use of these drugs came to be associated with a plethora of nonwestern religious traditions and ethnic cultures, especially those of Native American tribes, rhetorically unified as a monolithic ideal by the questionable suggestion that "primitive" peoples have dodged artificial symbolic representations erected by civilization to mediate between self and world. Thus romanticized, primitives appeared to preserve our psychic nature, and the mystical substances historically sacralized by some tribes would provide a point of access to their ecological authenticity. This psychedelic narrative played out as an appropriative fantasy, a celebration of idealized, feminized societies and their special botanical knowledge – a bestowal of dubious nobility upon indigenes nonetheless still considered savage. This myth helped to crystallize – even institutionalize – the notion that authentic subjectivity is not individual but expansive, holistic, and ecological.

If 1960s drug experiments exemplified countercultural attempts to access such a condition, Native writers of the period contested the myths

62   The Entheogenic Landscape

to which their lives were said to correspond. This chapter accordingly examines the presymbolic myth of ecological authenticity in relation to both the primitivist accounts of ecological belonging that developed and deployed it and texts authored by members of communities whose lifeways served as distorted countercultural touchstones. Texts such as Peter Matthiessen's *The Snow Leopard* (1978) and Acoma Pueblo poet Simon J. Ortiz's *Woven Stone* (1992), a compendium of three collections published between 1976 and 1980, trace this myth's significance to both environmental writing and Native American writers' contestation of its chief assumptions.[6] *The Snow Leopard* calls into question the effects of countercultural drug experiments even as Matthiessen looks to a psychedelic rhetoric of "consciousness expansion" to make sense of his dissolutive experience in the Himalayan Mountains. That rhetoric takes shape over the course of a seeming identification with the entirety of the ecosystem – one that the author articulates as a reversion to primitive and possibly even prelinguistic consciousness. Matthiessen recognizes, however, that his rhetoric of ecological authenticity proves only to be that: a strategy for representing a self-erasure that does not entirely come to pass, an originary condition that does not quite exist, a subjectivity only willfully undifferentiated from its material context.

Less reflexive writers than Matthiessen claimed that Native peoples best characterized such reversion. Ortiz and countless others disputed this view, teasing out inaccuracies in the idealization of Native cultures that underwrote it, as well as foregrounding the matters of environmental justice it effaced. Ortiz makes for an excellent companion to the countercultural figures examined in the following pages because his work so assiduously addresses the tendency of progressive and radical settlers to glorify the "authenticity" of Native peoples, especially in environmentalist contexts. His poetry exhibits no special interest in psychedelics *per se*, but it foregrounds the degree to which conceptions of authenticity – including ecological authenticity – take shape in the narratives that articulate them, and often at the expense of those the word is used to describe. The figures who in this time wielded ecological authenticity as an environmentalist value presented the concept as an unmediated facet of reality. Writers such as Ortiz, however, acknowledge that it took shape in part through misunderstood values haphazardly borrowed from Native cultures. Identity and affiliation with the land emerge out of language and narrative, not when one strips them away. In fact, the only dissolutions to be found in Ortiz's poetry are those that occur when colonial forces rob his people of their traditions. Effacing Native cultures even as they declared them authentic,

The Countercultural Psyche

countercultural figures occluded the actual political conditions facing such communities – in many cases, matters of environmental justice of the sort that Ortiz emphasizes in his writing. In this respect, Ortiz foregrounds other approaches to identity and environment even as his investigation of settler appropriations troubles the parallel discourse of ecological authenticity. Ortiz's poetry helps us draw a distinction between narratives that assert authentic identification with the land and narratives that recognize their own role in constructing such relationships. The "illusion of the ego," Matthiessen writes, may well be "the dream that separates us from a true perception of the whole ... the lost paradise of our 'true nature.'"[7] Those dreams, Ortiz suggests, are nonetheless worth having. They are the narratives that hold environmental communities together.

The Countercultural Psyche

On 13 January 1967, the *Berkeley Barb* ran a promotion for the Human Be-In that occupied San Francisco's Golden Gate State Park the next day. "In unity we shall shower the country with waves of ecstasy and purification," the banner read. "Fear will be washed away; ignorance will be exposed to sunlight; profits and empire will lie drying on deserted beaches." Gary Snyder declared in the same issue that participants would stand together as "primitives of an unknown culture ... with new ethics and new states of mind."[8] Snyder joined fellow beat-generation alum Allen Ginsberg as two of the most high-profile guests in attendance, preaching peace and, as Snyder's comment makes clear, the primitive social forms they believed would propagate it. To former SDS president Todd Gitlin, the two "beat-turned-countercultural hands" embodied "two impulses" pursued by the counterculture: the "libertarian side" that "wanted to overturn repression in the name of the id," and the communitarian, "spiritual side" that "long[ed] for group experience that would transcend the limits of individual ego." Like the New Left that preceded it, the broader counterculture, in its rare moments of mass organization, appeared to pursue revolution in simultaneously individual and collective registers. For this reason, Gitlin wrote in retrospect, the audience's participation readily took the form of "a confluence of politics (on behalf of the outside and the future) and psychedelia (on behalf of the inside and the present)."[9]

Psychedelic substances illustrate a point of contradiction at the heart of the counterculture's messy, no-holds-barred approach to liberation. How does one extrapolate a socially useful strategy from so profoundly private an experience as a drug trip? Where the New Left collapsed under the weight of its ambition and violence, the counterculture fizzled along lines of exhausted personalism and corporate usurpation. The socially transformative political vision of the New Left fueled the ire of many a hippie, but for others, including Kesey and disgraced Harvard lecturer and drug guru *par excellence* Timothy Leary, "all political systems were equal oppressors and power-trippers."[10] Naturally, this approach rankled do-or-die New Leftists and other righteous radicals. Murray Bookchin, for one, disagreed with the notion that LSD could revolutionize society merely by unlocking more "peaceful and communal . . . natural, spontaneous selves." Rampant drug use at political meetings "irritated him" because, sooner rather than later, "joints would come out, and then the next thing he knew, people wouldn't be talking anymore."[11] Perhaps the most tangible feeling Leary's famous directive to "turn on," "tune in," and "drop out" inspired was a hefty measure of ambivalence. Leary drew not only the scorn of politicos but also the criticism of fellow-travelers like Ginsberg, who had participated in Leary's early Harvard experiments. "Everyone in Berkeley is all bugged because they say this drop-out thing doesn't really mean anything," Ginsberg allegedly told Leary at a party on Alan Watts's houseboat shortly after the events at Golden Gate Park, worrying that "what you're gonna cultivate is a lot of freaked-out hippies goofing around and throwing bottles through windows when they flip out on LSD."[12] Despite many proponents' belief that a principled use of psychedelics could alter consciousness to the point of social change, others dropped acid just for the high. The Age of Aquarius was an undisciplined experiment.

For Leary especially, the point of psychedelic experimentation was not to overturn repressive social structures through sustained political attention, but to change the very structure of consciousness so that the world would follow. Psychedelics could chemically, *biophysically* activate liberation. As soon as Albert Hofmann, who first synthesized LSD in 1938, accidentally consumed the compound in 1943, he began to publicize what he believed to be its revolutionary capabilities. Leary came to a similar conclusion when he ingested psilocybin mushrooms in 1960. The trip proved to be "the deepest religious experience of my life," one that convinced him that mind-altering drugs, organic and synthetic alike, "could free man's consciousness and bring about a new conception of man, his psychology and philosophy." LSD inaugurated a "historical movement that would inevitably change man at the very center of his nature."[13]

Leary's words gesture toward the depth-psychology undertones of hallucinogen discourse. Consciousness-altering substances invite a number of applications, from the familiar *psychedelic* ("mind manifesting") to the more obscure *psycholytic* ("psyche loosening"), *psychotomimetic* ("madness mimicking"), and *entheogenic* ("connecting to the spirit within"). These functions depend on users' intentions and their "set" and "setting," their "interiorized feelings, hopes, fears, and expectations" and the "external situation in which the interior journey will take place."[14] Leary, his associate Richard Alpert (later rechristened as Ram Dass), and their graduate assistant Ralph Metzner first stressed these terms in *The Psychedelic Experience*, a manual they coauthored in 1964, prior to their dismissal from Harvard and following a series of experiments conducted at the Massachusetts Correctional Institute at Concord, in which Ginsberg and Watts both participated. The "mind-manifesting" properties of LSD, Watts later wrote, had "really begun to awaken psychotherapists from their studiedly pedestrian and reductionist attitudes to life."[15] The general academic thrust of psychedelic research in the postwar era tended toward two applications its scholars viewed as intimately related: the healing of neurotic minds and the liberation of "normal" minds, a mission shared with the midcentury Freudian Left. Years after his graduate study under Leary, Metzner wrote that hallucinogens, coupled with "more or less standard interactions using a Freudian perspective," would "loosen" the patient's ego defenses so that he or she "would become more vividly aware of his or her previously unconscious emotional dynamics."[16] That such agents might challenge the status quo rather than simply undermine the psychiatric establishment occurred to a number of physicians and psychiatrists, including Metzner in his later clinical work, R. D. Laing, and Humphrey Osmond, the medical doctor who first administered mescaline to Aldous Huxley. The "other world" perceived under the influence of mescaline, Huxley wrote in *The Doors of Perception* (1954), "was not the world of visions; it existed out there . . . in the realm of objective fact." The flowers that held his attention during his first trip "so intensely signified . . . nothing more, and nothing less, than what they were – a transience that was yet eternal life, a perpetual perishing that was at the same time pure Being."[17] Psychedelics revealed to Huxley and these psychiatrists not a series of illusions, but the existence of an intrinsic – and now unveiled – perceptual consciousness attuned to matter's ephemerality.

In this respect, the hallucinogen discourse of the 1950s, 1960s, and 1970s dovetailed with the radical psychoanalysis circulating in leftist political circles. "The Freudian method of analysis never appealed to me," Watts writes, "though I would neither deny its usefulness nor the tremendous importance of Freud himself, especially when one considers the wider cultural implications of his thought as discussed, for example, by Norman O. Brown."[18] Like his contemporary Herbert Marcuse, Brown found that "the path of sublimation," the motive force of civilization, bespeaks a universal "human neurosis," and that "the bitter facts of contemporary history suggest that mankind is reaching the end of this road." However, Brown split with Marcuse over the question of political revolution, situating his own revisionary psychoanalysis within the nonpolitical frame of countercultural mouthpieces like the drug prophets. Unlike Marcuse, who believed state and corporate overreach directly correlate with surplus repression, Brown believed that individuals have complete control over their potential self-liberation. In *Life Against Death* (1959), he argued that Freud misinterpreted the relationship between Eros and Thanatos, pleasure and the death drive, because Freud himself implies that in earliest infancy these two drives are joined as one in a "union of the self with a whole world of love and pleasure," a "blissful state" unmarred by dualism, "no self and other, no subject-object . . . only timeless experience of being one with the world, only instinctual fusion and undifferentiated unity." The pleasures of such intimate merger, he argued, strain against civilization and its "conditions of repression." The life instinct persists "in the unconscious," demanding "union with others and the world around us based . . . on narcissism and erotic exuberance," the recovery of a "Dionysian" consciousness "which does not observe the limit, but overflows."[19] One need only tap into it, through means that Brown himself never made particularly clear.

These ideas appealed to figures such as Leary and Kesey, who sought to manifest an "erotic life based on the pre-Oedipal Eden." As part of a "universal body," the individual's body signified less "location or flesh" than "a field of energy" such that "ego, character, personality were mere illusion. Id was now the impersonal energy embracing all mankind." Huxley experienced such coalescence the first time he ingested mescaline and fixated on a chair's legs, "actually *being* them – or rather being myself in them; or, to be still more accurate (for 'I' was not involved in the case, nor in a certain sense were 'they') being my Not-self in the Not-self which was the chair."[20] Leary referred to this phenomenon as "ego-loss."

This psychedelic assumption of merger "institutionalized" what Gitlin referred to as the "rituals and habits" by which seemingly antagonistic "hip collectivity and the cultivation of individual experience could cohabit."[21] Acid tests, peyote circles, and ayahuasca rituals developed as a series of institutions to collapse conflict between individual and collective liberation by figuring the individual *as* the collective and the collective *as* the individual. Unlike Leary, however, Huxley maintained no illusions about the universal appeal of psychedelic experience. In addition to the "happily transfigured majority" of celebrants, there also existed "a minority that finds in the drug only hell or purgatory." Huxley did not reckon himself "so foolish as to equate" psychedelic euphoria with enlightenment; rather, he considered mind-altering substances "potentially helpful" but "not necessary to salvation."[22] In this respect, Huxley vindicated the equally temperate advocacy of Watts, who, despite his optimism regarding LSD's transformative promise, also distrusted its "injudicious use." Despite his sympathy for – even celebration of – the experience of identity with God that psychedelics facilitated, he uncharacteristically commiserated with psychiatrists who found themselves unable "to distinguish between a megalomaniac who thinks he is Jesus Christ and a genuine mystic." This distinction – the difference between Charles Manson on the one hand and himself on the other – illuminates Watts's eventual disappointment in Leary's method of spreading the good word. By the end of the decade Watts had grown "concerned, if mildly, at the direction of Timothy's enthusiasm, for to his own circle of friends and students he had become a charismatic religious leader who, well trained as he was in psychology, knew very little about religion and mysticism and their pitfalls." Watts experienced Leary's gradual conversion "into a popular store-front messiah" as evidence of his friend having fallen prey to what Carl Jung called "inflation."[23] Watts considered himself a mystic and Leary a megalomaniac: one experienced the diminishment of his ego and the other its exaggeration.

Peter Matthiessen's Psychedelics of Water, Wind, and Stone

Watts and Huxley did not suffer their misgivings alone. In *Desert Solitaire*, Abbey writes that the afternoon sun "is like a drug. The light is psychedelic . . . I feel no temptation to sleep or to relax into occult dreams but rather an opposite effect which sharpens and heightens vision, touch, hearing, taste and smell." Abbey's use of the word "psychedelic" is intriguing, especially given his later description of LSD, whose benefits he seems to be outlining, as one of "the symptoms of discontent and desperation with which most Americans are now familiar." Abbey thought little of voguish drug experiments and the individuals who orchestrated or reported on them. He referred to Leary and Wolfe as "apologists for the glossy technocracy rising around us in walls of aluminum and glass." His journals recall his sole LSD experiment – not without a touch of

68 The Entheogenic Landscape

disappointment – as an "uncomfortable and inconclusive failure: the stars quivered in a cloudy cobweb but the big spider-God failed to appear." Nor did Abbey find a sustained mystical practice any more useful in this regard, as his correspondence with Annie Dillard makes plain.[24]

Peter Matthiessen voices a similar objection to hallucinogens in *The Snow Leopard*, though he places far more faith in the sort of Buddhist practice advocated by Watts than Abbey did. *The Snow Leopard* is Matthiessen's first-person account of his march to the Himalayan interior with field biologist George Schaller in 1973. Schaller, who made the journey to study the mating habits of indigenous *bharal* blue sheep at the isolated Shey Gompa, hoped to catch a glimpse of the elusive snow leopard, whose invisibility furnished Matthiessen with a convenient symbol of his own search for wholeness following the death of his wife Deborah. Matthiessen doubted the ability of psychedelics to facilitate his recovery, but his pointed juxtaposition of his participation in LSD experiments in the late 1960s with his joyful embrace of dissolution in the remote Himalayas reveals how environmental writers like himself (and Abbey) deployed imagery borrowed from acid tests to articulate their changing conceptions of selfhood. *The Snow Leopard* demonstrates how assumptions common to psychedelic experimentation have contributed to environmentalist narratives of fusion with one's surroundings.

Early in *The Snow Leopard*, Matthiessen recalls "working seriously with a renegade psychiatrist who was making bold, early experiments" into LSD as an instrument of therapy (44). After a brief stint working for the CIA, an experience Matthiessen described in 2014 as having "pushed me leftward," he toured Peru in 1959 to research *The Cloud Forest: A Chronicle of the South American Wilderness* (1961), where he experimented with ayahuasca or *yajé*, "a hallucinogen of morbid effect used by shamans of the Amazon tribes to induce states that we call 'supernatural'" (43).[25] The experience, "though frightening," convinced Matthiessen that "this family of chemicals ... might lead to another way of seeing, and not in the slow labor of ascetic discipline but in cool efficiency and speed" (44). When he introduces his wife to mescaline, though, Deborah "freaks out": "her armor had cracked, and all the night winds of the world went howling through" (46). The couple learned early what Huxley had widely publicized: that these were "heaven and hell" substances, capable of profound horrors and pleasures that paradoxically dovetailed in the same apprehension that one's sense of self could fall apart. Horror could presage what Matthiessen considered psychedelic success: "only later did we discover that all thoughts, laughter, and emotions had been not similar but *just the same, one mind, one Mind,* even to this: that as we held each other, both bodies turned into sapling trees that flowed into each other, grew together in one strong trunk that pushed a taproot deeper and deeper into the ground" (46–7). Matthiessen's account joins an almost covetous desire for union with imagery of the natural world, a rhizomatic root system illustrative of the complex ecologies he hoped to capture in his nonfiction. The sensation's transience, however, spoiled its pleasures. Even this "success" proved something of a disappointment, because still "an 'I' remained, aware that something-was-happening because of drugs. At no time did 'I' dissolve into the miracle."

The ephemeral quality of the high alienated Matthiessen from this "way of seeing" that so resembled Kesey's explosive intersubjectivity. Later, he joined the chorus against Leary's showmanship. "In those days," Matthiessen writes, "instant gurus were turning up as thick as bean sprouts, but true teachers were very hard to find" (46). LSD provided neither a "path" nor a "way of life," but a temporarily "blissful passage ... that in my ignorance I took for religious experience" (44). Like Watts, Matthiessen "neither miss[ed] nor regret[ed]" his psychedelic experimentation. "Drugs can clear away the past, enhance the present," he writes, but "[l]acking the temper of ascetic discipline, the drug vision remains a dream that cannot be brought over into daily life. Old mists may be banished ... but the alien chemical agent forms another mist, maintaining the separation of the 'I' from true experience of the One" (47). Central to Matthiessen's refusal is his contention that drugs lack "discipline." Their result is unsustainable. Regardless, he continued to seek a sense of wholeness that drugs could not provide, especially after his wife's death, and his psychedelic past remained a useful reference against which to elucidate that later work.

Matthiessen's method is ultimately more spiritual than hallucinogenic. He and his wife became students of Zen Buddhism in 1961. At a weekend retreat shortly thereafter, Matthiessen "chanted the Kannon Sutra with such fury that I 'lost' myself, forgot the self" (106). Notably, he describes this sensation as "liberation – not change, but transformation – a profound vision of ... identity with universal life, past, present, and future" (18). He later describes this act of liberation as "the obliteration of the ego." In Tantric practice, he writes, "the student may displace the ego," and in Zen meditation "one seeks to empty out the mind, to return it to the clear, pure stillness of a seashell or flower petal. When body and mind are one, then the whole being ... may be laid open to the *experience* that individual existence, ego, the 'reality' of matter and phenomena are no more than fleeting and illusory arrangements of molecules" (91).

Matthiessen deploys a psychoanalytic rhetoric of the ego and its dissolution to describe his spiritual practice and, ultimately, his engagement with the Himalayan ecosystem. By specifically likening the "empty" individual to a seashell or flower petal, Matthiessen draws lines of affinity among narcissistic expansiveness, spirituality, and artifacts of the nonhuman world. These spiritual connections often supplemented, or were supplemented by, LSD ingestion among more temperate users than Kesey who combined Buddhism with mind-altering substances. Ram Dass, Leary's counterpart at Harvard, preferred quieter, more introspective and spiritual experiments. During the events of *The Electric Kool-Acid Test*, Dass turns Kesey away from his East Coast retreat to dodge his "manic screaming orgies in public places."[26] Watts, for his part, appreciated that the Buddha never called "wenching and boozing ... *sin*," but lamented what he perceived as Leary and Kesey's empty sideshow mysticism. Leary missed the mark of the rigorous "intellectual structure" that Harvard's Department of Social Relations expected of him, and which Watts himself tried to create for his friend. Watts saw in psychedelic experience a means of apprehending the fact that man is not external to or determined by nature, but part and parcel with it, an "essentially mystical view that man and universe are inseparable."[27]

Watts preached Zen Buddhism as "a way and a view of life which does not belong to any of the formal categories of modern Western thought," neither religion nor philosophy nor psychology but a "way of liberation" whose "essential insights," unlike the divisions generated by Western science, "are universal." One of those insights, Watts taught, is that reality permits no duality, especially not one between human and nature. The "liberated man ... sees that the skin may just as well be regarded as what joins us to our environment as what separates us from it." Buddhism offered Watts, a convert from the cold exclusivity of Anglican Christianity, a sense of intimacy, of vision and sensation, "the nature-wisdom of Taoism" and the clarity of *prajna*, "a way of experiencing ultimate reality so unencumbered with concepts and propositions that it is called *sunya*, the Void." The point of *prajna* – Buddhist insight – is "not to reduce the human mind to a moronic vacuity, but to bring into play its innate and spontaneous intelligence by using it without forcing it."[28] Matthiessen daydreams about channeling this very reflex in reaction to a snow leopard's pounce, a moment in which he "might truly perceive it and be free" (257). "Naturalness" and "spontaneity" take on the same resonance in Watts's Zen Buddhism that they do in Bookchin's social ecology – a sign not of these thinkers' identity or mutual influence, but of the fact that these countercultural conversations focused on a remarkably consistent set of ideas.

Chief among these ideas remained the narrative of Freud's *Civilization and Its Discontents*. In *Nature, Man and Woman* (1958), Watts writes that the ego "is set over against nature as the dissociated soul or mind." He favorably cites at length Freud's theory of primary narcissism – the notion that "originally the ego includes everything" – and articulates an analogous biological dimension, "a world of interdependent relationships, where things are intelligible only in terms of each other" in "a seamless unity." Our psychic origins might be rediscovered through the abandonment of ego according to the teachings of Zen, Tao, and other Eastern traditions. Zen's Taoist influence especially takes on the function not of revolution but of personal transformation, much as for Brown a (rather unclear) psychoanalytic introspection and release would lead to a unified subject. Brown viewed psychoanalytic prehistory as the unseen force that motivated the mysticisms of his day, and radical psychoanalysis as a logic that could complete "what religion tries to do, namely, make the unconscious conscious." Watts praised likeminded intellectuals and analysts who "have recognized that regression may sometimes be important in the service of maturation." We learn more from the "baby's vision of the world ... the 'oceanic feeling' in which there is no differentiation between I and All," than we do from the "cancer" that results when "powerful people with sticks and guns" prod our growth according to "differentiation" and "the emergence of the articulate ego from the primal id."[29]

Amid this convergence of Buddhist and psychoanalytic rhetoric, Matthiessen "felt 'good,' like a 'good child,' entirely safe" while chanting the Kannon Sutra (106). "No ego was involved" in this state of calm, grace, and care, which adhered over the course of his wife's illness. "For the first time since unremembered childhood, I was not alone," he writes: "the one who acted in this manner was not 'I,'" in fact "there was no separate 'I'" (107). The notion that the child possesses a sense of ecological infinity charms Matthiessen, even inspires in him a feeling akin to envy when he fondly recalls his young son abandoning his toys during the summer to watch the birds and the trees. The boy stood "at rest in the very center of the universe, a part of things, unaware of endings and beginnings, still in unison with the primordial nature of creation, letting all light and phenomena pour through. Ecstasy is identity with all existence ... there was no 'self' to separate him from the bird or flower" (41–2). The text, like *Desert Solitaire* ten years before, repeatedly identifies the natural world with childhood and infancy; and like Brown and Watts, Matthiessen holds that

72 The Entheogenic Landscape

social context represses this wider worldview, bereft of an "I" to anchor it. Mature self-consciousness heralds a change in subjectivity: the "armor of the 'I' begins to form, the construction and desperate assertion of separate identity." Matthiessen is hopeful, however, that "to shatter or dissolve it brings about the reunion with all universal life that mystics seek, the homegoing, the return to the lost paradise of our 'true nature'" (66). One must find a way to reverse repression, to regain a lost sense of omnipresence, of connection, and of ecology.

Spiritual discipline lastingly fulfills the same function as psychedelic vision in that both structure themselves according to a common psychoanalytic vocabulary.[30] In the Himalayas, "consciousness expansion" is spiritual, infantile, *and* "hallucinogenic," but Matthiessen's Buddhist training has apparently resolved the heaven-and-hell tension he and Deborah navigated under the influence of mescaline and LSD. "In the snow mountains," Matthiessen feels "open, clear, and childlike once again," and when he loses his sense of self, "the heartbeat I heard was the heart of the world, I breathed with the mighty risings and declines of the earth, and this evanescence seemed less frightening than exalting" (168, 43). The reversal of repression Matthiessen believes possible is both temporal and spatial, characteristic of childhood and endemic to the landscape. The farther Matthiessen and Schaller travel from "civilization," the more readily they cast off "the screens of modern life" (265).

For Matthiessen, Zen engagement with a wilderness locale constitutes a psychedelics of ecology, an expansion of consciousness inclusive of all matter living and nonliving. His spiritual commitment to self-evacuation – what he describes as embodying the "void" – amplifies in the Himalayas. At high altitudes, Matthiessen feels the ground, like a heart, almost beating "with its own energy . . . that energy pours through me, joining my body with the sun." Among the "sheep dung, light, and the fleeting aggregate of atoms that is 'I,' there is no particle of difference . . . . I grow into these mountains like a moss" (232). Just before Matthiessen leaves the Shey monastery, preparing for his return journey, he intuits that "the dying grass, the notes of southbound birds in the mountain sky are no more fleeting than the rock itself, no more so and no less – all is the same. The mountain withdraws into stillness, my body dissolves into the sunlight, tears fall that have nothing to do with 'I'" (248). Matthiessen's identification with this "fleeting aggregate of atoms" emphasizes the cyclical characteristics of ecology, whose continuity he seizes upon to make peace with his wife's death. Tantric practice encourages the bereaved "to realize that everything in the Universe, being inseparably related, is therefore holy" (93). Buddhist

Peter Matthiessen's Psychedelics of Water, Wind, and Stone 73

Tibetans in the region practice "air burial," a custom according to which "the body of the deceased is set out on a wild crag ... to be rended and devoured by the wild beasts ... all is returned into the elements, death into life" (231). Matthiessen attempts to settle his grief via Buddhism's repudiation of lack, which Gary Snyder referred to as "needless craving" primarily "caused by social factors."[31] Long before the birth of Buddhism, Matthiessen writes, the Upanishadic Vedas "already included the idea that mortal desire – since it implies lack – had no place in the highest state of being," the "unification of the self" (17). Matthiessen's apprehension of cyclical material interchange momentarily appears to salve his wife's absence. Given her ephemeral biological composition, Deborah's body – and her self – had always been simultaneously dead and alive, both nothing and everything. So, too, is Matthiessen himself.

The potential violence of that realization repeats throughout *The Snow Leopard* in desolate wilderness places in terms analogous to those circulated by drug gurus. Matthiessen expresses a keen desire to be ripped apart by the earth: "If only [the mountains] would fly apart, consume us in a fire of white light" (235). The hint of glee lurking in these words turns up also in Wolfe's depiction of an acid trip: "The *experience* of the barrier between the subjective and the objective, the personal and the impersonal, the *I* and the *not-I* disappearing ... that *feeling!*"[32] Matthiessen's wilderness psychedelia reads as a beatific, even joyous celebration of what Terry Gifford describes as antipastoral sensibility, an embrace of "natural violence ... the neutrality of a nature that cannot be invested with that long list of pastoral comforts." Matthiessen urges readers to welcome rather than fear the pointlessness or indifference of biological infinitude, an enthusiasm reminiscent of Henry David Thoreau's fearful yet "thrilling" experience of "nature's extremity" atop Ktaadn in *The Maine Woods* (1864).[33] *The Snow Leopard*'s mysticism takes part in – and updates for its moment – an American narrative tradition of self-destabilization in nature that Matthiessen reads in the metaphysics of William James, the "transparent eyeball" of Ralph Waldo Emerson, and the simultaneously individualistic and all-encompassing "barbaric yawp" of Walt Whitman (62–3).

The Snow Leopard sits at an intersection between the countercultural surge in Eastern spirituality and a tradition of self-erasure in American nature writing, and it deploys the current imagery of psychedelic euphoria to join them.[34] "Left alone, I am overtaken by that northern void – no wind, no cloud, no track, no bird," Matthiessen writes. "This stillness to which all returns, this is reality ... such transience and insignificance are exalting, terrifying, all at once, like the sudden discovery, in meditation, of

74 The Entheogenic Landscape

one's own transparence" (173). Reality signifies, for Matthiessen, his own transience, which he experiences subjectively as a form of merger. Still, like Huxley before him, he experiences his dissolution and expansion of consciousness as a profoundly solitary transformation, sometimes chemical yet ultimately deeply personal. Part of Matthiessen's disappointment with the drug trip is his recognition that it is a mirage, covering over the fact that the high proceeds as an isolated synaptic incident occurring in his brain. Just as Deborah displayed a radically different reaction to mescaline – one bereft of Matthiessen's own joyful sensation of merger – Schaller does not share his companion's spiritual vision. Furthermore, he laments that for his spiritual exercise as well as for his drug saga, "as long as I remain an 'I' who is conscious of the void and stands apart from it, there remains a snow mist on the mirror" (174). The goal of total self-elimination is as unattainable for Matthiessen as it was for Abbey, given that the dismissal of the ego requires an ego-position from which to express it. He struggles to reconcile the holistic vision he strives for in his writing with his own authorial interpretation of Buddhism and the landscape. He finds himself aware, that is, that his experience of dissolution is not quite the unmediated glimpse of universal ecological authenticity he thinks it is, but instead filtered through a narrative he cobbles together from spiritual and psychedelic influences.

"The Hallucinogenic Oceans of the Mind" from East to West

The precision of Matthiessen's spiritualism led him to scrutinize his assumptions and beliefs with a rigor that the "protestant lawlessness" of beat-generation flirtations and the vapid personalism of New-Age commodification often precluded.[35] With the exception of Snyder, beat writers engaged Zen for the spontaneous style it inspired at least as often as they did for its coherent theology. Allen Ginsberg's back-cover plug for his 1968 collection of poetry *Planet News* touted his poetry's place in a "continuing tradition of ancient Nature Language" that "mediates between psychedelic inspiration and humane ecology & integrates acid classic Unitive Vision with democratic eyeball particulars," a series of sensually detailed images of pastoral landscapes in poems like "Wales Visitation." Ginsberg was not the only beat writer to situate his work in an environmental literary tradition while drawing from the "Unitive Vision" of acid, Buddhism, and other countercultural chestnuts. In *The Dharma Bums* (1958), Jack Kerouac's stand-in protagonist Ray deploys Mahayana Buddhist concepts like

"The Hallucinogenic Oceans of the Mind" from East to West   75

samsara, signifying cyclical change, and *tathata*, "suchness," in tandem as he attempts to evacuate his sense of self in the face of what he experiences as nature's material reality. Snyder, on whom Kerouac based the character Japhy Ryder, took umbrage at what he considered Kerouac's sloppy representation of Zen, but communicated a similar, if more disciplined, sentiment. In *The Old Ways* (1977), Snyder writes that the poet and philosopher share the yogin's "deep sense of communication with nature," an aesthetic knowledge that forcibly suggests "that we are all composite beings . . . changing constantly in time. There is no 'self' to be found in that, and yet oddly enough, there is." Snyder identifies and tries to resolve his own paradox – that there exists a coherent self that recognizes its own formlessness over time – by presenting it as a matter of repression, a symptom of "a culture that alienates itself from the very ground of its own being – from the wilderness outside" and "the wilderness within." He implores readers of his Pulitzer Prize-winning *Turtle Island* (1969) to recognize that the Anglo-American as well as the Buddhist East Asian or Native American "is a swirl in the flow," and that "all share such views at the deepest levels of their old cultural traditions – African, Asian, or European. Hark again to those roots, to see our ancient solidarity."[36]

Snyder's gesture to shared characteristics among "old cultural traditions" repressed in the modern West reverberated throughout the literature of the decade. In the Tibetan Himalayas, Matthiessen is "struck by the resemblances between our native Americans and these Mongol peoples," between their manners of dress which "suggest the Pueblo Indians and the Navajo" and their "animistic kinship with the world around" (53–4). In these encounters, Matthiessen confronts "the existence and perpetuation of a body of profound intuitive knowledge" (55). These similarly primitive peoples remain closer to our essential yet forgotten nature, "the practice of what Westerners, having lost the secrets, refer to with mixed fascination and contempt as 'mysticism' or 'the occult' but which for the less alienated cultures, past and present, is only another aspect of reality" (55). Ostensibly free of sociocultural alienation, the "entranced Brahman staring into the fire" and the "Pueblo sacred dancer" both "achieve the same obliteration of the ego" (90–1). For Matthiessen, a "primitive" dismissal of ego provides access to ecological reality, a human essence germane to the turbulent politics of his era. "If we are on the verge of postcivilization," Snyder writes, "then our next step must take account of the primitive worldview which has traditionally and intelligently tried to open and keep open lines of communication with the forces of nature." Such a perspective, he mused, "can be reconstructed from the unconscious."[37] The history and culture of individual tribes do not matter so much as the fact that all of them are – for the sake of argument – *originary*.

Despite their great care for the individuals and peoples with whom they interacted, Snyder and Matthiessen's rhetoric verges on the homogeneous. Matthiessen later noted that, prior to the research and experiences he detailed in *Indian Country* (1979) and *In the Spirit of Crazy Horse* (1980), and "like most people with more appreciation than understanding of the Indian vision," he had "clung to a romantic conception of 'traditional Indians,' aloof from activism and politics and somehow spiritually untouched by western progress."[38] Both Matthiessen and Snyder struggled against an impulse to lump diverse populations into a single, ecologically friendly camp of ego-free primitives, which manifested in countless other, more superficial articulations of spiritual environmentalism. This inclination found its broader cultural apotheosis in an omnipresent speech allegedly delivered by Chief Seattle in 1887, in reality penned by a white screenwriter and disseminated as an anti-pollution television spot by the Southern Baptist Convention in 1972. Seattle's "authentic" oration, Philip J. Deloria writes, "pasted together the classic tropes of Indian Americanism" even as it "erased contemporary social realities." Like Iron Eyes Cody's Crying Indian, the Seattle speech "linked people in one aboriginal, nature-loving family … bound by a universal web of blood connections and their relations to the earth."[39]

These images of "Ecological Indians," to borrow a term from Shepard Krech, have more often than not been "applied in North America to all indigenous people" as an ideological foil to a Western civilization that "ruined … pristine, unspoilt nature." In the back-to-the-land movement such figures "constituted fertile soil for those seeking alternative 'counter-cultural' lives."[40] Communes across the American Southwest populated compounds with a potpourri of religious iconography imported from across the Pacific as well as from Pueblo and Navajo neighbors. To supplement its showcase of practical instruments for communal living, Stewart Brand's *Whole Earth Catalog* included a registry of spiritual texts ranging from the *I Ching* and Watts's accessible Zen handbooks to volumes on shamanism and Indigenous heritage, even mystical interpretations of cybernetics. Despite his unapologetically aggressive "enthusiasm for business and unfettered capitalism," Brand found the "feelings of unity with the universe" provoked by flirtations with Indigenous spirituality, as well as his friend Kesey's acid tests, indispensable to ecological politics.[41] Communards supplemented watered-down social ecology with Native

"The Hallucinogenic Oceans of the Mind" from East to West 77

American and East Asian paraphernalia in an attempt to position themselves counter to Western artifice. Tibetans and Native Americans could therefore play similar roles in the environmental drama enacted by counterculturalists. In *The Snow Leopard*, Matthiessen frames both as originary, and therefore free of alienation, and therefore authentic. Native Americans, Gitlin writes, were "triply attractive" for their oppression, primitive intuition, and sadly vanishing authenticity.[42]

Such fashions – on the part of white radicals – facilitated efforts "to encounter the authentic amidst the anxiety of urban industrial and post-industrial life," a series of activities that, for a counterculture raging against the backdrop of the Cold War, came to "address anxieties focused on a perceived lack of personal identity." To adorn oneself in beads and amulets was to broadcast "that one's sympathies lay with both the past and the present targets . . . of United States imperialism."[43] Solidarity and even identification with victims of American foreign policy became fashionable among New Left militants over the course of the Vietnam War. SDS coalesced around its white members' impression that marginalized Americans – specifically Blacks and the poor – constituted a demographic more authentic than their own. The exclusion of these groups from the liberal status quo paradoxically rendered them less existentially (though more politically) alienated than SDS's white, middle-class base.[44]

The New Age that would soon blossom from the counterculture's commercialized corpse, however, pursued an emphasis on individual liberty increasingly bereft of SDS's strident socialism or the counterculture's exhausted communalism. Nonwestern spirituality and the fledgling practice of transpersonal psychology contributed two important ingredients to the individualized, personal "transformation" that characterized the New Age in place of a cohesive platform.[45] Transpersonal psychology recycled the same elements of psychoanalysis that attracted both the Freudian Left and the drug prophets, packaging them as a cure for alienation based on ego-transcendence – even developmental regression – which, alongside deep ecology, came to inform primitivist rhetoric in certain circles of ecopsychology in the 1990s. That political concerns fell by the wayside is not particularly surprising. The counterculture had long venerated avowedly apolitical gurus like Leary and Brown, who steered audiences away from action and toward a psychic transformation that manifested more often than not in lifestyle choices.

From the time of the counterculture's heyday in the 1960s through its declension in the 1970s, psychedelics consistently provided a point of contact between rebels seeking liberation and a homogenized primitive

78   The Entheogenic Landscape

tradition they believed held the keys. Upon breaking Leary out of jail in 1970, the Weather Underground declared that "LSD and grass, like the herbs and cactus and mushrooms of the American Indians, will help us make a future world where it will be possible to live in peace."[46] In an interview, Ralph Metzner used the word "trickster" to describe his former mentor, grafting vague Native American iconography onto countercultural drug mythology.[47] The Neo-American Church took LSD as its primary sacrament when it raucously imitated the Native American Church, which combined elements of Christian theology with entheogenic peyote rituals intended to connect devotees to deities and, by association, the natural world. "In sacramentalizing the use of peyote," Huxley writes, the Native American Church "fused" the "two great appetites of the soul – the urge to independence and self-determination and the urge to self-transcendence," thereby facilitating the sort of institutionalized individual/collective collapse that gurus such as Leary and psychoanalytical scholars such as Brown encouraged.[48]

The natural occurrence of peyote and other organic hallucinogens also strengthened their appeal as "valid antidotes to environmental destruction," an application attributed to their supposedly "unique ability for humans to realize that they are part of a much larger imbrication with the environment."[49] Organic chemistry has often informed this association. Ayahuasca's psychoactive properties, for example, derive from the presence of dimethyltryptamine (DMT) in *Psychotria viridis* leaves native to the Amazon basin. DMT alone has little effect on human physiology when ingested. The stomach enzyme monoamine oxidase (MAO) naturally degrades and metabolizes the compound. The second ingredient, the bark of the *Banisteriopsis caapi* vine, introduces harmine and harmaline beta-carboline alkaloids to the gut to inhibit MAO, enabling the body's direct absorption of DMT into the blood stream to the brain.[50] In spite of the passage of postwar sanctions against clinical hallucinogen research, a cadre of ethnobotanists continued to evangelize the shamanic lineage of such compounds. Terence and Dennis McKenna, two especially prominent New-Age luminaries, found they could mimic ayahuasca's interface between compound and axon through a combination of mushrooms and *B. caapi* bark, "the closest approximation to smoking synthetic tryptamine (DMT) that we have found in nature."[51]

This molecular correspondence inspired the brothers' charming idea that the consumption of ayahuasca, mushrooms, or other organic hallucinogens – a collection of substances Metzner once referred to as "plant teachers" – enables plant and human to directly converse.[52] In *The Archaic*

"The Hallucinogenic Oceans of the Mind" from East to West 79

Revival (1998), Terence McKenna describes the initial phases of the psilo-cybin trip as "a dialogue ... between the ego and ... larger, more inte-grated parts of the psyche that are normally hidden from view," which, when reduced to their constitutive series of chemical reactions in the brain, are continuous with the ecosystem itself. A 1971 experiment at La Chorrera in Colombia convinced Terence that "the mushroom was in fact a kind of intelligent entity ... able during the trance to communicate its personality as a presence in the inward-turned perceptions of its beholder." Dennis felt he "was downloading explicit instructions from the Teacher" as his "own DNA interlaced with the DNA of a mushroom." The plant "transmitted ... a set of procedures for creating, and then fixing, the mercury of my own consciousness," a chemical synthesis resulting in a biological manifestation of Carl Jung's "individuated self," a "fully realized person, aware of both the personal and collective aspects of the self."[53]

The notion that the ecosystem speaks to us through psychedelic plant compounds has enjoyed remarkable longevity. "If the plant really is talking to the person, many people hear the same thing: we are all one," wrote the journalist Ariel Levy in a 2016 *New Yorker* article detailing ayahuasca's enduring mystique. "Some believe that the plants delivering this message are serving their own interests, because if humans think we are one with everything we might be less prone to trash the natural world .... But this sensation of harmony and interconnection with the universe – what Freud described as the 'oceanic feeling' – is also a desirable high."[54] Levy's reference to Freud is significant: it obliquely nods toward the striking abundance of psychoanalytic terminology coursing through hallucinogen discourse in both clinical and autobiographical literature. What the McKennas termed "the shamanic function" of ayahuasca healing "also includes a psychoanalytic capability." The plant scientist Charles Grob accurately notes that in years past, "during a time of psychoanalytic preeminence," shamanic healers "were judged to be mentally ill." That "illness," however, was precisely the point for organic hallucinogens' most fervent devotees, who embraced the notion that Indigenous knowledge held the psychedelic secret to "erasing established patterns of behavior by letting the ego melt under its influence."[55] In a series of "yage letters" exchanged with William Burroughs, Ginsberg – gifted a parcel of aya-huasca by Matthiessen when they crossed paths in Lima, Peru – wondered at the "fearful" and "almost schizophrenic alteration of consciousness" generated by the mixture. The sensation appealed to New-Age psycho-nauts like the McKennas, who actively linked schizophrenia directly to

80   The Entheogenic Landscape

shamanic practice. The primary difference between psychosis and Indigenous ritual, the McKennas write, "must be sought in the degree of cultural acceptance of this ... altered perception of reality."[56] Their interpretation of schizophrenia as an expression of authentic consciousness dressed in New-Age rhetoric the midcentury antipsychiatry of analysts such as R. D. Laing and Thomas Szasz, who, like Marcuse, rejected the normative objectives of mainstream ego psychology. The ego, Terence McKenna writes, "developed" from earlier forms of consciousness "as a necessary means of adapting to socialization." In the millennia since, it has become such a detriment to ourselves and our environment that we must "reconnect" with "a globally conscious, ecologically sensitive ... kind of consciousness that we can access only ... through self-discipline, psychotherapy, [and] psychedelics." The modest experiment at La Chorrera would "trigger an end to history, throw open the gates of a paradise out of time and invite humanity to walk in."[57]

The brothers' call for psychic reorganization is a dual mandate for psychic and social liberation of a piece with the psychoanalytic leftism influential to the 1960s counterculture. Ayahuasca and psilocybin furnish ships on which to sail "the hallucinogenic oceans of the mind" lurking beneath the repressively civilized ego.[58] Metzner likewise suggested that clinically, psycholytic therapy might achieve "an even deeper psychic opening – to birth and prebirth memories." This equivalence among infancy, nature, and hallucinogenic experience also crops up in Richard Schultes and Albert Hofmann's seminal *Plants of the Gods* (1979). The "ultimate goal of indigenous ayahuasca ritual," they write, culminates in a "return to the maternal womb." Terence McKenna tags the *Stropharia cubensis* mushroom as "the Ur plant, our umbilicus to the feminine mind of the planet."[59] These (male) writers' chosen class of adjective is significant. "Feminine" suggests that the holistic sensation derived from organic hallucinogens represents the recovery of a primary, maternal, and unified condition of subjective continuity with the ecosystem, a "dissolution of boundaries between self and world" that survives in "feminine, foreign and exotic, and transcendental experiences."[60]

McKenna's psychedelic primitivism evokes a familiar litany of sliding associations among women, racial and ethnic others, and the land. As his comments make clear, proponents of psychedelics have long deployed a familiar narrative: that of a golden, pre-civilizational past, a disastrous present, and a future potentially glorious only insofar as it resembles the past. This script overlaps what Ursula K. Heise refers to as the "story template" that has frequently characterized mainstream environmentalism from the nineteenth century to the present: "the idea that modern society has degraded a natural world that used to be beautiful, harmonious, and self-sustaining and that might disappear completely if modern humans do not change their way of life."[61] As one might expect, the ideal of "anti-modern authenticity" conjured by this decontextualized pastiche of psychedelic vision, generic Indigenous ritual, and *I Ching*-inspired ecological mysticism "rarely engaged real Indians, for it was not only unnecessary but inconvenient to do so." Native Americans and their artifacts often, though not always, served as "temporal Others, reflections of a primitive stage of cultural existence outside modernity," representations of primary wholeness that could be "exceedingly limiting, even dehumanizing, particularly at a moment when many Indian people were generating new ways of living in a changing world."[62] Simon Ortiz noted in a 2010 interview that romantic stereotypes have flourished among Native as well as nonnative peoples, but the gulf between ideal and ordinary Native Americans – the "tragic, degraded figures" who did not match the primitivist narrative – puts the lie to the notion of authenticity as many deployed it.[63]

Psychedelic Primitivism's Presymbolic Myth

Ortiz's comments about self-imposed romantic stereotypes gesture to the tendency among certain Native activists to in fact encourage these associations – a point that the next chapter will take up in more detail. What I want to emphasize now is that countercultural settlers established their ideas about ecological authenticity on very real Native practices – attachments to the land, engagements with hallucinogenic plant compounds – that they nonetheless misinterpreted chiefly due to their assumptions about psychic development. "What were the natural, the primitive, the unrefined, the holy unspoiled child, the pagan body," Todd Gitlin writes, "if not *the repressed* ... the animal spirit now reviving from beneath the fraudulent surface of American life?"[64] A familiar, ad-hoc psychoanalytic narrative about primary, infantile consciousness fused psychedelic experience with diverse "primitive" cultures in the white counterculture's ecological imagination, obscuring the complex cultural practices that partially informed the concept of ecological authenticity to begin with. More specifically, gurus chiefly imagined that psychedelics provided access to the ecological authenticity they presumed "primitive" peoples enjoy by melting away one's symbolic faculties.

A pervasive linguistic theme dominates countercultural assumptions about both drugs and Indigenous peoples, linking both together by asserting

82 The Entheogenic Landscape

their shared psychosocial innocence. On the one hand, true indigenes live unburdened by the ego and the symbolically mediated social baggage that shapes it. On the other, psychedelic substances work their magic by stripping away the symbol systems that negotiate between self and environment. Through the reinvigoration of hallucinogenic ritual and shamanism, Terence McKenna writes, we might accomplish the "revival of the Archaic – or preindustrial and preliterate – attitude toward community, substance use, and nature."[65] The operative word in McKenna's promise is "preliterate." Countercultural gurus collapsed infantile psychology and nonwestern peoples together by arguing that because both exist in a primitive stage of development, they both enjoy an unmediated – and therefore expansive and ecological – state of consciousness. "The belief in the omnipotence of thoughts," Brown writes, is "a characteristic feature" not only of the infantile developmental stage but also of "primitive adults." More specifically, "the child and the primitive man are satisfied with play and imitative representation" rather than sophisticated symbolic communication.[66] Brown and McKenna both contended that Indigenous communities are *favorably* regressed, and the key to their regression lies in an underdeveloped use of language, a mode of perception untethered to representation, an unmediated experience also characteristic of the psychedelic episode.

This presymbolic myth circulated among figures looking to link the expansive vision of Eastern and/or Western spirituality with environmental concerns. When Watts met Snyder in San Francisco, he commented that the poet "*is* just exactly what I have been trying to *say*."[67] For both Watts and Matthiessen, direct, unmediated perception and experience – whatever that might look like – stood in spiritual contrast to "meaningless" attempts "to capture what cannot be expressed, knowing that mere words will remain" (212). In his *Snow Leopard* era, symbolic representation seemed to Matthiessen to impede his unification with the landscape: "the secret place *where we have always been* is overgrown with thorns and thickets of 'ideas,'" of "masks and screens, defenses . . . propped up by ideas and words" (44–5, 91). Symbols interfere with spontaneity. "Compare the wild, free paintings of the child" – as well as the "bold sumi painting" of Zen artists – "with the stiff, pinched 'pictures' these become as the painter notices the painting and tries to portray 'reality' as others see it" (42). It is at this point, when reaction, sensation, and amateur impressionism give way to representation, that the "armor of the 'I' begins to form." Infant, East Asian mystic, and Native American shaman join forces in their environmental merger.

These perspectives suffer from a glaring and – as Matthiessen and Watts knew well – unsolvable complication. The "primitive" practices – and

Psychedelic Primitivism's Presymbolic Myth

hallucinogenic substances that may or may not have accompanied them – to which countercultural spiritualists appealed in a bid to access ecological authenticity are themselves highly structured rituals that accumulate centuries' worth of symbolic gestures, despite whatever liquification a given ritual might promise. As a result, the "symbolic value" affixed by New-Age communards to "Indian" artifacts like tipis reads as irony.[68] Huxley recognized this inability to transcend representation, although he did believe psychedelic drugs possessed the capacity to mitigate it (at least momentarily). In *Heaven and Hell* (1956), he lamented "the verbal notions" by which "our perceptions of the external world are habitually clouded" – necessarily so, for without "language and the other symbol systems," our "sensations, feelings, insights, fancies – all these are ... incommunicable." At the same time, he believed "we must preserve and, if necessary, intensify our ability to look at the world directly and not through that half opaque medium of concepts," an alteration made possible "by taking the appropriate drug." Huxley directs his readers' attention to the "close similarity between induced or spontaneous visionary experience" and the sensorium of "man in his primal state of innocence." Under the influence of mescaline, Huxley believed, one "recovers some of the perceptual innocence of childhood, when the sensum was not immediately and automatically subordinated to the concept." Without the occasional mystical and/or psychedelic reprieve, we are, "as it were, petrified by language," subject to the mercy of what Huxley, borrowing a phrase from Henri Bergson, called "the reducing valve." To sift through and retain only what is practical in an overwhelming mass of sensual perception, "man has invented and endlessly elaborated those symbol-systems and implicit philosophies which we call languages ... . What comes out at the other end is a measly trickle," a psyche truncated by signs whose unconscious "antipodes" quietly retain "all the freshness, all the naked intensity, of experiences which have never been verbalized ... entirely natural in the sense of being entirely unsophisticated by language."[69]

Huxley's "reducing valve" appears to refer to both ego *and* symbolic language – they are in his writing closely associated. By the time Watts wrote his memoir in 1973, he had also come to believe something similar: "that my ego is a marriage between my (necessarily false) image or concept of myself, and the chronic muscular tension which a child learns in *trying* to do things which must happen spontaneously." Watts presents an account of the ego as tension between representational image and biology, in the process challenging his hero Carl Jung, whom he believed "bewitched by the grammatical convention that the verb must have a subject."[70] Jung famously busied his career with symbols, especially those he believed "cannot be derived from ... personal experience," the series of unconscious "archaic remnants" he believed reflect "the biological, prehistoric, and unconscious development of the mind in archaic man, whose psyche was still close to that of the animal." To varying degrees, Huxley and the McKennas, who greatly admired Jung, viewed psychedelics with this development in mind: as a paring knife that made it possible to "peel the unconscious, layer by layer," back to its seed, the primitive psyche of "even the amoeba."[71] The McKennas even contended that a primordial ingestion of psychedelics "triggered the invention of language," a claim they supported with characteristically fanciful evidence: a faint "buzzing" sound produced by the consumption of *S. cubensis*. At La Chorrera, Dennis *tried to imitate these noises with my vocal cords ... Suddenly, it was as if the sound and my voice locked onto each other and the sound was my voice.*[72] Language, the brothers suggest, is external to the human subject, a system in which individuals become implicated first through psychedelic experimentation and then through socialization.

In light of Western hallucinogen discourse's extensive reliance on psychoanalysis for its vocabulary, the McKennas' perspective lends a distinctively Lacanian flavor to the psychedelic mythologies they helped to circulate. I do not mean to suggest that the brothers explicitly established their thought on Lacanian psychoanalysis. Rather, I want to point out that they asked questions about subjectivity that resonated with Jacques Lacan's own (albeit with different results). Within the span of two decades, the McKennas, Huxley, Lacan, and even Matthiessen, Watts, and Snyder, to a lesser extent, shared an interest in language as the component structuring experiences of subjectivity. Terence McKenna refers to the ecosystem as the "Other" and, in Lacanian fashion, means that designation to signify symbolic order. After the La Chorrera experiment, the brothers proposed that ayahuasca's humming "waveform" – which they took to be the foundation of human language – produces consciousness "holographically" by "encoding" sensory perception onto the brain, even if the resulting image "bears little resemblance to the object photographed."[73] Their schema reflects Lacan's insistence on the incommensurability between language and the real objects it represents. It also strikingly evokes the Lacanian mirror stage, during which the ego forms in infancy as an imaginary image – an "I" that emerges through discourse – with which the subject identifies. All subsequent perception filters through the same symbolic register.[74]

At the very least, Lacanian ideas help to elucidate the McKennas' conception of what hallucinogens accomplish. The brothers believed the human ego to be a construction predicated on language, generated by the ecosystem but, as a mediating symbol between self and world, nonetheless an obstacle to directly interfacing with it. One is ordinarily casually ignorant of our implication in this "syntactical web that holds both language and the world together," but tryptamines, Terence argues, enable us to perceive the system as a *language which becomes and which is the things it describes.*" In the McKennas' mythos, hallucinogens play a role that resembles what Lacan describes as the ever-elusive "trove of signifiers," an imaginary key to grasping the system directly rather than via symbolic mediation. If tryptamines gave rise to the conscious ego, they could also undo it by revealing and breaking down its construction, collapsing the distinction between symbol and referent and establishing "channels of direct communication with the Other."[75] By breaking down the chain of signification, hallucinogens break apart the ego that is a product of that chain, enabling the brothers to better interface with their surroundings. The significance of the McKennas' theory lies not in its certainty that language exists as a relational field that draws us into cultural formations, but in its assertion that our relation to the field, and therefore to culture, must come undone.

The McKennas' suggestion that psychedelics enable access to prelinguistic subjectivity – and therefore ecological authenticity – rests heavily on their assumption that the shamans from whom they derived their knowledge represent a primary, ecologically attuned tradition. That assumption prompted them and other gurus to conflate *all* Indigenous peoples believed free of civilizational corruptions under the rubric of an authentic identity obscured in developed peoples beneath the callous and imprecise veneer of symbolic representation. The figure of this Ecological Indian, however, "masks cultural diversity" and "serves to deflect any desire to fathom or confront the evidence for relationships between Indians and the environment."[76] As a result, the practical environmental issues facing Native communities also tend to fall by the wayside.

Simon Ortiz, Oral Tradition, and Environmental Justice

Countercultural figures, despite their understanding of ecological authenticity as an unmediated condition, in part modeled the idea on a misguided understanding of Native environmentalism. The Acoma Pueblo poet Simon Ortiz is acutely aware of how readily appeals to "primitive" insight map over entire populations, deifying ecological authenticity yet eliminating tribal distinctions, to the detriment of pressing social, economic, and

86 The Entheogenic Landscape

environmental concerns facing those communities. Over the course of the eight years following the McKenna brothers' experiment at La Chorrera, as Matthiessen drafted what would become *The Snow Leopard*, Ortiz published the three collections of poetry he would later gather in a single volume, *Woven Stone*. Like the works of these other writers, Ortiz's poetry demonstrates a keen interest in subjectivity, language, and indigeneity, but differentiates itself by undertaking a far more nuanced exploration of Native identity, its relation to language and ecology, and the political and environmental concerns that contour it – matters of tantamount personal and practical importance to Ortiz.

In *Woven Stone*, among other works, Ortiz does two things worth mentioning in the context of this chapter. First, he articulates the sort of connection to the earth often attributed to Native cultures in terms of its narrative basis, rather than psychic primacy. Second, he interrogates settler projections of authenticity onto those same cultures. It is significant that *Woven Stone*'s concluding volume, *Fight Back: For the Sake of the People, For the Sake of the Land* (1980), a cycle of poems and prose dedicated to an historical view of environmental racism, ends with a poem that responds to an assertion of authenticity posed by white hobbyists rather than explicitly addressing matters of environmental justice. In the poem, Ortiz describes receiving an unsolicited call from a woman who asks him if he will participate in a parade to add some "authenticity" to its traditional Indian display, typically enacted by white performers. Like the tribe of Haight-Ashbury hippies playing Indian in Ortiz's satirical story "The San Francisco Indians," the organizer "want[s] to make it real," to "put a real Indian on a float ... Maybe even a medicine man.'" *Woven Stone* closes with Ortiz's flat refusal: "'No,' I said. No."[77]

What Ortiz rejects is a vision of authenticity such as the McKennas wielded it – that is, the prescription of a pristine, essential identity ostensibly unspoiled by the colonial forces that have otherwise occupied it. The expectation that Indigenous peoples would happily, reflexively enact "certain timeless 'spiritual' or 'traditional' knowledges" takes for granted Natives' subjective harmony with the natural world and disregards what Joni Adamson refers to as a "capacity to make changes." Native writers such as Ortiz are rarely interested in iconography associated with the "'pristine wilderness areas' celebrated by many mainstream American environmentalists." Ortiz's poetry concerns itself largely with regional fallout from the open-pit uranium mines that dot the Four Corners region, declared a National Sacrifice Area by Richard Nixon in 1972. The romantic vision of Native peoples that often accompanies the wilderness idea

Simon Ortiz, Oral Tradition, and Environmental Justice   87

glorifies, as the McKennas do, "the Exotic Other who lives far away, perhaps in a rain forest, perhaps doing some kind of 'authentic' or archaic work in nature," and "gives us permission to ignore the Other who lives next door, working in a field or a factory or a mine."[78] Ortiz's relationship with his environment stems from shared land and circumstance, not from shared psyche. His fellow laborers in the local uranium mines "were mostly working-class whites . . . hardworking, earnest, loyal to their group . . . and I identified with them" (22). Native knowledges of ecological relationships emerge in these accounts not as inherent but as culturally articulated over time. For writers like Ortiz, language and stories are the source of identity, not a cowl covering it up.

Most of the poems in *Woven Stone*, especially those reprinted from *Going for the Rain* (1976) and *A Good Journey* (1977), are deeply personal, connecting recollections of childhood events with physical features of the landscape. Ortiz writes that he was "pretty impressionable" in his youth, so much so that beat-generation writing by the likes of Ginsberg and Snyder "struck" him "as if by a revelation." One detects in Ortiz's words a tone of fond regret that gently chastises the sharp equivalence he drew in adolescence between the Zen Buddhist influence in their works and the Indigenous spiritual tradition with which he grew up. More lastingly influential to Ortiz was the beats' poetic emphasis on "the idea of experience, writing from and about experience, and writing as experience" (19). Ortiz makes clear that the speaker in these poems is almost exclusively himself, but his emphasis on personal history takes on broader implications in light of his perspective on story, narrative, and language. In "Spreading Wings on Wind" (121–3), Ortiz reminds himself "that I am only one part / among many parts" (lines 2–3). His voice becomes one contribution among many to a collective identity that includes the environs of the Acoma Pueblo.

It is precisely this sort of interconnective aesthetics to which figures such as the McKennas gravitated, and which inspired their understanding of "primitive" peoples as the arbiters of a more authentic, ecological consciousness. Later in the poem, Ortiz refers to himself as "a transparent breathing" (line 6) – an image that recalls Matthiessen's Buddhist reflection in the Himalayas. However, it is important to recognize that Ortiz's goal is not to eliminate the distinctive voice that calls the "many parts" to attention, even in poems such as "Between Albuquerque and Santa Fe" (205–11), whose section "Back into the Womb, the Center" reads as if it could have singlehandedly inspired the McKennas' ethnobotany. Ortiz writes of "one of the certain places / that is the center of the center," a deep

88   The Entheogenic Landscape

"crotch" in the hills where he can "go back 10,000 years" (lines 34–5, 37, 47). It would be a mistake to read in these lines a desire to eliminate self-identity through a fantasy of regression. Ortiz's sense of traveling "back 10,000 years" does not rely on the stripping away of his linguistic faculties or subjective merger with stones and plants – it is, to the contrary, self-consciously a function of the narrative he is telling about the continuity of matter in the ecosystem.

That sense of continuity, while deeply significant to his sense of identity, does not inspire in Ortiz an impulse toward merger. Nor, he makes plain, does that goal characterize Native cultures in general, despite the settler counterculture's adoption of Native valuations of interconnection. To the contrary, Ortiz highlights the role played by individual mediating selves in communicating and caring for ecological systems, and he does so by explicitly punctuating the "wholeness" of the material world with the more local perspectives and relationships that make it meaningful. In "My Children, and a Prayer for Us" (125–6), Ortiz implores his son to "always see the wholeness / of what is around you" (lines 9–10). That "wholeness" indeed signifies the complexities of ecological interconnection. Leslie Marmon Silko, a member of the neighboring Laguna Pueblo, likewise references her tribe's keen attention to continuities and cycles. "Corncobs and husks, the rinds and stalks and animal bones were not regarded by the ancient people as filth or garbage," but as momentary arrangements of matter "merely resting at a midpoint in their journey back to dust. Human remains are not so different."[79] Ortiz expresses the same sentiment in "A Birthday Kid Poem" (212–3), in which he comforts the addressee in a moment of pain: "Bone and flesh are ephemeral / in the count of centuries after all." However, he counsels also that his young listener love and respect himself and his kinship circles "well and appropriately," and avoid "dream[ing] so fantastically / that you lose the reality / that dreams are" (lines 3–4, 7, 16–8). Sense of self and social conventions together take on the quality of an illusion that is no less real for its mediating presence. Ortiz understands selfhood as Silko does: as a "myth, the web of memories and ideas that create an identity." The same narratives, Silko writes, link one's sense of identity to one's surroundings. The "process of identification with place" foregrounded in these stories and poems, Robert M. Nelson notes, is not one of merger, but one of "identity with whatever tribal traditions – encoded in stories and ceremony – happen also to have come about in these places."[80]

Woven Stone's affirmation that relationships with environments arise through kinship structures articulated through tales and histories places it

Simon Ortiz, Oral Tradition, and Environmental Justice 89

squarely in the tradition of writers such as N. Scott Momaday, work that throughout the "Native American Renaissance" foregrounded how traditional tales have generated customs retroactively branded "ecological." "Native artistry," Craig S. Womack writes, "is not pure aesthetics, or art for art's sake: as often as not Indian writers are trying to *invoke* as much as *evoke*." What Snyder cursorily describes as the Pueblo's "ultimate democracy," in which "plants and animals are also . . . given a place and a voice," arises not from primordial merger but from a collective sequence of narration, the spiritual yet pragmatic practice of oral tradition and its modern precipitates.[81] Representations structure a people's understanding of itself and its relation to the world. To willingly and collectively alter the narrative is to suggest changes to the way in which a people lives. Pueblo tradition, Silko writes, "sought a communal truth, not an absolute truth . . . . This truth lived somewhere within the web of differing versions, disputes over minor points, and outright contradictions tangling with old feuds and village rivalries." Oral tradition comprises "the consciousness of the people" along contingent, constructive lines, not through a fantasy of psychic merger.[82]

Ortiz foregrounds the creative, generative, and functional aspects of oral tradition in his poetry and prose. In so doing, he emphasizes how *any* relationship with the nonhuman necessarily takes shape through language, rhetoric, and narrative, despite how a McKenna might interpret these tales. Stories told at Aacqu – the Acoma Pueblo – "tied me into the communal body of my people and heritage" (9). Those who told stories of the history of Deetseyamah – Ortiz's hometown – "realized they knew, *in their own language*, the place" (4). Language, in this sense, constitutes the experience of environment, renders it intelligible. "Song at the very beginning was experience," Ortiz writes. "There was no division between experience and expression. Even now, I don't think there is much a division except arbitrary." Ortiz means not to collapse distinctions between sign and referent – such distinctions, he believes, are beside the point – but to emphasize that narrative representation is "made substantial by its context – that is its reality, both that which is there and what is brought about by the song."[83] One's perception of reality substantially relies on how his or her culture approaches it.

Identity is no different. In his poetry, Ortiz develops at length his conviction that "we are who we are in our own consciousness and the language that we express it in" (26). In "Language" (49–51), he describes carrying his infant daughter to bed. "I patted her back," he writes, "and she fell asleep making small universal sounds" (lines 4–5). These biological tics are communicative but formless, universally animal yet lacking discernible meaning. The remainder of the poem relates a linguistic education. Ortiz positions his daughter in front of a mirror, where, after a "murmur sound," she begins to persistently mimic her reflection, turning back to smile at her father as she does so. The child's articulations of verbal concepts accompany her identification with her own image in the reflective surface, just as they do for the infant of Lacan's mirror stage. To know "the language of movements – sights – / possibilities and impossibilities," the speaker explains, one has to "become a part / of it – a word is the poem – child / upon hearing a sound hears the poem" (lines 10, 28–30). The fragmented line, "of it – a word is the poem – child," sandwiches the "word" between "it" (language) and the child. The word is also "the poem," an invocatory act that gives shape and comprehensibility to an identity or relationship by articulating it. The child begins to grasp a sense of who she is because she begins to articulate herself. Her self-identity is a constructed, changing thing, not reducible to the biological aspects of the ecosystem to which she nonetheless exists in relation. Given this construction's social origin, one cannot entirely control it, Ortiz writes in a later essay.[84] Socially contingent language practices furnish the primary means of understanding and being in the world. The arc of the poem corresponds with a comment Ortiz makes in his introduction to *Woven Stone*. "Since we're all human with the same human feelings and responses to feelings, we understand and share hurt, love, anger, joy, sadness, elation, a gamut of emotions," he writes. "However, human cultures are different from each other, and unique, and we have different and unique languages" (6). It is possible, he suggests, to understand that humans possess a similar biological default that underwrites our ability to perceive and react to events in the world, while still recognizing cultural differences whose narrative conventions render that condition distinctively meaningful.

Those narratives constitute not only the "consciousness we have of our selves" but also "our responsible care for and relationships we have with our communities and communal lands" (27). In both their content and form – which exhibits the repetitive, invocatory cadence of oral tradition – many of Ortiz's poems reflect his conviction that stories also catalyze human alteration of environment. For example, "We Have Been Told Many Things but We Know This to Be True" (324–5), far from suggesting that the Acoma Pueblo exist in a facile state of ecological harmony, places emphasis on the inevitability of one's impact on the land. The tribe's relationship with the natural world is not psychically harmonious, but tenuous. The world is not balanced but constantly shifting, and one must

Simon Ortiz, Oral Tradition, and Environmental Justice   91

work hard to stay alive amidst change. Survival, Silko writes, *necessitated* Native peoples' stories.[85] The oral tradition's catalogue of sustainable environmental practices emphasizes the catastrophes they were designed to withstand, including those induced by colonial activities and those brought about by the people themselves "when [they] had not paid careful heed to their responsibilities" in properly maintaining their agriculture or in times of intratribal conflict (345). Ortiz describes in great detail "the destruction caused by liquor" in his community, which "caused family tension, arguments, distrust, fear, pain" (11), as well as his tribe's own tendency toward "ethnocentrism among ourselves and racism" (28). He explicitly aims to capture in his own poetry his sense that oral tradition "does not ignore bad times and mistakes that people have made throughout their history. And it is told in mythic proportion in order to impress upon those hearing that there are important lessons, values, and principles to be learned" (345). Action and reflection, not idealized essence, govern these tales.

The great irony of psychedelic primitivism's presymbolic myth is that the Native valuation of material interconnection that animates it is itself a series of stories, not an ecologically authentic essence that representation covers up. In suggesting that Native peoples lack the capacity for representation, that perspective at best ignores the cultural and political work those narratives have performed and continue to perform, as well as downplays or neglects the political challenges those peoples face. Ortiz neither romanticizes his people nor grants some erroneous balance or unity to the ecosystem. Images of merger in *Woven Stone* correspond not to sustainable environmental practice but to imperialism. In "Pain" (113), the "disintegration" of the speaker's identity – tied intimately, bodily, to his or her home – comes about not through any wish on the speaker's part, but as the result of various U.S. federal policies. The Indian boarding schools Ortiz attended as a child existed "to break or sever ties to culture, family, and tribe" (8). The Termination and Relocation program begun in 1953 cancelled services to reservations that colonial land seizure had delimited to begin with, engineering the swift depopulation of Native homelands and "further fracturing and weakening ... communities" (15). The rending of stories connecting the tribe internally and to environmental markers of their region, as well as to the region's colonial alteration, brings about the very sort of dissolution described by the McKennas: the evisceration of narratives and linguistic traditions that make environmental care possible. In the third section of his "San Diego Poem" (165–8), Ortiz surmises that "America has obliterated my sense of comprehension. / Without this comprehension, I am emptied / of any substance" (lines 27–9). The literary primacy of this "comprehension" – the matrix of narratives and representations particular to a people – forcibly resists the countercultural and New-Age myth of presymbolic primitivism, itself a colonial dissolution of lived Indigenous experience and the artworks that express it.

Narrative, Self, and Environment

Ortiz and fellow Native writers belonging to tribes other than the Acoma Pueblo do not often seek to represent ecological authenticity. They concern themselves with the particular environmental considerations of a place-specific people. The counterculture's interest in East Asian and Native American environmental traditions often merely maintained a hoary and injurious discourse that imagines noble primitives inhabiting a wilderness untouched by human culture. As Ortiz, Silko, Krech, and numerous other writers and critics have pointed out, when Native Americans have not acted "properly" ecological, "they have at times eagerly been condemned, accused of not acting as Indians should, and held to standards that they and their accusers have seldom met." The standard of purity is rigorous: "the forces that draw lines of protection around sacred, wild, 'new lands,'" Adamson writes, are often "the same forces that write off other landscapes as 'fallen.'"[86] Ortiz witnessed the "fall" of his own homeland as the uranium boom that hit the Acoma Pueblo in the mid-1950s rendered its sophisticated irrigation systems nearly impotent. The Grants Uranium Belt drained much of the water needed to cultivate Aacqu's fields and poisoned the volume reserved for drinking (363). The destruction of Acoma Pueblo farmland especially damaged the community's ability to support itself and retain "control of [its] destiny" – for Ortiz the tantamount political issue facing his tribe (23–4).

Ortiz's vision of environmentalism aims not to preserve a landscape but to navigate and overcome the social, economic, and political constraints that limit a community's ability to sustainably maintain its region. In other words, his project is one of environmental justice, though it is worth mentioning that it emerges from the same valuation of interconnection that animated countercultural and New-Age narratives of ecological authenticity – a bifurcated lineage that the next chapter will consider in more detail. For Ortiz, however, representation is not only an indelible facet of identity and environment. It is also a politically crucial one. "We need to insist on Native American self-sufficiency," he writes, adding that "a major source of this language of coming into being comes from the work of writers such as myself" (27). In his short introduction to *A Good Journey*, Ortiz explains his intention "to have the poetry show the energy that language is, the way that the energy is used and transformed into vision" (151). Snyder, too, places great stock in "the almost magical capacity of language" to illuminate "that we are interdependent energy-fields ... expressed in each person as a superb mind" and "complex body."[87] The narratives that structure identity also project potential futures, not only as "a matter of preserving and protecting Indian lands as some kind of natural wilderness," Ortiz writes, but as "a matter of how those lands can be productive in terms which are Indian people's to make" (360).

The question that *Woven Stone* raises in the context of countercultural mythmaking is: *Which narrative of ecological relationship is more beneficial?* One that insists we strive for an evacuated sense of subjective merger, or one through which we imagine practical changes based on social, economic, and environmental challenges? Ortiz's own answer is clear: "too often we look abstractly at a romanticized future that is impractical," he writes (32). Rather than indulge in such fantasies, "America must give back" to both the landscapes colonial activity has despoiled and the peoples it has displaced (331). Amidst his strident preservationism, Matthiessen also pays keen attention to matters of social justice. The Himalayan landscape is "hallucinatory" only when his narrative proceeds as primitivist romance. The vision dissipates when "mountain children" with "big bellies of malnutrition" wander into view (38). In the pages following these encounters, Matthiessen "look[s] at paradise askance" (24). Pressing political matters constantly invade, tarnish, and implore readers to rethink the primitivist narrative. These interruptions also call into question Matthiessen's reverence for a certain vision of the Buddha, who "never involved himself in social justice," for "self-realization is the greatest contribution one can make to one's fellow man" (18). The "Bodhisattva smile" of Matthiessen's Sherpa "would shine impartially on rape or resurrection" (242). Emptied of social significance, the mystic's transcendence leaves no room or reason to act against normative injustices. Zen, Watts also admits, can be a deeply apolitical doctrine. It "lies beyond the ethical standpoint, whose sanctions must be found, not in reality itself, but in the mutual agreement of human beings."[88]

This comment ironically nods toward the potentially pragmatic dimensions of an otherwise aloof corpus that coincidentally supplied substantial inspiration for New-Age navel-gazing. "If the ego were to disappear," Watts writes, "or rather, to be seen as a useful fiction, there would no longer be the duality of subject and object, experiencer and experience," but instead an "organism-environment field." The notion that an ego is something of a "useful fiction" – a contingent and constructed sense of self – does not discount the fact that egos have effects in and on the world. Identities change over time, and from Watts's Zen perspective "it is the very transitoriness of the world which is the sign of its . . . actual identity with the indivisible and immeasurable infinity of Brahman." At the same time, Watts does not believe that the reality of material flux implies that the "illusion" of "the manifold world of facts and events" must "vanish from sight" and "merge in a boundless ocean of vaguely luminous space." Such an impression "implies a duality" between culture and nature, or language and reality, and "nothing is more artificial than the notion of artificiality."[89] Identities and personalities have weight. They make things happen.

The sheer sincerity of Matthiessen's investment in Zen, in contrast to the often merely hip engagements taking place across the counterculture and New Age, encouraged him to consistently trouble his assumptions about it until his death in 2014. That same measure of healthy skepticism allowed him to decide, in the early 1970s, that he was "not ready" for Watts's "progressive disentanglement of one's Self . . . from every identification."[90] Matthiessen embraced not the void but the "mist" that separated him from it. Nothing "has changed" for him by the end of his trek: "I am still beset by the same old lusts and ego and emotions, the endless nagging details and irritations – that aching gap between what I know and what I am" (298). The indifference of both entheogenic and ascetic spiritualism to the political circumstances of people's lives dissatisfies him. "In spiritual ambition," Matthiessen writes, "I have neglected my children and done myself harm" (298). Despite the almost melancholic ambivalence this conclusion inspires, Matthiessen comes close in *The Snow Leopard*'s final pages to sharing Ortiz's certainty that "being real in a real world is loving and respecting myself" (32). The line is sentimental, almost banal, but it drives home *Woven Stone*'s organizing argument. Perhaps the self is an illusion born of language, but why should that origin make it any less real? Self-identity – constructed, interpreted, shifty, and contradictory – is itself a narrative worth maintaining for the relationships to which it grants meaning and the political action it makes possible. Real environmental work proceeds from collective narratives that account for and value the survival of multiple interests. By contrast, the notion of ecological authenticity – and its sheer rejection of the social formations we negotiate – seems only a means of excusing oneself from addressing social and environmental problems at all.

CHAPTER 3

The Universal Wilderness
Race, Cultural Nationalism, and an Identity Politics for the State of Nature

Ultimately nature rules. That is the great democratic gift the earth offers us – that sweet death to which we all inevitably go – into that final communion. No race, no class, no gender, nothing can keep any of us from dying into that death where we are made one.

Bell Hooks, *Belonging: A Culture of Place*

... particularity can never be simply left behind or obliterated. The notion of escaping from it into a realm of entirely universal maxims which belong to man as such ... is an illusion and an illusion with painful consequences.

Alasdair MacIntyre, *After Virtue*

By the end of *Song of Solomon* (1977), Toni Morrison's protagonist, Macon "Milkman" Dead, appears to have glimpsed the sort of direct, prelinguistic correspondence between self and other that eluded Peter Matthiessen during his Himalayan travels. Milkman, having tracked down his family's ancestral homeland in Appalachian Virginia, joins his estranged kin on a trek through the region's foothills. The patterns of communication among the locals, their hunting dogs, even the soil underfoot inspire in Milkman a sense of intimate continuity with his surroundings, "as though there was some cord or pulse of information they shared." The hunters "whispered to the trees, whispered to the ground." These dialogues arise "not [from] language" but from "what there was before language," a sense of homology with fellow creatures and "the earth itself, for that matter."[1] Conceiving of the forest as untouched, primordial wilderness enables Milkman to believe that it brackets and preserves what is essential from what is socially contrived. That sensations of merger accumulate around these exchanges situates Milkman's experience squarely in the discourse of ecological mysticism circulating at the time of *Song of Solomon*'s composition.

These passages foreground how representations of dissolution often proceed from a certain egalitarianism, an initial recognition of diverse yet

96 The Universal Wilderness

coequal human and nonhuman voices that dissolution's aesthetics of merger nonetheless ultimately smothers. Milkman's experience first "widen[s] the circle," as Nobel laureate and one-time Christian mystic Albert Schweitzer once put it. Schweitzer, whose name graces Rachel Carson's dedication to *Silent Spring*, was doubly prophetic when it came to postwar environmentalism. Like Alan Watts, a fellow student of East Asian religions, Schweitzer regretfully acknowledged mysticism's ethical poverty. As a result, he sought to temper spirituality with a program of ethical expansion that environmentalist litigation would carry on after his death. Just as nations progressively granted rights to women and ethnic minorities, so too could they welcome elements of the natural world into liberal community. "By reason of the quite universal idea . . . of participation in a common nature," Schweitzer wrote in 1936, one is "compelled to declare the unity of mankind with all created beings."[2] As his words illustrate, environmental ethics has long tread a fine rhetorical line between extending rights to nonhuman individuals and, more holistically, conferring such rights on the "unity" of ecosystems as a whole, such that the individuals who comprise them appear to metaphysically congeal. At the level of representation, philosophical distinctions between individual and collective turn fuzzy.

Milkman's dissolutions parallel this instability, but their greatest significance to *Song of Solomon*'s narrative emerges from how Morrison arranges them in relation to other elements in the novel. Both *Song of Solomon* and its protagonist come of age at a time of widespread cultural nationalism. In the novel, such sympathies reside in the character of Guitar, who, like many of his real-world Black-nationalist counterparts, eschews the shortcomings of liberal universalism – the sort that informed Schweitzer's "circle" – in favor of racial particularism. By the end of the 1970s, the idealistic luster of what Donald Pease refers to as the liberal narrative's "social symbolic order" had soured amid diverse articulations of how it "systematically separated an abstract, disembodied subject from resistant materialities, such as race, class, and gender."[3] Not too long after, the deep ecologists Bill Devall and George Sessions would draw on the work of Murray Bookchin to argue that, rather than institutionalize as part of the liberal state, environmentalism should also "follow the minority tradition."[4] On the one hand, such a statement could gesture toward the sort of communitarian politics typical of environmental justice – for example, commitments that seek to redress "how Blacks encounter another set of environmental hazards in addition to the universal burden on all, and hence receive a double dose of ecological backfires."[5] On the other, it might

The Universal Wilderness 97

refer – as Devall and Sessions indeed do – to the wisdom of "primal societies." The writers clarify that they do not seek "a revival of the Romantic version of primal peoples as 'noble savages,'" as Terence and Dennis McKenna might, but nor do they tend to tackle the sort of asymmetrical harms common to environmental justice activism.[6] I want to suggest that what they're after instead is a share in the claims to authenticity common among diverse identity politics of the preceding years.

This chapter considers how appeals to ecological authenticity constitute a point at which two scales of political rhetoric – the universal and the particular – intersect. Many of the figures examined thus far have presented ecological authenticity as an originary, unmediated condition. However, the previous two chapters have suggested that, throughout the 1960s, they nonetheless also relied heavily on psychoanalytic narratives and misinterpreted Native values to make their appeals. This chapter continues that trend by situating the ideal of ecological authenticity in the flourishing field of identity politics along lines of race, ethnicity, and gender that bloomed across the 1960s and 1970s. In this context, environmentalism emerged as an atypical new social movement committed to maintaining universals, the ideal or material conditions all people allegedly share in common (though the shape of what counts as "universal" remains hotly debated). At the same time, throughout the 1970s and 1980s writers such as Devall and Sessions mimicked the logic that animated appeals to racial or ethnic authenticity across a variety of social movements, even as they maintained their commitment to ecology's universal scope. It's worth recalling that white student radicals on the New Left tended to frame the Black communities with which they worked in terms of their perceived authenticity – their distance from repressive civilization. As the previous chapter suggested, some environmentalists also perceived Indigenous communities as the privileged site not only of authenticity but also, paradoxically, a *universal* version of it.

These writers did not just appropriate Native valuations of ecology. Their consistent claims to expansive identity with the ecosystem arose alongside cultural movements that produced race and ethnicity as models of identity with which we are more familiar, even as those appeals erased the material needs of these other communities. Their psychoanalytic narrative frames subjectivity in a radically different way than other movements did, but their appeals to authenticity also rest substantially on an understanding of sociopolitical dispossession borrowed especially from Black activists, as previous chapters have briefly noted. This chapter takes

98 The Universal Wilderness

up this point in greater detail. Such engagements with "minority tradition" signal the extent to which the appeals to ecological authenticity considered thus far gesture toward consolidation as a loose yet consistent identity politics of their own – an identity politics of ecology, uniquely inclusive of all peoples and matter, but one whose arguments often mirrored those of more particular traditions given their concurrent emergence. Just as Black Power, for example, scorned the civil rights movement for the strong influence postwar liberal universalism had on its program, so too does the IPE presume to move beyond the natural-rights philosophy of the era's standard – though at the time no less radical – environmental ethics. Voices in both traditions also mobilized a rhetoric of romantic authenticity, one whose complex history has included institutions of systemic racism as well as primitivist treatment of racial and ethnic others. As Simon Ortiz's poetry makes plain, literature produced by writers belonging to marginalized communities has often contested the premises underlying such narratives (even when members of those very communities perpetuate them, as this chapter will show). Native and Black Americans have often distrusted mainstream environmentalism for its historical tendency to "overwrite" their social, cultural, and economic situations, often as a result of viewing them as "'closer to nature' – whether in negative terms as 'backward' or in positive terms as 'noble savages,'" as Sarah Jaquette Ray observes.[7] Even as diverse cultural nationalisms began fervently contesting narratives of liberal universalism in the 1970s, the IPE posited a new universalism that erased the very peoples from whom it derived much of its rhetorical inspiration, as well as those in whom it tended to locate ecological authenticity to begin with.

Song of Solomon offers insight into these developments for its remarkable juxtaposition of two representations of authenticity: the racially particular and the ecologically universal. Morrison is doubtless as suspicious of liberalism's universalist pretense as her Black Power contemporaries. All the same, she has explicitly expressed a distrust toward the primacy some such radicals granted to racial essence in their work. By contrast, ecology appears to be the one concept to which Morrison does affix a certain unifying, even intrinsic importance. Commenting on "global changes in terrain and weather that can radically alter human environment," she makes clear her perspective that mitigating climate crisis, local ecological collapse, and species extinction requires "thinking about generations to come as more than a century or so of one's own family line, group stability, gender, sex, race, religion."[8] Cultural movements, while potentially useful in the short term, seem to strike her as inconsequential – and possibly harmful – to ensuring the future of our species. As I will argue, *Song of Solomon* likewise foregrounds ecological interconnection as a universal force that destabilizes the factionalism of identity politics.

That said, Morrison's skepticism toward the racial essentialism espoused by characters like Guitar extends to the cultural narratives with which Milkman's dissolution resonates. The conflict *Song of Solomon* stages between Milkman and Guitar places the dissolution motif in dialogue with Black nationalism's sporadic essentialist tendency. The result is twofold. First, this arrangement illuminates how the IPE draws on narratives borrowed from other identity politics, in the process reminding us that many such movements, emerging as they did at the same political moment, often shared certain recurring attitudes (toward capitalism and the state) and values (especially authentic expression). Second, it enables Morrison to altogether refute the ideal of romantic authenticity on which both paradigms have rested. If she refuses to endorse Guitar's politics, she also incisively critiques Milkman's psychic state of nature – the very sort that typifies the IPE. Such an approach to environment, she suggests, only replicates in altered, identitarian form an American wilderness narrative that has long shuffled people of color and women out of the picture. That is, her depiction casts the IPE as an identity politics that favors a masculine stance (much like Black nationalism), revealing several of its ideological liabilities. The alternative vision that emerges by the novel's end is more evocative of nascent environmental justice coalitions – traditions that themselves have important roots in the era's cultural nationalisms. As such, this chapter reads *Song of Solomon* against both liberal environmentalisms and cultural nationalisms to illuminate how the IPE effects a cross-pollination between them, as well as to suggest that it's not the only tradition to do so.

The New Universalism: Environmentalism Beyond Natural Rights

By the time ecology entered mainstream discourse, environmentalists had already expanded the scope of liberalism. On 17 September 1970, the United States Court of Appeals of California heard suit brought by the Sierra Club against Walt Disney Enterprises, which planned to develop a valley in the southern Sierra range as a ski resort. The court ruled against the organization because neither it nor its members suffered injury. The Sierra Club appealed the case to the Supreme Court in 1971. In preparation, Christopher Stone developed an argument for the preservation of the valley based on his contention that if the Sierra Club could not claim damages, *something* could. Stone argued for an extension of rights to the valley's trees by ethical expansion. "Originally each man had regard only for himself and those of a very narrow circle about him," he reasoned, but rights had since been extended – "imperfectly" – to "prisoners, aliens, women ... the insane, Blacks, fetuses, and Indians."[9] Nonhuman individuals, he argued, also possess rights, on which human industry infringes. Numerous similar defenses of nonhuman rights and interests arose in the years surrounding the case, culminating in significant legal milestones such as the Wilderness Act of 1964, the Marine Mammal Protection Act of 1972, and the Endangered Species Act of 1973. Ideas and texts such as Richard Ryder's "speciesism," Richard and Val Routley's "human chauvinism," and Tom Regan's *The Case for Animal Rights* (1983) came to prominence, comprising a postwar ethics that maintained nonhuman others and/or nature as a whole have intrinsic value and possess rights of their own. These philosophers typically drew on and applied to nonhuman elements the natural rights tradition of political philosophy, a universalist lineage that "posits the existence of an immutable human nature that, while its manifestation in different people involves variations across culture, genetics, upbringing, race, gender, and historical context, is nevertheless fixed."[10]

As the environmental historian Roderick Frazier Nash has pointed out, post-*Silent Spring* environmentalists' frequent adoption of the counterculture's contrarian style has at times tended to encourage oversight or even ignorance of their protest's intellectual antecedents, including the "quintessentially American" fascination with natural-rights philosophy and the climate of liberal universalism that at least nominally maintained the postwar consensus.[11] Their frequent legal investment in causes ranging from civil rights to women's liberation indicates the extent to which student activists especially drew in part from an enduring, if inconsistent, philosophical tradition shared with their liberal rivals. From a New Left perspective, American liberal universalism was not wrong, but it had *failed*, neglecting to protect select demographics, especially along lines of race. The decade's unrest arose in large part from dissatisfaction – on the part of coalitions of color as well as the predominantly white political counterculture – with postwar liberals' universalist abstractions, a righteous anger directed against the social blunders of the liberal narrative and the "utterly equal ... subject position devoid of any particularity whatsoever" it guaranteed.[12] That same political philosophy informed many of the ethicists who argued, legally and academically, that nonhuman individuals possess rights – an argument that has weathered substantial (and often reasonable) critique across its

The New Universalism: Environmentalism Beyond Natural Rights 101

permutations. How, for example, could Christopher Stone presume to speak for the wants and needs of nonhuman nature? Edward Abbey stumbled across a similar problem in his attempts to respect Utah's desert landscape "as it is in itself."

To the extent that ethics are socially agreed-upon, self-imposed restraints on behavior, Stone sought to organize a new environmentalist narrative, not to make an argument about nature's authenticity. There is a difference between asserting the fundamental reality of such claims and recognizing the social potential of their contrivance. In response to global environmental change, French polymath Michel Serres likewise proposed in 1990 a "natural contract" between human society and the Earth as a unified entity. This contract would balance scientific and legal discourse, checking the potentially totalizing influence of science while drawing from science's ability to "show us the object's point of view, as it were, just as the other contracts showed us, by the bond or ligature of their obligations . . . the point of view of the other partners in accord. The natural contract leads us to consider the world's point of view in its totality." By this logic, the contract *produces* the subject's voice, in this case the demands of the Earth as an organic personage that "speaks to us in terms of forces, bonds, and interactions."[13] Serres is well aware of the creative narrativity of his account. He frames his natural contract, as well as the humanistic social contracts that inspire it, as a series of pragmatic parables.

That narrative, however, tilts along the axis of its universalism. Serres ends his treatise with imagery of the self's subjective disintegration and unification with the planet during an earthquake: "Who am I? A tremor of nothingness . . . for a moment of profound happiness, the spasmodic Earth comes to unite herself with my shaky body. Who am I, now, for several seconds? Earth herself."[14] Do the rights of the earth – here envisioned in its organic totality – nullify the rights granted to its citizenry? Environmental ethics' "broadening of value," Holmes Rolston wrote in 1975, prompts us to consider if, rather than merely "universalize 'person,'" we "ought to again universalize, recognizing the intrinsic value of every ecobiotic component."[15] These words pinpoint a certain trouble regarding what counts as "universal" in the context of environmental ethics – the ethics itself or the subject to which a given principle applies – that emerged promptly among the field's modern originators. Aldo Leopold wrote that his foundational land ethic "simply enlarges the boundaries of the community to include waters, plants, and animals, or collectively: the land."[16] Leopold's representation of "the land" as a rights-bearing organism in its own right would potentially eclipse the rights claimed by its constituent

102   The Universal Wilderness

parts. My point is not that a consideration of all such stakeholders is not important – it certainly is, from any environmentalist perspective – but that reliance on a natural-rights idiom generated conflicts in such work's argumentative scope.

Other writers encouraged the holistic perspective more systematically and earnestly than Leopold. Arne Naess, the Norwegian founder of deep ecology, underscored the "inherent" or "intrinsic" worth of nonhuman nature as a whole. Devall and Sessions, Naess's colleagues, drew from eighteenth and nineteenth-century organicism to supplement the natural-rights basis of deep ecology's foundational values, "ecological egalitarianism" and "self-realization." In the process, their rhetoric at times functioned to extend such recognition primarily to systems in their entirety, as self-possessed organisms in their own right. Eugene C. Hargrove, in *Beyond Spaceship Earth* (1986), later sought to expand the implications of James Lovelock's Gaia hypothesis – the notion that Earth constitutes a single organic system – by envisioning the solar system itself as a discrete organism with rights to self-determination and freedom from human interference. I do not mean to suggest that such writers found human-scale ethical concerns of no importance. Naess, Devall, and Sessions all vociferously addressed the micro as well as the macro.

What I do want to point out is that the heavier one's investment in such expansive rhetoric grows, the steeper the argument appears to tilt toward an ontologically (rather than ethically) holistic understanding of universality. Rights-based ethics in classical American liberalism has typically functioned for the protection of individuals against "aggregates" such as institutions and majorities. But even as rights-of-nature activists and philosophers aimed in the 1970s and 1980s to expand the circle of rights to include animals, plants, and minerals, biocentric notions of ethical holism "led the most radical moral philosophers of recent times to conclusions that devalued the individual life relative to the integrity, diversity, and continuation of the ecosystem."[17] The more holistic one's metaphysics, the less persons themselves appear to matter.

One senses an analogous contradiction at play in Morrison's *Song of Solomon* and its critical commentary. Fleeing various "demands" made on him by family and friends in Michigan, Milkman travels southeast in search of gold allegedly stashed in the mountains by his Aunt Pilate decades before. On the way, he locates his sundered kinfolk in Shalimar, Virginia, and temporarily integrates into their routine. While hunting, he falls behind and pauses to rest beneath a sweet-gum tree. There, "on the ground," Milkman's "self – the cocoon that was 'personality' – gave way":

The New Universalism: Environmentalism Beyond Natural Rights 103

> He could barely see his own hand, and couldn't see his feet. He was only his breath, coming slower now, and his thoughts. The rest of him had disappeared. So the thoughts came, unobstructed by other people, by things, even by the sight of himself. There was nothing to help him – not his money, his car, his father's reputation, his suit, or his shoes. In fact they hampered him . . . . His watch and his two hundred dollars would be of no help out here, where all a man had was what he was born with, or had learned to use. (277)

Milkman's dissolution occurs at a pivotal moment in the novel's plot, just before he narrowly escapes an attempt on his life. Throwing off a garrote, Milkman exhales "a living breath this time, not a dying one" (279). The experience strips away the bourgeois trappings of Macon Sr.'s industry – the shoes, the suit, the pecuniary symbols of capitalism itself – until all that remains to Milkman is "what he was born with." The passage leads the reader to understand that Milkman has accessed something elemental to himself. Critics have often focused on this dissolution as a climactic consolidation of identity. That he now expels a "living breath" suggests that he has also undergone a fundamental transformation, a "movement from alienation to authenticity." What begins as a quest for material gain – a treasure hunt for Pilate's trove – segues into an acquisition of self-knowledge based on "the dismantling of his personality."[18] Such perspectives partake of a shared, paradoxical equation among self-coherence, racial or family history, and dissolution, and fail to explain how Milkman's soupy sense of merger calcifies into anything like a solid, true, "unique self." The forest does not mystically fix Milkman's broken personality. The primacy he grants to the rhythms of the system erases his person altogether.

The more Milkman perceives the boundaries between himself and his environment fading, the less of a self he is. When Milkman "walks the earth," Morrison comments in an interview, "he feels a part of it, and that is his coming of age, the beginning of his ability to connect with the past and perceive the world as alive."[19] That she refers to Milkman's dissolution as the "beginning" of a process signals its defiance of the identity-consolidation interpretation. In light of Morrison's clarification, the scene reads almost as an attempt to first recover an impression of what Bell Hooks, in a personal essay, describes as our shared status as "people of the earth." To walk and work the land, Hooks writes, is to glimpse this commonality, "even when that land was owned by white oppressors." Despite their mastery, slaveholders and Jim-Crow landowners lacked any power to "make the sun or the rains come," her grandfather once told her. "We can all see that ultimately we all bow down to the forces of nature. Big white boss may think he can outsmart nature but the small farmer know."

104 The Universal Wilderness

By Hooks's estimation, any intimate relationship with the earth reveals that white supremacy lacks the authority it appears to wield and that all folks – Black, white, or otherwise – exist in like subordination to ecological rhythms.[20] Still, one's experience of those conditions might change depending on sociocultural factors.

For Milkman in the woods, ecological interconnection likewise reveals itself as a force binding together all individuals, regardless of race, gender, class, or species. Ecology is truly, materially universal. That universal vision, however, seems to level the interconnected chorus of voices within its bounds, molding itself according to the contours of a single organic body. Wes Berry suggests that this moment seems out of step with "what we expect from African-American writers – namely, narratives that reinforce the importance of asserting and gaining subjectivity."[21] Morrison is no doubt aware of her defiance of expectations (if such expectations can even be summed up so crisply). Her departure, such as it is, is more critical than it is sincere, and markedly cognizant of the complex role played by race in environmentalist debates of the 1970s.

After all, Christopher Stone is not the only ethicist to have invoked racial, ethnic, or tribal identity to strengthen a case against regional or species degradation. Comparisons between nature and slave have enjoyed special prominence. In 1975, Richard Ryder commented, "When we examine the arguments used by slave-owners in the past, we can see a striking similarity with the view expressed today by those who defend the exploitation of animals." Aldo Leopold takes the "enslavement" of the earth as his point of departure, and Abbey writes that in their damming Glen Canyon and the Colorado River had been "sold down the river." Theodore Roszak describes nature as a "downtrodden nigger" in *Person/Planet* (1977), and Wendell Berry declares that "if we begin by making niggers of people, we have ended by making a nigger of the world." In 1984, a member of the Animal Liberation Front likened the organization to the Underground Railroad.[22] On the one hand, these comparisons bespeak a certain liberal momentum generated in the wake of the civil rights movement. On the other, such rhetoric implicitly reiterates old equations between racial or ethnic minorities and animals or the land itself.

In this respect, the conceptual flattening of African Americans and trees reflects the sort of unintentional racial reductionism that Morrison observes upholding "the routine bestiality of those who had founded and settled this country."[23] Paul Outka has examined how nationalistic and literary sentiment surrounding wilderness in the late nineteenth and early twentieth centuries explicitly exoticized, excluded, or romanticized the slavery of Blacks, and "the terrible historical legacy of making people of color signify the natural" often formed "a prelude to exploiting both." That legacy continues to resonate in environmental politics. "Knowledge" grasped in alignments of land with other, Lauret Savoy notes, is often "the product of invention and stereotype," ignorant of the extent to which "meanings assigned by cultural values, assumptions, or preconditions" have contributed to relations with environment – a point the previous chapter developed at length. Furthermore, the tendency to view environment in terms of what Dorceta Taylor refers to as "white middle class male environmental activism," inclusive of New-Age mysticism as well as mainstream preservationism, misunderstands the environmental concerns of people of color and economically disadvantaged communities.[24] These groups, often facing regional and economic displacement, have increasingly challenged the presumed universality of such accounts, as well as stereotypes enshrining their environmental purity. For example, in 1964 the National Indian Youth Council (NIYC) responded to arrests of Native fishermen in the Pacific Northwest by staging a series of "fish-ins" modeled after the civil rights movement's sit-ins.[25] The altercation, which pitted conservation law against cultural tradition, is representative of the broader climate of distrust toward liberal universalism that permeated the 1960s and 1970s among communities of color.

Cultural Nationalism and Racial Authenticity

Even as environmentalists upped the ante on liberal universalism, other sectors of 1970s political culture called the entire enterprise into question, often on the basis of racial and ethnic particularity. On 20 November 1969, an intertribal coalition of student activists calling itself Indians of All Tribes seized Alcatraz Island in San Francisco Bay. Under the de facto leadership of the Mohawk student Richard Oakes, the organization established on the island a colony intended to resuscitate "old Indian ways" through militant self-assertion and Native-centric education, institutionalized in a small university, museum, and "ecology center." In its earliest days, the occupation positioned Native peoples at the forefront of what was not yet called environmental justice, as participants called for both self-determination and redress to the environmental ills that had befallen their tribes at the hands of mismanaged or overtly racist corporate and governmental policy. The coalition's lack of centralized organization also reflected "their ideals of unity and consensus and a rejection of the idea of hierarchy," write Paul Chaat Smith and Robert Allen Warrior. Activists in

106 The Universal Wilderness

attendance "had drunk deeply from the well of anarchism popular among student radicals of the time."[26] The occupation broadcast growing Indigenous unrest in the United States while demonstrating the pervasive influence of the decade's student movements and their theoretical touchstones.

The Alcatraz occupation marked one node in a fertile network of resistance to assimilation by people of color, fueled by the decade's liberation rhetoric. One year previously, an intertribal march on Washington, D.C., organized largely by NIYC leaders, protested what Simon Ortiz refers to in *Woven Stone* as the "shaky" integrity of tribal cultures at midcentury, "constantly under attack by U.S. education, values, attitudes, influences, politics, and its economy," as well as more overtly draconian policies of Termination and Relocation.[27] Ortiz understands his own literary production as an essential component of Native resistance against such forces, an effort to define and maintain cultural identity and promote self-sufficiency by "keeping the stories alive." The oral tradition's constitutive "link between literature and social realities," Craig S. Womack writes, is part of Native literatures' "national character" – that is, their distinction from American literature writ large.[28] NIYC co-founder Mel Thom (Paiute) also had cultural nationalism on his mind when he drafted the intertribal march's statement to Secretary of the Interior Stewart Udall, a declaration "that Indian people have the right to separate but equal communities within the American system."[29]

Thom's demand neatly summarizes the separatist atmosphere that pervaded the new social movements as 1960s utopianism waned and 1970s factionalism waxed. A wave of Native-American, African-American, Chicano, Asian-American, and even white ethnic political pluralism and cultural production contributed to a decade-defining "ideological debate between universalism and diversity."[30] Postwar American liberalism's approach to race centered on a moral appeal to universal subjectivity of the sort that rights-of-nature ethicists mobilized on behalf of nonhuman environment. The civil rights movement's program capitalized on Northern States' liberal momentum, advancing an agenda focused on racial integration and liberal individualism that would mesh comfortably with the existing socioeconomic order. Leaders such as Bayard Rustin and Martin Luther King, Jr., stirred positive racial consciousness and pride in Black cultural strength in order to advance Black interests and nourish a broader liberal-universalist goal. By elevating their followers' sense of self-worth, they might in turn "spur a parallel transformation of white consciousness, prompting an understanding that racism limited the

Cultural Nationalism and Racial Authenticity 107

development of the full humanity of its perpetuators, as well as its targets." Activists also emphasized the importance of socioeconomic equality to this breakthrough in legal and political equity. However, despite the Kennedy and Johnson administrations' devotion to activist government, the postwar liberal order generally shied away from the social-democratic inclinations of its New-Deal precedent, favoring a peremptory anticommunist ethos and platform of economic growth emboldened by postwar plenty. Liberals' keen fixation on reforming the Jim Crow South fortified widespread oversight of economic hardship – and its attendant racial tension – in the urban North and West.[31] After the 1965 Watts riots, this undercurrent exploded onto the national scene. Widespread dissatisfaction with the limitations of liberal policy prodded racial and ethnic politics toward a critique of assimilation and liberal universalism altogether.

Assimilation critique formed the cornerstone of the period's cultural nationalisms and the multiplying politics of difference. In 1967, Charles V. Hamilton and Kwame Ture (né Stokely Carmichael) described integration as "a subterfuge for the maintenance of white supremacy," a demand for adaptation to a sociopolitical situation whose values historically included the exclusion and alienation of the very community to which they belonged.[32] Black nationalists' vociferous repudiation of the political status quo in the 1960s targeted the very basis of liberal universalism, which Ture and Hamilton framed as "a kind of pragmatic contradiction," to borrow a phrase from political theorist Charles Taylor. Drawing attention to the white dominance of the political establishment revealed liberalism as nothing more than "a particularism masquerading as the universal," one of many possible ethnic paradigms, but the one that wielded the power to establish hegemony.[33] This idea percolated in organizations such as Malcom X's Nation of Islam, Max Stanford's Revolutionary Action Movement (RAM), and, increasingly, the SNCC under Ture and the Congress of Racial Equality (CORE) under Floyd McKissick. Black nationalism in the 1960s differed from its predecessors in that it largely "set the tone for radicalism of that period," laying the groundwork for SDS, radical feminism, and the antiwar movement over the following decade, as well as the "ethnic revival" that steadily came to redirect American liberalism toward political pluralism.[34] The NIYC, for example, augmented the staid National Congress of American Indians (NCAI) and its program of cultural preservation, self-determination, and treaty enforcement with militant tactics borrowed chiefly from SNCC and SDS. From SNCC especially the NIYC derived a twofold agenda focused on tribally tailored educational curricula and direct-action community organizing to combat the influence of

108 The Universal Wilderness

Eurocentric politics, economics, and culture. Under the leadership of Mel Thom and fellow co-founder Clyde Warrior (Ponca), the organization grew increasingly militant alongside its peers. In 1966, enflamed by Ture's eruptive call for "Black Power!" in Mississippi one month prior, Warrior painted "Red Power!" on the side of his car at a Fourth of July festival in Oklahoma City.[35]

The myriad incarnations of Black nationalism that proliferated in the 1960s generally organized according to their idiosyncratic interpretations of several "key themes": (1) a rejection of assimilation to a putatively universal but actually white standard; (2) an identification with colonized and postcolonial peoples; and (3) a claim to distinctive cultural characteristics with ancient roots.[36] The combination of these currents demanded a platform of political separatism or, at the very least, community control and access to economic resources. Just as Warrior argued that governance of War on Poverty programming must be delivered into the hands of activist reservation leaders to buttress self-determination, so Malcolm X's Organization for Afro-American Unity sought control over local institutions and resource management. Ture and Hamilton proposed a "closed ranks" strategy according to which Black communities "lead and run their own organizations," thereby "convey[ing] the revolutionary idea ... that black people are able to do things themselves."[37] Even as it encouraged self-sufficiency and neighborhood growth, however, the influence of "black economic development" on community programming also invited participation in the same system of capitalist enterprise Black-nationalist leaders identified with restrictive white liberalism.

This connection features prominently in *Song of Solomon*, which dramatizes the sort of universalism critique undertaken by Black-nationalist leadership. Milkman's father, Macon Sr., an influential landlord with a cruel reputation, convinces himself that his Black neighbors will rent or buy lakeside summer homes if he offers them because "white people do it all the time" (34). When his daughter, First Corinthians, counters that "Negroes don't like the water," he responds that Black buyers will "like it if they own it." Corinthians does not accept her father's logic. She announces, regarding a local bar owner, "I don't care what she owns. I care about what she is." Their debate rests at the center of the novel's pervasive preoccupation with an uneasy distinction characters draw between what people *are* and what they *do*. Macon measures one's worth according to his or her accumulation and exertion of capital – according to what actions a person takes from an assumed position of equality determined by a fixed economic order. *Song of Solomon* hardly looks fondly on

Cultural Nationalism and Racial Authenticity 109

his capitalist zeal. His industriousness is a twisted reflection of Black self-reliance, an "homage to his own father's life and death" through worship of "property, good solid property, the bountifulness of life ... distorted ... for the sake of gain" (300). In Macon, the novel critically rehearses Robert S. Browne's characterization of integration in his widely circulated 1968 _New York Times Magazine_ article, "The Case for Two Americas – One White, One Black." Integrationists, Browne writes, want "to be 'in' American society" – that is, to live as the middle-class white population does. Separatists, by contrast, strive "to reclaim [their] group individuality and have that individuality recognized as equal with other major cultural groups."[38] In light of this debate's centrality to racial politics of the 1960s and 1970s, Macon and Corinthians's disagreement rehashes a conflict between liberal universalism and racial authenticity.

If Macon is the novel's resident capitalist-integrationist, Milkman's confidant Guitar is its local Black nationalist for several reasons. One passage in particular, a remarkably scathing and misogynistic example of nationalist rhetoric's occasional tendency to "strong racial chauvinism," captures the specificity of Guitar's political sympathies.[39] Women, he tells Milkman, "want your living life . . . . White women, same thing. They want us, you know, 'universal,' human, no 'race consciousness.' Tame, except in bed. They want a little racial loincloth in the bed. But outside the bed they want us to be individuals" (222). Guitar's invective illustrates how Black nationalism's "turn toward violence" often established its "idealized image of the tough, fearless, macho revolutionary outlaw" according to the same dismissive gender stereotypes deployed by the dominant culture it sought to dismantle, as well as by the white student left's largely male leadership.[40] Guitar masculinizes racial consciousness in service to a distinction he means to draw between blackness and its emasculated antithesis, the "universal ... individual." Guitar's simultaneous disparagement of the "individual" and the "universal" condemns a subjectivity founded on supposedly global standards of equality in favor of Black identity marked by oppression and assumed coherence. Milkman's perfunctory disinterest in such matters disqualifies him – at least while his characteristic political apathy endures – from the racial consciousness Guitar believes indispensable to Black identity. For Guitar, however, Milkman's insouciance is an intrinsic function of "who you are and what you are" (104).

In contrast to Macon, Guitar evaluates his neighbors according not to what they do or buy but to what they are. He participates in 1960s cultural nationalism's common, though certainly by no means ubiquitous, consolidation of authenticity along "fixed, given channels of fellowship."[41] In *Black Power* (1967), Ture and Hamilton contend that "to reclaim our history and our identity," it would be necessary to cultivate a "new consciousness among black people."[42] That consciousness would not be new so much as it would be recovered. Black nationalism's "narrative of the past" held that slavery "had robbed Africans of their identity." To reclaim what RAM's Max Stanford referred to as "consciousness of our own kind of self" would require extricating a fundamental Black culture and identity from the white. This idea reached a popular Black audience largely through orators such as Malcolm X and artists such as Amiri Baraka and Eldridge Cleaver, who actively sought "to represent an 'authentic' voice of the black masses, and an alternative vision to that of the dominant middle-class civil rights leadership."[43] Black-nationalist leaders' rhetorical interest in uncovering unique, even inborn characteristics came to associate racial membership with a certain narrative of authenticity, one that would adhere across an entire population. Baraka, for example, once declared that an artist such as himself "is supposed to be right in the center of his community . . . . fully integrated into the will of his people, has to *be* the people himself, and not be any different."[44] Cultural production would capture a certain romantic homogeneity, a racial unity that would further the interests of the community in defiance of the white civilization that would oppress and repress it.

Guitar's brand of Black nationalism premises itself not on cultural production but on the numerical equalization of fixed and opposed identities, but it retains the suggestion that *self* and *race* are, to a certain extent, coterminous values. By *Song of Solomon*'s midpoint, Guitar comes to oversee the shadowy operations of the Seven Days, an organization that mathematically seeks to answer Malcolm X's charge that "the African American people insure ourselves that justice is done – whatever the price and *by any means necessary*" – to recoup the "over 5,000 Afro-Americans . . . lynched since the Emancipation Proclamation."[45] Its vigilante members randomly execute whites "as indifferent[ly] as rain" every time a Black person is killed in order to keep "the ratio the same" (154–5). The Days premise their mission on a system of justice that treats racial lives as a matter of calculation, as equal percentages opposing one another on a balance sheet. Their utilitarian motives compel them to "keep the numbers the same" (154). For Guitar, execution is also consistent with what James T. Stewart described in 1968 as "natural aesthetic styles."[46] Murder is a matter of racial aesthetics for both whites and Blacks. It signifies one's fundamental perversion and the other's authentic virtue. The Days "believed the crimes they committed were

Cultural Nationalism and Racial Authenticity

legitimate because they were committed in the heat of passion" (100), a justification that leans heavily on the same sort of appeal to spontaneity that underwrote the era's broad politics of authenticity, from SDS's student activism to Murray Bookchin's social ecology. The Days judge white-on-white violence as a form of madness but take pride in their assumption that "members of their own race killed one another for good reasons" like "violation of another's turf," "refusal to obey the laws of hospitality," or "verbal insults impugning their virility, honesty, humanity, and mental health" (100). The "lunatic" nature of white killings, Guitar explains to Milkman, is innate: "It doesn't matter who" has killed a Black man. "Each and every one of them could do it . . . . There are no innocent white people, because every one of them is a potential nigger-killer, if not an actual one" (155). A capacity for wanton murder is an ingrained feature of the white race, "in the structure of their chromosomes" (157). Homicidal styles express racial authenticity at the level of biology.

In this respect, Morrison makes of Guitar's racial politics a violent caricature of Black nationalism. To be clear, she specifically targets not its direct-action tactics – nor the many gains Black-nationalist politics have made in Black communities – but its sporadic authenticity rhetoric, an occasional tendency to reiterate and ratify "old romantic racialist ideas that confused Afro-American 'cultural' identity with a 'racial' one."[47] Guitar emphasizes community, but he homogenizes and decontextualizes it, viewing each person as a nearly insignificant component of a larger racial body defined by certain essential characteristics. "What I'm doing isn't about hating white people," he explains to Milkman. "It's about loving us. About loving you. My whole life is love" (159). His pledge ironically echoes his earlier condemnation of a white woman, the ex-wife of a colleague who "came home to find her with another . . . black man," who "discovered that his white wife loved not only him, not only this other black man, but the whole race" (128–9). The striking similarity between these passages draws attention to the novel's critical stance toward the Seven Days' rigid conception of racial identity and membership. According to this standard – inflexibly constructed yet framed as essential truth – Milkman is either loyal to the race via the Days or he isn't. Guitar's promise that "we don't off Negros" might exclude those who do not conform to the interests of the organization (161). Guitar begins to hunt Milkman through Appalachia late in the novel because he believes Milkman has betrayed the Days – and therefore the race – by locating and claiming Pilate's rumored gold for himself. Guitar subordinates his personal plans for the cash to what he claims to be the needs of his clan: "I need the bread . . . Not *me. Us*" (225).

This slippage between *me* and *us*, evocative of Baraka's perspective on community leadership, draws attention to Guitar's tendency to racially homogenize his self-identity – in this case, a dubiously magnanimous move that packages his own desires in nationalist rhetoric, thereby calling into question the credibility of racial authenticity altogether.

Song of Solomon's parody of racial essentialism foregrounds a number of its political shortcomings. First, and most importantly, it ignores social and economic variations among Black, mixed-race, and other communities of color. Second, it discourages partnerships among peoples, organizations, and communities with common goals. Third, it relies on what Julianne Newmark calls "retrogression," an "active and ideological nostalgia for a mythic past of racial uniformity."[48] That narrative in particular has rendered cultural nationalisms susceptible to continuity with the very systems against which they have struggled. For example, the Red Power movement attracted trenchant criticism from Native writers such as Gerald Vizenor (Anishinaabe) for its crystallization of putatively authentic stereotypes. When the American Indian Movement's (AIM) "Trail of Broken Treaties" march on Washington devolved into an occupation of the Bureau of Indian Affairs building in 1972, militants erected a tipi on the lawn, decorating their hair with feathers and their faces with paints. Ortiz, like Vizenor, has been critical of this strategy. Tribes the world over, he writes, "can't take Indigeneity for granted." If on the one hand it is difficult to maintain Indigenous identity in the face of assimilation, on the other "it is too easy to be Indigenous, especially to be the very image of the Indian who is a foil and fool to the dominant culture and society."[49] In contrast to Ortiz's self-conscious maintenance of identity according to a multitude of "elements and factors having to do with land, culture, and community," AIM often leaned on a rhetoric of primal authenticity to boost their political cachet. Some members of Indians of All Tribes did similarly on Alcatraz, festooning the island with "primitive" emblems designed to emphasize their ecological unity. If on the one hand the occupation's commitment to self-determination and policy change predicted the environmental justice movement, on the other its appeals to romanticized "old Indian ways" informed the concurrent development of the IPE.

Racial Particularity and Ecological Authenticity: A Reflective Stalemate

Each of these trends – the slide into ontological universalism on the part of environmental writing, the appeal to authenticity on the part of various cultural nationalisms – contributes an ingredient to our understanding of ecological authenticity discourse as its own form of identity politics. When *Song of Solomon* places these elements in juxtaposition in the characters of Milkman and Guitar, it illuminates how the IPE borrows narrative elements from other traditions organized around race or ethnicity – the "minority traditions" to which Devall and Sessions would later refer. Appeals to ecological authenticity form along a psychoanalytic narrative introduced at midcentury, but they subsist because they remain in keeping with the political climate, proffering one identity politics among many others that concurrently, though in most cases more justifiably, grew out of the same atmosphere of sociopolitical alienation in the 1960s.

Song of Solomon itself appeared in 1977, fast on the heels of cultural nationalism's postwar heyday. Morrison herself, however, preferred to avoid the idiom of "the black community ... because it came to mean something much different in the sixties and seventies, as though we had to forge one – but it had seemed to me that it was always there." In her essays, she reflects fondly on the neighborhood of her youth, when "[w]e thought little about 'unity' because we loved those differences among us" and "had rent parties that were truer manifestations of community love and sharing than any slogan ever invented for us."[50] Modern Black nationalism's "increased cultural production in the form of 'authentic' black rituals and traditions" struck Morrison as an expression of "political expediency" that "ran roughshod over some valuable and tender roots." Even the dangerous and sorrowful aspects of the past are valuable and "at risk of being lost" amid certain Afrocentric projects to "create" a Black culture, to "rush to move away from the past." Literature might instead offer an opportunity to recover and represent history "as life lived."[51]

Morrison's flair for "keeping our troubled relics" to maintain healthy historical perspective bespeaks her reservation toward the romanticism underlying both a politics of racial authenticity and the common critical interpretation that Milkman's sojourn constitutes "an ennobling tradition through which a community can reconnect itself to a primeval state 'before language.'"[52] In fact, her treatment of Guitar and Milkman draws parallels between the former's strict identitarianism and the latter's dissolutive universalism. In developing a conflict between these two characters, Morrison has also placed racial and ecological authenticity in opposition. Their juxtaposition accentuates their commonality. They share a narrative logic wherein what has been lost, obscured, or alienated is reclaimed. Their structural similarity reveals Milkman's dissolution, and the cultural narratives it reflects, for what it is: its own form of essentialist yet universal identity politics. That many environmentalists of the period (explicitly in the case of Devall and Sessions yet implicitly in the case of writers like McKenna and even Abbey and Matthiessen) envision their ecological narratives in keeping with the era's "minority traditions" – that is, oppressed and repressed cultural alternatives explored by a variety of identity politics – reinforces this relationship.

Guitar and Milkman's quarrel originates in Milkman's own perennial sense of alienation. Throughout *Song of Solomon*, he struggles to compensate for his disjointed self-perception and social disaffection. Studying his reflection, Milkman notes that he "had a fine enough face. Eyes women complimented him on, a firm jaw line, splendid teeth. Taken apart, it looked all right . . . . But it lacked coherence, a coming together of the features into a total self. It was all very tentative, the way he looked" (69). His concern belies the posture of masculine swagger he adopts on the street. He tries to hide a congenital limp with "the strut of a very young man trying to appear more sophisticated than he was" and takes pains to maintain an air of "masculine flippancy" (62, 96). A "snorting, horse-galloping glee as old as desire" he feels after punching his father heralds "infinite possibilities and enormous responsibilities . . . but he was not prepared to take advantage of the former, or accept the burden of the latter" (68). The novel consistently characterizes Milkman in terms of aimless, frenetically useless momentum coupled with self-absorbed disinterest; when his family makes reasonable demands of him, he "felt abused" (123). His malaise reads like teenage angst channeled through a man in his mid-thirties: "Boredom, which had begun as a mild infection, now took over him completely. No activity seemed worth doing, no conversation worth having" (90). Morrison herself views the character as "a man running away from some obligations and himself," a representation of masculinity's "outward . . . rhythm" and potentially destructive consequences.[53] The gendered dimensions of Milkman's movements merit further attention (to be given shortly), but the character interprets his own aimlessness as a lack of personal fulfillment. Enter Guitar and his plea for racial consciousness, which Milkman largely ignores. Instead, he flees on his cross-country saga, followed closely by his now-homicidal friend.

Their first encounter occurs beneath the sweet-gum tree that inspires Milkman's dissolution and identification with the wilderness scene. The tree itself seems to save Milkman from assassination, though at the time Milkman senses little distinction between it and his body: "Feeling both tense and relaxed, he sank his fingers into the grass. He tried to listen with his fingertips, to hear what, if anything, the earth had to say, and it told him quickly that someone was standing behind him" (279). The attempted execution physically manifests Milkman's impression that Guitar's racial politics, too, constitute yet another oppressive, even deadly "demand" holding him down. The wilderness itself, on the other hand, appears to evacuate such burdensome social forms. That Milkman feels "exhilarated by simply walking the earth" (279) appears to signify a resolution of his alienation, accomplished by movement from urban restlessness to "redemptive intimacy and affinity with the natural environment."[54] The forest signifies a shared order, which Milkman's mother Ruth earlier defines as "wilderness where there was system, or the logic of lions, trees, toads, and birds" (138). Milkman perceives the system as primary, prelinguistic, predating socially mediated identities. Within this state of nature, he perceives a universal character among all species most immediately at the level of communication but also, implicitly, at the level of ontology, in terms of "what he was born with." Dogs, hunters, trees, and "the earth itself" unite in the shape of the wilderness.

Song of Solomon's placement of Milkman's dissolution in pointed opposition to Guitar's violent racial essentialism signals the centrality of their relationship to the novel. They dovetail in their commitments to idealized authenticity. From Guitar's perspective, as well as that of numerous Black nationalists working at the time of Morrison's writing, Black degeneracy (either adherence to the capitalist order or the failure of Black institutions) results from the machinations of white culture's imposition on African Americans' essential nature. First slavery and then Jim Crow and Northern ghettoization alienated Blacks from their roots. Liberal universalism – and its history of racism and imperialism – dilutes a people's origins. At times, such commentary walks a fine line between complex material critique and renewed romanticism. The philosopher Kwame Anthony Appiah has pointed out that Black American culture "is centrally shaped by American society and institutions; it cannot be seen as constructed solely within African-American communities."[55] Identity is dialogic, in conversation among cultures and individuals within cultures. Any discourse of authenticity risks invoking an idealized past of ethnic or racial uniformity.

Nonetheless, this sort of recourse to lost origins is precisely what Devall and Sessions mean when they refer to "the minority tradition." They infuse ecology with the moral outrage of systemic dispossession, just as the New Left did for psychic authenticity in general, also by drawing lines of affinity between their own alienation and the oppression of Black (and Native) communities. Similarly, Milkman's dissolution structurally reflects Guitar's politics. In the wilderness context, Milkman appears to participate in an exercise advanced by one deep ecologist in 1989: to "shake off . . . the grasp of our conscious egos." For both figures, the "conscious ego" seems something of an imposition, yet another "particular masquerading as a universal." If for Black nationalists like Guitar it is white culture and its liberal platitudes that obscures one's essence, for these others it is social forms in general, including the ego. Milkman's self momentarily registers as a "case of mistaken identity, a millennia-long amnesia" repressing his originary, holistic identity with the earth itself.[56] Devall and Sessions's practice of ecological "self-realization," a psychic condition "experienced and integrated with the whole of nature," likewise resembles Guitar's rhetoric in substantial yet often unrecognized ways. For these figures, "human self-interest and the interest of the ecosystem were one and the same," just as for Guitar the interests of individual and race are identical. Both perspectives "come with notions of how a proper person of that kind behaves."[57]

The IPE is an identity politics precisely because it places ultimate political value upon a standard that unites its constituents. It differs from Guitar's racial authenticity, however, in that it collects *everything* under its purview, rather than one particular people or culture. Both accounts – the universal and the particular – are carefully calibrated narratives that masquerade as essential truths. These "scripts," as Appiah calls them, become oppressive when unbalanced by an historical understanding of identity.[58] Guitar's behavior provides a case in point. Milkman's, however, is no less totalitarian. Because of the self-erasure that accompanies Milkman's dissolution, the universal experience does not ultimately provide any real challenge to Guitar's totalizing essentialism. Milkman stands between two alternatives that propose to mend the cracks he perceives in his self-identity. Both of these positions, however, demarcate cohesion not at the level of the individual or its constitutive interactions within a community, but at the level of a homogeneous collective that eliminates inter- and intracommunity variation, as well as the self.

Such boundary-blurring appears throughout Morrison's corpus as a critical exercise rather than as an affirmation of romantic authenticity. For example, fantasies of maternal merger from both the mother's and child's perspectives feature prominently, as in the stylistically experimental passages in *Beloved* (1987) in which Sethe, Denver, and Beloved's voices seem to merge in such a way that mother and daughters become indistinguishable: "I am not separate from her there is no place where I stop."[59] For Milkman, however, intimacy with Ruth instead carries undertones of both discomfort, for its limitation of his independence, and shame, for the rumors that circulate about their relationship. A similar sense of abjection marks the otherwise gratifying "wilderness" of characters like Hagar in *Song of Solomon*, Beloved in *Beloved*, and Florens in *A Mercy* (2008), for all of whom "wilderness" seems to signify a lack of normative boundaries. Florens is "nothing but wilderness. No constraint. No mind," according to an ex-lover. Her fellow farmworkers note that the "docile creature they knew had turned feral." These judgments originate in men who project wilderness onto Florens as a threatening feminine attribute, but Florens herself seems enamored of the transformation. "You say I am wilderness. I am," she confirms, appropriating the characterization. "I am become wilderness but I am also Florens. In full. Unforgiven. Unforgiving . . . . Free."[60] Despite her confidence, Florens's announcement nonetheless identifies her "with a 'nature' that is impulsive, dangerous, without boundaries, which presumably requires the order and restraint represented by man." As Jennifer Terry points out, that association does not exist in a cultural vacuum, but arises from "a familiar patriarchal hierarchy in which woman is corporeal, irrational, excessive, and aligned with the nonhuman world as opposed to masculinized civilization."[61] Florens's reference to her "fullness" is double-edged. Even as she embraces a powerful sensation of wholeness, she fails to recognize how the experience plays into established narratives.

For Morrison, the cultural dimensions of the wilderness concept are of far more importance than its environmental references. "Wildness" finds expression in *Beloved*'s Sethe as a sensibility "whitefolks planted." The "jungle" within Sethe is predicated on something cultivated and, perhaps more importantly, *interpreted* negatively by a dominant culture.[62] Morrison similarly appraises Guitar's character, whom she intends to epitomize a certain "freedom of the will" that has come into conflict with social conventions and racial hierarchies. Guitar numbers among "the misunderstood people in the world. There's a wildness that they have, a nice wildness," one that is "pre-Christ in the best sense. It's Eve." At the same time, this wildness or wilderness (Morrison uses the two words almost interchangeably) "has bad effects in society," but only because "society says" that Black folks and Black men in particular are "not supposed to have it." As such, "when you take away the vocabulary of denigration, what you have is somebody who is fearless and who is comfortable with that fearlessness."[63] Morrison's words – particularly her emphasis on wildness and "Eve" – conflate three values: nature, the feminine, and the precivilizational. Her favorable reflection on "nice wildness" suggests that the conflict between

Milkman and Guitar arises because the former has lost his originary condition, his "wildness," while the latter has been perverted by context. More importantly, the passage implies that, due to their sociocultural mediation, wildness or wilderness will always be untrustworthy concepts. Wilderness is a cultural construction that collapses Black into savagery through the deployment of naturalized and feminized imagery.

Milkman experiences wilderness in his dissolution as an expansive psychic nature set apart from social forms. Morrison uses such universalist imagery, however, to question and critique its assumptions. Affiliation, she writes, does not signify intrinsic, homogeneous group cohesion, but comprises "all sorts of voices, each of which is profoundly different. Because what strikes me about African American culture *is* its variety." Her affection for the particular bespeaks a suspicion of claims to universality she nonetheless plots in her characters. She writes, "Even when I'm talking about universal concepts, I try to see how people, such as myself, would look at these universal concepts, how they would respond to them."[64] In her fiction, Morrison is less interested in showcasing ecology's universal aspects than she is in probing the implications of the perceptions, actions, and relations it engenders.

Toni Morrison's Skeptical State of Nature: Race, Gender, and Wilderness

The Wilderness Act and a major Civil Rights Act both passed in 1964, three years before Ture and Hamilton made popular the Black-nationalist critique that American liberalism functions as a white particular masquerading as a colorblind universal. The Wilderness Act, Carolyn Finney points out, itself presumed a certain "universality of ideals," including the importance of pristine natural spaces to the national imaginary. The Act's assumptions overlooked the fact that segregation remained rampant in many parts of the country. Black and other families of color found it difficult, if not dangerous, to visit national parks in light of inherited associations of slave-hunting and lynching with "white and hostile terrain" and the very real threat of white retaliation. The discourse surrounding America's foundational "clean state of wilderness" has historically relied on material programs of exclusion, colonization, dispossession, and slavery. The wilderness narrative itself has largely functioned as a particular masquerading as a universal, a "narrative ... constructed about the environment that is deemed at once authentic and universal and that denies the complexity of experiences that nondominant groups have encountered historically."[65]

Unlike the traditional wilderness ideal or, more generally, the liberalism Guitar's Black nationalism vilifies, Milkman's dissolutive experience is not precisely a particular masquerading as a universal. Rather, it is a true universal – ecological interconnection – made to deny the value of any particular. In this respect, however, it relies on the same discursive oversight of which these other traditions stand accused. By plotting this feature in Milkman's expansive self-erasure, Morrison bends a critical eye toward the premises underlying the IPE's own brand of universalism, namely its presumption of ontological unity. In doing so, *Song of Solomon* elucidates the IPE's continuity with universalism's contested lineage not only in American liberalism, but also across environmental and literary history. If the IPE revises the traditional American wilderness narrative, it often does so in such a way that preserves its status as a white wilderness – that is, fundamentally colonial, in terms of gender as well as of race. That is, if the IPE is an identity politics, it is one whose underlying assumptions favor of an historically masculine (and typically white) stance.

Morrison is particularly skeptical of the "'universal' yearnings" that characterize "Young America," as well as the nation's founding mythologies of pristine, untouched environment. She critiques the antediluvian romance directly in *A Mercy* as it manifests in the white Jacob Vaark's vista of "forests untouched since Noah, shorelines beautiful enough to bring tears, wild food for the taking," all of which he claims upon arrival in the New World.[66] The "primal encounters" that "form the backbone of the classic American literary canon" figure freedom in the pastoral mode, "in terms of man's ability to master the natural environment," a tradition Morrison consistently critiques throughout her oeuvre. The putatively ubiquitous "rights of man ... upon which the nation was founded," Morrison writes, have always existed in counterbalance to "the hierarchy of race." The "constituted Africanism, deployed as rawness and savagery," that she observes in early American texts "provided the staging ground and arena for the elaboration of the quintessential American identity."[67] Throughout literary history, romantic protagonists have simultaneously conquered that state of nature and, having seized it from unworthy savages, embraced it. The wilderness narrative is intimately related to this national myth, "informed by ... the linkage of wilderness to whiteness, wherein both become naturalized and universalized."[68] What begins as an identification of other with nature transforms into a narrative of white domestication founded on the retroactive establishment of universal principles of freedom denied to that very other.

120   The Universal Wilderness

The location of liberty in an idealized nature no doubt informs those critics who have framed wilderness as a "broad geographical metaphor for search, discovery, and achievement of self," an "alternative space" to the fenced plantation or the Northern ghetto, passage into which "is but one step toward the recovery of wholeness," of both "individual and group identity."[69] Despite the benignly egalitarian appearance of such a state of nature, Morrison is acutely aware of this idea's discursive manufacture and mediation throughout American history. At the very least, her characters cannot sympathize with it. In *A Mercy*, Florens finds in the New World wilderness a hostility painted by unfriendly, watching eyes; in *Beloved*, characters associate lynching with trees themselves; and in *Song of Solomon*, Macon and Pilate acutely fear white hunters in the wilderness as children. What these moments have in common is that in each instance wilderness derives its terror from human presence. "All the affectionate things" that Macon and his sister Pilate had known in their backyard "became ominous signs of a presence that was searching for them" (168). Wilderness is never pure, untouched, or neutral. It resonates with associations, with the protective stewardship of Macon and Pilate's father or with the malevolence of white men who would seize his land. Morrison's interest in representing the personal rather than the universal, coupled with her characters' interactions with nonhuman others, foregrounds the extent of that state of nature's sociocultural mediation, especially along lines of race, ethnicity, and gender.

The relationship between Macon Sr. and Pilate informs how these politics play out in the novel in relation to wilderness. Given Macon's often cruel adherence to liberal individualism, it is remarkable that he changes his script when he disparages Pilate as a "snake": "It ain't what she did; it's what she is" (54). Macon tends to appraise the members of his community in terms of self-determination – what they do rather than who they are – but he makes a notable exception for his sister. As Macon's distaste aptly illustrates, who or what Pilate is seems far less important than what other characters make of her, how they see her, or how they use her. The novel very pointedly delivers impressions of Pilate chiefly through the words, thoughts, and perceptions of other characters, rather than through direct narration or description (with the exception of one scene late in the novel). Though readers get a glimpse of Pilate's migratory history, that background filters through Ruth's impressions of the story. Even her seemingly neutral depiction at the novel's beginning, which identifies her not by name but by her clothes and voice, her "powerful contralto" and "knitted navy cap pulled far down over her forehead," passes through the

Toni Morrison's Skeptical State of Nature 121

perspective of a crowd that "nudged each other and snickered" at the singing woman (5–6). Macon is ashamed of his sister's "odd, murky, and unkempt" presentation, and he "tremble[s] with the thought of the white men in the bank … discovering this raggedly bootlegger was his sister" (20). She chews pine needles, a habit picked up in childhood, so that she "smelled even then like a forest," and her ramshackle house seems "to be rising from rather than settling into the ground" (27). Pilate, her daughter Reba, and her granddaughter Hagar, Macon comments, "ate what they had or came across or had a craving for" (29). Macon animalizes his sister and her offspring, identifies them with the trees and animals that populated the forest he and Pilate became lost in as children.

Pilate appears to loom large in the novel as a mystically naturalistic power because other characters, including Macon, build her up to mythic proportions. The locals believe that she possesses "the power to step out of her skin, set a bush afire from fifty yards, and turn a man into a ripe rutabaga – all on account of the fact that she had no navel" (94). Pilate "borned herself," the midwife Circe tells Milkman (244). The absence of this primary symbol of human gestation "convinced people that she had not come into this world through normal channels; had never lain, floated, or grown in some warm and liquid place" (28). Rather than contest this claim, Milkman takes it as another detail of his aunt's history as Circe rather fantastically relates it. The notion that Pilate played some arcane role in her own creation is as much a facet of the tall tale of Pilate's gold as the gold itself, yet Milkman hurriedly accepts both details as consistent with the narrative. The inscrutability of Pilate's physical body renders her a larger-than-life, even transcendent figure in the imaginations of the people close to her. She has nothing to show for her time spent in the womb, but the folklore other characters build up around her suggests that Pilate herself functions as a sort of womb, an enveloping presence to which all characters gravitate.

Many critics likewise identify Pilate with Morrison's customary maternal imagery. A more accurate interpretation would account for the extent to which other characters project this quality onto her. Their superstitions contrast sharply with the only scene in which the novel directly narrates Pilate's actions without the lens of another character's perception. Toward the end of *Song of Solomon*, when Hagar returns home from a confrontation with her lover Milkman, Pilate, shorn of her typically majestic reception, appears a frantic, doting grandmother, trying desperately to catch Hagar's eye. When her granddaughter finally responds, Pilate is "thrilled at the sound of [her] voice" (308). The exchange marks the first

122   The Universal Wilderness

and only instance in which the reader gets a sense of Pilate's thoughts and emotions beyond what she verbally reports to Ruth earlier. Pilate is neither omniscient nor supernatural. She is a weary, anxious parent, wracked by fear and the knowledge that she has no control over her granddaughter's deteriorating health, despite the mythology gathered around her. She and Reba have pampered Hagar throughout the entire novel, "spoiled her, and she, as a favor to their indulgence, hid as best she could the fact that they embarrassed her" (150–1). Despite her mask of cool, aloof power, Pilate tries remarkably hard to manage her surroundings and her people, and to win their love.

The juxtaposition of these examples illustrates the extent to which Macon and others render Pilate at once more than and less than human by taking seriously the myths they have built up around her. Milkman comes to idolize his aunt. "Was that something? Wow!" he whispers to Hagar after Pilate coolly threatens a man who has mistreated Reba (95). His words paint him as a star-struck boy meeting a superhero. At his first sight of her, he "knew that . . . nothing – not the wisdom of his father nor the caution of the world – could keep him from her" (36). Readers' impressions of Pilate's death at the novel's conclusion also arrive from Milkman's perspective. He lays her body down and looks up to see that two "birds circled round them. One dived into the new grave and scooped something shiny in its beak before it flew away. Now he knew why he loved her so. Without ever leaving the ground, she could fly" (336). The passage calls attention to how Milkman sentimentalizes Pilate for the same reasons that Macon distrusts or is disgusted by her. To Macon, Pilate is "ugly, dirty, poor, and drunk" (37). To Milkman, she is not "dirty; unkempt, yes, but not dirty" (38). Her house is "the only one he knew that achieved comfort without one article of comfort in it . . . . peace was there, energy, singing, and now his own remembrances" (301). The house is a refuge from which Milkman takes (literally, in the case of a sack of bones he confuses for treasure) but to which he does not give in return. Pilate and her house become loci of retreat and gratification that Milkman does not intend to reciprocate. She tellingly remarks to her nephew during their first meeting, "I ain't the one with the wants. You the one who want something" (37). Milkman's disdainful treatment of his cousin and lover Hagar, whom he regards at best with derision and at worst as property, accentuates the degree of his self-interest. Even as he "stretched his carefree boyhood out for thirty-one years," he "tired of her," as a child grows weary of a stuffed animal (98, 91). Milkman's air of persecuted self-absorption tends toward the narcissistic in relation to the women in his family, whom he

Toni Morrison's Skeptical State of Nature

understands not as individuals but as extensions of himself. "Never had he thought of his mother as a person, a separate individual, with a life apart from allowing or interfering with his own," and he "had never been able to really distinguish" his sisters "(or their roles) from his mother" (75, 68). In Milkman, Morrison's theme of maternal merger takes on a tone not of gynocentric intimacy but of chauvinistic instrumentalism.

The difference between these other women and Pilate is that Milkman pastoralizes his aunt. What I mean by "pastoralize" is that he treats Pilate much as he treats the Virginia woodlands, as a precursor to his experience of the latter. For Milkman, both woman and wilderness function as devices "of retreat and return." Insofar as he associates Pilate with the earth, both become "idealized descriptions of [the] countryside."[70] Milkman cleaves to Pilate because he believes she has something to give him, some expansive experience or essential knowledge from which he can return to his quotidian routine feeling more satisfied and complete than before. Significantly, he also naturalizes his aunt, treating her as an extension of the earth in the same fashion in which his father associates her with trees, animals, and soil. "Pervading everything" in Pilate's house "was the odor of pine and fermenting fruit," and to the young Milkman she "looked like a tall black tree" (39). The imagery links his later dissolution beneath the sweet-gum with his aunt, whom he also associates with a certain expansiveness, and her role in the community with the womb.

Milkman's dissolutions, like Abbey's, proceed from an old pastoral logic associating wilderness with woman. Pilate's home comes to represent "prelapsarian nature," and Pilate herself appears "to play Earth Mother to the questing male protagonist."[71] These sorts of observations are common to criticism of the novel but bear some revision. Pilate only "plays Earth Mother" to Milkman in his own perception of her. Morrison herself does not take for granted the "'natural woman' that feminist theory has rejected." Rather, she introduces the idea in order to critique it, as she does through Lina's reflexive inner monologue in *A Mercy*. Lina, a young Native woman, finds solace in imagining herself "one more thing that moved in the natural world. She cawed with birds, chatted with plants, spoke to squirrels, sang to the cow and opened her mouth to rain." Such identification not only provides Lina comfort in her bondage, but also "echoes the oppositional definitions of savagery and civility shaped by early European Americans" and "potentially reflects the modern turn to a representative other for access to 'authentic' relations."[72] These "authentic relations" are precisely the universal rhythms Milkman projects onto Pilate and feels in the woods.

124   The Universal Wilderness

Song of Solomon passes judgment on Milkman for his indulgence in the exhausted colonial tendency to identify land with woman. Morrison is explicitly critical of this naturalistic kind of "special soul ... some magic blacker than everybody else's and more mysterious." She is just as critical of Black writers, such as Baraka and Cleaver, who evoke this sort of romance as she is of whites – and even more so of what that sort of equation has meant for women in *any* literature. "Soul," she writes, "is what the master allows you when you don't have anything else."[73] Even identitarian uses of such imagery merely recapitulate unhelpful divisions between white civilization and racial savagery, men and women. Such illusive fire would nonetheless seem to characterize Pilate for both *Song of Solomon*'s dramatis personae and her commentators. Morrison herself, however, understands the character as fulfilling a crucial role played by what she calls "elders," the "sort of timeless people whose relationships to the characters are benevolent, instructive, and protective." Representations of such nearly transcendental figures easily lapse into romanticism, mysticism, or Mammy-ism. Morrison's solution lies in a distinction she seems to draw between essence and history. An elder distills knowledge not from her nature but from her experience. A character derives "solace" from the figure's story and "not from the contemplation of serene nature as in a lot of mainstream white literature."[74] If Milkman appears to learn little from his time with Pilate (he chooses to mine her, like a colonial landscape, for gold), it is precisely because he does identify her with that "serene nature." In the context of this relationship, the dissolution that later expands his consciousness similarly reeks of such tropes, proceeding as a masculine projection of feminine expansiveness onto the land, a "universal" vision that erases the material needs of the Black men and women who occupy it. The IPE's wilderness might be psychic rather than spatial, but it retains many of that narrative's most tired elements.

An Admission of Fabrication

The masculine valence of Milkman's narcissistic self-inflation among the women in his family and the feminine valence of his self-erasure in the womblike wilderness differ only in terms of their gendered registers. Both have the same effect: they erase distinctions. The crucial detail of Milkman's apprehension of a universal, racially blind, and essential identity in the wilderness is his loss of a coherent sense of selfhood and ability to detect or respect it in others. As he follows the hunters, "he found himself exhilarated by simply walking the earth. Walking it like he belonged on it;

An Admission of Fabrication 125

like his legs were stalks, tree trunks, a part of his body that extended down down down into the rock and soil, and were comfortable there – on the earth and on the place where he walked. And he did not limp" (281). Notably, as Milkman feels his sense of selfhood drift away, he also feels his disability ease. In the forest, his masculine performance is no longer necessary, and would even obscure what in the moment seems to him a more natural identification that encapsulates tree, ground, and dog, the entirety of the forest. At the same time, the disappearance of an idiosyncratic limp, a distinctively individualized aspect of his body, signifies the disappearance of the person. As Milkman attends to the universal tenor of each individual voice in the forest, the less distinction he perceives between hunter and dog, Milkman and tree. He takes wilderness to emblematize an ecological basis to identity that undermines both the transgressions of whites against Blacks and the limitations of an essential conception of racial authenticity.

On one hand, the experience counters Guitar's factional politics of identity, which actively mean Milkman harm. However, on the other, it undercuts the appetite for self-coherence that has driven Milkman's narrative thus far. His perception of dissolution flattens all residents of the Shalimar forest, living or nonliving. That primordial state of nature is relatively indifferent to the integrity of the elements that comprise it, including Milkman himself. It is worth pointing out that he finds himself unable to react to his would-be assassination until he resumes thinking of himself as an "I," when he throws Guitar off of him beneath the sweet-gum. The tree itself appears to warn him against his impending murder, but at other points in the novel Milkman's apprehension of ecological interconnectivity itself heralds his death, much as Annie Dillard's reflections on "fecundity" do in *Pilgrim at Tinker Creek*. When Milkman travels to Danville, Pennsylvania, in search of a cave where Pilate allegedly left her gold, he stops beside the wall of a mansion in which Macon and Pilate sheltered as children. At first "oblivious to the universe of wood life that did live there in layers of ivy," he gradually grows aware of the complexity among the vines, "grown so thick he could have sunk his arm in it up to the elbow. Life that crawled, life that slunk and crept and never closed its eyes. Birth, life, and death – each took place on the hidden side of a leaf." (219). Milkman's expansive sensation in Shalimar provides what he considers a welcome reprieve from the demands made on him by various characters, but his discomfort here also betrays a certain ambivalence.

It is tempting to say that Milkman comes out of this experience having learned something about himself or his community, as many critics have

126   The Universal Wilderness

done. On the contrary, he spends his final days in Shalimar and his trip back to Michigan romanticizing a man who abandoned his wife and children, choosing to interpret ancestral folklore in a way that merely sanctions his own behavior prior to departure. Milkman "could hardly wait to get home" to share with Macon, Pilate, and anyone who will listen his discovery of a distant forebear's Appalachian fame (329). Local legend tells that Solomon literally took flight from the foothills back to Africa. His magnificent departure links a parable of Black-nationalist aspirations with Milkman's own personal history, drawing critical attention to both. Solomon, like Milkman himself, left a distraught woman behind him, a point that Milkman at first overlooks. He does not reconsider the myth until the novel's final pages, only after Pilate has forcefully announced her presence as an individual separate from Milkman's narcissistic fantasies by smacking him across the head with a pan. Hagar has died in his absence: "He had hurt her, left her, and now she was dead – he was certain of it. He had left her. While he dreamt of flying, Hagar was dying" (332). The epiphany demystifies Solomon in Milkman's imagination, and he confronts the fact that his ancestor "left [his wife] behind and twenty children . . . . Who looked after those twenty children?" (332). He faces this conclusion not in the revelatory light of some purifying wilderness, but in Pilate's "unkempt" basement, back in the city.

The Solomon myth remains important to the characters' understanding of family, history, and community, but its interpretation and resonance shift. The "ancestor acknowledgment" central to mythmaking, Kimberly Ruffin notes, has operated as "a powerful activity in shaping collective identity." Nonetheless, those stories must demonstrate a certain flexibility to be of use, a shifting of value depending on context so as to "create meaning and reality based in a connection to place."[75] Morrison's contention is that an elder's narrative is what renders her an important figure in the community and its literature, not her "serene nature." In this respect, Morrison joins Simon Ortiz and Leslie Marmon Silko in their understanding of narrative's adaptive role.

By the end of the novel, the characters – Milkman and Pilate in particular – must content themselves with fragments of stories that may well be false. Despite Milkman's lengthy investigation from Michigan to Danville to Shalimar and back again to each, he never turns up any firm answers to his questions about his people. He receives only myths and multiple versions of the same stories, with many inconsistencies. The motivations underlying each event and action throughout his family history remain vexingly opaque. Milkman's questions are largely consistent with the era's Black-nationalist historical narrative, according to which "slavemasters had changed Africans' names and religions, and thus severed connections with the past."[76] He wonders why his grandmother "want[ed] her husband to keep that awful name," Macon Dead, inscribed by a drunk white man in clerical error. "To wipe out the past?" Milkman asks. "What past? Slavery?" (293). He later tells Guitar that the eldest Macon took the name "like a fuckin sheep. Somebody should have shot him" (89). Maintaining an original name, his vitriol implies, would have been a more honorable retention of accurate history, even of truer personhood. The name Macon "hid from view the real names of people, places, and things. Names that had meaning" (329). "Real" names ostensibly signify something true about a person – their heritage and origin, who they are. Milkman never finds any answers in his search for authentic history. One must assume that there are none, or that such answers are undiscoverable. The only verifiable information Milkman gathers over the course of his travels is the disclosure of his grandmother Sing's Native American blood, and therefore of his own mixed-race heritage.

Milkman's ancestry deals a deadlier blow to the notion of racial authenticity than his equally essentialist dissolution ever could. For this reason, the novel itself does not take Milkman's view on names. Morrison herself "never knew the real names of my father's friends." The colonial decimation of ancestral and tribal denominations left "a huge psychological scar," she writes, but the alternative offers its own means of self-determination. "The best thing you can do," she tells an interviewer, "is take another name which is yours because it reflects something about you or your own choice."[77] Milkman's own name, like almost every other name in the novel, is a fabrication inspired by an act or event (in Milkman's case, an embarrassingly long breastfeeding period). His name expresses not who he essentially is, but who he has been to his community. He ultimately takes pride in this point by the end of the novel, exultantly reciting in his head the myriad names of his people, "Names they got from yearnings, gestures, flaws, events, mistakes, weaknesses. Names that bore witness" (330). On the one hand, this tradition is remarkably individualistic, rooted in agency and self-direction. On the other, these names are collective articulations, manifestations of relationships and shared culture. As Guitar tells Milkman early in the novel, "Niggers get their names the way they get everything else – the best way they can. The best way they can" (88). It is ironic that this statement comes from Guitar, the novel's paragon of inviolable and homogeneous racial authenticity, but its aphoristic ring draws attention to the crucial role the sentiment plays in the novel.

128   The Universal Wilderness

The significance *Song of Solomon* grants to names indicates its stance on Milkman's sojourn in the universalizing wilderness. That experience not only is temporary, but also robs him of the identifiers his community has built up around him and which give him a sense of self-identity to begin with. Chasing a purportedly natural condition for its universality might be downright destructive, given that Milkman's abandonment of commitments and responsibilities leaves people like Hagar by the wayside. What the experience does provide is an admission of fabrication – an understanding that one dialogically constructs identity rather than discovers it in primordial nature. *Song of Solomon* fully endorses neither the essentialism that underwrites Guitar's racial politics nor the universalist promise of Milkman's wilderness romance, but it does argue for the necessary and positive failure of any stringently unifying sense of identity. Pilate speaks to this conclusion early in the narrative. "You think dark is just one color, but it ain't," she tells Milkman in his childhood. "There're five or six kinds of black. Some silky, some woolly. Some just empty . . . . And it don't stay still. It moves and changes from one kind of black to another" (40–1). Pilate is describing the Pennsylvania woodlands, but her words also gesture to the pervasive theme the novel cultivates in the conflict it stages between Milkman and Guitar. Blackness – or any other identity – is a construction collectively articulated by people. It might originate in a divisively racist history, but it changes and is ultimately open to what these characters make of it. Pilate's point applies to nature, wilderness, and even ecology just as compellingly.

A Brief Comment on Community and Environment

That Morrison affixes global importance to matters of climate change and health signals a certain tension between universal and particular concerns in her work, which operates almost as a caution to readers exploring "constitutive link[s] between intrahuman oppression and ecological violence."[78] Specifically, *Song of Solomon* illuminates how such vital connections, when drawn without sufficient care, can collapse into the sort of authentic identifications that suffused the primitivist counterculture. On the one hand, the "heightened awareness" of environmental issues among many Black, Native, Latinx, and economically disadvantaged communities – rural or urban – often points to the exposures to environmental harm that constitute environmental racism, the practice of channeling environmental policy or practice "to provide benefits for whites while shifting costs to people of color."[79] James

A Brief Comment on Community and Environment 129

Cone, the founder of Black liberation theology, once declared that those who "struggle against environmental degradation but do not incorporate in it a disciplined and sustained fight against white supremacy" are as "anti-ecological" as those "who fight against white racism but fail to connect it to the degradation of the earth."[80] Numerous critical readings of *Song of Solomon* have aligned Black America with environment. Many, however, have also moved past matters of social justice to focus on how the narrative links "characters' self-hatred and angry confusion" to "a psyche cut off from ancestral or communal wellsprings" and "chart[s] a moving and powerful repossession of selfhood."[81] As this comment illustrates, to emphasize correspondences between minority identity and ecology is also frequently, though certainly not always, to reiterate an equation of authentic racial or ethnic identity with the land.

It would be a mistake to say that *Song of Solomon* draws such lines of affinity between people of color and the earth. Milkman's dissolution, though it might appear to reclaim a particular "psyche cut off from ... communal wellsprings," in fact universalizes the wilderness as a flat representation of ecological authenticity, rather than identify it with a specific racial or ethnic identity. The novel's actual "coupling of racism and ecological alienation" takes place at the level of history, not of essence.[82] Macon and Pilate wander the countryside as children because white men have murdered their father and unlawfully seized his land. Dispossession has a profound impact on these characters' actions, but the novel is far more interested in the role played by land in communitarian self-determination than in its spatialization of ecological authenticity. *Song of Solomon* personifies the image of a communal farm to issue, "like a sermon," its own declaration of community premised on shared interests and self-making:

> Never mind you can't tell one letter from another, never mind you born a slave, never mind you lose your name ... Here, this here, is what a man can do if he puts his mind to it and his back in it .... We got a home in this rock, don't you see! ... Grab this land! Take it, hold it, my brothers, make it, my brothers, shake it, squeeze it, turn it, twist it, beat it, kick it, kiss it, whip it, stomp it, dig it, plow it, seed it, reap it, rent it, buy it, sell it, own it, build it, multiply it, and pass it on – can you hear me? Pass it on! (235)

The farm's voice ties locals into kinship with the earth, not identification – an environmental vision drastically different from the essential holism Milkman assumes in the wilderness. At this point, his apprehension of ecological authenticity would appear to merely reiterate the narcissism with which he approaches the women in his family.

The sentiment expressed in this passage is not interested in the totalizing universals that make up Milkman's dissolution, the IPE, or even the more flexible liberal vision misdoubted by modern Black-nationalist leaders. It is concerned not with pristine, wild nature, but environment broadly conceived as the place "where we live, where we work, where we play, and where we learn" – the understanding advanced by the environmental justice movement.[83] It views identity and environment not as unchanging or interchangeable essences, but as mutually constituted points of social negotiation. It is regionalist – even bioregionalist – and committed to self-determination while emphasizing respect for environment. In the context of the debate surrounding postwar liberalism it resembles not the foundationalism of rights-of-nature philosophers but the contingent historicism of communitarian thinkers such as Charles Taylor, Elizabeth Anderson, Michael J. Sandel, and Alasdair MacIntyre (quoted in this chapter's epigraph) – not to mention scholars of race from James Baldwin to Morrison herself. It wanders into what Joni Adamson calls the "middle place between universalism and particularity."[84]

Song of Solomon does not engage the political dimensions of this environmental vision, but it is nonetheless notable that Morrison published the novel just as the myriad threads of the environmental justice movement began to coalesce. The movement – less a cohesive campaign than a consistent yet adaptable platform uniting diverse stakeholders – focuses less on cultivating a politics of authenticity than on restructuring how environmental politics, practice, and policy play out. It "grew organically" out of the meeting between local environmental struggles and the direct-democracy strategies and direct-action tactics employed by social movements of the 1960s and 1970s, including the civil rights movement and Native land-rights struggles, as well as the anti-toxics movement and, to a lesser extent, traditional environmentalism.[85] The community self-determination platform that cultural nationalisms such as Black Power and Red Power cultivated among their constituencies especially informed the movement as well. A "Principles of Environmental Justice" statement delivered at the 2001 People of Color Environmental Leadership Summit in Washington, D.C., declared that environmental justice "demands that public policy be based on mutual respect and justice for all peoples, free from any form of discrimination or bias," but also "affirms the fundamental right to political, economic, cultural and environmental self-determination of all peoples."[86] On the one hand, environmental justice writ large is a normative protest, seeking to hold liberal government accountable to the standards it holds to be universal. On the other, its

A Brief Comment on Community and Environment   131

leaders often recycle cultural-nationalist calls for community self-determination, all too often aware of "the traditional dangers" of leaving political matters in the hands "of others with good intentions" – that is, the likelihood that "the outcome might not provide . . . substantive changes," just as civil rights' faith in liberalism failed to do for Black Power.[87]

My point in drawing attention to these influences is to highlight that the political clashes of the 1960s and 1970s informed environmentalist traditions other than the IPE – traditions that have not only tangibly advanced the causes of underrepresented communities, but also, at the very least, avoided the troubling homogenization that characterizes appeals to ecological authenticity. The "Principles of Environmental Justice" statement also "affirms the sacredness of Mother Earth, ecological unity and the interdependence of all species," elevating interconnection to the forefront of its system of values, much like the IPE. "For us," one activist nonetheless wrote in 1991, "the issues of the environment do not stand alone by themselves. They are . . . woven into an overall framework of social, racial and economic justice."[88] These documents emphasize assemblage, but they do so in a way that does not pit "real" ecology against "artificial" civilization. For this writer, at least, material interconnection binds all of these phenomena together: there is no "true" identity apart from her identity at the intersection of myriad environmental, social, and economic forces. The concerns of environmental justice have had little to do with "nature," either spatial or psychic. The movement, broadly speaking, has also tended to recognize, as intersectional groups such as the Combahee River Collective did as early as the 1960s and 1970s, that notions of racial, ethnic, or gendered essence only (and often violently) oversimplify, rather than capture, matters of identity. Environmental justice, Adamson writes, "can only begin when members of these diverse groups proceed with the hard work of recognizing the other groups' specific experiences."[89] The environmental justice narrative holds that there are no universals in such matters.

Such an approach has yielded concrete, productive gains for people of color in terms of community self-determination and relationship to environment in a way that Milkman's nominally universal yet profoundly self-absorbed dissolution does not. The deliberative process central to environmental justice coalition-building recognizes that one *creates* a vision of environmental well-being through conversation as opposed to *discovering* one through revelation – the psychical or at times mystical ecological work demanded by the IPE. It also recognizes that it is impossible to recognize a "single bad actor" in either racism or environmental catastrophe, as the IPE has so often singled out civilization writ large.[90] These processes are complex assemblages. They impact not only romanticized people of color, allegedly cloven from psychic "wellsprings," but also other socioeconomically disadvantaged communities, such as predominantly white townships of central Appalachia. Environmental justice has encouraged intersection among such communities instead of flattening them according to a single ideological standard. Rather than authenticate certain identities, it has inspired narratives about relationships across identity and environment, as Terry Tempest Williams's *Refuge* (1991), for example, traces interactions across gender, religion, and region. The IPE, on the other hand, negates the very possibility of intersectional critique or political coalition. Nonetheless, as the next chapter will show, certain identity communities have in fact adopted the IPE in an effort to bolster their particular self-determinations.

CHAPTER 4

The Essential Ecosystem
Reproduction, Network, and Biological Reduction

You aren't and can't be apart from nature. We're all part of the biological universe: men as well as women.
Margaret Atwood, interviewed by Karla Hammond

Thrust aside, completely removed from culture, this nature – the repository of essentialism and stasis – nonetheless remains dangerously intact.
Stacy Alaimo, *Bodily Natures*

Environmental justice emerged in the 1970s alongside work by feminist theorists such as Marjorie Spiegel, Susan Griffin, Gena Corea, and Adrienne Rich, as well as with anti-toxics and civil-rights coalitions. Like critics of color, these scholar-activists reproached liberal "extensionists" such as Christopher Stone "for extending ... a masculine justice framework to include nonhumans." Feminist writers and other artists contributed to environmentalism an imminent critique of its most enduring assumptions, especially longstanding gendered narratives positing "a masculinist 'self'" that would either enshrine liberal individualism or "overcome the dualism between the human individual and nature." A rigorous ecofeminism, Val Plumwood wrote in 1994, would by contrast seek to deconstruct affiliated woman/man and nature/culture dualisms, as well as balance the "climate of ... false choice" between "approaches which critique anthropocentrism" and "focus primarily on forms of human domination" – that is, between deep and social ecology.[1]

The crisp term "ecofeminism," however, lends itself a misleading air of integrity. Broadly, ecofeminism is any position that views feminist and environmental matters as deeply inextricable, much as James Cone's Black liberation theology perceived environment and race. As an activist cause, ecofeminism has been a global project, one with especially important roots in the May 1968 uprisings in France and decolonial protest movements such as India's *Chipko Andolan*. As a body of scholarship, its parameters

134 The Essential Ecosystem

have encircled numerous camps, hermeneutics, and texts tethered by their common interest in the historical relationship between the domination of women and the domination of nature. In the 1970s and 1980s, one of the greatest fault lines dividing ecofeminists ran along the idea that "women have some epistemic privilege in both deconstructing naturism and articulating a new environmental ethic or ethics."[2] Whence comes that privilege? From women's social situation? If so, which women's? Or does it derive instead from women's very biology?

These questions should appear familiar to any student of feminism writ large. They rehash in an environmentalist context many of the concerns that busied the women's movement in general in the 1970s. Debates over what defines *woman* to begin with dominated much of the conversation. Not incidentally, many feminists of the era pitted the "wholeness" and "integrity" of womanhood or lesbianism against the "alienated" and "death-devoted sickness of male-inspired civilization."[3] One feminist strategy – one among many – worked to build not only a community but also a sense of shared identity using a rhetoric of essential womanhood, oppressed in like manner to the Black constituencies mobilizing around the same time and likewise committed to expressing a certain authentic womanhood or lesbianism in art, literature, and political life.[4] At the same time, critics and analysts such as Juliet Mitchell, Dorothy Dinnerstein, and later Carol Gilligan and Nancy Chodorow began to draw from yet also critique the sort of psychoanalytic thought that governed midcentury social theory and spurred the 1960s' proliferating politics of authenticity. Perhaps more rigorously than any other movement that emerged from the decade, second-wave feminism explored the relationship between subjectivity and "repressive civilization," though for feminist activists the word "repressive" rhymed with "patriarchal." In some cases, feminist understandings of gendered essence concurrently took shape according to the same basic logic as the IPE: a true self – or woman – lay buried beneath mounds of intertwined oppression and repression.

This overlap set the stage for a cross-pollination between feminism and the IPE narrative, which not only borrowed from other movements but also influenced them. This chapter examines how feminist debates surrounding essentialism paralleled the IPE even as that narrative informed certain feminists, specifically a loose yet prominent faction that arose in the 1970s and persisted throughout the New Age of the 1980s and 1990s. What Catherine Roach terms "nature feminism" (to distinguish it from ecofeminism writ large) joined ecology with gender essentialism, invoking the IPE narrative to argue that women share

The Essential Ecosystem   135

a privileged ecological perspective.[5] "Women have always thought like mountains," the poet Sharon Doubiago wrote in 1989. "There's nothing like the experience of one's belly growing into a mountain to teach you this." As Doubiago's comment aptly illustrates, nature-feminist authenticity largely took the form of biologism, "a particular form of essentialism in which women's essence is defined in terms of their biological capacities."[6] As Black feminists from the 1970s to the present have especially made clear, "gender essentialism" is a strategy mostly particular to white feminists, at least those neglectful of the political challenges posed by what Kimberlé Crenshaw would later call "intersectionality."[7] Nature feminists embraced, with an ecological spin, the routine colonial trope of land-as-woman discussed in previous chapters, subsuming differences along lines of race and other indexes under a monolithic ideal of ecologically unified "woman" – an erasure typical in other iterations of the IPE.

This chapter also aims to show that the logic of the IPE undermines the identitarian cause that nature feminists have intended it to support. In this respect, nature feminism serves as one of many possible examples of the fact that the IPE compromises any identity movement that would adopt its narratives. Because ecology is a universal condition, appeals to ecological authenticity cancel out the social identities such movements often aim to fortify. Margaret Atwood dramatizes this point in her 1972 novel *Surfacing*, whose unnamed narrator's attempt to access her "natural woman[hood]" serves only to progressively accentuate her shifting role as "part of the landscape." Her bodily matter "could be anything, a tree, a deer skeleton, a rock."[8] Atwood herself notes that like other Canadian women protagonists of the late twentieth century, the narrator retreats "into the woods" to dispel a series of social expectations affixed to womanhood by men who seek to control that identity. Like many texts written by feminist women in the 1970s, the novel "has largely been read as a narrative of … self-discovery."[9] I argue the opposite: that *Surfacing* reads far more compellingly as a narrative of self-undiscovery. The narrator's refusal of the gender roles expected of her inspires a series of dissolutions in Québécois lake country. As she searches the wilderness for her missing father, she casts aside the "layers" of her identity she believes tailored by men in an attempt to recover her natural – even biological – self. Her comprehension of her environment's ecological complexity, however, leads her to approach biology in such a way that "woman" ceases to hold any meaning for her. The most natural thing about her, she concludes, is her bodily matter's dynamic interplay with its ecosystem. Her fixation on (and identification

136   The Essential Ecosystem

with) matter's circulation expands a particular essentialism – *woman* – into a universal one – *ecology*.

In *Surfacing*, women's capacity for reproduction cedes the floor to the human body's more generic capacity for what Donna Haraway calls "replication," ecological cycles of life and death, consumption and defecation.[10] In this respect, the novel resonates with feminist projects to sever sexuality from reproduction. Like the postmodern feminists whose careers have paralleled her own, Atwood has been deeply suspicious of "the body" as a potentially reductive concept, one that is always inscribed with shifting cultural meanings even when understood in terms of its material elements. *Surfacing*'s narrator cannot successfully sustain a dissolution of bounded selfhood, but she nonetheless undermines stable conceptions of ideas like "body," "woman," and even "subject." As such, the novel also resonates with the networked paradigm that concurrently began to dethrone psychoanalysis as a major basis for social thought in the 1970s, heralding a shift in emphasis from subjectivity to complex webs of agency and interaction that subvert the subject altogether.

That networked frame undergirds what has been called the "material turn" in contemporary feminist thought, as well as the humanities and social sciences more generally. "Identity" tends to carry derogatory connotations in new-materialist scholarship, which often treats the concept as a restrictive, categorical relic that persists despite the fact that the physical sciences have established time and again that matter – including the matter that constitutes human bodies – is not static but endlessly dynamic, constantly shifting and undermining subjective stability at a biophysical level. New-materialist philosophers continue the feminist debates surrounding essentialism that started in the 1970s, in some cases announcing "the death of the subject (if not the subject position)" altogether. At the same time, as Linda Garber points out of certain queer theorists, such writers also often "find the need" to "strategically" redeploy subjectivity to make political sense.[11] For new materialists, this work often proceeds by drawing on established feminist models of situated political subjectivity, many of which arose in contest with the gendered essentialisms of the sort peddled by nature feminists. In such writing, the subject and its death exist not only in tension, but in dialectical relation. How would one recognize the subject's death if one did not speak from a situated subject position from which to observe it?

What this point makes clear is that the questions occasioned by the IPE endure in today's intellectual debates. Those debates proceed from the same concerns that animated the conversation surrounding the IPE narrative in the 1960s and 1970s: subjectivity's uncertainty in light of ecology and other physical sciences, and its political necessity in the face of ongoing racial, ethnic, and gendered violence. The conversation, that is to say, continues. Moreover, identity's fall from grace amid the material turn does not necessarily preclude appeals to nature or essence. After all, the IPE proposes the death of one subject merely to make room for another. It simply expands subjectivity beyond the discrete individual to fit the ecosystem as a whole. New materialists have especially emphasized the ontological aspects of networks – their "vitality." At what point do such arguments about the ontology of the network come to reify the idea of ecological authenticity? It would be impossible to reckon with the material turn's vast intellectual diversity and extensive literature in the space of a single chapter, let alone an entire book. What I want to focus on is how reading Atwood from the 1970s to the present illuminates lines of continuity between defunct elements of identitarian nature feminism and specific moments in nominally anti-identitarian new materialism. As one might expect, the thread that connects them runs along the at least implicit persistence of psychoanalytic narratives in these conversations. *Surfacing*'s plot shifts from nature feminism's identification with reproductive capacity to a broader identification with *replicative* capacity – a sort of "matter essentialism" that underwrites certain instances of the material turn. This transition raises important questions about authenticity's political purchase. How deep does one go in search of essence? To gender? To the body? To matter in general? Atwood draws attention to how authenticity's ever-receding limits expand the idea to the point of political uselessness.

Surfacing's Identity Crises: Gender and Nature in the 1970s

The measure of sanctity granted to selfhood in the radical political climate of the 1960s does not inspire in *Surfacing*'s narrator any profound sense of liberation, meaning, or fulfillment. In the novel, such guarantees emanate chiefly from male voices – as they often did among organizations like SDS and SNCC – whose thinly veiled chauvinism would dictate the terms of both "liberation" and "woman." Accompanying the narrator north are her boyfriend Joe, her friend Anna, and Anna's horny husband David, who appeals to the narrator as a liberated, "groovy chick" in a bid to sleep with her. When she refuses his advances, he dismisses her as a "tight-ass bitch" (152). All the while, she represses her memory of an abortion mandated by a former (married) lover, who "talked about it as though it was legal, simple, like getting a wart removed" (145). These suitors unite in a casual approach to sex, the narrator's body, and their assumption that willing intercourse defines her identity as a "groovy chick" for whom an abortion must be as banal as a trip to the grocer. David's chauvinism conspicuously limns the boisterous countercultural bravado of his Canadian nationalism, a disinclination toward "rotten capitalist bastard" American imperialism shared with many characters in the novel (8). That Atwood prominently juxtaposes David's radical sympathies with his crass sexism, so that these characteristics come together in the narrator's perception, speaks to the often-misogynistic rhetoric and behavior associated with the New Left, counterculture, and other movements, despite these groups' commitment to cultural revolution.

The Women's Liberation Movement amply documented the Left's sexual double standards in the early 1970s, invigorating numerous forays into gender identity. Robin Morgan excoriated the "counterfeit Left" for its gendered division of labor, priorities, and gratification in a 1970 essay, the same year she compiled the widely read feminist anthology *Sisterhood Is Powerful*. As a young writer at an "American radical magazine," Susan Griffin, one of the earliest and most popular voices in ecofeminism, grew "disturbed" by the "clearly prejudicial attitude which the radical employers had toward their female staff."[12] The great irony of such treatment, as Griffin knew well, was that she and other women suffered it at the hands of so-called "new men" who aligned themselves with qualities "co-opted" from women's "traditional realm." The counterculture and "antiwar, antiestablishment, ecological, back-to-the-land movement of the sixties and seventies was a movement in large part of young males taking on traditional female … values," including "love, conscience, unconscious-ness, compassion, sensitivity, sensuality, [and] nature."[13] This sort of argument preserved without troubling the gendered dualism of its milieu.

Essential womanhood has lost much of its political luster, especially in academic circles, but such distinctions have remained at least influential enough to inform numerous readings of *Surfacing* as an essentialist romance that casts the narrator's encounters with sexism and capitalism against her "search for authenticity and truth."[14] One must nonetheless account for the fact that Atwood has consistently rebuffed feminist labels often attached to her work. She heartily dismisses the idea, advanced by one interviewer, that her novels do or even can "espouse a feminist pos-ition," and even wryly incorporates her ambivalence regarding feminist criticism in her fiction (Elaine, the protagonist of her 1988 novel *Cat's Eye*, laments the ease with which some women uncritically read her work).[15] Atwood's distaste stems less from disagreement with feminist theory and history (much of which has animated her own activism and indeed informed her writing over the course of her career) than from the idealism in which feminists at times couched their politics in the early 1970s. She would not count her early fiction among what Lisa Maria Hogeland describes as the decade's "consciousness-raising novels," literary "assertion[s] of feminist identity" plotted according to "women's sense of themselves *as women*," not because she did not consider herself a feminist, but because she questioned – indeed, continues to question – the extent to which individual experience can comprehensively represent collective identity. Like feminists of color who gradually prodded feminism away from this perspective, Atwood explicitly (though certainly less meticulously or, lately, even sufficiently) rejects the notion that "'women' are a fixed quantity . . . . There is no single, simple, static 'women's point of view.'"[16] Her suspicion targets not feminism as such, but the idea that there is such a thing as a monolithic and essential "woman."

Given Atwood's outspoken suspicion of essential womanhood, as well as the notion that fiction should perform the work of the manifesto, it is remarkable that so many critics have reviewed *Surfacing*, as Atwood herself notes, "almost exclusively as a feminist or ecological treatise," a series of "equations" according to which "man is to woman as culture is to nature ... as the United States is to Canada as dominator is to dominated."[17] Shortly after *Surfacing*'s publication, a 1976 "Women and Religion" special issue of *Signs*, dedicated to the question of what values a "feminist theology" might entail, featured several articles about the novel, all of which addressed whether such a theology should "retain a traditional and symbolic association between women and nature." The articles "warily" agreed that feminism writ large should – and did – embrace a spiritual vision of women's special, innate, and "organic" gifts, and, more certainly, that *Surfacing* explores and vindicates this theme. Atwood responded to these essays with a mixture of pleasant flattery and cordial disagreement. "My own view," she writes, "is that my novel is not a treatise at all, but a novel." Her narrator "need not correspond to either the real or the desirable," but she might still "have something we can learn."[18]

The narrator indeed teaches readers much about the logic animating the "natural woman" interpretation common to *Surfacing* criticism by refusing to exemplify it. Such readings align the novel with early ecofeminist tracts like Mary Daly's *Gyn/Ecology: The Metaethics of Radical Feminism* (1978) and Griffin's *Woman and Nature: The Roaring Inside Her* (1978), both of which responded to the cultural narrative that "woman is both inferior ...

and closer to nature" largely by embracing and reversing it, disparaging instead the rational "culture" of men. Women, Griffin writes, "*are leaves of ivy and sprigs of wallflower. We are women. We rise from the wave.... We are women and nature.*" Daly more aggressively advocated for women's particular, innate gifts, as well as the coming domination they guaranteed. "Gyn/Ecology," she writes, is "the process of ... dis-covering, de-veloping the complex web of living/loving relationships *of our own kind*," the act of "creating our Selves ... hearing the call of the wild, naming our wisdom."[19] It would only be a matter of time before women's natural intuition overturned men's manufactured dominance.

Critiques of Western "value dualisms" that link women to nature and men to culture tend to move in two different directions: toward deconstructing the dualism or toward leaning into the offended half. The second approach – exemplified by Daly and (cautiously) by Griffin – implies that the problem lies in the devaluation of feminine roles and the consequent devaluation of nature in like kind, rather than in the dualism itself. As Rosemary Radford Ruether pointed out in 1992, at the height of debate over ecofeminist epistemology, counternarratives that propose an originary "prepatriarchal paradise" in which "women and female modes of relationality dominated" uphold familiar gender distinctions, as well as their associations with nature and culture. Those narratives presume *de facto* gender roles that somehow exist prior to the patriarchal phenomena that establish them.[20] Despite differences in women's experiences (not to mention massive political divisions), the notion that women, when left to their own devices, always have and always will "live at peace with themselves and with the natural world" has been a mainstay of feminist utopian writing – one that Plumwood believed risks replacing "the 'angel in the house' version of women by the 'angel in the ecosystem' version."[21] It also adds a gendered twist to the notion of ecological authenticity.

The bulk of ecofeminist theory vulnerable to this criticism, Karla Armbruster suggests, has proceeded chiefly from the re-essentializing tradition of (primarily white) cultural feminisms in the 1970s and 1980s that focused on physical connections to the earth through menstrual cycles and childbirth. Nature feminism attends to "women's unique, felt sense of connection to the natural world." Fertility, pregnancy, and breastfeeding "ground women's consciousness in the knowledge of being coterminous with nature" in a way that men's is not.[22] Such accounts have varied in execution from the early 1970s to the present but typically rest on a general platform that can be broken down as follows: (1) all women (2) have always (3) possessed a privileged ecological consciousness that men do not. This position questions neither predominant nature/culture and woman/man dualisms nor their relationship. It merely shifts value from one side to the other. In extreme cases, work like Daly's *Gyn/Ecology* so ferociously defends women's special ecological sensitivity that "the male is negated as a fellow human," reversing the skewed balance of value and contradicting the egalitarian thrust of feminist activism, all while downplaying the fact that though men do not menstruate or give birth, they do partake in other biological processes like eating, making waste, and dying.[23] While Griffin cautiously embraced this trend (at the time, she found its "emotional accuracy" appealing), she notes that within this feminist enclave "it was being suggested, as it had also been during the nineteenth century, that men, valuing power, produce nations, conflict and wars, and that women, valuing life, produce relationship, continuity and peace" – an alignment Griffin herself rejects as "far too simple a description of men and women in contemporary society."[24]

Surfacing likewise resists commentary that celebrates the novel for its engagement with "a more general move among some feminists toward reasserting the very old idea that there is a magical power in the female body." To argue that the narrator discovers (or recovers) a stable and essential gender identity is to ignore the novel's conclusion. The only thing with which the narrator emerges from the wilderness is a sense that to remain submerged would only define her in terms of the "back-to-nature cliché" already applied to women by the very culture she seeks to escape, while to actually surface as a "new woman" would be to re-enter the patriarchal system she flees.[25] To align oneself with nature in such a context, Plumwood notes, would be to unavoidably take part in this narrative's pervasive gendered history, to define oneself "as passive, as non-agent or non-subject, as the 'environment' or invisible background conditions against which the 'foreground' achievements of reason or culture (provided typically by the white, male expert or entrepreneur) take place."[26] Atwood herself is keenly aware of this particular overlap between traditional and feminist appeals to natural womanhood. *The Handmaid's Tale* (1985) ends with an epilogue featuring conference proceedings that postdate the novel's totalitarian events by a century. At one point, the speaker reflects specifically on the patriarchal Gilead regime's calculated decision to implement matriarchal education and "particicution" ceremonies, in which enslaved women execute scapegoated men in controlled doses. "There are echoes here of the fertility rites of early Earth-goddess cults," the lecturer remarks. "Gilead was, although undoubtedly patriarchal in form, occasionally matriarchal in content." This moment complicates the novel's overarching critique, which targets the identification of women with their biology. Gilead's childbearing handmaids are "two-legged wombs," human "containers" whose uniforms are "the color of blood, which defines us."[27] At the time of the novel's publication, feminist protest that framed reproductive technology as "the vehicle that will ... destroy the claim to reproduction that is the foundation of women's identity" unwittingly defended the institutional valorization of motherhood taken to an extreme in *Handmaid*, which many feminists sought and still seek to deconstruct. Atwood trusts neither this perspective nor the inverse argument "that reproductive technologies have given women control over their motherhood – and thereby over their own lives."[28] The question of reproductive control points to how *Handmaid*'s abortion sanctions and *Surfacing*'s abortion mandates carry the same significance in the grand scheme of Atwood's corpus. The traumatic aspect of the narrator's abortion in *Surfacing* is not the death of her unborn child or her hand in the procedure but the coercion by which she undergoes it. The abortion, Atwood explains, "was forced. That's not an 'antiabortion' stand. It's an anticoercion stand." Her work, as a whole, critiques various ideals of natural womanhood not for their specific demands (for fecundity or risk-free promiscuity, for example) but in general, insofar as men (or women) expect adherence to them.[29]

The reduction of specific individuals or identities to biological ideals is one of Atwood's enduring literary preoccupations, one that typically plays out thematically as an oppressive de-individualization of human subjects. In *Handmaid* the state mandates and codifies this process. In *Oryx and Crake* (2003), the first volume of Atwood's *MaddAddam* trilogy, the titular wunderkind Crake breeds biogenetically altered, docile sub-humans according to anatomical, physiological, and sexual ideals to replace *Homo sapiens* following their induced extinction. Both novels examine biologism in terms of its biopolitical imposition by either the state or the corporation. Each text's authoritarian locus, Gilead's theocratic hierarchy and Crake's supply chain, de-emphasizes the particular identity or identities of the individuals and populations they police and modify, granting primacy not to the subject *qua* subject but to the biological body alone (specifically its reproductive capacity). According to Commander Fred, the hierarch who keeps *Handmaid*'s protagonist Offred in sexual bondage, Gilead has nobly "return[ed] things to Nature's norm." The handmaids' overseers instruct them to "identify with your body," a directive that *Handmaid* frames as restrictive and totalitarian but *Surfacing*'s narrator nonetheless appears to follow of her own volition.[30] *Surfacing*'s interest in a character

Depth and Nature Feminism 143

who pursues this end of her own accord reverses these later texts' authoritarian model *avant la lettre*. The narrator flees toward a de-individualized, expansively biological identity to escape the patriarchal system that Atwood's mature works recast as the very force driving such identification.

It would be a mistake to assume that Atwood's attitude regarding this theme is more laudatory in *Surfacing* merely because biologism is pursued rather than imposed. In light of the idea's trajectory across Atwood's career, *Surfacing* reads almost as a gently cautionary tale, one that at least tangentially addresses (eco)feminist tendencies to "glorify the feminine uncritically" and "imply ... that the 'feminine perspective' is a unified perspective."[31] If the novel does not explicitly critique the early ecofeminism that gained purchase at the time of its publication, it nonetheless deconstructs its premises through the narrative example of an individual who takes such appeals to natural or essential identity literally. *Surfacing* is Atwood's own attempt to answer a question she would pose over twenty years later: "What accounts for [the] urge to claim kinship, and to see wilderness as salvation?"[32] I would add my own question to Atwood's: What forms of subjectivity might such "salvation" entail? Atwood's interest clearly transcends the obvious point that humans are materially bound up in the more-than-human world, probing instead what accounts for an urge to *identify* with wilderness – that is, nature somehow untouched by culture – and what such an identification might look like. If the narrator emerges in the final pages transformed by her "descent into primeval, preconscious awareness as a reborn woman who has discovered identity, meaning, and purpose," one must ask what shape that identity takes.[33]

Depth and Nature Feminism

Freud identified women with a lack of "civilization" that corresponded to what he considered women's weaker development of ego boundaries. A number of feminists seized on and upended this sort of equation in the 1970s, denigrating "civilization" as a patriarchal construct and revaluing the "wholeness" of women's repressed primacy. When nature feminists joined this reversal with their environmentalism, they effectively made a gendered claim to ecological authenticity. Nature feminists (and also, often to nature feminists' chagrin, many deep-ecologist men) celebrated the association between women and psychic nature, often using a rhetoric inherited from the student movements of the preceding decade. We "no longer feel ourselves to be a part of this earth," Griffin writes, because "civilization" brainwashes us "to disown a part of our own being . . . . We have traded our real existence, our real feelings for a delusion." Because women are "divided against ourselves," they must struggle to recover their ecological birthright – a perspective in keeping with feminist consciousness-raising of the 1970s.[34] However, if recovering ecological authenticity is a matter of accessing a state of psychic nature, and if psychic nature exists free of patriarchy and its gendered repressions, would not such a recovery wipe those gendered distinctions away? Such an argument takes for granted existing cultural assumptions about women's inherent affinity with nature – their freedom from civilization, their organic lack of boundaries – and speaks to a more general confusion in nature-feminist writing as to "whether women's epistemic privilege is the result of biology, socialization, or both."[35] Griffin's reliance on the IPE's familiar developmental narrative undercuts the notion that women are by default more ecologically attuned than men.

At the time of Griffin's writing, feminist psychoanalysis more stridently sought to address the "uncomplicated opposition between women's perceived unity with nature and male-associated culture's alienation from it," mostly in an effort to contest and revise the dated assumptions about women's psychology that governed how mainstream ego psychologists tended to analyze – and normalize – women.[36] The decade's work culminated in Carol Gilligan's *In a Different Voice* (1982), which challenged the notion that the perceived "dissociations" in women's "voice" signal women's developmental deficiency even as it upheld gendered distinctions. According to Gilligan, cultural constraints differentiate the psychic development of women, whom she characterizes by "a struggle for connection" rather than "a problem in achieving separation." Women offer "a relational voice: a voice that insists on staying in connection . . . so that psychological separations which have so long been justified in the name of autonomy, selfhood, and freedom no longer appear the *sine qua non* of human development but as a human problem." At the same time, she rejects the notion that intimacy and interrelationship are qualities "intuitive" or "instinctive" to women alone.[37] If women are more ecologically attuned than men, this predilection is the result of socialization, not biology, in that contemporary culture does not limit in women, as it does in men, a natural *human* capacity for interconnection. Nancy Chodorow likewise dismissed the instinctual argument, leveling her critique toward not only the psychoanalytic establishment but also the era's "alternate sexual politics" that "tended toward an essentialist position" – that is, cultural feminists. The psychoanalytic narrative of infantile separation-individuation – the origin of "ego boundaries" and "the first 'me'-'not-me' division, in the

Depth and Nature Feminism 145

development of the 'I,' or self" – suggested to Chodorow that "ideologies of difference ... are produced, socially, psychologically, and culturally, by people," not by biological inclination. Social forces, she writes, lead boys to fixate "on a more fixed 'me'-'not-me' distinction . ... By contrast, the female's self is less separate." Unlike men, women's "core gender identity" is "built upon, and does not contradict, her primary sense of oneness and identification with her mother ... a relational connection to the world."[38]

In other words, psychoanalysis suggested to these feminist writers that women's presumed capacity for interconnection is in fact a universal trait, traceable to common psychic origins that civilization not only represses, but also parses out based on gender. These analysts located gender difference in culture rather than biology, arguing that social life represses universal psychic origins less thoroughly in women than in men. In effect, they responded to and revised in feminist terms the sort of social theory that organized the program of the New Left and counterculture, identifying certain cultural assumptions about women with *everyone*, rather than women alone. They "suggest that, developmentally, the maternal identification represents and is experienced as generically human for children of both genders."[39] The phrase "generically human" signals the extent to which these writers refigured psychical connection, expansiveness, and even holism, which both patriarchal nature/culture dualism and nature feminism identified with women, as an essentially *human* trait that Western civilization represses only in men. Women are closer to nature than men only because men have lost sight of shared subjective origins. On the one hand, these conclusions would confirm one of nature feminism's two contradictory angles: the notion that women already possess a privileged ecological orientation (an assumption that nonetheless downplays differences *among* women). On the other, they complicate the competing notion that women must recover an orientation they've lost. Nature feminists would have nothing to recover – only men would.

This narrative of universal yet socially diffracted connectivity manifests in both *Surfacing* and *Woman and Nature*. Despite Griffin's proclamation that "[t]his earth is my sister," her paired contentions that "*we have made up boundaries*" and that "*this earth is made from our bodies*" imply that her conception of ecological integration is more universalist than it first appears. That feminism "had allowed me to reach a deeper self ... an earlier, pre-social being who had come to life in me" seems at once specific to her idea of women and yet universally applicable.[40] That "deeper self" is "pre-social," altogether defiant of gendered expectations of either men or women. Griffin's claim to essential sorority with the earth unites women

146 The Essential Ecosystem

against a common enemy – men and modernity – but accompanies a more general argument running through *Woman and Nature* that identification with the ecosystem is an essentially universal trait that patriarchal culture has regretfully repressed. "Men . . . need not be the enemy," according to another writer. "Though they have been groomed since early childhood to become the enactors of patriarchy, they began life in the arms of women." Such an argument does indeed appeal to the ostensibly "holistic proclivities of women," identifying material continuity with a gendered position (the mother). Men, however, now appear to partake of "the same organic flow of life," but only insofar as they dredge up their "deepest selves," their primal identification "of human consciousness with the radical energy of matter throughout the universe."[41] Woman's primal psyche, however, ostensibly remains at least partially intact – a claim that finds expression in Griffin's dissolution rhetoric: "*we know ourselves to be made of this earth, because we know sunlight moves through us, water moves through us, everything moves, everything changes, and the daughters are returned to their mothers.*"[42] Griffin attempts to reach ecological awareness by mapping identity onto the ecosystem as a whole.

Surfacing's omnipresent imagery of submersion blatantly illustrates this interest in psychic depth. In so doing, however, the novel confronts the extent to which nature feminism's engagement with the IPE – its reliance on a narrative that pits civilization against ecological authenticity – represents a universalist impulse that undermines its claims to essential womanhood. Like Griffin, the narrator accesses "a self more whole than I had allowed to live before . . . a self untouched by convention, a self not molded to society's idea of who a woman should be."[43] This work begins when she recalls her repressed abortion, a memory that resurfaces when she encounters her father's fetus-like corpse drifting at the bottom of a lake. Underwater, the narrator's vocabulary evokes excavation: "Pale green, then darkness, layer after layer, deeper than before" (143). The deeper she digs into the water, the deeper she plumbs her psyche, peeling back "layer after layer." The first casualty of this process is the housewife image she constructed of herself to sanitize the trauma of her coerced abortion, an ideal inspired by childhood images of pious young women "holding up cans of cleanser, knitting, smiling, modeling toeless high heels and nylons with dark seams" (91). The narrator's recollection of her abortion concretizes her muddled memories but also kicks off a series of attempts to go deeper, to peel back *all* gendered expectations, to reacquire a more natural sense of identity she believes known but forgotten.

Depth and Nature Feminism

In a political context in which "men define reality and women are defined in terms of men," the narrator attempts not to be a woman at all.[44] I mean not to suggest that the narrator's experience as a woman is in any way incidental to *Surfacing*'s plot, but to point out that her intention is not to embrace but to *escape* fixed conceptions of womanhood, precisely because these characteristics have always been imposed. Her successive abandonment of false selves, represented variously throughout the novel by clothing, makeup, and the managed expression of expected affects, occurs as the gradual dismissal of repressions defined by gendered assumptions. "Everything from history must be eliminated," she declares as she disrobes: "these husks are not needed any longer" (181–2). Her rebellion responds most immediately to the sexy dress, deferential behavior, and feminine accoutrements demanded by David and his ilk. Anna, the narrator fears, has become "a seamed and folded imitation of a magazine picture that is itself an imitation of a woman who is also an imitation, the original nowhere." Her slavish application of makeup especially strikes the narrator as a manifestation of "gradual" social dissimulation that "takes a little of you at a time" and "leaves the shell" (169–70). Makeup manufactures a particular woman for David's consumption and represents the mis-guided, coerced identity the narrator believes she must strip away. After she trashes David's film stock of voyeuristic footage featuring Anna's naked body, the narrator feels the sun "sear away the wrong form that encases me . . . I dip my head beneath the water . . . When I am clean I come up out of the lake, leaving my false body floated on the surface, a cloth decoy" (183). In the nonhuman natural world, the narrator believes she exhumes a more essential identity, one untouched by gendered prescriptions.

When the narrator indulges the notion that to embrace the "natural" is to discover a more essential identity, she comes to experience identity in terms that resonate with the primary psychic state described by Chodorow, not the essential womanhood celebrated by Daly. In this respect, Atwood is interested in essence insofar as she believes the very idea might pulverize the claims to specificity that appeals to essence have often been used to support. The narrator discovers in the ecosystem not essential womanhood but essential humanhood, the network of organic fluctuations experienced by the human body in its environment. This encounter challenges both traditional and feminist alignments of female/feminine with nature and male/masculine with culture. Any appeal to nature or essence, Atwood suggests, has little to do with identity positions, because it ultimately speaks chiefly to the universal fact that human organisms consist of matter. In other words, any nature-feminist argument for identification with the

148 The Essential Ecosystem

ecosystem lapses into the IPE, striking from its program the very gendered distinctions it means to reinforce.

"The First True Human": Narcissistic Fantasy and Material Complexity

The second half of *Surfacing* largely plays out as a shift from identification with reproduction to identification with replication – or identification with *woman* to identification with *ecosystem*, an illustrative slide from nature feminism into the IPE. Late in the novel, the narrator seduces her boyfriend Joe in the woods after over 150 pages spent refusing his advances. Their intercourse is a matter of heat, of animal urges: "pleasure is redundant, the animals don't have pleasure. I guide him into me, it's the right season, I hurry. He trembles and then I can feel my lost child surfacing within me, forgiving me, rising from the lake where it has been prisoned for so long" (165). Critics have often taken this scene of impregnation quite literally, yet in the final pages the narrator comments that the fetus within her is "perhaps not real" (197). The "primeval one . . . shape of a goldfish now in my belly, undergoing its watery changes," is not a child. It's an idea or sensibility on the part of the narrator herself, growing within her, "the first one, the first true human" (198).

In pronouncing this improbable fetus the first "true" human, the narrator questions what it means to be human and invalidates the subjectivity of the people with whom she has to this point interacted. Prior to this passage, the narrator lobs the word "human" only as an epithet. She initially rebuffs Joe's sexual advances because "I saw he was human, I didn't want him in me, sacrilege, he was one of the killers" (148). When David accuses the narrator of "hating" men, she realizes that "it wasn't the men I hated, it was the Americans, the human beings, men and women both. They'd had their chance" (155). Two details merit attention. First, the narrator conflates the word "American" with "human." Second, she ends her condemnation with a striking indictment. David, Anna, and Joe have "had their chance." In other words, the narrator identifies her companions not with human nature but with its perversion. To be "American" is to no longer be a *real* human. Among the novel's characters, "America" signifies "something coming up over the border which isn't necessarily a good thing," an aversion Atwood, in an interview, claims to be "a very widespread feeling in the country itself."[45] Americans are "the kind who catch more than they can eat and they'd do it with dynamite if they could get away with it" (63). The narrator describes the influx of American business

"The First True Human" 149

and tourism in Northern Quebec as a "disease . . . spreading up from the south" (3). The bug is also catching. By the end of the novel, David, Anna, even remote lakeside villagers "are all Americans now," slowly but surely "turning to metal, skins galvanizing, heads congealing to brass knobs, components and intricate wires ripening inside" (173, 160).

A certain anti-modernity animates the narrator's words, a distrust of industry and of the United States as its chief harbinger. If America is less a country and more an economic force that infects or dominates Canada – and this is a position that Atwood has avowed for the greater part of her career – then we are all Americans in the global twentieth and twenty-first centuries, regardless of national origin. Americanness has less to do with nationality than it does with capitalism and power, the wanton exercise of which the narrator witnesses when she stumbles across a heron left grotesquely gutted and hanging on a portage route. The reason its executioners "had strung it up like a lynch victim," she concludes, was to "prove that they could do it, they had the power to kill" (118). It ultimately "doesn't matter" that these marauding "Americans" are fellow Canadians on holiday. "Secondhand American" infests them – as well as David and Anna – "like mange or lichen" (153–4). This possibility terrifies the narrator not only for its environmental implications, but also because the heron-killers mistake her, too, for an American vacationer.

To be "American," then, is to have deviated from an origin – to be false or artificial. The narrator's assumption of the "first *true* human" mantle troubles the critical commonplace that she dismisses the category of "human" altogether. Her intention is not to transcend the human, but to recover a more authentic instantiation of it – the quintessential vector of the IPE. Her fetus' actual existence is beside the point. Its significance lies in its function as a symbol of material interchange among organisms, whether inside or outside the body. The image helps the narrator to redefine her identity in purely biological terms, as an essential condition uncluttered by boundaries between body and environment. As such, she identifies with the lake country ecosystem itself, in its entirety, because her material dispersal is the most natural thing about her. A final, anguished assertion of coherent selfhood – "I'm here!" – meets with overwhelming indifference (177). In response to the ecosystem's silence, the narrator's sense of bounded self-identity falls apart:

> I'm ice-clear, transparent, my bones and the child inside me showing through the green webs of my flesh, the ribs are shadows, the muscles jelly, the trees are like this too, they shimmer, their cores glow through

the wood and bark . . . . The boulders float, melt, everything is made of water, even the rocks . . . . I lean against a tree, I am a tree leaning . . . . I am not an animal or a tree, I am the thing in which the trees and animals move and grow, I am a place. (187)

Her dissolution reads as an endeavor to pinpoint something essentially human at a base, ecological level. She "wanted to be whole," but she equates being whole as an individual with the whole of the ecosystem (147). A solid, unfractured identity comprises not a bounded, individual psyche but multiple bodies interacting without mediation. Artificial taxonomies have no meaning over the course of her dissolution. She observes in her parents' garden "weeds and legitimate plants alike, there is no distinction . . . . The garden is a stunt, a trick. It could not exist without the fence" (186). Concepts like "inside" and "outside" cease to hold meaning. An expansive psychic state, inclusive of her environment, characterizes the narrator's whole self.

The poignant image of a fetus that is likely not really in the narrator's womb signifies the threshold not of a child's birth but of the narrator's *re*birth backward in psychoanalytic history. Her impression of expansive wholeness arises upon discovery of her father's body lurking beneath the surface of the lake, weighed down by a heavy camera he used to photograph Indigenous paintings on the cliffs overhanging the water. She spies him "below me, drifting towards me from the furthest level where there was no life, a dark oval trailing limbs. It was blurred but it had eyes, they were open, it was something I knew about, a dead thing" (143). At first, she mistakes the body for her drowned brother, "hair floating around the face, image I'd kept from before I was born" (144). This line refers to a dream she relates early in the novel, in which she imagines herself as her mother, gazing into the same water at the end of a dock at her brother's upturned face, "eyes open and unconscious . . . I can remember it as clearly as if I saw it, and perhaps I did see it: I believe that an unborn baby had its eyes open and can look out through the walls of the mother's stomach, like a frog in a jar" (28). The dream conjures images of a pickled fetus, apprehensions of death, and sensations of dissolution into a greater body in the water. Significantly, the narrator also identifies with this fetal image via a circuit of images, perspectives, and memories she overlays in the dream. First, she joins her own point of view with her mother's. Second, she conflates her brother with her aborted fetus, floating "in a bottle curled up, staring" (144). (The narrator makes this association explicit. Her initial misidentification of the shadow in the lake with her brother's drowned body is what jolts her memory of the abortion.) She then identifies her mother/self with

"*The First True Human*" 151

her brother/fetus as she imagines peering into the water, meeting the body's "eyes open and unconscious." The surface of the lake takes on the reflective properties of a mirror, so that she ultimately imagines narrator, brother, mother, and fetus collapsed into one. Lastly, she projects this composite onto her father's bloated corpse.

In light of this series of projections and identifications, the indistinct mass at the bottom of the lake, her father's decomposition, appears to inspire not only the memory of abortion but also the imagination of intrauterine life and perspective. What the narrator believes she represses, and what returns, is not simply her memory of abortion, but a retroactive fantasy of oceanic experience as a fetus or infant. The lake takes on the characteristics of a womb to harbor a fetal, amphibious, and narcissistically expansive narrator, free of subjective boundaries between herself and the other characters. Fetal representations in the 1970s often visualized their subjects "via distancing codes of scientific omniscience, isolated from the female uterus and therefore cut off from any spatial identificatory cues." Accompanying commentary frequently observed that the human fetus appears indistinguishable from that of other mammals.[46] *Surfacing's* narrator likewise views her fetus, both the one she aborted and the one she believes she currently cultivates, in nonhuman – or, more accurately, "*true* human" – terms. If the narrator also seems to obscure her own personhood, she erases herself only as a cohesive, singular self. She continues to feel intimately, corporeally present, but she imagines her matter dispersed, spread out across plants, animals, and soil.

The suspected pregnancy at first appears to place the narrator squarely in the discourse of women's essential sorority with nature, but her repetition of the term "human" undermines this association. To be authentically ecological, Atwood suggests, is not to be a woman but to be indistinct, to abandon self-identity in favor of the identity of the collective. The narrator is, after all, unsure if the fetus she aborted is "part of myself or a separate creature" (144). In imagining herself to be simultaneously mother and fetus, the narrator also collapses the distinction between the two. The fetus ceases to be a distinct entity. It is simply more of herself, which is to say more of the ecosystem. In turn, she loses track of her own outlines, imagining herself as a fetus suspended and nourished in the amnion of the lake, indistinguishable from the ecosystem that sustains her. The imaginary fetus, which is in her but also *is* her, "buds, it sends out fronds . . . . In the morning I will be able to see it: it will be covered with shining fur" (165). Her fetus-self is simultaneously plant and animal. It sprouts and proliferates. It is matter.

152   The Essential Ecosystem

In this respect, reproduction – and the monopoly on ecological consciousness that nature feminists derived from it – comes to play second fiddle to "metamorphosis" (171), transmissions of matter among organisms of the sort Donna Haraway partially captures in her term "replication." This redefinition decouples reproduction from insemination and pregnancy, and thence from any stable ideal of strictly defined, biological womanhood. Furthermore, it conceives of all humans in terms of matter's reproductive potential. "I love the fact that . . . genomes of bacteria, fungi, protists, and such . . . play in a symphony necessary to my being alive," Haraway writes. "I love that when 'I' die, all these benign and dangerous symbionts will take over and use whatever is left of 'my' body, if only for a while."[47] *Surfacing*'s narrator not only embraces the myriad replications that constitute her biological existence, but also identifies with their very intransience. She rejects her identity as a woman even as she embraces her identity as a reproducer, specifically because she feels this quality to be more of a generically human attribute than a particularly female one. She arrives at this conclusion via the same sort of indulgence in natural identity that structured nature-feminist work of the 1970s and, later, the 1980s. There is no difference between an essential man and an essential woman when one considers the most authentic thing about both of them to be their participation in the networked ecosystem.

Depth and Network

The political philosopher Cary Wolfe writes of Haraway's 1985 "Cyborg Manifesto" as the "locus classicus" of contemporary posthumanism, a rangy body of thought that crystallizes post-structural criticism and the open systems theory associated with postwar thinkers such as Gregory Bateson. Systems theory emerged in the 1950s and 1960s to conceptualize interactions among actors and events in terms of complex networks, intricate structures of feedback and influence that also helped to explain ecology. In the 1970s, the notion of an "open" system made room for "unpredictability, creativity, and emergence" in networked models of interdependence. These models, and their emphasis on irreducible interconnection, furnished a perspective by which "we can no longer talk of *the* body or even, for that matter, of *a* body in the traditional sense . . . . Rather, 'the body' is now seen as a kind of *virtuality*" – a normative concept that nonetheless has material effects.[48] Posthumanism, like ecofeminism, is a variegated umbrella, but in general functions as a conceptual frame that "displaces the traditional humanistic unity of the subject" by taking into

Depth and Network

153

account the myriad ways in which historical location and physical reality both constitute and undermine "our flexible and multiple identities."[49] The subject emerges as relational and embodied, rather than discrete or abstract, and resistant to universalist assumptions of the sort made by Marxist historical materialism, classical liberalism, and normative ego psychology.

Atwood's work bears witness to the transition from psychoanalytic to networked models of desire and subjectivity that played out in intellectual circles over the second half of the twentieth century. Her typically fastidious treatment of psychoanalysis (as novels such as 1969's *The Edible Woman* and 1996's *Alias Grace* attest) belies her distrust of the inflexible assumptions regarding gender that dominated its institutional uses in the 1950s and 1960s. *Surfacing* appeared at a moment when the reductive conclusions reached by ego psychology and nature feminism alike increasingly clashed with emerging postmodernist disbelief in fixed identity categories. At the same time, Atwood's interest in ecological science acquainted her with the systems approaches gaining purchase in the humanities and social sciences, as well as in the New Age. Zen Buddhist figures such as Paul Goodman and Alan Watts informed the whole-earth Gaia spirituality of writers such as Joanna Macy, who paired "the Buddha's central teaching of dependent co-arising" with a scientific menu cherry-picked chiefly from systems theory: "what I am, as systems theorists have helped me see, is a 'flow-through' . . . of matter, energy, and information." James Lovelock, who originated the systems-oriented Gaia hypothesis, took pains to discourage and even dismantle idealistic, prescriptive applications of his descriptive work. All the same, numerous writers have mobilized his hypothesis as a form of what the sociologist and philosopher Bruno Latour recently referred to as "political religion," positing Gaia as a sort of networked yet materially homogeneous identity, a "cybernetics of the self" that discloses a "continuous chain of events" rather than "clear lines demarcating a separate . . . categorical 'I.'"[50] Despite the measured exploration of Buddhist and cybernetic ideas that often plays out in such writing, impassioned declarations of "what I am" have the effect of drawing subjective equivalence between the self and the planet as a whole.

I draw attention to this example because it illustrates how a rhetoric of depth continued to play an important role in social thought amid changing hermeneutics in the late twentieth century. Psychoanalysis began losing critical territory for a variety of reasons, the most important of which was perhaps the reputation of mainstream analysis in the United States, which came under heavy assault in feminist and poststructuralist criticism for its

154 The Essential Ecosystem

normative assumptions about the solidity of the ego and its proper expression in men and women. One might also say that it was precisely the emergence of ecology that spelled political psychoanalysis' general doom, given that its own networked perspective, alongside the cybernetic model developing in postwar computer science, helped to shift the way social theorists viewed subjectivity altogether – a shift that occasioned the IPE's transformation of psychoanalytic narratives to begin with. That said, though psychoanalysis' ensuing decline in North America never really halted, its methodologies have remained influential to literary studies, cultural and political history, and even, significantly, the very network paradigm that, among others, has come to supplant it.[51]

One should not ignore the extent to which psychoanalytic ideas have played a role in network's articulation. Even the work of Gilles Deleuze and Félix Guattari – one of posthumanist philosophy's primary influences – relies substantially on the notion of psychic depth to effect the critique of psychoanalysis it mobilized open systems theory to make. The very first words of *Anti-Oedipus* (1972), published the same year as *Surfacing*, draw a correspondence between open systems and quintessential psychoanalytic principles:

> It is at work everywhere, functioning smoothly at times, at other times in fits and starts. It breaths, it heats, it eats. It shits and fucks. What a mistake to have ever said *the* id. Everywhere *it* is machines – real ones, not figurative ones: machines driving other machines, with all the necessary couplings and connections. An organ-machine is plugged into an energy-source-machine: the one produces a flow that the other interrupts. A breast is a machine that produces milk, and the mouth a machine coupled to it.[52]

This passage articulates its overt interest in network according to an unruly "it," a plural yet monist id that Deleuze and Guattari immediately, and not incidentally, channel through the breast, maintaining the mother's psychoanalytic resonance with the expansive, unregulated desire of infantile narcissism. "Deterritorialized" flows of desire resist the Oedipal complex, which Deleuze and Guattari interpret as a structure of repression deployed by capitalism rather than the *de facto* structure of subjectivity. Desire is productive, not deficient. It constitutes a deconstructed subject constantly in process, rather than a calcified ego. This critique of the foundational narrative of psychoanalytic practice – the Oedipal drama – proceeds in large part as a recovery of desire's originary condition from the prescriptive malice of analytic institutions. In other words, the authors refute the narrative's direction, but not necessarily the psychoanalytic concepts that structure it.

Depth and Network

Deleuze and Guattari broke with the Left Freudian veneration of classical psychoanalysis, but they did so while pursuing the same goal of liberating the nature of repressed, unconscious content.[53] Their project found expression in the figure of the schizophrenic and his or her "process of desire," according to which "the self and the non-self, outside and inside ... have [no] meaning whatsoever." The schizophrenic, they write, experiences "nature as a process of production" and effectively grasps that "there is no such thing as relatively independent spheres or circuits: production is immediately consumption ... without any sort of mediation." Human and nature are not "like two opposite terms confronting each other ... rather, they are one and the same essential reality, the producer-product." This line notably highlights the extent to which Deleuze and Guattari underwrite their project with continued appeals to what is natural, real, and essential. Processes of desire (or "production") signify base reality: "the human essence of nature and the natural essence of man become one within nature in the form of production or industry." Despite their emphasis on "becoming" and "production" – a process ontology – Deleuze and Guattari find recourse to "natural essence" an important rhetorical tactic in their ambition to "undo the expressive Oedipal unconscious, always artificial, repressive and repressed, mediated by the family, in order to attain the immediate productive unconscious." Their interest in dispelling the "artificial" bespeaks an equally keen interest in uncovering something "natural": an "immediate productive unconscious." Capitalism, the family, and other such institutions comprise an illusion masking one's true "producing/product identity ... an enormous undifferentiated object."[54]

Of course, Deleuze and Guattari did not actively participate in the ongoing articulation of an identity politics of ecology. However, the psychoanalytic narrative they maintain in their work has no doubt impacted how later scholars (who *are* interested in ecology and environment) have structured their arguments. My point is that networks and psychic origins often get rhetorically conflated, even in the nominally anti-essentialist work that has been hugely influential to (post)humanistic thinking about networks today. *Surfacing* narrativizes the interplay between depth and network that occurred as systems theory and psychoanalysis passed each other in the 1970s. The capitalist artifice Deleuze and Guattari ecstatically deconstruct finds an analogue in *Surfacing*'s "America," which, much like late capitalism, infects and solidifies its essentially indeterminate hosts as bounded, gendered, consumer subjects. To strip away these forms is to access the truth of "becoming." On the shore, on the trees, "on the sodden trunks are colonies of plants, feeding on disintegration . . . Out of the leaf nests the flowers rise, pure white, flesh of gnats and midges, petals now, metamorphosis" (171). The lake country ecosystem does not take holistic shape so much as it reveals itself to the narrator in its myriad transformations. Energy flows from one organism to the next as each nourishes and constitutes and is nourished and constituted by others. The ecosystem comprises what Rosi Braidotti refers to as "radical transversal relations" rather than "holistic fusion."[55] The narrator's matter constantly transforms, "the swamp around me smolders, energy of decay turning to growth, green fire. I remember the heron; by now it will be insects, frogs, fish, other herons. My body also changes, the creature in me, plant-animal, sends out filaments in me; I ferry it secure between death and life, I multiply" (172). Essence reduces not to a discrete gendered identity, but to flow and immanence. The elimination of categorical distinctions destabilizes lines between "inside" and "outside," the individual and its surroundings.

This perspective becomes a matter of essential identity – and of the IPE – as a result of its indulgence in what Latour refers to as "the individual versus society paradigm."[56] The narrator comes to view matter as the most – if not the only – natural aspect of the human subject. As such, her obsessive conviction that she can only be her genuine self (or not-self) after she has done away with socially mediated characteristics frames identity such that it has little to do with particulars, preferences, choices, and contexts, and everything to do with sheer matter and its movement. The narrative effects of this line of reasoning force one to confront the implications of what the contemporary political theorist Jane Bennett, to take one example, means when she writes of "the rhetorical advantage of calling to mind a childhood sense of the world as filled with all sorts of animate beings, some human, some not." Bennett's goal is to illuminate a "positive ontology of vital matter," the irrepressible activity and influence of nonhuman objects that comes together to constitute a blanket "distributive agency."[57] It is not discrete persons, other organisms, or even inanimate things that act on the world, she writes, but systems. Bennett's tendency to frame such vitality as the special (dare I say repressed?) purview of infancy at least rhetorically advances the idea that it is childhood's *social innocence* that grants it privileged perceptual access to this reality. This idea is not particularly novel. The foreword to a 1995 ecopsychology volume co-edited by Theodore Roszak links the "'liveliness' of matter" to infantile psychology. Not coincidentally, it also praises how psychedelics mimic the infant's "psychoid view of material intentionality," a compliment Deleuze and Guattari also pay to peyote in *A Thousand Plateaus* (1980).[58]

Such incidental concurrence with ecopsychology and New-Age mysticism speaks less to Deleuze and Guattari's agreement on matters of drug use than their participation in the era's broad interest in paring psychoanalysis back to its basics, a project that might – or might not – undermine unitary subjectivity. Work like Bennett's, for example, risks reproducing the ecological narrative of the IPE. The "impersonal" assemblage she describes is rhizomatic, to use *A Thousand Plateaus*' oft-touted term. "Any point" of it "can be connected to anything other, and must be." Her articulation of this idea in terms of psychic origins, however, contradicts the notion that the rhizome's complexity renders it "a stranger to any idea of . . . deep structure."[59] Socialized adults remain embedded in assemblages whether they recognize it or not; unsocialized infants, however, experience that integration as a form of subjectivity, which, in an ideal world, we might regain. Despite their comments to the contrary, Deleuze and Guattari's own rhetorical investment in an opposition between the network's reality and capitalism's artificiality itself posits a sort of "deep structure" – a stratification between what they term "molar" unities and "molecular" becomings. Given the considerable influence of these ideas, one must ask to what extent their overlap of psychoanalytic narratives and systems models has helped keep the IPE alive. Together, Bennett's appeals to childhood and tendency to collapse self into other in the flashy jargon of "distributive agency" demonstrate the extent to which current scholarship preserves features of the IPE, maintaining its appeal to ecological authenticity in terms of material flux rather than holism.

New Materialisms, Old Narratives

The philosopher Elizabeth Grosz writes that Deleuze "can neither be classified as a materialist nor as an idealist. His work is oriented in both directions without any assumption of a break between them." Philosophical materialism thrives on its assertion of concrete, observable, *real* phenomena. However, the "plane of immanence," or ongoing transformation, that grounds materialist accounts of "becoming" and "emergence" takes shape as a certain "incorporeal" element, "the subsistence of the ideal *in* the material," that philosophy has never satisfactorily resolved. The unavoidable persistence of abstract concepts in materialist writing highlights the extent to which the reality it aims to describe takes shape according to narratives that "make this materiality conceivable."[60] The "new" materialisms of the past decades are no different. Although such literature "calls for a move away from epistemology toward ontology, for a move away from representation toward questions of the 'real,'" by necessity it also relies on its own representational conventions.[61]

Self-described or otherwise identified new materialists participate in broader posthumanist efforts to trouble exceptional human subjectivity, aiming to cultivate opposition to the "dialectics of self and other" that result when humans delimit themselves by "escaping or repressing" (note the word choice) their dynamic molecular composition.[62] Such scholarship "conceives of matter itself as lively or as exhibiting agency," influencing how we understand ourselves and the world even as we try to do so. As Diana Coole and Samantha Frost write in the introduction to their field-defining anthology *New Materialisms* (2010), matter "becomes" rather than "is." The ambitious scope of that rhetoric – especially when coupled to a narrative of repression – opens for discussion the possibility that some such scholarship might keep alive a politics of ecological authenticity.[63] Scholars of color, especially, have already suggested that such writing potentially invokes a certain "universal or generic . . . 'matter'" that brings to mind the "universal woman" that animated nature feminism. When explicit or implicit references to "repression" pop up, one must also ask to what extent such work treats matter much as it accuses social constructionists of treating the body: as a "primordial" slate "on which society and culture went to work."[64] At times, new-materialist theory has even sought to recover a scientific realism that sidesteps representation altogether. If physics and the life sciences have taught us anything, it's that "material phenomena" *do* consist of "open, complex systems with porous boundaries." All the same, the idea that one can faithfully capture or subjectively embody "the truth or essence of matter" is itself a representational ideal.[65]

To be fair, that sort of objective tends to emerge more out of recycled narratives – inherited, as I've suggested, from psychoanalysis' persistence in the network paradigm – than from intention. Most new materialists – the physicist and critic Karen Barad foremost among them – seek instead to integrate our understandings of reality and representation by examining the impact of the "agent ontologies" they describe.[66] It's worth noting, too, that such an approach is not particularly new. Indigenous philosophies have long upheld the agency of nonhuman entities, as well as the notion that representations – as Chapter 2 discussed in detail – play an integral role in *invoking* reality as we understand it. The role played by language and social construction in work by Simon Ortiz, Toni Morrison, and Peter Matthiessen calls into question the notion that representations obscure a truer reality that we could otherwise access. *Surfacing* undertakes a similar sort of investigation, with an eye toward the interaction between network

New Materialisms, Old Narratives

and psychic depth taking place at the time of Atwood's writing. "In one of the languages," the narrator notes, in reference to non-Western dialects, "there are no nouns, only verbs held for a longer moment" (187). To Atwood herself, the narrator's ordeal is "a visionary experience in which language is transformed," a linguistic frame in which "things are not seen as discrete concrete separate objects" but as a "general matrix which manifests in certain ways." Atwood's interest should come as no surprise given *Surfacing*'s moment of composition. Zen Buddhism charmed Alan Watts as much for its East-Asian languages of expression as for its spirituality. Grammatical convention determines "what experiences shall be called objects and what shall be called events or actions." As such, "one who thinks in Chinese has little difficulty in seeing that objects are also events, that our world is a collection of processes rather than entities," due to its comparatively relaxed distinction between nouns and verbs, or linguistic representations of *being* and *doing*. Atwood notes that in certain Indigenous tongues native to present-day Quebec, "you wouldn't say a deer is running across a field. You'd say it manifests itself as the quality of deerness engaged in the activity of running."[67] Such morphology does not identify anything intrinsically unique about the collection of matter called "deer." Deer are only deer because they remain relatively consistent in how they physically develop, move, eat, shit, reproduce, and die. The essence of deer – biological matter, physical energy – is identical to the essence of, say, cat or human. Deer just come together a little differently.

Identity emerges in Atwood's novel, as well as in writing by Watts, Ortiz, and others, as a function of the way in which *how* we know mutually influences *what* we know. Identities and their relations rely, in this sense, on creating new or revisiting existing ways of articulating, and thereby conceiving, "what we do and what we make," as Grosz writes – expressive processes that "may give us an identity, but always an identity that is directed to our next activity, rather than to the categories that may serve to describe us."[68] Her words reflect the extent to which current scholars participate in the same project that Watts and others hoped to popularize in the 1960s, in response to the same, ongoing questions about the status of subjectivity in the face of complex networks. To a certain extent, writers then as now undertook an effort to imagine subjects not as "individuals with inherent attributes, anterior to their representation," but as what Barad calls "performative" articulations of various phenomena, in which language plays a key role. In this frame, the relation between reality and discourse resembles Lasik surgery. A contact lens or pair of glasses can be removed from the eye, but Lasik modifies the eye while being a part of it.

Properties of discernible objects and formal boundaries between nature and culture or human and nonhuman arise and accrue meaning through "specific agential intra-actions," not through intrinsic features.[69] Identities are not inherent but still very real, generated in encounters and the narratives we tell about them.

One could proceed from these insights in one of two ways. One could take what Haraway once described as a "diffractive" perspective, the aim of which is "not really ... the overcoming of epistemic impediments to grasping nature, nor even the ontology of matter per se," but understanding "the concrete, particular, and situated lives of beings." This pragmatic approach emphasizes the analysis of various material phenomena and their dynamic sociopolitical effects "as opposed to discovery of immutable truths."[70] On the other hand, one could stop at physicists' revelation of our essentially dynamic material constitution, making a political investment of this reality's disclosure. Quantum mechanics drastically changes the status of "things" from solid, definable entities to complex, relative, "elusive," and inherently indeterminate series of relations. Much new-materialist work mobilizes these observations to contest Cartesian humanism and Newtonian science, according to which "material objects are identifiably discrete."[71] Matter is undeniably unstable, constantly shifting, and often unverifiable. At the same time, the boundaries drawn by inherited humanistic wisdom have also had real social and political effects. Without a doubt, it is the form and content of these effects that new-materialist critics wish to interrogate. However, the preponderance of words like "repression" and "recovery" in many such works tends to circumscribe them according to a depth narrative, a disclosure of our essential immanence and indeterminacy, of a primary and *ideal* lack of boundaries in our self-definition. The new materialisms emerge chiefly from continental theories of deconstruction and phenomenology, but this rhetoric draws its energy from appeals to ecological authenticity.

These flourishes frame the new-materialist project in terms of a reinterpreted wilderness narrative, or a firm distinction between nature and culture. To be sure, Coole and Frost's emphasis on matter's dynamism, for example, does not "simply replace 'nature' with 'matter' and leave the rest of the conceptual edifice undisturbed." At the same time, an almost utopian haste among other new materialists "to dissolve identity into difference" seems to privilege ostensibly natural subjectivity over the social questions with which new materialists claim to reconcile it. When new materialists discuss matter according to psychic depth, especially – as when, for example, Melissa Orlie draws on Freud to call for "a return ... to

New Materialisms, Old Narratives 161

that sense of unity with nature as all of matter" – they risk the ahistoricism of their IPE forebears.[72] As Braidotti rightly notes, scholars belonging to disenfranchised communities have more often than not been "suspicious of deconstructing a subject-position, which historically they have never gained the right to," for good reason. To be denied subjectivity – whether by systemic oppression or by new-materialist philosophy – is to be "deprived of an identity that can provide me with a possible life in my society."[73]

For this reason, one must attend to the tenuous difference between fostering an alternative conception of subjectivity and excavating an ostensibly repressed yet natural one. The narrator of *Surfacing* tumbles from the first to the second mindset when she decides not to repurpose an alternative grammar. Instead, much like the McKenna brothers, she dubiously attempts to abandon language wholesale, given its distasteful social construction. "Language divides us into fragments," she says. "I wanted to be whole" (147). The narrator's words demonstrate the means by which network might rhetorically crystallize into yet another expression of holism and, more to the point, holistic identity. It doesn't matter if the material transformations she apprehends and undergoes are "imminent" or "emergent." The fact that she visualizes them as a matter of essence makes of them a blanket, universal, and authentic condition.

My point is that the IPE's particular essentialist rhetoric – its narrative of repression and recovery, as well as the binary logic of real interconnectivity and artificial social forms that propels it – persists despite millennial emphasis on "constant emergence, attraction, repulsion, fluctuation, and shifting of nodes of charge." Contemporary academic trends that challenge notions of mostly static or balanced nature risk enthroning material interchange in the empty seat of essence. One merely posits new universals and totalities to replace old ones. Although new materialists across the board profess an "antipathy toward oppositional thinking," a particularly important opposition between new and old ways of thinking matter occasionally replaces the old binaries. The Cartesian view of matter and the "fashionable" postmodernist fetish for linguistic construction are not merely inaccurate. They are cultural layers that generate false identities, which in turn cover up and prevent our understanding of and posthumanist delight in the fact that our "existence depends from one moment to the next on myriad micro-organisms and diverse higher species, on our own hazily understood bodily and cellular reactions."[74] When writers such as Grosz, Coole, and Frost contest "the overwhelming dominance ... of identity politics," they target not the sort exemplified by nature feminists like Griffin and Daly, but the "proliferation of subject positions" that accompanied the rise of social construction as an intellectual paradigm. When feminism concerns itself with "the vagaries" of subjectivity, Grosz writes, it "abdicates the right to speak about the real, about the world, about matter, about nature, and in exchange, cages itself in the reign of the 'I.'"[75] This comment is especially noteworthy. It suggests that "I" am not in fact "real." Only the dynamic matter that constitutes one's body is real.

This perspective differs from nature feminism only insofar as it replaces "reproduction" with "replication," swapping a gendered essentialism for a universal one. It maintains a familiar distrust of "I" as an artificial social construct. For Grosz, identity is problematic because it so often totalizes the communities to which it affixes characteristics. By contrast, "pure difference in itself, this process of self-differentiation that has no self before it begins its becoming, is the undermining of all identities, unities, cohesions." Neel Ahuja gestures to just this sort of statement when he notes that posthumanist discourse "continues to invest the breakdown of species 'boundaries' with a certain idealism."[76] Any materialist assertion that a "false impression of self" cleaves us from a "visceral sense of the matter that exposes us" reiterates the IPE's wilderness narrative – its investment in a primary condition in which, as Orlie puts it, "the ego is one with all of matter." In these instances, such accounts differ only marginally from Latour's "political religion," the pious holism that informs "dynamic, rather than static" Gaia spirituality, as well as other nature-feminist narratives of "*imminent*" subjective merger.[77] Grosz does ultimately land on the more pragmatic suggestion that identity might shed its categorical limitations when envisioned as "what I do, what I make . . . not who I am." Too often, however, the material soup from which such "becomings" arise itself seems to become yet another matter of "who I am." As a result, one reads echoes of the IPE in assertions like Braidotti's that "[w]hat we most truly desire is to surrender the self."[78]

Atwood has lampooned this sort of idealized "merger with the web of non-human forces" numerous times over the course of her career, most recently in *The Year of the Flood* (2009), the second volume of the *MaddAddam* trilogy, and its local political religion, the God's Gardeners vegetarian doomsday cult. The novel ends with the Gardeners having survived the viral elimination of humanity featured in *Oryx and Crake*. The sect's numbers soon dwindle, however, as predators slowly pick them off. "Via the conduit of a wild dog pack," one celebrant "made the ultimate Gift to her fellow Creatures, and has become part of God's great dance of proteins."[79] That kind of "ultimate subtraction is after all only another phase in a generative process," Braidotti writes. "We may call it death, but in a monistic ontology of vitalist materialism, it has rather to do with radical immanence." The asymmetrical privilege Braidotti grants to matter sets a politically distasteful precedent. "Of course repugnant and unbearable events do happen," she writes, but posthumanist ethics consists in "reworking these events in the direction of positive relations" by accepting "the fundamental meaninglessness of the hurt, the injustice, the injury one has suffered. 'Why me?' is the refrain most commonly heard in situations of extreme distress.... The answer is plain: actually, for no reason at all."[80]

One wonders where to go from here, politically speaking. Hannes Bergthaller shrewdly notes that when one takes seriously such a "flat" ontology, "it becomes very difficult ... to come up with a principled reason that any particular species or habitat ought to be protected," including human populations, communities, and individuals.[81] Identities marked by race, gender, disability, age, sexual orientation, and otherwise have material origins and consequences. They do exist, have existed, and do materially impact the lives of individuals occupying those positions – sometimes deleteriously, sometimes beneficially. The positive, productive aspects of identity and community especially risk getting lost in the play of matter venerated by accounts such as Braidotti's. What humans truly desire, she writes, is to "disappear by merging into the generative flow of becoming, the precondition for which is the loss, disappearance, and disruption of the ... self."[82] Merger comes to resemble a death drive, a cessation of tension such that one's extinction facilitates circulation throughout the ecosystem. As a consequence, politics as such would seem to become quite unnecessary. All that matters is matter's constant flux. Everything else is artifice.

Still, it's important to keep in mind that other, "diffractive" route proposed by Haraway and undertaken by careful materialists such as Barad, for whom ontology and social representation are always two sides to the same coin. The conjoined approach to ecology and narrative taken by these writers – as well as Ortiz, Morrison, Watts, Matthiessen, and (spoiler alert) Atwood – takes up and finds wanting the notion that under our repressions lies some materially expansive psychic paradise. If nothing else, the previous chapters have demonstrated that the history of the IPE is one of contestation – of a series of dialogues about the role of subjectivity in a networked ecology. My point is that this conversation – between the IPE narrative, on the one hand, and those who complicate its erasure of social forms, on the other – carries on in contemporary posthumanist conversations. That legacy is no accident, either. New materialism, object-oriented

164   The Essential Ecosystem

ontology, speculative realism: all of these paradigms emerge as modes of examining a subject compromised by the introduction of complex networks such as ecology to our social thought. They arise, that is, along the same line of questioning that gave shape to the IPE fifty years ago. In some cases, they also retain the elements of psychoanalytic thought that saturated that debate from the beginning – narratives that, as writers like Braidotti show, might pave the way for a certain political quietism that the rest of this chapter (as well as the next one) will consider in more detail. New-materialist writing starts to veer into the IPE's essentialist territory specifically when the idiom of repression enters the picture, recasting social forms as an aberration rather than component of the network.

An Appeal to Obliteration

One makes of a network a wilderness – a nature overwritten by culture – when one counterposes it against, instead of enmeshes it with, social forms that ostensibly repress it. In such a scenario, an appeal to the natural or authentic also constitutes an appeal to the universal, in that it obliterates material distinctions among individuals and communities. Death plays an integral role in this transformation for Atwood as well as for Braidotti. The protagonist of her 1990 short story "Death by Landscape," reflecting on the disappearance of her childhood friend Lucy in the same lake country in which *Surfacing* takes place, comments that "a dead person is a body; a body occupies space, it exists somewhere. You can see it; you put it in a box and bury it . . . But Lucy is not in a box, or in the ground. Because she is nowhere definite, she could be anywhere . . . . She is here. She is entirely alive." Life and death come together in the ecosystem's material composition taken as a whole. "The only way the speaker could actually get into the landscape," Atwood commented in an interview, "was by dying."[83] If the narrator of *Surfacing* seems to identify with that same landscape, she also comes to recognize death – decomposition and material dispersal – as the only means to physically sustain that identification. For this reason, she also ultimately abandons it.

Surfacing invites skepticism toward not only feminist essentialism but also similar attitudes toward network gaining traction at the time of Atwood's writing. To define individuals by matter *tout court* de-emphasizes, if not destroys outright, those to whom such definitions affix, no less than to define woman by biology has historically tended to do. At the conclusion of *The Handmaid's Tale*, out of desperation and acquiescence in the face of potential extinction, Offred pleads that she will

An Appeal to Obliteration 165

"obliterate myself, if that's what you really want; I'll empty myself, truly, become a chalice." In a moment of fear, Offred offers to trade one form of annihilation for another: the cessation of her life in favor of the extinction of her subjectivity. She accepts her biologistic station as vessel, as woman identified entirely with ovary and womb. When the handmaids pray, "Oh God, obliterate me. Make me fruitful. Mortify my flesh, that I may be multiplied. Let me be fulfilled," they validate the repressive regime under which they serve as incubators by glorifying dissolution of selfhood in favor of reproductive capacity. Individual women are entirely interchangeable. When the state executes one handmaid, another of the same designation takes her place. What matters is her matter. In those moments when Offred seems to internalize the Gileadean doctrine that women equal their wombs, she assents to "sink down into my body as into a swamp, fenland . . . Treacherous ground, my own territory. I become the earth."[84] The holistic, impersonal shape taken by Offred's muted horror and resigned acceptance of her gendered station chillingly reflects the rhetoric employed by *Surfacing*'s narrator as she attempts, by contrast, to *escape* prescriptions of proper womanhood. The narrator de-individualizes herself by way of appeals to nature similar, though by no means identical, to those levied by the Gileadean patriarchy. Even if the narrator more or less successfully decouples sexual reproduction from her conception of material essence, she nonetheless obliterates her self as such.

The narrator takes seriously this sort of appeal to the natural, essential, or authentic. In tracing such logic to its limits, however, Atwood suggests that to follow it through is to ultimately, and perhaps unwittingly, make the claim that death is not only inevitable but also crudely desirable. The narrator's de-individualized sense of ecological authenticity invites her death. To be truly spread out across the ecosystem, as she imagines she most naturally is and must be, is to let that ecosystem take of one's body what it will. Through her death her matter will experience continued life throughout the ecosystem. For this reason, her initial despair at the news of her father's death gives way to acceptance and attraction. The narrator's companions "find me inappropriate" when they learn that her father's body has been found: "they think I should be filled with death, I should be in mourning. But nothing has died, everything is alive, everything is waiting to become alive" (160). When the narrator beholds what she takes to be her father's ghost, she notes that it takes not a familiar corporeal shape but the vague and unspecified form of "what my father has become. I knew he wasn't dead" (193). This announcement reads less as a literal confirmation than as an affirmation

166   The Essential Ecosystem

that her father's matter now circulates more freely in the lake and the soil, up through roots into leaves and the bellies of mobile creatures, "back into the earth, the air, the water" (194). Death signifies for the narrator not the snuffing out of a life but its efflorescence and expansion.

As the narrator imagines herself "approach[ing] the condition" her parents "have entered," however, she grows increasingly ambivalent regarding its requirements, not because she does not desire to dismiss her socially determined self but because she finds doing so quite impossible. Their "condition" lacks boundaries. Her parents, being dead and diffuse, "can't be anywhere that's marked out, enclosed ... they are against borders" (186). She laments having arranged a conventional burial for her mother because coffins exist "to lock the dead in, preserve them," and keep them from "spreading or changing into anything else" (151). The cabin, fences, and paths she helped her mother and father to build now appear reprehensibly artificial. Like her incorporeal father, she "wants ... the borders abolished" and "the forest to flow back" (192–3). Boundaries subsist on manmade concepts – "fence" or "wall" or "man" or "woman" – whose deconstruction facilitates the narrator's conception of an expansive, primary condition. At the same time, moments of recoherence punctuate her merger: "I have to get up, I get up. Through the ground, break surface, I'm standing now; separate again" (188). The narrator finds her attempted dispensation with self-identity impossible to complete because she paradoxically yet necessarily maintains a perspective from which to effect her self-erasure. She finds herself in a complex double-bind. She longs to sustain her expansive identification as an expression of ostensibly natural subjectivity. However, in order to seamlessly merge with the ecosystem – that is, in order to truly divest herself of an "I" – she must die. At the same time, she requires a situated perspective from which to maintain that sense of merger to begin with. She does not want to die, but to express an essential identity that she cannot comprehend without the very sense of "I" – and all the experiences, predilections, and memories that go with it – that she considers a veneer obscuring her nature and intends to dismiss. The novel's punctuated moments of recoherence, during which her personality reasserts itself, signify her acknowledgment of this dilemma.

The ease and abruptness with which the narrator slides back into the self-identity she earlier denounces as a fiction seems almost disappointing. She speaks of assuming boundaries as one who dons a pair of shoes: "I place my feet" in a pair of footprints found on a path "and find that they are my

An Appeal to Obliteration 167

own" (193). The line inverts the narrator's earlier distaste for the "cloth decoy" of dress, makeup, and emotions that she eagerly sheds in an attempt to escape social construction. The footprints are "my own." They demarcate a sense of coherence, of being more or less "whole" not in terms of the ecosystem but in terms of self. The narrator's self is, like Offred's in *The Handmaid's Tale*, "a thing I must now compose, as one composes a speech. What I must present is a made thing, not something born."[85] Both women lament the managed impression of selfhood intimated in these passages, but they also exemplify what Grosz means when she writes that "acts that constitute oppression also form the conditions under which other kinds of inventions . . . become possible."[86] Offred privately celebrates when her Commander gifts her a tube of lipstick because it seems to her a small instrument of liberation, a perhaps ineffectual yet also personally meaningful means to craft and take control of an identity otherwise entirely determined by the state. Social construction, in this light, appears a creative, positive, and potentially consequential force. Offred momentarily becomes free to shape her identity in a context in which others ordinarily define her by her fruitfulness. The self-determinative orientation of Atwood's later work illuminates the implications of *Surfacing*'s ambivalent conclusion, which does not corroborate the critical claim that the narrator discovers and strengthens her sense of identity in the woods. If anything, the narrator's identity is more uncertain than ever. Atwood, however, leads us to believe that such uncertainty is what stands between the narrator and the extinction she invites. Placing her feet in her footprints, she concedes that choices, experiences, affiliations, and performances, while perhaps not as "natural" as flesh and blood, constitute identities worth claiming.

In tracing the narrator's failure to build a sustainable sense of identity on a purely "natural" basis, *Surfacing* takes an anti-essentialist stance, a position visible in other texts of Atwood's oeuvre. The novel's conclusively contingent representation of self as process rather than essence is one she continues to take up and explore in her work. Nature offers neither "total salvation" nor "resurrection" (196). The narrator's casual yet uneasy acceptance that she "must return to the city and the pervasive menace, the Americans," treats with the "American" not as an artifice obscuring essence but as a function of human action no less "natural" than its potential, as-yet unimagined alternatives. To "live in the usual way, defining . . . love by its failures, power by its loss, its renunciation," is to approach subjectivity as an ongoing project, defined not by essence but by relationships and reactions (195). The narrator returns to Joe at the novel's conclusion precisely because "he isn't an American . . . he isn't anything, he is only half formed, and for that reason I can trust him" (198). That she considers Joe's lack of fixed identity a respectable and desirable condition signals her revised understanding of identity as a plastic and pragmatic thing. Moving forward, she "refuse[s] to be a victim" (197). If she accepts her identity as a constructed aspect of her person, she also determines to direct that construction herself, in defiance of men like David as well as the economic forces that would dominate both women and other organisms.

That the narrator cannot escape narratives of identity – self-directed or otherwise – also illuminates how the IPE is as much a construction as any. The narrator's willing self-obliteration occurs in response to the domination and imposed definition of both women and their environment as the latter groans under the pressure of encroaching industrial tourism. However, her perspective willfully and paradoxically ignores the material validity of these discursive forces, which she deems harmful yet ethereal, unsubstantial enough to entirely strip away. Ecofeminists outside the nature-feminist tradition have emphasized that "connections and potential for communion between any group of humans and nonhuman nature is an important step toward overcoming the dualisms that structure our culture's thinking," but also that "relying *only* on connection can collapse the self/other dualism into an undifferentiated whole." The real/artificial binary reiterated by nature-feminist and occasionally new-materialist rhetoric tends to collapse dynamic networks into just this sort of unity. Other ecofeminists have instead considered "how to negotiate connection and difference," acknowledging "the other as neither alien to and discontinuous from self nor assimilated to or an extension of self" – and it's small wonder that such critics have recently drawn substantially on theorists such as Barad and Haraway for this sort of work.[87]

This uneasy middle ground is precisely the uncomfortable yet manageable territory into which *Surfacing*'s narrator has wandered by the end of the novel. She intimately embraces the vast cavalcade of organisms and forces that constitute her but she forgoes a complete dissolution. To borrow a phrase from Haraway, she recognizes that "to be one is always to *become with* many," not to "*become* many." Like Morrison, as well as many ecofeminists of color, Atwood "take[s] seriously non-individualist modes of identity formation," a project that "refuses not only a notion of a universal 'woman,' but even the possibility of an unproblematic individual 'woman.'"[88] Identities are shared and negotiated constructions, built in partnership with and/or reaction to fellow humans, institutions, and nonhuman others. As such, Atwood neither takes for granted nor neglects ecology's generic influence in *Surfacing*. Instead, she suggests that to recognize the material conditions universal to the human species requires culturally mediated and collectively generated identity positions from which to do so. Accordingly, the novel leaves the shape of that potential open-ended.

CHAPTER 5

The Death of the Supertramp
Psychoanalytic Narratives and American Wilderness

> ... the authentic inaugurating act of a would-be biocentrist should
> properly consist of suicide, since by staying alive he uses up another
> creature's resources – even its very life.... everybody is an anthropocen-
> trist, except corpses pushing up daisies: they are the real biocentrists, giving
> their all so others can live.
>
> Harold Fromm, "Aldo Leopold"

> ... think to your next death. Will your flesh and bones back into the cycle.
> Surrender. Love the plump worms you will become.
>
> John Seed and Joanna Macy, "Gaia Meditations"

On the shores of the Teklanika River, a tributary that feeds the Yukon's central Alaska drainage basin, one can find embedded in a stone cairn a small plaque that reads, "Rester C'est Exister Voyager C'est Vivre."[1] The memorial commemorates the death of Claire Ackermann, a Swiss back-packer who, in 2010, drowned in the river's current, dragged to the bottom by the same rope to which she tied herself in an attempt to safely cross during the Teklanika's typically turbulent summer. Those same rough waters barred passage to Christopher McCandless late in the summer of 1992, two years after he quietly donated his savings to Oxfam American and vacated his apartment near Emory University. Several months later, two parties of hikers and hunters found McCandless's body decomposing in an abandoned bus on the Stampede Trail south of Denali, little more than five miles west of the river. Four years after that, Jon Krakauer published *Into the Wild* (1996), a reconstructed account of McCandless's cross-country travels, over the course of which the man fashioned himself as a self-renouncing ascetic icon: the "Supertramp," an alter ego styled as a paragon of authentic selfhood, unfettered by social custom, continuous with his environment. In Alaska, McCandless believed himself finally "free from society at last," able to begin his "real life."[2] Ackermann's adventure – and, more tragically, her death – purposefully mirrored McCandless's. She and her boyfriend traveled the Stampede Trail in homage to the Supertramp, dead eighteen years almost to the day.

That Supertramp figure, however, is largely a fictional assemblage, despite the historically verifiable life and death of a man named Christopher Johnson McCandless. Krakauer pieced together the man's travels from a woefully incomplete archive of letters, journals, and interviews. A host of Alaska residents, toxicologists, documentarians, and other commentators continue to fabricate, elaborate, and interrogate the story. *Into the Wild* sits at the center of this ongoing narrative, and the Supertramp figure that emerges from McCandless's writings and Krakauer's commentary lionizes wilderness "as a space devoid of culture, devoid of civilization . . . the realm of the real" and of "*authentic* experience of the world." More than any other figure discussed thus far, McCandless takes seriously a "developmental model of history" that "posits humans and their modern trappings as somehow like the layers of an onion."[3] At the center of this existential pellet rests the expansive ecological authenticity hypothesized by the IPE's psychoanalytic narrative. To enter the putatively untouched Alaskan bush, the Supertramp reasons, is to shuck off his false, socially mediated self, repressed by a postindustrial America obsessed with capital and consumer comforts, and to recover a harmony within ecology somehow devoid of cultural influence, a wilderness somehow free of ideology.

Into the Wild's continued success evidences widespread fascination with the Supertramp, especially with the relationship between his ideas and his mysterious death. The book, expanded from a 1993 article in *Outside* magazine, has remained a bestseller since its publication (as recently as 2018, it still ranked second in "Travel Writing" on Amazon). Krakauer's treatment of the man's motivations, as well as Sean Penn's 2007 film adaptation, "helped elevate the McCandless saga to the status of modern myth," writes Diana Saverin in another *Outside* article. The "McCandless pilgrims" she profiles for the 2013 story follow his footsteps along the Stampede Trail to "ponder the impact that McCandless's antimaterialist ethic, free-spirited travels, and time in the Alaskan wild has had on how they perceive the world." Saverin's account of scouting the Teklanika River is almost comical. Dazed hikers seem to pop out from behind almost every bush, lost, hungry, stranded, or worse, but all having followed McCandless's lead.[4] The article's humor in no way diminishes its urgency. At best, ill-equipped strays have taken a life-threatening dip five hundred meters down a glacial river in attempted imitation of their hero. At worst, people have died.

172　　　　　　　　The Death of the Supertramp

This final chapter traces the IPE to this very limit: a commitment to ecological authenticity such that dissolution into the ecosystem is taken to its biophysical extreme in death. Accordingly, it starts by examining the extent to which the Supertramp represents the IPE's apotheosis. It ends by considering the degree to which his cult popularity reflects – and perhaps even contributes to – an American wilderness narrative reshaped by the IPE, a myth that draws a psychic rather than spatial distinction between nature and civilization. This transition raises serious questions about popular, if not academic, representations of environment. With death as its logical implication, the political pretension of the IPE comes to resemble more of a political nihilism. Chapter 4 gestured toward this conclusion. This chapter fleshes it out.

It also argues that *Into the Wild* demonstrates the extent to which wilderness has become a repository for the superannuated psychoanalytic elements of midcentury social theory. Krakauer frames the Supertramp's assumption that he accesses a totally unmediated condition in terms of a longstanding American wilderness narrative, pointing to writers such as Henry David Thoreau and Jack London, whom McCandless greatly admired. At the same time, the man's obsession with essential identity revises and situates those narratives in a distinctively contemporary moment. The notion that one might peel back the layers of civilization's various repressions recalls the Freudian Left's midcentury social theory. McCandless gestures frequently to a romantic wilderness tradition of generations past, but his most salient touchstones proceed from the New Left and counterculture of the 1960s. His affinity with certain environmental thinkers of his generation – particularly deep ecologists such as those quoted in this chapter's epigraph – furthermore points to the foundational role played by psychoanalysis across genres. Like ecofeminism, deep ecology is a philosophically diverse body of thought. However, as in other cases, the surfeit of dissolution rhetoric in its texts has contributed to an atmosphere of ecological authenticity that has had profound cultural effects, not least on individuals such as McCandless. Psychoanalysis' influence on the American zeitgeist had already long been in decline by the time of *Into the Wild*'s publication, but McCandless's logic makes clear that the introduction of Freudian thought to American environmentalism has endured. *Into the Wild* even brings the IPE's debt to Herbert Marcuse full circle, from its origin in his theory of "repressive civilization" to its capitulation to what he called "repressive desublimation" – the capitalist appropriation of the psyche's liberation. Increased traffic to McCandless's "magic bus" has resulted in a site "once wild" but "now . . . worn with use," a commodity in its own right.[5]

The Death of the Supertramp   173

The nihilism occasioned by the IPE is therefore twofold: on the one hand, the death of the ecologically authentic subject, and on the other, the death of meaningful environmentalist politics. McCandless has helped to inspire what I term a *neoliberal wilderness* discourse, one that puts the idea of ecological authenticity up for sale. Wilderness has always been a site of consumption, but the IPE's alteration of the idea's significance – from geographical location to authentic identity – has changed the shape of what, exactly, one is consuming. If for past generations wilderness chiefly signified an untouched environment that situated retreat and recreation, for our contemporary moment wilderness additionally offers a type of identity that one inhabits, crafts, or buys. Nowhere does this transition make itself more apparent than in the DIY self-erasures of McCandless's cult following, which participates in a marketplace of authenticity – and with the Supertramp as model, to be authentic might require one to disappear from the arena of environmental politics altogether.

However, despite the fact that *Into the Wild*'s publicity has played a substantial role in wilderness' conflation with consumer identity, I suggest that we read it as a text critical of its subject. Krakauer traces the IPE's psychoanalytic narrative to its limits and finds it wanting as an environmentalist model. He does so by representing McCandless less as a biographically accurate figure and more as a persona determined by Krakauer's own interpretation of pervasive wilderness narratives. *Into the Wild* isn't about McCandless – it's about Krakauer's relationship with the idea of McCandless. I first examine how Krakauer positions himself in conversation with the always-absent Supertramp and go on to suggest that he does so in order to stage an unresolved debate between two different perspectives. The first is McCandless's IPE, which relies on a sharp division between nature and civilization to conceptualize a natural identity totally spread across the ecosystem. The second is Krakauer's own view that nature and civilization are falsely divided concepts, and his consequent understanding that socially mediated selfhood is the inescapable yet beneficial impetus behind environmental thinking in the first place. Krakauer's nuanced representation of the Supertramp's various preoccupations – with his parents and his name, especially – inform *Into the Wild*'s sharp portrayal and subtly uncharitable treatment of the IPE and the developmental saga that underwrites it. The text's meticulous attention to how McCandless styles himself as an "ascetic superhero" – a persona paradoxically premised on both self-erasure and self-inflation – especially foregrounds the IPE's contradictions. Krakauer himself contests IPE dogma through his ambivalent perspective toward identity and his implicit thesis

174 The Death of the Supertramp

regarding McCandless's death. In dying, the Supertramp succeeds in holistically identifying with the ecosystem in the only way possible: as carrion.

Characterizing Chris McCandless

One might consider death the most radical move possible in terms of biocentrism, the acceptance of ecology's distributive aspects and the conviction not only that one will die, but also that one's carcass will provide an inestimable service to the ecosystem after death. A pictographic belt McCandless crafted under the tutelage of his friend Ron Franz boldly features his legal initials, C. J. M., surrounding a skull-and-crossbones – a symbol of his death as Christopher McCandless and rebirth as Alexander Supertramp. Krakauer represents McCandless's quest as one for the replete ecological authenticity with which figures discussed previously have merely toyed, foregrounding McCandless's serious alignment of an expansive, indistinct sense of selfhood with his wilderness locale. The Supertramp is a true believer. He presumes his ego or self has dissolved and that he is no longer individual but dispersed throughout the ecosystem. His self-styled "Supertramp" label paradoxically lauds his sense of ascetic superiority even as it invokes a certain timelessness, even immortality, that gestures toward what he considers the purity of an ecosystem in which the self as such vanishes. That immortality manifests, as it does in *Surfacing*, as dead matter's persistent vitality in the ecosystem. According to Krakauer, McCandless decided not to take his own life but to let the natural (albeit unclear) death to which he fell prey run its course. McCandless ended his journey as a piece of meat, a fate Krakauer frames as a more or less noble outcome in that it consummated the Supertramp's quest.

Perhaps more importantly, the Supertramp's almost mythological cultural resonance has granted McCandless a certain degree of immortality as a character, even if McCandless, the person, neither wanted nor expected to die. Krakauer adamantly contests the charge that the young man was "bent on suicide from the beginning" (134), although a number of Alaskan locals, reporters, and filmmakers have vigorously challenged Krakauer's speculation on cause of death over the past twenty years. Ron Lamothe, in his 2007 documentary *The Call of the Wild*, notes that Krakauer had not updated *Into the Wild* by the time of the film's production to reflect new information relevant to McCandless's autopsy. Lamothe disputes other details as well. Interviews with trappers who maintain a cabin mentioned in the text reveal that McCandless likely followed their dog trail to find the

Characterizing Chris McCandless

abandoned bus in which he died, a point Krakauer omits. At the same time, such an omission could be said to strengthen Krakauer's representation of McCandless's zealous self-isolation. This "idealized McCandless," Lamothe confesses, "matters most to me."[6] That is, Lamothe is most fascinated not by Christopher McCandless the real person, but by Alexander Supertramp, the persona invented by McCandless but largely crafted by Krakauer. The facts of the McCandless case remain disputed, but Lamothe's admission illustrates how little the actual, historical series of events matters when analyzing Krakauer's work, which the author himself acknowledges as at least in part a work of fiction he imagined. Despite the almost pious investment in authenticity observed among McCandless's most fervent fans, the Supertramp is always subject to the mediating presence of his commentators.

McCandless is a character – the Supertramp figure the real McCandless invented – and a character who, as imagined by Krakauer, accepts his death as a final dissolution. Krakauer also becomes a character in this narrative, a youthful interlocutor whose past experiences and convictions overlapped substantially with McCandless's own. Despite the author's showcase of McCandless's journals, interviews with people he met across the United States, and observations and memories about places of adventure and refuge, the reader never quite receives McCandless's own account. Instead, one witnesses Krakauer's speculation and interpretation. Krakauer makes no claim to distance. In his author's note, he writes of "vague, unsettling parallels between events in [McCandless's] life and those in my own." He declines "to be an impartial biographer" and "interrupt[s] McCandless's story with fragments of a narrative drawn from my own youth. I do so in the hope that my experiences will throw some oblique light on the enigma of Chris McCandless." Krakauer means these autobiographical vignettes to fill gaps left in McCandless's own record, where photographic and epistolary evidence do not exist. McCandless and Krakauer constitute each other as characters in dialogue.

Krakauer himself, however, challenges McCandless's earnest dualism between nature and culture, "real life" and artifice, as early as the first chapter challenging the notion that one might exist entirely free of sociocultural influence. He develops the Supertramp character not only through his writings and interactions, but also through his literary influences and cultural antecedents. When McCandless arrived in Alaska in April 1992, he scrawled a Thoreauvian creed in his notebook: "*I am reborn. This is my dawn. Real life has just begun. Deliberate living: Conscious attention to the basics of life, and a constant attention to your immediate environment and its*

176   The Death of the Supertramp

concerns" (168). The words "Reality," "Truth," and "Real" repeat among McCandless's numerous messages, scribbled in books or carved into buses, and indicate a conscious effort at rhetorical self-representation as having recovered some natural identity that the average person represses. The Supertramp takes for a roadmap and elevates to universal significance the codes established by well-published figures before him. Krakauer's pointed observation that McCandless entirely ignored his forebears' own hypocrisies (Jack London only spent a single winter in the north, for example) highlights the extent to which McCandless discursively constructs both "truth" and the wilderness in which he finds it.

Even more notable, however, is the fact that Krakauer counts this Supertramp character among a series of "countercultural idealists" who hoped to make of Alaska an environment of self-liberation (72*ff*.). Like his predecessors, McCandless "believed that wealth was shameful, corrupting, inherently evil" (115). Shortly after commencing his university studies, "Chris started complaining about all the rich kids at Emory" (123). Several years prior to graduation he announced that "he would no longer give or accept gifts," and he "upbraided" his parents Walt and Billie "for expressing their desire to buy him a new car as a graduation present and offering to pay for law school" (20). Among the documents he left behind can be found a 1992 doodle in the center of which he prominently scribbled "Down With The Program!"[7] McCandless's "seemingly anomalous political positions" are mercurial yet always anti-establishment. Despite the fact that he "was a vocal admirer" of Ronald Reagan, his fierce anti-centralism reads more convincingly in the tradition of Murray Bookchin's ecological anarchism. He once remarked of hunting licensure, "How I feed myself is none of the government's business. Fuck their stupid rules" (6). At the same time, he tempered his boisterous libertarianism with avid, even revolutionary civic-mindedness, as when he "spoke seriously to his friends about smuggling weapons" into South Africa to aid "the struggle to end apartheid" (113). Krakauer does not necessarily paint the Supertramp as a latter-day New Leftist or countercultural icon, but the inclusion of such details foregrounds the fact that though McCandless looked for guidance to writers of the late nineteenth and early twentieth centuries (especially Thoreau, London, Boris Pasternak, and Leo Tolstoy), his perspective on wilderness takes as one major thread of inspiration the confluence of postwar radical movements organized around issues of alienation, authenticity, and ecology.

The anti-industrial impetus behind McCandless's white, upper-middle-class malaise, though indeed reflective of early twentieth century

Depth and Deep Ecology 177

environmentalism, is more representative of the existentialist alienation felt by the equally white and middle-class Movement of the 1960s. If McCandless idolizes (and frequently misreads) writers like London and Thoreau, he does not quite fall into the tradition of romantic idealism. Instead, he goes the whole hog: McCandless believes his self or ego has actually dissolved and that he is no longer individual but dispersed throughout the ecosystem. At the outset of his account, Krakauer writes that McCandless changed his name and hitched cross-country to Alaska "in search of raw, transcendent experience" (23). McCandless himself expressed an intention "to wallow in unfiltered experience." The expansiveness of his proclamations, coupled with Krakauer's repetitive imagery of submersion and dispersal, voices a desire not merely to affirm one's place in the ecosystem, but to *be* the ecosystem. McCandless effaces his sense of self-identity in favor of identification with the ecosystem as a whole. In this way, he believes he has sacrificed a repressed and limited sense of self for a more natural identity. He can never quite achieve this goal, but he nonetheless earnestly *believes* he achieves it.

Of course, this narrative depends on the conceptual balkanization of "real" nature and "artificial" civilization. McCandless fervently presumes a "vital need for wilderness, wild places, to . . . become more mature," in the divisive yet self-constituting way deep ecologists Bill Devall and George Sessions articulated the concept shortly before McCandless's departure.[8] Krakauer remains suspicious of this notion throughout *Into the Wild*, despite his youthful comprehension of wilderness isolation as the locus of wholeness and plentitude. Of the various "countercultural idealists" in whose company *Into the Wild* situates the Supertramp, Krakauer reflects most harshly on an anonymous man who "passed through the village of Tanana in the early 1970s, who announced that he intended to spend the rest of his life 'communing with Nature.'" A search party discovered among the man's recovered belongings "a diary filled with incoherent rambling about truth and beauty and recondite ecological theory" (72). The man's disappearance and his interest in "recondite ecological theory" are important and related details. Krakauer's tongue-in-cheek reference to the man's choice in literature announces his dismissive opinion of the pro-nature/anti-culture narrative that characterizes the IPE, even as he locates McCandless in that tradition.

Depth and Deep Ecology

Krakauer frames *Into the Wild*'s critique of the IPE's assumptions and consequences as a dialogue between the divergent perspectives of Krakauer and Supertramp characters. The text's young Krakauer, semi-autobiographical yet pointedly rendered in juxtaposition to McCandless, relates how his own faith in the purity of wilderness crumbled after a series of near-death experiences. On the face of Devils Thumb, a sheer mountain south of Juneau, Alaska, where "the unnamed peaks towering over the glacier were bigger and comelier and infinitely more menacing than they would have been were I in the company of another person" (138), Krakauer experiences a sense of wholeness he paradoxically believes made possible only by an absence – that of civilization. The fantasy shatters when he becomes frustrated with his lack of control over natural forces and the appearance of manmade technologies. Starving on the mountain in the aftermath of a blizzard, he hears a plane fly overhead and, slowly, recede. "As silence again settled over the glacier," Krakauer "felt abandoned, vulnerable, lost. I realized that I was sobbing" (141). Krakauer's sudden awareness of his utter inability to police any supposed border between nature and civilization heralds also his recognition of the extent to which he has constructed his own idea of wilderness. "Like McCandless, I was a raw youth who mistook passion for insight and acted according to an obscure, gap-ridden logic" (153). At the center of that logic sits the premise that if freed of civilization one might act in seamless harmony with one's surroundings.

"Insight," in the context of perceived wilderness isolation, takes on the connotation of "instinct," especially insofar as the young Krakauer believed himself to possess the ability to automatically and suitably react to his environment. This same conviction, phrased similarly in terms of "intuition," played a starring role in the deep ecology movement in the 1980s and early 1990s, even as McCandless set his sights north. Arne Naess developed deep ecology with Sessions in 1984 as a position, not a theory, "a nontechnical statement of principles around which, it is hoped, people with different *ultimate* understandings of themselves, society, and nonhuman nature, could unite." Such principles, as Sessions and Devall laid them out one year later, revolve most saliently around two interconnected points: that nonhuman life (or matter in general) has intrinsic value independent of human use, and that humans must curb their "interference" in the earth's operation. Theoretically, however, a number of deep ecologists often rested their justifications for this general platform on a recognizable appeal to the "intuition" of "immediate, spontaneous experience."[9] Just as Bookchin did for ecological anarchism, deep ecology's founding writers championed spontaneity as a primary method by which to celebrate both unity and diversity. Unlike social ecology, however, deep

Depth and Deep Ecology

ecology's foundational narratives often explicitly expressed this capacity in terms of a repressed, authentic "self."

Krakauer frames McCandless's ecological affiliations in nearly identical terms, thereby situating him squarely in the IPE's narrative form. Wilderness is for McCandless the authentic locus of deep-ecological "self-realization," a locale in which to recuperate identity at its most natural. "We underestimate" the self, Naess wrote in 1988. "We tend to confuse it with the narrow ego," but "increased self-realization implies broadening and deepening of the *self.*"[10] Devall and Sessions address their volume on deep ecology to "the reader seeking a more authentic existence and integrity of character" – a reader like McCandless himself. Their outline of the "real work" required to become "a whole person," or "'self-in-Self' where 'Self' stands for organic wholeness," resembles a suggestion made by at least one ecopsychologist that we "become whole again" by retreating to the wilderness to "*be* wilderness." The word "again" is significant. It implies that in wilderness we *re*-access something forgotten, a repressed, "primordial self."[11] This capital-S "Self," Devall and Sessions write, includes "not only me, an individual human, but all humans, whales, grizzly bears, whole rain forest ecosystems, mountains and rivers, the tiniest microbes in the soil, and so on." The ego, they add, comprises only a "narrow" or "social" self, a clarification that suggests the expanded self they praise is "whole," primary, and of more material consequence than any socially mediated identity position.[12]

McCandless targeted the artificiality of this "narrow" self with great invective. His unrest stemmed from his association of social status – which for him included characteristics like names and personalities – with repression. Despite Krakauer's plea that fair commentary must avoid psychologizing McCandless's parental relationships, Krakauer himself (reluctantly) traces the man's distrust of authority and government to disagreements with his father Walt. In the context of the narrative, McCandless's outspoken distaste for Walt (or for "civilization," for that matter) do not arise until he discovers, by chance, that his father maintained two families without divorcing his first wife for many years after Chris was born, a fact both of his parents aimed to keep hidden indefinitely. The most compelling detail of this account is Krakauer's suggestion that Chris comes to identify Walt's financial success and upper-middle-class comfort with hypocrisies and secrets. McCandless's dissatisfaction consequently emerges from his sudden consciousness of what Krakauer frames as a primary repression. Krakauer locates McCandless's sense of alienation in his father's artifice, such that McCandless comes to associate duplicity with

180   The Death of the Supertramp

his father's charm and wealth, with his successful navigation of capitalist civilization. Nature comes to strike him as profoundly "real" by comparison.

At first glance, the attention *Into the Wild* pays to Chris's relationship with Walt seems to sustain the habit of psychologizing McCandless that Krakauer condemns in other commentators. Krakauer in fact does something more nuanced: he self-consciously writes McCandless according to the nature/culture binary that the man himself took so seriously. He crafts a character typified by his own ideology in order to examine it. To pathologize McCandless, Krakauer suggests, would be to downplay or even efface the role played by the cultural narrative in which the Supertramp figure participates, even if that narrative is itself fundamentally psychoanalytical. Krakauer's expressed intention is to examine that narrative by drawing attention to the effects of the dualism in which McCandless so fervently believes, and by undermining what he considers the simplistic charge that the man was merely neurotic, "a narcissist who perished out of arrogance and stupidity" (184). As Krakauer rightly notes, "It probably misses the point to castigate McCandless for being ill prepared . . . . he was fully aware when he entered the bush that he had given himself a perilously slim margin for error. He knew precisely what was at stake." Rather than approach nature "as an antagonist that would inevitably submit to force," McCandless "went too far in the opposite direction. He tried to live entirely off the country" (182). Krakauer's point – biographically speculative yet fundamental to the Supertramp character he devises – is that though McCandless did not intend to die, he recognized the possibility that he *might* die as a dimension of the putatively authentic condition he hoped to approach. Like other countercultural tramps, McCandless "had an impractical fascination with the harsh side of nature," but though he "was rash, untutored in the ways of the backcountry, and incautious to the point of foolhardiness, he wasn't incompetent – he wouldn't have lasted 113 days if he were" (8). Krakauer writes as if McCandless is different or notable precisely because he more or less knows what he's doing but perishes anyway.

The Supertramp can be described as narcissistic only in terms of the psychoanalytic narrative in which he participates – that is, in terms of his attempt to regress through developmental time, to subjectively fuse with his surroundings in a way that recalls the infant of Freud's schema. He assumes that in the wilderness scene he merges with his environment while still existing *as* the Supertramp. Such an intention tests the metaphysical limits of ecology's most basic principle: that organisms exist interdependently in a complex biophysical matrix. In 1995, the deep ecologist

Warwick Fox defended deep ecology by clarifying that he did not believe "that I literally *am* that tree over there, for example," but that his "*sense* of self . . . can expand to include the tree even though I and the tree remain physically 'separate.'"[13] Fox's writing, like Naess, Sessions, and Devall's, is intricate enough to assure readers that he did not, in fact, become a tree in the process of composition. Still, one must question the extent to which such rhetorical flourishes – especially when so ubiquitous they seem characteristic, even constitutive – can benefit environmentalism, given the elisions between self and other they imply. Self-dismissal in this regard does not dispense with ego, as Val Plumwood and other ecofeminists pointed out at deep ecology's heyday. It shores up the self to expansive proportions according to the IPE's standard of universal authenticity, which derives its legitimacy from the supposed primacy of natural psychic expansiveness. One of the unavoidable contradictions of such erasure is its *elevated* egoism, by which "the larger world becomes part of our own interests." To erase the self by expanding it is to efface the other, a drawback incidentally betrayed by Naess's cheerful certainty that "if we progress far enough, the very notion of 'environment' becomes unnecessary."[14] Such an account downplays productive differences among individuals and groups in favor of an ahistorical mass of indistinguishability based on the impermanence of biological composition. Its representation also rests insecurely on a rhetorical two-step that the Supertramp also dances between framing his identity simultaneously as *nothing* and *everything* – a paradox that ties all of these figures together in the IPE's historically specific psychoanalytic narrative.

The Ascetic Superhero's Boast

Arguably, that psychoanalytic narrative most clearly alerts us to its presence in the contradictory shape of the Supertramp's name, a self-congratulatory boast of self-disappearance. That paradox remains in keeping with a general pattern in McCandless's behavior, a tension between his claims to authenticity and how he represents it. A collection of McCandless's photographs and writings prefaces its contents with a "note of authenticity" in which its photo editor claims that the "images on the cover and inside of this book are Christopher Johnson McCandless's photographs as he saw his world during his two-year journey. None of Chris's images were manipulated or retouched for this book."[15] The volume treats the images as spontaneous representations of McCandless in the wild, even in those frames he very clearly

182 The Death of the Supertramp

staged or for which he posed. In one such image, he moodily glances toward the sunset as the camera captures his profile. Despite the fact that McCandless himself extensively manipulates these images' content, the book presents itself as a collection of impartial wildlife photography, observing an unrestrained creature in its natural habitat, just as Edward Abbey imagined himself twenty-five years prior.

The disjunction between McCandless's claims to authenticity and his manipulation of the media that represent him serves as one facet of the complex relationship the character has with the notion of the "natural," and signals one of *Into the Wild*'s most forceful subtexts. McCandless takes great pains to *invent* what he considers to be natural throughout his adventure. The more meticulously he (or his curators) tries to stage these photos to portray something putatively authentic about his sojourn in the wilderness, the less spontaneous the photos themselves turn out to be. The same is true for his journals, which the text accompanying these images attempts to replicate in McCandless's stilted, third-person present tense. (It is unclear if these entries are McCandless's own, the mediating words of his father Walt, or the guiding interpretation of one or more of the volume's editors. The voice seems left intentionally ambiguous in order to lend another veneer of realism to the photographic timeline.) Krakauer's reproductions of McCandless's entries read similarly: "*He lived on the streets with bums, tramps, and winos for several weeks. Vegas would not be the end of his story, however*" (37). McCandless's journals take the perspective of a disinterested observer, a rhetorical move intended to spice the genuine flavor of the journey.

McCandless's insistent fabrication of his narrative predicted the inexpertly mimetic found footage collected in Werner Herzog's 2005 documentary *Grizzly Man*, a film whose own attention to matters of ecological authenticity further demystifies the Supertramp myth. The film's subject, Timothy Treadwell, also died in Alaska, in 2003, at the paws of his ursine friends. Herzog praises Treadwell for capturing "glorious spontaneous moments" as a filmmaker – an appreciation for cinematic realism ironically undermined by Herzog's wry attention to the multiple takes required for Treadwell to pose himself as the unadulterated subject of a nature documentary. Herzog almost comically draws attention to the extent to which Treadwell painstakingly obscures his companion Amie Huguenard's presence in his camp in order to maintain "his stylization as the lone guardian of the grizzlies." At one point, Treadwell mutters that he's "supposed to be alone" as he pushes Huguenard out of a candid shot.[16] Herzog's focus on Treadwell's inept maintenance of his solitary façade illuminates

McCandless's own willful construction of boundaries between natural and civilizational spheres. The Supertramp must repetitively fabricate a clean division between them to maintain his impression that he moves from one mode to the other. He recognizes the persistence of anthropogenic activity in putatively natural spaces but forcibly resists these artifacts, often by merely omitting them from his personal narrative. For example, he devises "an elegant solution" to the fact that, by 1992, "there were no more blank spots on the map": "He simply got rid of the map. In his own mind, if nowhere else, the *terra* would thereby remain *incognita*" (174). He clearly understands that Alaska is by no means a pure Eden untouched by the civilization he flees, but he constantly pushes back against this knowledge to restructure nature as a region independent of human influence. It is perhaps because of the Supertramp's self-consciousness that Krakauer treats him not as an incompetent naïf but as a wary participant in a longer history of wilderness retreat.

From Krakauer's perspective, the most relevant representative of that fellowship is Everett Ruess, who disappeared in Utah's Davis Gulch at twenty-one in 1934. Beyond drawing a few parallels between the two figures' lives (and deaths), Krakauer does not elaborate on what, exactly, makes Ruess a particularly important antecedent. Ruess's letters, however, illuminate the role played by the name *Supertramp* in McCandless's self-fashioning, as well as what naming reveals about McCandless's motivations and the narratives in which he participates. In his final letter, Ruess asked his brother Waldo, "Do you blame me . . . for staying here, where I feel that I belong and am one with the world around me?" The question expresses more than mere affection for the desert. Like McCandless, Ruess had a high opinion of his perspective – a sense that "civilization" writ large is morally wrong and primordial wilderness morally right – and he measured others accordingly. He quit university studies because he felt his "lofty unconquerable soul" could no longer "remain imprisoned in that academic backwater." He granted respect to only one faculty member, an English professor who graded him highly despite his truancy. "In spite of all his shortcomings and handicaps he was able to see that here was a student of unusually high caliber!" Ruess wrote to a friend in 1933. "*Let us congratulate him* on his insight!!"[17]

Ruess's swollen opinion of himself (like McCandless's) is significant for its seeming conflict with his often-expressed desire to disappear. It is precisely that will to erasure, however, that constitutes Ruess's self-regard. "Art needs an audience, or it will die," he wrote in a 1931 letter. It would not be a stretch to assume that Ruess considered his biography a work of art. Many of his letters are second drafts, closely edited reproductions from his diary, altered not only for clarity but also for continuity. His selection of a suitable brush name came to be intimately bound up with this process by which he, like McCandless, edited his own narrative for consumption. The friend who helped him design his first pseudonym, Lan Rameau, "thought it was quite euphonic and distinctive" – far better than "Ruess" and its "freakish . . . affectation of Frenchiness."[18] Ruess's urge to distance himself from civilized "affectations" nonetheless entailed his measured consideration of a listening and reading audience party to that departure. He cycled through several such self-designations before he finally settled on the Latin word "Nemo," the name he "twice etched . . . into the soft Navajo sandstone" of Davis Gulch just before he disappeared (93).

"Nemo" translates to "nobody." Its inscription captures a contradictory announcement of one's own self-erasure. Writing in 1942, shortly after Ruess's disappearance, Wallace Stegner wondered if the signature expressed "a cryptic notice to the world that he intended to disappear, to cast off his identity," a sacrifice perhaps intended to pay "the price of immortality."[19] Stegner intends "immortality" to signify the longevity of romantic myth. How tenuously, he wondered, would Ruess's fabulous self-erasure stick in the wilderness narrative? Quite well, it turns out. *Into the Wild* catapulted the incident back into the popular imagination. Ruess, Krakauer muses, "no doubt" found himself "moved by the same impulse that compelled Chris McCandless to inscribe 'Alexander Supertramp/May 1992' on the wall of the Sushana bus" (89). Like McCandless's assumption of the Supertramp mantle, Ruess's graffito expresses the "competitive dimension of asceticism," a commitment to renunciation traditionally characteristic of Christian mystics. Each alias – Nemo and Supertramp – rehashes in a wilderness context what the critic Geoffrey Harpham refers to as "the far from idle boast of one monk to another: 'I am deader than you.'"[20] The question of whether Ruess intended to remove himself from or contribute to cultural forms misses the point. The assumption of the name Nemo constitutes an alchemy of both impulses. McCandless likewise intended his disposal of formally recognized identity to convey formlessness and fluidity to an audience. When Jim Gallien, the last person to see McCandless alive, asked for his name, he allegedly responded, "Just Alex." The more concrete label "Supertramp" ironically announced McCandless's presence while bragging of his status as the ultimate loner, an ascetic superhero.

Into the Wild's *Freudian Narrative* 185

This rebaptism doubly dispels the self and shores it up to mythic proportions. The ascetic superhero's boast encapsulates a contradictory double impulse to self-aggrandizement and self-erasure in an isolated wilderness presumed to induce it. In assuming the Supertramp mantle, McCandless makes of himself a cultural icon premised on its own disappearance. The same inclination to represent oneself simultaneously as grandiose and irrelevant characterized Treadwell, who "stylized himself as Prince Valiant, fighting the bad guys with schemes to do harm to the bears." Like McCandless and Ruess, Treadwell demonstrated a flair for the boast: "I am right on the precipice . . . Come here and try to do what I do. You will die." Also like McCandless and Ruess, so did he. Most importantly, however, he similarly premised his lofty self-image on self-erasure. At *Grizzly Man*'s midpoint, an ecologist reads a letter in which Treadwell declares, "I have to mutually mutate into a wild animal to handle the life I lead" – a project the ecologist describes as an almost religious impulse to "connect so deeply that you're no longer human."[21]

That the ecologist references spiritual fervor and self-erasure in the same breath should come as no surprise. McCandless, Ruess, and Treadwell's off-putting identifications with nothingness resonate strongly with the "oceanic feeling" that Freud described in *Civilization and Its Discontents* as "a sensation of 'eternity.'" For Freud, such a feeling most often characterizes religious sentiment, an outpouring of beatific yet infantile communion that exists in "counterpart" to the civilized ego as a feeling of "limitlessness and of a bond with the universe."[22] That notion has also played a prominent role in the IPE narrative. By erasing from his identity the formal mark of his civilized ego – his legal name – McCandless believes he has begun to construct a situation in which he recovers a primary limitlessness. Of course, the Supertramp persona merely imposes a new name with a new self, bigger but nonetheless articulated *as a self*. He claims for himself an expansive identity that renders him everything and nothing at once. Devoid of discrete selfhood, at one with the wild, he might also *be* the wild, an expanded "Self" spanning the system.

Into the Wild's Freudian Narrative

McCandless's journals and letters compose a narrative according to which his experience (at least after he arrives in Alaska) is entirely extra-civilizational, pure of human influence. *Into the Wild* draws a parallel between this civilization/nature dualism and a related self/non-self dualism that preserves the IPE's psychoanalytic origins long after the decline of the

Freudian Left's immediate cultural influence in the 1960s. McCandless's alignment of instinct and fulfillment with nature, and repression and frustration with civilization, bespeaks the endurance of *Civilization and Its Discontents'* representation of nature/culture conflict. The tensions within Freud's developmental schema, however, illuminate the contradictions that surface in McCandless's wilderness logic.

Freud argued that the individual sacrifices the joys of infantile narcissism (a subjective sense of oneness with the world) for the realities of ego development (a bounded sense of self). Humankind, he writes, strives above all to be happy, a project that pursues both a positive and negative aim: to experience strong feelings of pleasure and to eliminate threatening feelings of pain. The "pleasure principle" of infancy dictates that the individual pursue those feelings of pleasure to mitigate discomfort, and this project, for Freud, "dominates the operation of the mental apparatus from the start," though "its program is at loggerheads with the whole world." This impasse arises because to pursue "unrestricted satisfaction" headfirst, despite being "the most enticing method of conducting one's life," would be to self-destructively place "enjoyment before caution." The ego forms partially as a defense to separate the self from anything that might be a source of pain. The origins of suffering number three: from within the body, from the external world, and from harms caused by other people. To curtail such pain, one comes to "differentiate between what is internal – what belongs to the ego – and what is external – what emanates from the outer world." The advent of such discrimination marks the emergence of the "reality principle." As the realities of need, and of others' needs, continue to violate omnipotent perceptions, the individual enters into social contract and accepts civilization to curb the excesses of pleasure.[23]

Just as Freud aligns the pre-civilizational with the gratifications of an expansive non-ego and the civilizational with the sacrifice of a limited ego, the Supertramp aligns ego fluidity with "nature" and separates these terms from "civilization." In the Freudian narrative, the abdication of the former to the latter catalyzes an abiding tension between individual and society that tears the individual between his or her own desires and the pressures of civilization. The price of civilization is diminishment, the sacrifice of a "feeling of happiness derived from the satisfaction of a wild instinctual impulse untamed by the ego ... incomparably more intense than that derived from sating an instinct that has been tamed."[24] This introduction of boundaries polices a line not only between self (ego) and other, but also between nature and civilization. The state of nature at the heart of this

Into the Wild's *Freudian Narrative* 187

developmental saga privileges an overflowing of pleasure and gratification unseen on the stage of civilization, which diminishes that pleasure. Krakauer represents McCandless's philosophy in almost identical terms. For the Supertramp, however, the dispersed pleasures of ecological interconnection are far more real than any reality principle of civilization, which comprises artifice, wealth, and waste. He strives for personal fulfillment and gratification premised, paradoxically, on the diminishment of his personality's boundaries. Krakauer frames this dissolution in terms of identification with the Denali ecosystem as a whole.

Freud himself briefly entertained the notion that one might entirely reject human company to combat the experience of pain. "Against the suffering which may come upon one from human relationships the readiest safeguard is voluntary isolation," he writes. "Against the dreaded external world one can only defend oneself by some kind of turning away from it, if one intends to solve the task by oneself."[25] McCandless does indeed intend to solve the task by himself, taking great pains to fabricate a narrative according to which his environment is devoid of all human influence. He "didn't want to see a single person, no airplanes, no sign of civilization. He wanted to prove to himself that he could make it on his own, without anybody else's help" (159). The contradiction at the heart of McCandless's narrative lies in his self-proclaimed identity as the ultimate loner (the Supertramp), which he nonetheless steadily forges in the brief yet intense relationships he experiences with acquaintances across the country and the more enduring ones he maintains with his literary heroes.

For McCandless, such social attachments somehow exist separately from "reality." Freud, on the other hand, seems to collapse "human relationships" and "external world" into one another. The source of harm directed against the self stems from an environment defined by its human character. The painful "external world" includes the human as well as the nonhuman. Freud nonetheless endorses fraternization. There exists "another and better path" than turning away from one's neighbors: "that of becoming a member of the human community, and ... going over to the attack against nature and subjecting her to the human will."[26] One might say that Freud, like McCandless, weds civilization to ecological degradation (even if the idea of ecological degradation did not exist as such in 1930). Human alteration of environment is for Freud a relatively positive development (nature is, after all, one of the three sources of pain against which the ego defines itself). At the same time, he articulates the state of nature that predates the realty principle as a realm of pleasure. Both "nature" and "civilization," divided along the blurry line between pleasure and reality principles, are by Freud's logic ambivalent

188 The Death of the Supertramp

concepts that invoke both pleasure and pain, even if civilization yields the greater return on repressive investment. McCandless, on the other hand, would prefer to "wallow in unfiltered experience" – to dispense with the human element altogether by reclaiming his pre-civilizational narcissism. For Freud civilization operates like a vaccine – a small harm meant to forestall greater pain – but for McCandless a civilization defined by repression is itself the chief harm plaguing the individual.

The Supertramp intends his own asceticism – a turning-away from civilization's reality principle – to counteract the asceticism that Freud (and his Left Freudian interlocutors) suggested constitutes civilization in the first place – a turning-away from nature's pleasure principle. Self-denial forms the cornerstone of ethics and social cohesion, the very possibility of communal life and therefore cultural formations in general. In Freud's developmental narrative, the development of the ego is nothing if not an ascetic renunciation of pleasure, one that generates in social life a certain "disquiet, an ambivalent yearning for the precultural, postcultural, anti-cultural, or extracultural."[27] Despite the fact that McCandless "entertained no illusions that he was trekking into a land of milk and honey," Krakauer represents his sojourn in terms of a primary, pervasive pleasure. The Supertramp, he writes, "seems to have been driven by a variety of lust that supplanted sexual desire," which "paled beside the prospect of rough congress with nature, with the cosmos itself" (66). On the one hand, Krakauer's rhetoric echoes Abbey's tired yet no less troubling insinuation in *Desert Solitaire* that male wanderers screw their way into sensations of ecological dispersal. On the other (and this is a point *Wild Abandon*'s conclusion will consider at more length), this kind of metaphorical copu-lation also evokes the sort of intimacy imagined by the narrator of *Surfacing*, inclusive of decay as well as of sex itself.

Krakauer represents the Supertramp's desire as pre-sexual, spread out, inclusive of the polymorphous pleasures retroactively experienced by the ego-less infant of Freud's theory. The seeming contradiction between McCandless's bitter isolation and his irrepressible satisfaction neatly exem-plifies the ambivalence central to ascetic self-renunciation, inclusive of "any act of self-denial undertaken as a strategy of empowerment or gratification."[28] If the smooth operation of human culture relies on a renunciation of the full pleasure available to a person, how does the exercise of asceticism also signify the pursuit of pleasure? *Into the Wild* unifies the Supertramp's renunciation – his turning-away from civilization – with the very pleasure that social and ethical asceticism represses. For a wilderness ascetic such as McCandless, the civilizing relinquishment of pleasure circles

Into the Wild's *Freudian Narrative*   189

around on itself and reverses its terms. He intends his brand of disavowal to separate him from civilization rather than initiate him into it, to return him to a sphere of "natural" and ego-indistinct pleasure. The Supertramp does not quit civilization to be alone, but to be in intimate contact with *everything*.

McCandless's investment in this expansive account of identity – the deep ecologist's singular "Self" – leads him to generalize nature as a static landscape and ignore the actual, dynamic conditions of the biosphere. During a trip to the Gulf of California, he subsists on nothing more than five pounds of rice and the little marine life he is able to fish, "an experience that would later convince him he could survive on similarly meager rations in the Alaska bush" (36). McCandless's tendency is to flatten nature into a homogeneous landscape with which he holistically identifies. By contrast, Krakauer's own focus on human interactions with ecologically diverse locales demonstrates his more nuanced understanding of regional variation and the roles played by narrative and politics in our comprehension of and impact on environment. His attention also enables him to clarify that McCandless's camp "scarcely qualifies as wilderness by Alaska standards" (165). The George Parks Highway, Denali's National Park Service access road, and a handful of then-unoccupied cabins closely triangulated the patch of forest surrounding the famous Fairbanks bus, "rusting incongruously in the fireweed beside the Stampede Trail" (10). McCandless's decision to squat in an abandoned vehicle – something less wild, perhaps, than the forest itself – drives home his sheer dedication to a fantasy of merger premised on the abandonment of civilization. "*Two Years He Walks The Earth . . . . No Longer To Be Poisoned By The Civilization He Flees*," reads an inscription at the site (163). One of the greatest ironies of McCandless's persistent denial of human narratives and technologies is his decision to carve this declaration of freedom into the bus rather than something more stereotypically "natural," like a tree. One assumes that he views the bus much as he does himself: as having departed civilization.

Despite Krakauer's cognizance of McCandless's hypocrisies, what seems important even to the author is that McCandless nonetheless *perceives* a gulf between human and nonhuman spheres. His maintenance of pure, untouched wilderness facilitates his conviction that he has accessed a natural, ecological "Self" otherwise quelled by a limited social self. Moments of rupture in the Supertramp's subjective continuity with the natural world accordingly provoke extreme ambivalence toward the ecosystems with which he identifies. His reaction to a dust storm that interrupts his merger with the Gulf of California, for example, shatters his fantasy. In his journal he writes, "*he screams and beats canoe with oar. The oar breaks. Alex has one spare oar. He calms himself. If loses second oar is dead. . . . This incident led Alexander to decide to abandon canoe and return north"* (36). This passage especially foregrounds a constant fluctuation between fantasied omnipotence and loss of control that characterizes the Supertramp's expansive personal narrative, as well as the fact that the journals often position McCandless himself as the audience for his own dissolution. McCandless's powerlessness over weather conditions momentarily shatters his assumption that identification with the Gulf ecosystem somehow mitigates the environment's indifference toward his survival. The storm has barely passed, however, before he simply shifts his perspective by following a new path that cannot be thwarted by maritime squalls, thereby reconstructing and maintaining his fragile identification.

McCandless *believes* his patch of wilderness to be isolated from repressive civilization, a willful bifurcation that structures his claim to ecological authenticity. As with most of his assumptions, however, the details of the Supertramp's experience put the lie to his presumed instinctual ability to comfortably thrive in his surroundings simultaneously *as* the ecosystem yet also as a discrete body. McCandless required a field guide to identify edible plants. Even so, his character in *Into the Wild* dies precisely because he misidentifies them. Previously, he scrawled in his terse journal that he "Must Revamp My Soul + Regain Deliberate Consciousness" after mishandling the preservation of a moose carcass.[29] His turmoil, occasioned by the corpse's occupation by flies and maggots, seems somewhat misplaced. The meat is only wasted on him, not the ecosystem at large. His desperation at this moment resonates with Treadwell's deep sadness over a slain fox in *Grizzly Man*. Herzog suggests that Treadwell "seemed to ignore the fact that in nature there are predators." His apparent ignorance, however, did not stifle his bush pilot's impression that the man "would have been happy if nobody had found [his] remains." Assuming that this perspective was in fact Treadwell's own, Herzog's comment that there exists in wilderness "no kinship . . . only the overwhelming indifference of nature" seems to miss the point.[30] Such "overwhelming indifference" is precisely the kind of kinship Treadwell and McCandless demand (intentionally or otherwise) when they presume to identify *tout court* with a dynamic ecosystem that will inevitably recycle their corporeal matter after death.

Fatal Dissolutions

In 1982, Edward Abbey wrote that he hoped his "own last vision" would not be the artifice of a manmade hospital but "the spectacle of distant

Fatal Dissolutions 191

canyon walls, the profile of a mesa against the sky, the gleam of a river far below. These are the things I want to take with me in my dying moments, if I too must die, and taking them with and within me . . . become a part of them."[31] Two of Treadwell's friends express a similar sentiment at the end of *Grizzly Man*. As they scatter his ashes, they observe that Treadwell "finally figured a way out to live here forever." Abbey's imagination of expansion in death, as well as the words of Treadwell's companions, recalls *Surfacing*'s narrator's conclusion that death alone comprises a total foreclosure of self-identity, via the body's material dissemination. McCandless's own photo captions insist that he shares this sensibility – that "Alex understands the circle of life" – and the text of *Into the Wild* suggests that McCandless might even expect that final dissolution.[32] At the time of his death the Supertramp succumbs more or less gracefully to whatever killed him. "He must have been very brave and very strong, at the end, not to do himself in," observes his mother (202). By dying "naturally," by unidentified herbaceous poison rather than rifle, McCandless achieves dispersal without rewriting his narrative. His acceptance of death at the hands of forces outside his control reads as a conscious choice to holistically integrate with the ecosystem in the only comprehensive way possible: by decomposing. To commit suicide would be to deny this recognition. That the Supertramp decides not to, Krakauer suggests, signals the unexpected fulfillment of his goal.

Krakauer's bittersweet reflection on this morbid success is despondently favorable. He approaches McCandless's fate with a great degree of reverence – even fascination – throughout the narrative. He remains convinced that at the end of his life McCandless felt much as he himself did on the brink of death at Devils Thumb. "The hint of what was concealed in those shadows terrified me, but I caught sight of something in the glimpse, some forbidden and elemental riddle," Krakauer writes. "In my case – and, I believe, in the case of Chris McCandless – that was a very different thing from wanting to die" (156). One must ask, however, what it was about the death of the Supertramp that preempted what Krakauer would describe only one year later, following a brush with mortality on Mount Everest, as the "downward spiral into the nightmarish territory of the mad" he experienced upon witnessing death firsthand. Krakauer professes a certain admiration for the Supertramp and his "tragedy" that seems incommensurate with the Himalayan "calamity" he describes in *Into Thin Air* (1997), "so far beyond anything I'd ever imagined that my brain simply shorted out," which occurred within months of *Into the Wild*'s publication.[33] The disparity seems related to intention. McCandless's journals and Krakauer's hesitation on Devils Thumb gesture toward the two figures' shared desire not for death but for life in total subjective cohesion with the wild around them – two objectives that in the end might be relatively indistinguishable.

Into the Wild's narrative fascination with McCandless's demise in Alaska communicates Krakauer's interest in the total elimination of ambivalence between self and ecology that accompanies self-extinction. Prior to the Everest disaster he would chronicle one year later, however, Krakauer had never "seen death at close range." We must assume that he includes the McCandless episode when he writes that, before 1996, "Mortality had remained a conveniently hypothetical concept, an idea to ponder in the abstract."[34] That abstraction is precisely what is at issue for McCandless as well as for Krakauer. The Supertramp figure comes to believe he can escape harm and find gratification in a pre-civilizational wilderness scene precisely because he categorically abstracts nature from civilization, ecology from the self.

The identity the Supertramp locates in wilderness takes for its constitution little more than the first law of thermodynamics. It conceptually crystallizes as a static category the constant transmutation of matter and energy. One year before McCandless vacated his apartment at Emory, Naess also articulated identity in terms of a dynamic "relational field" that encapsulates "the totality of our interrelated experience." As if paving a path for new materialists of the next generation, Naess suggests that one best intuits "material things," including people, as "junctions," not as discrete entities. "The same things appear differently to us, with dissimilar qualities at various times, but they are nonetheless the same things."[35] More zealously than a contemporary new materialist, however, Naess means to offer in part an argument for what constitutes authentic subjectivity, and his totalizing rhetoric consistently advances matter itself as his answer. Another, more fanciful way of phrasing such a perspective would be to say that if one has buried their deceased cat in the backyard, the wildflowers that grow over its grave are the same as the cat. Any transmission of matter or energy renders all organisms more or less identical over time. This interpretation is only true if one takes units of energy as the sole value by which to classify matter. One might easily consider someone identical to their cat if one understood them not as human and cat but as two collections of particles that just happened to organize in different ways.

Into the Wild's engagement with Freud's final developmental schema foregrounds the role played by psychoanalytic narratives in such deep-ecological work, as well as in the IPE as a broad rhetorical position. An "identification with all life" proceeds naturally as "preconscious memory"

Fatal Dissolutions 193

improves, one of Naess's collaborators wrote in 1988, and accrues until we realize "that the distinction between 'life' and 'lifeless' is a human construct. Every atom in the body existed before organic life emerged 4000 million years ago." In the same volume, the Gaia spiritualist Joanna Macy implores us to "shift free from identifying solely with your latest human form," if only because "it may well be, if things continue the way they are going, that we will all return for a spell to non-organic life. We'd be radioactive for quite a while, but we are built to endure."[36]

Macy's thought experiment makes uncomfortably explicit what the IPE's logic ultimately implies. If proper environmentalism entails reducing individuals to their material substrates, then what stake does one have in whether one lives or dies – or, for that matter, if human activity substantially alters the biosphere and its climate? The IPE insists on its ideological purity – its authenticity – but absent a framework of normative values its rhetoric suggests that we have no good reason to mitigate individual death or even largescale catastrophe if we understand these irruptions as inevitable and, in the long run, minimal alterations to a single body. As Val Plumwood noted in 1993, it is not quite clear how "dissolving self boundaries is supposed to provide the basis for an environmental ethic. The analysis of humans as metaphysically unified with the cosmic whole will be equally true whatever relation humans stand in with nature."[37] Humans are intimately bound up with ecological systems regardless of the narratives we tell about them or, for that matter, identity. To take seriously a sense of dissolution of selfhood into the ecosystem so that the system itself becomes one's identity seems only to hasten the arrival of the mortal moment at which one does, physically and completely, disperse. Macy and her colleague John Seed, however, boldly invite their readers to "think to your next death. Will your flesh and bones back into the cycle. Surrender. Love the plump worms you will become."[38] Regardless of the writers' intention, this particular rhetoric of dissolution implies that the death of an individual, species, or even entire ecosystem does not matter as long as its remnants fertilize others. Such a position represents an extreme limit to environmental politics, as well as the logical consummation of the IPE's narrative. *Civilization and Its Discontents* gives way to *Beyond the Pleasure Principle*: the oceanic feeling's narcissistic urge toward unity lapses into the death drive's attempted termination of social tension. An appeal to psychic prehistory as an expression of ecological holism, even over geological time, facilitates a roundabout nihilism by suggesting that our essential oneness with the system discounts the meaningfulness of actions – destructive or

194 The Death of the Supertramp

generative – on the part of individuals, cultures or societies, even the entire species.

Krakauer's interest in McCandless's death suggests that the writer is concerned more with considering these very limits than with McCandless's level of preparation. He seems most fascinated, that is, by the possibility that casualty signifies a counterintuitive type of success. He commends the Supertramp for consummating his dissolution. At the same time, it would be a mistake to assume that Krakauer views this kind of accomplishment favorably. Up to his time of death, McCandless does not appear to recognize the required annihilation at the heart of his project. Krakauer "was stirred by the dark mystery of mortality" when he climbed Devils Thumb, but he "wasn't suicidal" (155–6). Neither, he thinks, was McCandless when he trekked into a wilderness of his own making. The seriousness with which he observed the IPE narrative, however, made that outcome all but inevitable. *Into the Wild*'s progression insinuates that an unwavering belief in and commitment to self-dissolution in a wilderness divorced from civilization, taken to its physical extreme, can only culminate in total biological dissolution – death.

By contrast, Krakauer places melancholy faith in ambivalence itself, a self-conscious maintenance of tension between selfhood and ecology. As he questions McCandless's motivations throughout the text he also cultivates, by way of his own anecdotes, an understanding that one's ego does not comfortably mesh with environment as a flawless, unified "Self." On Devils Thumb the young Krakauer reconsiders the dissolutive logic at the heart of his own wilderness narrative. He initially assumes that (a) the mountain, as wilderness, exists independently of human influence; (b) its separation from civilization renders it the realm of "natural" selfhood; and (c) because of this last point, nothing in the wilderness could possibly upset his subjective merger with his environment. Experience, of course, teaches differently, and rattles young Krakauer's belief that he might dissolve comfortably and physically into unity with the mountain landscape without dying. The author's fascination with McCandless's death wavers precisely because of this experience, during which he recognizes his subordination to the ecosystem but also realizes he wants to survive. The incident's significance lies in Krakauer's newfound investment in his self-identity's altered recoherence.

One must therefore read *Into the Wild* as a text skeptical of "recondite ecological theory," the IPE narrative the Supertramp takes quite seriously, for two reasons. First, Krakauer *does* frame McCandless's dissolution in terms of an ongoing cultural narrative, not as an explosion of pure authenticity. Second, he implicitly concludes that to identify with the entire ecosystem is to lose any perspective from which to have a stake in how an environment changes, including changes to the status of one's own continued existence. From a political perspective, then, to make this sort of identification is to foreclose the possibility of an environmentalist ethic that defines which sorts of changes are desirable and which are not. One sacrifices community for indistinguishability. One wonders what such a perspective contributes to a sustainable environmentalism that takes continued human existence as one of its aims. To earnestly believe that wilderness frees oneself of socially mediated identity is to sentence oneself to death.

The Neoliberal Wilderness

This chapter, which has joined the previous one in bringing *Wild Abandon*'s history of the IPE to the present, ends on a speculative note, with the proposal of a tentative concept intended to capture what we mean when we talk about wilderness today. Despite the cautionary tale furnished by the Supertramp's death, *Into the Wild* has enjoyed remarkable staying power precisely for his ideas. The Facebook group "Into The Wild changed my life" boasts nearly seven thousand members (as of 2019). The name seems to reference Penn's film adaptation rather than Krakauer's narrative. Many of its active members seem oblivious to the book's existence, as well as to its more nuanced and critical treatment of the Supertramp figure. The immense popularity of *Into the Wild*'s self-styled spiritual successors, especially Cheryl Strayed's 2012 memoir *Wild: From Lost to Found on the Pacific Crest Trail*, demonstrates the endurance of the wilderness idea in the American cultural imaginary, despite the steady emergence of more complex ecological accounts of the natural world over the past sixty years. Perhaps more arrestingly, these examples illustrate the persistent *commercial* appeal of wilderness.

My contention over the past several chapters has been that the IPE not only makes of ecology a wilderness, but also modifies wilderness such that it signifies not only nonhuman spaces but also a primary psychic condition. The IPE's discursive elasticity has propelled deep ecology's trademark alignment of wilderness with authentic identity to the forefront of popular and casual representations of the natural world. This convergence has increasingly come to coexist rather happily with commercial endeavors of the sort once derided by deep ecologists themselves. For example, the saleable aspects of the Canadian lake country featured in *Surfacing* inform the minor character Bill Malmstrom's interest in capitalizing on its "rural charm." About halfway through the novel, he approaches the narrator at her cabin with a development proposition, a plan for "a kind of retreat lodge, where the members could meditate and observe . . . the beauties of nature." The narrator's discovery of her father's corpse quickly overshadows this two-page exchange, but the moment merits attention. Malmstrom "had trimmed gray hair and an executive moustache like the shirt ads, the vodka ads; his clothes were woodsy, semi-worn, verging on the authentic."[39] This final observation, as well as the slightly snide tone in which Atwood captures it, catches the eye. What does it mean to "verge" on the authentic? For that matter, what is it about Malmstrom's sartorial presentation that qualifies?

One might ask the same question of Brandon Burk, a public Instagram user who in August 2016 shared a photograph to his account featuring a young, full-bearded man clad in burnt orange flannel by Pendleton Woolen Mills and a designer backpack by Red Clouds Collective.[40] Burk frames the man against the landscape of the Albion Basin south of Salt Lake City, Utah. Amid a flood of hashtags (codes that categorize searchable online content) listed beneath the image, one finds advertisements for the young man's sported brands and textiles (#mypendleton, #rawdenim, and my personal favorite, #flannel) interspersed with more picaresque slogans such as #keepitwild, #lifeofadventure, #mylifeoutdoors, and, most notably, #liveauthentic. The image pointedly juxtaposes designer goods, an appeal to authenticity, and a remote wilderness locale in an effort to rhetorically associate products with a putatively natural lifestyle. As of 2019, users have deployed the #liveauthentic handle to tag roughly 30 million posts. About a quarter million more appear misplaced by a variation or spelling error, such as #liveauthentically or #liveauthentice. The hashtag originated with *FOLK Lifestyle*, a Kentucky-based magazine and online store whose site features portfolios of landscape photography, an "Authentic Lives" profile series, and a page where visitors can "Shop Authentic."[41] Appeals to a wilderness aesthetic are mainstays of American advertising. This particular campaign is notable, however, for its explicit appeal to authentic *identity*, as well as its tendency to align this term with wilderness imagery. In these rustically arranged scenes dwells the authentic human: a young, typically white, able-bodied individual who buys clothing, rucksacks, and accessories as genuine as he or she is. The message is clear. In order to enjoy a legitimate relationship with the natural world, one simply *must* purchase these items.

The Neoliberal Wilderness 197

More interesting still is the #liveauthentic tag's companion, #livenaked, which features a titillating cascade of bare backsides foregrounded by hot springs, fields of wheat, and, in at least two instances, horses. These images, which more convincingly attempt to inspire lifestyle than sales, rather comically foreground at least one contradiction at the heart of this campaign. They recall the narrator of *Surfacing*, whose authentic human is pure animal, shuffling naked about the forest for food and shelter, burning its clothes. It is hard to imagine such a figure placing value in artisanal coffee or a designer tarpaulin for her next foray into the woods. The #livenaked crowd ironically supplies a literal image to what McCandless's experience forcefully illustrates. The authentically ecological individual is a piece of meat. The chief contradiction among those who would claim to live the authentic life is that the individual who truly considers his or her identity holistically ecological would be unlikely to broadcast that conviction to others – a rhetorical paradox I referred to previously in this chapter as the ascetic superhero's boast. They would be foraging for food or rotting on the forest floor as food themselves. The ease of the hashtag's use obscures the complex discursive history behind authenticity, wilderness, and ecology's perceived relationship, as well as the environmentalist nihilism this rhetorical alignment begets.

The #liveauthentic wilderness aesthetic turns on a remarkably contradictory representation of selfhood. On the one hand, these images appeal to an authentic wilderness as the natural and real condition of human experience, as opposed to the assumedly inauthentic realm of culture. On the other, authenticity appears to chiefly inhere not in that extra-civilizational context, but in the accessories with which these individuals enhance their personal brands – items that are, of course, produced by and within the very culture that first perspective disavows. #liveauthentic images feature figures who claim an identity defined simultaneously by a presumed natural essence and by its construction according to the performance of rustic tropes aided by consumer products. This second, performative understanding of self resembles nothing if not the consumerist inauthenticity so vehemently rejected among the New Left. At the same time, the #liveauthentic emphasis on artisanship preserves the sort of "green consumerism" advocated by countercultural publications like the *Whole Earth Catalog*. The notion that wilderness circumscribes a venue for natural human subjectivity informs a DIY attitude regarding business and, to a lesser extent, environmentalism itself, with the latter emerging as a casualty to the former. One might describe this trend as a commercialization of disappearance that shuffles environmentalism into not only the realm of lifestyle choice but also the wilderness itself, where it remains hidden. After the death of the Supertramp, the IPE undergoes its almost inevitable "repressive desublimation" – the absorption into the marketplace that Marcuse observed taking place among other countercultural projects. McCandless's ethos itself goes up for sale.

To the extent that wilderness often constitutes a consumer product, the wilderness one consumes in the twenty-first century is no longer a recreational space but an identity. It is a *neoliberal wilderness*, a putatively universal and egalitarian stance that premises environmental consciousness on "individual psychic act[s] rather than a political practice, yielding a theory which emphasizes personal transformation and ignores social structure," as Plumwood once described deep ecology.[42] As previous chapters have suggested, it is also typically a *white* representation of environment – one that neglects the fact that environment, for people of color especially, exists in relation to complex socioeconomic problems of the sort that #liveauthentic folks might pass by as being merely artificial in comparison to wilderness. What came to pass for many countercultural projects has indeed come to pass for the IPE. Its psychoanalytic narrative facilitated synthesis with New-Age projects of psychotherapeutic betterment. The neoliberal wilderness is a self-help environmentalism. Are you authentically ecological enough? That is, do you have what it takes to disappear? The neoliberal wilderness institutionalizes the Supertramp's paradoxically self-effacing self-aggrandizement, in the process subsuming or otherwise ignoring the particular environmental concerns facing a variety of communities. Self-fashioning becomes synonymous with self-erasure, as well as the erasure of others. Of course, the more would-be environmentalists disappear, the fewer we actually have. The death of the Supertramp is the death of meaningful environmentalism occasioned by the identity politics of ecology.

CONCLUSION

Ecological Consistency

It wasn't that the world was "made up," that there weren't cells, but that the descriptive term "cells" is a name for an historical kind of interaction, not a name for a thing in and of itself. . . . I live materially-semiotically as an organism, and that's an historical kind of identity.
Donna Haraway, *How Like a Leaf*

Environmentalist literary and cultural criticism today seems caught between two revisionary impulses. On the one hand, critics working in the environmental humanities, like their colleagues in other fields, have responded to the vigorous rally issued by scholars such as Rita Felski, Sharon Marcus, and Stephen Best to consider alternative modes of reading that emphasize "making rather than unmaking."[1] The movement toward "post-critique" issues from a long-incubating distrust of literary historicism, of "paranoid" or "suspicious" reading practices that seek to unearth ideological depths lurking within texts, waiting for discovery to retroactively illuminate historical contexts. On the other hand, environmentalist critics especially have participated in the ongoing "material turn" in the humanities and social sciences. "Material ecocriticism" – new-materialist, vitalist, queer, and phenomenological approaches to literary and cultural studies – proceeds from Serenella Iovino and Serpil Oppermann's suggestion, in an introduction to these emergent reading practices, that "the world's material phenomena are knots in a vast network of agencies, which can be 'read' and interpreted as forming narratives, stories."[2] These post-critical and new-materialist currents in contemporary literary scholarship do not exist in opposition, though critics rarely, if ever, place them in conversation. Together, however, they suggest a great deal about how we read literature and environment now, and how environmentalist identity politics has impacted those practices.

My intention throughout *Wild Abandon* has been to tell a story about that environmentalist identity politics from its origins in the 1960s to the

200   Conclusion: Ecological Consistency

near present. The preponderant emphasis on authenticity that characterized postwar radicalism, as well as its psychoanalytic wellspring, has all but
dissipated from the American political scene, but the IPE's legacy nonetheless remains relevant today. As Chapter 4 suggested, the conversation
surrounding subjectivity that characterizes the IPE and its interaction with
politics organized around race, gender, and other social vectors is neither
dead nor dormant, but the very foundation for discussion in posthumanist
criticism, which emerges from the exact sort of observations and questions
that animated the IPE to begin with. To study in depth the contemporary
persistence and influence of the IPE would require an entirely new volume,
but focusing on current cultural criticism seems a useful place to pause.
Specifically, I want to contemplate how this conversation continues to split
thinking about ecology between, on the one hand, a wilderness model of
(psychic) nature cloven from (repressive) civilization and, on the other,
ways of treating identity and environment that flesh out, rather than
obscure, the role played by sociocultural formations in our understanding
of those ideas.

That second position is the one that *Wild Abandon*'s major texts have
occupied in dialogue with the IPE over the status of subjectivity. Those
texts do not function merely as "paranoid" revelations of underlying
ideologies gnawing at their cultural moment. *Song of Solomon*, *Woven
Stone*, and *Surfacing* envision tentative yet hopeful futures for identity
and environmental thought, even as they remain suspicious of the cultural
narratives circulating around ecology at the time of their publication.
Milkman eventually recognizes how his community sustains itself on
narratives rather than on a metric of authenticity. The speaker of Simon
Ortiz's poems mobilizes a similar facet of Acoma Pueblo culture to counter
settler myths about Native relationships with the land. *Surfacing*'s narrator,
though she recognizes her passive imbrication in ecological networks, exits
Canadian lake country determined to exercise a measure of agency on
behalf of the region and of herself as a discrete creature with desires of its
own. Jon Krakauer teases out the cultural narratives surrounding the
Supertramp precisely because the figure contrasts a more nuanced understanding of identity as a shifting, changeful thing. Every one of these texts
engages the notion of ecological authenticity. Every one of them also
prolongs the dissolution motif that grounds it, lingering over its tensions
and contradictions, upending the IPE's fixed, even universal conception of
identity. Every one of them ends instead with an affirmation of identity's
creativity, its ability to shift in response to challenges and in support of
shared communities – especially environmental communities, which exist

Conclusion: Ecological Consistency

because they take shape and endure as complex negotiations among cultural practices and the nonhuman world. They exist because those who belong to them sustain them. These texts suggest that to take the notion of ecological authenticity literally is to deny the discernible perspectives that make such contingent formations possible and necessary. They share a structure by which critique of ecological authenticity, as well as other pervasive narratives, is in fact what prompts their visions of contingent, adaptive environmental identities and communities.

These conclusions arise from a series of readings that I believe fit neatly into neither the "paranoid" nor "reparative" structures that Felski, for one, has respectively derided and praised. Such critical goals do not exist in opposition. I have indeed read these texts as unearthing and contesting the logic of the IPE. I have also read them in terms of how they gesture to messier ways of engaging the world that do not rely on an almost nihilistic rhetoric of disappearance. Perhaps it is precisely by "looking behind the text," as Felski writes, "for its hidden causes, determining conditions, and noxious motives" that we might discover "what it unfurls, calls forth, makes possible."[3] In fact, framing the second ambition within the first seems more necessary than ever, given the IPE's persistence. To take seriously the doctrine of ecological authenticity amidst rapid anthropogenic changes to the global climate would be, as Richard Rorty once wrote of politics in general, to "leave the fate of the United States" – or, more to the point, the earth – "to the operation of nonhuman forces," rather than "deciding to be an agent."[4] My point is not that such changes do not in fact stem from human activity, but that to rhetorically identify with the earth's ecological matrix as a whole robs one of any specific perspective from which to contest them, and also lets particularly culpable human actors off the hook. This latter criticism has been made multiple times of posthumanist models such as Jane Bennett's, whose "agency of assemblages" might appear to relocate accountability from the actor to the network as a whole. In the current critical idiom, all things are agents, but the actions of and harms suffered by discrete agents suffer drastic devaluation when entirely subordinated to or naturalistically defined by the networks they help to comprise.

That said, practices of material ecocriticism that draw on such models have also proceeded along simultaneously paranoid and reparative tracks, given such scholarship's attempt to unearth and recoup the buried agency of nonhuman objects and assemblages to begin with. That approach's originators have presented it as a uniquely generative methodology, one that seeks to translate "the way the agentic dimension of matter expresses

202 Conclusion: Ecological Consistency

itself." According to this approach, matter – like "literature and other cultural forms" – itself constitutes a text to be read, with meaning to interpret.[5] As Chapter 4 argued of the new materialisms in general, these contemporary reading practices participate in a long tradition of muddling through the subjectivity of what Peter Matthiessen described in 1978 as "these fleeting assemblies that we think of as our bodies," with an eye turned specifically to questions of representation. As Hanna Meißner puts it, "in our epistemic economy, any attempt to bring the material back in, or to acknowledge the agency of matter, *always is a representation*," even if new representations unsettle conventional wisdom.[6]

What kind of representations does such criticism produce? What kind of representations *of* representation, let alone ecology and identity? These materialist perspectives take their brief from the questions that gave rise to the IPE, but also from feminist and critical race theory. Current methodologies decenter the subject occasionally in ways that maintain the IPE, but they also point to a vocabulary for *re*centering the subject without essentialism. In this vein, I want to conclude by arguing for an environmentalist politics of *consistency*, rather than a politics of authenticity.

Material ecocriticism perpetuates the IPE when it keeps ecology positioned as a matter of repression. This sort of claim should not come as a surprise, given that it's been the basis of *Wild Abandon*'s entire argument. Despite psychoanalysis' gradual departure from mainstream political conversation, the narratives it contributed to midcentury social theory continue to influence writing of a radical persuasion, if only because that tradition remains one of the most important foundations of leftwing cultural criticism. I hope to have demonstrated that its psychoanalytic facets do not necessarily benefit environmental thinking. Nonetheless, they continue to exercise influence. For example, Norman O. Brown's 1959 comment that "the confrontation between psychoanalysis and the philosophy of organism" discloses "an erotic sense of reality" resonates deeply with current writing on ecology's "queer" capacity to "abolish rigid boundaries between and within species."[7] Like ecofeminism, queer ecology is an incredibly diverse subfield, representing some of the most vibrant environmentalist scholarship in cultural criticism. Altogether, it comprises a loose effort to examine, deconstruct, and reconcile the many uses and abuses of the elastic term "nature" and the ways in which the idea has obstructed a productive alliance between environmental studies and queer theory. Such criticism takes an anti-essentialist stance, examining texts that Nicole Seymour describes as "skeptical of identity and ... the natural bases of

Conclusion: Ecological Consistency 203

sexuality, gender, and race."[8] To do this work, however, some writers have drawn on queer theory's own psychoanalytic narratives.

In particular, Leo Bersani's argument that "the sexual shatters" the self has intermittently informed such scholarship. "Thinking ecologically ... requires rethinking subjectivity," write Angela Hume and Samila Rahimtoola in a recent issue of *Interdisciplinary Studies of Literature and Environment*. For these two critics, the alleged "antisocial thesis" in queer theory, a label affixed to writers such as Bersani, Lee Edelman, and Lauren Berlant, furnishes the most promising advancement toward "imagining an alternative to the fantasy of the sovereign subject":

> for these critics, the dissolution of the self during sex becomes the ground for rethinking both sovereignty and relationality in a social, political, and psychic sense . . . . Sex, here, shatters the psychic structures of the self, as well as the social relations that are based on the self's exercise of or abdication to power . . . . the self's encounter with nonsovereignty during sex becomes the site at which one can reconfigure subjectivity to acknowledge our fundamental porosity to and passivity in the world.[9]

Bersani wrote in 1987 that the "performance" of sex as power – that is, as a matter of heterosexual, normative gender roles – is "perhaps a repression of sex as self-abolition." An ecocritical flirtation with these ideas scaffolds ecological concepts over the shape of desire. Social constructions of sex and gender limit desire's fundamentally impersonal play across matter, the excavation of which might demolish the "sacrosanct value of selfhood" that engenders struggles for power, whether among individuals or between humans and environment.[10]

Such speculation on Bersani's legacy fails to account for his psychoanalytic framework. In its commitment to the Oedipal complex, mainstream analysis' "most serious limitation," he writes, is its refusal to "imagin[e] that we can find ourselves *already* in the world – there not as a result of our projections but as a sign of the natural extensibility of all being." The comment more or less reiterates Freud's remark that expansive infantile narcissism exists in "counterpart" to the civilized ego. Freud ridiculed the oceanic feeling, but Bersani built an entire theoretical edifice around it. The developmental myth that the ego replaces "a being we once had but may have lost," he writes, "divert[s] us . . . from our presence *already there*." The "psychological individuality" of the ego "could be thought of as merely the envelope of the more profound . . . part of [our]selves which is our sameness." To shatter the self in sex is to access something repressed by social convention. It is to reverse Freud's developmental narrative – to

204 Conclusion: Ecological Consistency

cast off the reality principle in reclamation of "impersonal narcissism." Even as he rejects the idea of fixed identity, sexual or otherwise, Bersani locates beneath the ego's "envelope" a different, rather unclear, yet suggestively universal essence: "our sameness."[11] He attracted the "antisocial" label for his contention that sex provides access to this condition by demolishing established social formations and identity categories.

Certain queer ecologists idealize this exact narrative. Were one to "self-shatter," one would at least temporarily cast off socially imposed identity structures to uncover the psychic/ecological payload hidden beneath. Ecology corresponds to psychic nature as social construction corresponds to repression – a familiar series of dualisms. Greta Gaard's inaugural argument that "ecological society . . . values sexual diversity and the erotic" rests on an explicit opposition she draws between Eros and rational Western thought.[12] The amorphous character of desire in her account speaks to queer ecologists' tendency to distance their work from sex itself. Timothy Morton barely mentions sexuality in his influential *PMLA* column on the subject, focusing instead on material intimacies. In this vein, queer ecology involves not only "the opening up of environmental understanding to explicitly non-heterosexual forms of relationship," but also "flows of desire that escape classical biology."[13] For Morton, attending to such exchanges reveals that "there is no authentic life-form . . . . We are embodied yet without essence. Organicism is holistic and substantialist, visualizing carbon-based life-forms . . . as the essence of livingness. Queer ecology must go wider, embracing silicon as well as carbon."[14] In one breath, Morton disposes of essentialism yet appeals to an "essence of livingness" – that is, molecular composition. He contests appeals to nature and essence by making a different appeal to nature and essence. The ecosystem's polymorphous perversity undermines the supposedly natural yet actually artificial boundaries of human sexuality.

This expansive vision of desire – what Bersani describes as "a more general phenomenon irreducible to what we ordinarily think of as sex" – is precisely the understanding Krakauer evokes in *Into the Wild* when he writes of the Supertramp's "rough congress . . . with the cosmos itself."[15] Hume and Rahimtoola reference Chris McCandless as one of traditional environmental writing's hallowed "autonomous subjects," poised to colonize an unconquered wilderness. To the contrary, he aims for precisely the sort of self-shattering these critics make central to their theory. Still, as previous chapters have suggested, this goal results in the same totalizing perspective, neglectful of complex matters of race, gender, and so forth, of which these critics accuse him. Self-shattering itself flattens these materially meaningful distinctions. The parallel between these critics and their target demonstrates the extent to which nominally anti-essentialist intellectuals partake of the same narratives that structure mainstream representations of wilderness, effectively reiterating the binaries between nature and culture they seek to overcome. They simply posit a new conception of "nature" or "essence" to replace the old ones. Queer ecology's tentative gestures to Bersani risk misinterpreting him and thereby reifying the IPE's narrative, largely because these references nod specifically to his idea that one might "shatter" the self without accounting for its psychoanalytic logic. In fact, Bersani himself abandoned the idea, in part for these very reasons. Merely reversing Freud's developmental narrative does not change it, but rather upholds its "political order and its conservative commitments" – namely, the oppositions it strikes between nature and civilization, as well as all the peoples variously identified with either end of that spectrum along lines of gender, ethnicity, race, or sexuality.[16] In other words, he threw out the idea because he recognized that it functioned as an appeal to authenticity that upended his otherwise anti-essentialist politics.

We need to similarly throw authenticity out of our theories and criticism about subjectivity and ecology, and recognize the places where it still persists despite our best intentions. The agential realism motivating much materialist scholarship has indeed called the entire concept into question, drawing attention to the way in which identities and texts alike arise in the process of "a particular entanglement" among a variety of forces and phenomena – a tactic that characterizes "suspicious" literary historicism as well. In this regard, criticism in general, at its best, "involve[s] reconsidering ideals of 'authentic' representation."[17] The ecological reality described by the IPE is not quite the reality the IPE thinks it is, but instead a creative fabrication. In 1982, Richard Poirier asked readers, "How would you like to disappear?" – a question that rightly draws attention to the important role played by *you* in representations of self-erasure.[18] Ecological authenticity masquerades as an impersonal condition, but dissolution requires an "I" for its articulation. At the same time, because humans "are, of course, a part of nature," as the sociologist Jane Jacobs commented in 1961, our social constructions are also "as natural, being a product of one form of nature, as are the colonies of prairie dogs or the beds of oysters."[19] For that matter, so are toxic waste disposal sites, racially biased urban planning, and anthropogenic climate crisis. Maintaining vast ontological distinctions between one's natural condition and artificial civilization – whether explicit or implicit, intentional or accidental – does not benefit environmentalism. To again borrow Val Plumwood's assessment,

206 Conclusion: Ecological Consistency

ecological interconnection "will be equally true whatever relation humans stand in with nature."[20] Environmentalist politics could not change our biophysical condition even if it tried – but it could help to establish the kind of future we want to secure. That problem is a matter of narrative.

The narrative of ecological authenticity fails not least because the dissolution for which it calls constitutes a "rather facile, even irresponsible celebration of 'self-defeat,'" as Bersani writes of self-shattering.[21] When one throws out the subject, one throws out the situated positions that make political action intelligible and necessary. This problem is precisely the one around which recent new-materialist deliberation circles. The IPE's persistence is really a testament to the fact that ecologically informed scholarship has yet to develop a cogent and dependable vocabulary for expressing the subject's coherence that does not rely on totalizing statements about nature, essence, or authenticity – one that accounts for difference and network but still leaves room for a solidity that makes self-identity and political organization possible. It would be unfair, though, to describe this problem as a failure on the part of environmentalist writers. It is, rather, a pervasive challenge inherent to the concept of ecology altogether – the one that gave rise to the IPE to begin with, and the one that contemporary materialist scholars largely write to solve.

What we need is a narrative of subjective *consistency* rather than authenticity. I choose this word for a reason: the American pragmatist philosopher Charles Sanders Peirce used it to describe identity – how it congeals in "what [one] does and thinks" and, I would add, what is done to and thought about one. Peirce's own thinking about what we today call "agent ontologies" required that he conceptualize subjectivity in a way that did not rest on naturalistic assumptions.[22] (It has also, not incidentally, informed some new-materialist writing today.) Identities are contested and negotiated terrain, subject to both biophysical and sociocultural forces, often born of prescriptive hardship – the racist and gendered narratives that have dominated the natural and human sciences of the past several centuries, for example – but also foundational to the communities through which people understand themselves, articulate their relationships with the world around them, and advocate for futures they need and desire. We recognize identities *as* identities not because they are intrinsic to people, but because people maintain certain aspects of those identities over time, for a variety of reasons, even as they construct, leave behind, or otherwise alter different aspects. Certainly, the experiences that contribute to those changes are rooted in real, material conditions, but narratives change over time as conditions do. Identity narratives are no different.

Conclusion: Ecological Consistency 207

A narrative of ecological consistency is precisely what emerges in *Wild Abandon*'s primary texts, in conversation with the more prescriptive ecological authenticity of the IPE. These works do acknowledge the foundational role played by material conditions of ecological interconnection in constituting and unsettling subjectivity. At the same time, not one of their authors – neither Edward Abbey nor Peter Matthiessen, Simon Ortiz nor Toni Morrison, Margaret Atwood nor Jon Krakauer – seems particularly satisfied with the notion that grounding a sense of identity entirely in the ecosystem might be politically useful. Feminists and scholars of color have long challenged the radical fantasy of "an imagined organic body to integrate our resistance." Donna Haraway penned her foundational "Cyborg Manifesto" (1985) to counter that very perspective, as well as to reconceptualize identity as a fluid phenomenon that "skips the step of original unity, of identification with nature in the Western sense."[23] All the same, a solid sense of identity *matters*. After all, the environmental justice movement mobilized around the material concerns of a variety of identity positions asymmetrically impacted by ecological harm – a "unity without uniformity" based on "agonistic respect . . . a key recognition of the other as a like, but separate, being."[24] The stakeholders in question emerge through a certain regularity in their experiences of environment. That consistency in turn mobilizes actors to get stuff done. Distinctions among identities – as well as matter in general – might be historically contingent, but their contrivance does not render them immaterial. "The distinctions through which they can be treated as coherent objects" are *pragmatic* boundaries, "preserving . . . operational autonomy by selecting which aspects of the environment matter." The figures of *Wild Abandon*'s texts likewise do not take universal material conditions to be identity's defining limit. They express an "affinity, not identity" with their surroundings along a variety of sociopolitical boundaries that make matter meaningful.[25] Those boundaries, though, are also *normative* constructions. They and our priorities can and often should change.

I began *Wild Abandon* by drawing a distinction between dissolution's political and literary uses based on how they *fortify* or *test* the concept of identity, respectively. To destroy boundaries is always to create new ones. The question is: *Which boundaries do we want?* Which are necessary and useful for maintaining increasingly uncertain human and nonhuman survival in an increasingly precarious world? Such questions are a matter of narrative, not essence. What *Wild Abandon*'s readings gesture toward is a simultaneously materialist and pragmatist account of boundaries that are shifting and changeful yet situated and meaningful. Those boundaries are most meaningful when they're consistent, not authentic: when they don't fix identity in place, but they also honestly and accurately reflect the environmental and sociopolitical experiences that arrange matter into the figurations by which we recognize and understand it. Ortiz, Morrison, and Atwood especially suggest that the strength of identity and community derives from taking charge of those boundaries. That process might indeed involve an imaginative dissolution, but one that comes full-circle, back to the self that articulates it. The tension between selfhood and ecology that these texts foreground might be the very basis for environmental action to begin with. That tension draws attention to and generates an awareness and comprehension of a shared ecological condition that nonetheless does not undermine the standpoints necessary to act politically. The question is not how to return to some natural state of affairs, but how to negotiate activity in such a way that sustains human life, as well as the lives of other creatures.

As its own identity narrative, though, the IPE also changes and adapts. *Wild Abandon* has traced some of the ways that has happened, but the notion of ecological authenticity is not a relic of the environmentalist past. It continues to structure the way people talk about the self and its role in the ecosystem. This book's primary interest has been how trends on the left – specifically, the anti-establishment attitude and commitment to authenticity common to cultural movements of the 1960s and 1970s – shaped the IPE's inverted developmental narrative. Those attitudes, though, are not limited to the radical left. What do we make of right-wing appeals to identity with the landscape of the sort that accompanied, for example, Ammon Bundy's occupation of the Malheur National Wildlife Refuge in 2016? The libertarianism that characterized the New Left and counterculture's use of psychoanalysis itself follows a complex discursive history, having largely shifted across the political aisle over the past fifty years. Bundy sought to remove his militias from the oversight of the liberal establishment, just as many of the IPE's earliest adherents did on the left. To what extent did he also understand this movement as a rebirth backward in psychoanalytic time? Where has this IPE narrative overlapped with or informed right-wing "blood-and-soil" nationalisms, whether in the United States or elsewhere? To what extent do these questions confront the IPE's white and masculine prejudices, driving home the extent to which it might after all become – even if it did not start out as – a reactionary identity politics, poised against more familiar cultural movements organized by women and people of color? How do contemporary movements, especially those that have more recently emerged around matters of

Conclusion: Ecological Consistency 209

(dis)ability and neurodiversity, continue to push back against the logic of ecological authenticity and its emphasis on psychic wholeness? How do continued appeals to such a condition unite voices on the right and the left in perhaps unintentional yet dubious ways? These questions lie beyond the scope of this book, but doubtless this direction is one of the most important in which *Wild Abandon*'s narrative goes next.

My sense is that because authenticity – as the New Left and counterculture understood the term – is not a value limited to a single ideology, the IPE is an ecological narrative with uncommon reach. It characterizes North American wilderness rhetoric in uncounted venues – from sovereign citizen movements to *Vogue* articles touting the psychic benefits of peyote – to the detriment of environmentalism writ large. The IPE narrative pulverizes boundaries, only to fix identity into a single, massive shape that devalues the global multitude of sociopolitical perspectives that have a stake in health, survival, and how environments change over time. Long gone from the political scene, psychoanalysis has nonetheless injected into the cultural imaginary an environmentalist neglect for this variety, as well as a general, often unintentional nihilism regarding the future of the planet and its inhabitants. Wilderness continues to loom large in political and literary culture. What do we learn when we read that narrative today? Nothing about ecology's authenticity, but a lot about what people think about it.

Notes

Introduction: Modern Environmentalism's Identity Politics

1. Stacy Alaimo, *Bodily Natures*, 20.
2. Dana Phillips, *The Truth of Ecology*, ix.
3. Gary Snyder, *The Practice of the Wild*, 92.
4. Greg Garrard, *Ecocriticism*, 66.
5. Paul Shepard, "Whatever Happened to Human Ecology?", 891; Rachel Carson, *Silent Spring*, 8. The phrase "subversive science" graced the title of one of Shepard's books but originated in an article by Paul B. Sears, "Ecology —A Subversive Subject" in *BioScience*, vol. 14, no, 7 (1964). Despite the term's political charisma, ecology has never been a unitary science. Since the late nineteenth century, the field has weathered numerous conflicts over approach. Despite these disagreements, many environmentalists in scientific and nonscientific circles alike have downplayed ecology's internal disunity to sanctify unity itself as an ethical standard. See Frank Benjamin Golley, *A History of the Ecosystem Concept in Ecology*.
6. Peter C. van Wyck, *Primitives in the Wilderness*, 11.
7. This phrase, an environmentalist commonplace today, finds its popular origins in Barry Commoner's *The Closing Circle*.
8. Snyder, *The Practice of the Wild*, 68.
9. Gabriel Breton, "The Ideology of the Person."
10. R. D. Laing, *The Politics of Experience*, xiv, xv and *The Divided Self*, 22; Doug Rossinow, *The Politics of Authenticity*, 250.
11. See Paul A. Robinson, *The Freudian Left*.
12. Juliet Mitchell, *Psychoanalysis and Feminism*, xviii.
13. Despite the centrality of imperatives to seek the "natural," many radical student groups and publications sought to distance themselves from the environmentalist label, pushing back against the thinly veiled racism that stemmed from a rash of sustainability studies that appeared in the late 1960s and early 1970s, including Commoner's *Closing Circle*, Garrett Hardin's "The

Tragedy of the Commons" (1967), and Paul Ehrlich's *The Population Bomb* (1968).

14. Rossinow, *The Politics of Authenticity*, 4.
15. See Rossinow, *The Politics of Authenticity* and Roderick Frazier Nash, *The Rights of Nature*.
16. Christopher McCandless, *Back to the Wild*, 175.
17. Sigmund Freud, *Civilization and Its Discontents*, 24, 28.
18. Harold F. Searles, *The Nonhuman Environment in Normal Development and in Schizophrenia*, 9, 30, 39.
19. Shepard, *Nature and Madness*, 7, 6; Theodore Roszak, "Where Psyche Meets Gaia," 14; Murray Bookchin, *The Ecology of Freedom*, 7; Rosi Braidotti, *The Posthuman*, 138.
20. Timothy Morton, *The Ecological Thought*, 47.
21. Roszak, *The Voice of the Earth*, 305.
22. Rossinow, *The Politics of Authenticity*, 16.
23. Richard Poirier, *The Renewal of Literature*, 182.
24. Ursula K. Heise, *Sense of Place and Sense of Planet*, 29.
25. Edward Abbey, *Desert Solitaire*, 209; Morton, *Ecology without Nature*, 182.
26. Heise, *Sense of Place and Sense of Planet*, 209, 67.
27. Rita Felski, *The Limits of Critique*, 12. See also Eve Kosofsky Sedgwick, *Epistemology of the Closet*.
28. Ralph Waldo Emerson, "Nature," 24. "Writing off the self" is Poirier's expression.
29. Poirier, *The Renewal of Literature*, 185, 183.
30. It would also be a mistake to confuse the IPE's rhetoric of dissolution with articulations of the sublime, which express temporary aesthetic shocks and experiences of diminishment. The IPE, on the other hand, maintains that one subjectively *equals* the environment that inspires that diminishment.
31. See Kwame Anthony Appiah, "Identity, Authenticity, Survival."
32. Poirier, *The Renewal of Literature*, 222.
33. Donna Haraway, *How Like a Leaf*, 24.
34. van Wyck, *Primitives in the Wilderness*, 10; Appiah, *The Lies That Bind*, 9–10; Morton, *Ecology without Nature*, 195.

1 The Ecological Alternative: Civilization, Selfhood, and Environment in the 1960s

1. See Robert Gottlieb, *Forcing the Spring*, 105–7.
2. Barry Weisberg, "The Politics of Ecology," 154, 155.
3. See James Bishop, *Epitaph for a Desert Anarchist*, 148.
4. Weisberg, "The Politics of Ecology," 158. See also Daniel G. Payne, *Voices in the Wilderness*.

212   *Notes to pages 28–35*

5. See James M. Cahalan, *Edward Abbey*, 124.
6. Wendell Berry, "A Few Words in Favor of Edward Abbey," 8.
7. Gregory Calvert, "In White America," 415, 413; Massimo Teodori, "Historical and Critical Notes," 36. See also Herbert Marcuse, *One-Dimensional Man* and *Eros and Civilization*.
8. David Gessner, *All the Wild that Remains*, 187.
9. Harold Alderman, "Abbey as Anarchist," 139, 143; Wendell Berry, "A Few Words," 5.
10. Students for a Democratic Society (SDS), *Port Huron Statement*, 172; Bob Gottlieb and Marge Piercy, "Movement for a Democratic Society," 407.
11. Peter Quigley, "Heraclitean Fire, Bakhtinian Laughter, and the Limits of Literary Judgment," 8–9.
12. Murray Bookchin, "Between the 30s and the 60s," 249, 250; *Anarchism, Marxism, and the Future of the Left: Interviews and Essays*, 67, 71; and "The Concept of Ecotechnologies and Ecocommunities," 74.
13. Bookchin, *Post-Scarcity Anarchism*, 69, 13.
14. Bookchin, *Interviews and Essays*, 82, 106, and "Between the 30s and the 60s," 250.
15. Bookchin, *The Modern Crisis*, 55.
16. Andrew McLaughlin, "The Heart of Deep Ecology," 90. Social ecology and deep ecology generally differentiate according to a distinction Andrew Light, in "Reconsidering Bookchin and Marcuse as Environmental Materialists," draws between "environmental materialism" on the one hand and "environmental ontology" on the other, for which social, economic, and political issues are the cause or symptom of environmental crisis, respectively.
17. William Hedgepath, "The Alternative," 329–30.
18. Bookchin, *Interviews and Essays*, 127.
19. Ecology Action East, "The Power to Destroy, the Power to Create," 164.
20. Bookchin, "Social Ecology versus Deep Ecology," 13.
21. Bookchin, *Interviews and Essays*, 119; Edward Abbey, *Down the River*, 121. See also Bob Sipchen, "Ecology's Family Feud." Abbey was hardly the Luddite Bookchin made him out to be, and even shared much of Bookchin's perspective on technology. In 1982, he wrote, "Without necessarily rejecting either science or technology, it seems to me that we can keep them as servants not masters." See *Down the River*, 158.
22. See John Clark, "What Is Social Ecology?", 9, 6.
23. Bookchin, *The Ecology of Freedom*, 323.
24. Abbey, *The Journey Home*, 228–9 and *Desert Solitaire*, xiii. *Desert Solitaire* cited in text for the remainder of Chapter 1.
25. Gabriel Breton, "The Ideology of the Person"; Hannes Bergthaller, "Paradox as Bedrock," 118.

Notes to pages 36–50   213

26. Abbey, *Down the River*, 108, 6; SDS, "America and New Era," 180.
27. See Scott Slovic, *Seeking Awareness in Nature Writing*, 137.
28. Abbey, *Down the River*, 7 and *One Life at a Time, Please*, 28; Daniel J. Philippon, *Conserving Words*, 229, 233.
29. Barry Lopez, *Arctic Dreams*, 11; Wallace Stegner, *Where the Bluebird Sings to the Lemonade Springs*, 4.
30. Greg Calvert and Carol Neiman, *A Disrupted History* 37; Tom Hayden, "The Politics of the Movement," 204.
31. SDS, *Port Huron Statement*, 166–7.
32. Sigmund Freud, *Civilization and Its Discontents*, 48, 29.
33. Theodore Roszak, *The Making of a Counter Culture*, 101.
34. Marcuse, *Eros and Civilization*, 166.
35. Marcuse, "Ecology and Revolution," 174.
36. Roszak, "Where Psyche Meets Gaia," 17.
37. Abbey, *Down the River*, 31–2, 3.
38. Glen A. Love, "Revaluing Nature," 233.
39. Paul Shepard, "Whatever Happened to Human Ecology?", 894 and "Ecology and Man—A Viewpoint," 2.
40. David Tagnani, "New Materialism, Ecomysticism, and the Resolution of Paradox in Edward Abbey," 318; Stacy Alaimo, *Bodily Natures*, 89.
41. Bergthaller, "Paradox as Bedrock," 118, 105, 109.
42. James I. McClintock, "Edward Abbey's 'Antidotes to Despair,'" 41.
43. Randall Roorda, *Dramas of Solitude*, xiii, xvi.
44. Abbey, *The Journey Home*, x.
45. Lawrence Buell, *The Environmental Imagination*, 73–4.
46. Lopez, *Crossing Open Ground*, 66.
47. James Hepworth, "The Poetry Center Interview," 44.
48. Stewart Brand, "Introduction."
49. Abbey, *The Journey Home*, 19; Barry Commoner, *The Closing Circle*, 33–48.
50. Hedgepath, "The Alternative," 330.
51. Weisberg, "The Politics of Ecology," 155.
52. Mario Savio, "Sproul Hall Steps."
53. Ecology Action East, "The Power to Destroy," 168.
54. Abbey, *Down the River*, 39.
55. Abbey, *The Journey Home*, 64.
56. Bookchin, *Post-Scarcity Anarchism*, 21, 41 and *The Modern Crisis*, 58.
57. Abbey, *Down the River*, 5.
58. Aldo Leopold, *A Sand County Almanac*, 137.
59. Freud, *Civilization and Its Discontents*, 24, 29.
60. Tom Lynch, *Xerophilia*, 219, 221.
61. Annie Dillard, *Pilgrim at Tinker Creek*, 16, 98.

214 *Notes to pages 51–60*

62. Ibid., 94, 101, 2–3.
63. Abbey, *Postcards from Ed*, 143, 95, 93.
64. Bookchin, "The Concept of Ecotechnologies and Ecocommunities," 74.
65. Tagnani, "New Materialism," 339, 343.
66. Ibid., 331. Tagnani almost certainly overstates the extent to which posthumanists in general believe in such an "expanded sense of identity." See especially Bruno Latour, "Why Gaia Is Not a God of Totality."
67. Norman O. Brown, *Life Against Death*, 307; Roszak, *The Making of a Counter Culture*, 88.
68. Roszak, *Person/Planet*, xxviii, xix.
69. Bookchin, *The Ecology of Freedom*, 315.
70. Bookchin, *The Modern Crisis*, 52; *The Ecology of Freedom*, 4, 8; and *Post-Scarcity Anarchism*, 18, 20.
71. Bookchin, *The Ecology of Freedom*, 330–1.
72. Bookchin, *The Modern Crisis*, 59, 60, 75 and *The Ecology of Freedom*, 24.
73. Bookchin, *The Modern Crisis*, 60–1.
74. Bookchin, *The Ecology of Freedom*, 21. Bookchin does not help his case when he writes that "we are the very 'knowingness' of nature, the embodiment of nature's evolution into intellect, mind and self-reflexivity" (38). The ecofeminist Val Plumwood convincingly reads social ecologists' frequent "incorporation of nature into the human sphere . . . as 'nature rendered self-conscious'" as a kind of self-inflation of a piece with deep ecology's identification impulse. See "The Ecopolitics Debate and the Politics of Nature," 70, as well as more thorough discussion in Chapter 5.
75. Barbara Katz Rothman, *The Tentative Pregnancy*, 114; Karen Newman, *Fetal Positions*, 10, 18, 97; Rosalind Pollack Petchesky, "Fetal Images," 268, 276.
76. Tagnani, "New Materialism," 338.
77. Bookchin, *The Modern Crisis*, 8, 47–8.
78. Philip J. Deloria, *Playing Indian*, 158.
79. Hayden, *Trial*, 94.

2 The Entheogenic Landscape: Psychedelic Primitives, Ecological Indians, and the American Counterculture

1. Edward Abbey, *Desert Solitaire*, 209.
2. Tom Wolfe, *The Electric Kool-Aid Acid Test*, 99, 8.
3. Todd Gitlin, *The Sixties*, 206. See also Martin A. Lee and Bruce Shlain, *Acid Dreams*, 119.
4. See Lee and Shlain, *Acid Dreams*, 132.
5. Arthur Versluis, *American Gurus*, 2, 110; Lee and Shlain, *Acid Dreams*, 64–8.

Notes to pages 62–73 215

6. *Woven Stone* gathers three of Ortiz's previously published collections of poetry: *Going for the Rain* (1976), *A Good Journey* (1977), and *Fight Back: For the Sake of the People, For the Sake of the Land* (1980).

7. Peter Matthiessen, *The Snow Leopard*, 66. Cited in text for the remainder of Chapter 2.

8. *Berkeley Barb*, 13 January 1967.

9. Gitlin, *The Sixties*, 208, xviii, xix, 208.

10. Ibid., 208.

11. Janet Biehl, *Ecology or Catastrophe*, 105–6.

12. See Don Lattin, *The Harvard Psychedelic Club*, 121.

13. Timothy Leary, "Turning on the World," 331, 343.

14. Terence McKenna, *Food of the Gods*, 248.

15. Alan Watts, *In My Own Way*, 354.

16. Ralph Metzner, "Hallucinogenic Drugs and Plants in Psychotherapy and Shamanism," 334.

17. Aldous Huxley, *The Doors of Perception* and *Heaven and Hell*, 16, 18.

18. Watts, *In My Own Way*, 329.

19. Norman O. Brown, *Life Against Death*, 320, 3, 8, 45, 4, 8, 307–8. The line beginning "no self and other" is from Allen J. Matusow, *The Unraveling of America*, 278.

20. Matusow, *The Unraveling of America*, 279; Huxley, *The Doors of Perception* and *Heaven and Hell*, 22, 64.

21. Gitlin, *The Sixties*, 206.

22. Huxley, *The Doors of Perception* and *Heaven and Hell*, 66, 73.

23. Watts, *In My Own Way*, 346, 347, 328, 350.

24. Abbey, *Desert Solitaire*, 155, 267 and *Down the River*, 83.

25. See Jeff Himmelman, "Peter Matthiessen's Homegoing."

26. Tom Wolfe, *The Electric Kool-Aid Acid Test*, 222.

27. Watts, *In My Own Way*, 81, 349.

28. Watts, *The Way of Zen*, 3, 4, 40, 21 and *In My Own Way*, 65.

29. Watts, *Nature, Man and Woman*, 12, 4; Brown, *Life Against Death*, 13; Watts, *In My Own Way*, 327–8. Watts's *Way of Zen* also features a discussion on Confucianism and Taoism's relationship and impact on Zen that strongly resembles Freud's developmental structure, even alludes to it (see 10–1).

30. Kesey's project of "total identification" found its roots in his own introduction to Freudian psychoanalysis, which an acquaintance briefed for him as a prelude to his first experiment with "psychomimetic drugs," which he intended to produce mild borderline states that would amplify oceanic feeling. See Tom Wolfe, *The Electric Kool-Aid Acid Test*, 36.

31. Gary Snyder, "Buddhism and the Coming Revolution," 251.

32. Tom Wolfe, *The Electric Kool-Aid Acid Test*, 40.

216 *Notes to pages 73–8*

33. Terry Gifford, *Pastoral*, 117–9; Randall Roorda, *Dramas of Solitude*, 55. This expression, Roorda argues, serves a primarily textual purpose. It is a function of Thoreau's narrative arc – a climax manufactured for the story – even as it "reflects an ascetic impulse . . . to self-sacrifice, in terms of which dissolution of personal identity is an attraction, consonant with recognition of the nonhuman."

34. For a more thorough discussion of Matthiessen's understanding of and engagement with the Emersonian tradition, see John Gatta, *Making Nature Sacred: Literature, Religion, and the Environment in America from the Puritans to the Present* (Oxford University Press, 2004) and SueEllen Campbell, "Science and Mysticism in the Himalayas: The Philosophical Journey of Peter Matthiessen and George Schaller" in the *Environmental Review*, vol. 12, no. 2 (1988), pp. 127–42.

35. The phrase "protestant lawlessness" is Watts's. See *Beat Zen, Square Zen and Zen*.

36. Snyder, *The Old Ways*, 13, 63–4 and *Turtle Island*, 106, 96.

37. Snyder, *Turtle Island*, 107 and "Buddhism and the Coming Revolution," 252.

38. Matthiessen, *In the Spirit of Crazy Horse*, xxiii. Following the publication of *Turtle Island*, numerous Native American authors, especially Leslie Marmon Silko, accused Snyder of cultural imperialism. Snyder responded by articulating his spiritualism in terms of its universal applicability or primary nature. See Sherry L. Smith, *Hippies, Indians, and the Fight for Red Power*, 63–4.

39. Philip J. Deloria, *Playing Indian*, 167. See also Rudolph Kaiser, "Chief Seattle's Speech(es)."

40. Shepard Krech, *The Ecological Indian*, 22, 16, 20.

41. Andrew G. Kirk, *Counterculture Green*, 9, 187; Chris Elcock, "From Acid Revolution to Entheogenic Evolution," 299.

42. Gitlin, *The Sixties*, 215.

43. Deloria, *Playing Indian*, 7, 129, 161.

44. See Doug Rossinow, *The Politics of Authenticity*.

45. See Bruce J. Schulman, *The Seventies*.

46. David Farber, "The Counterculture and the Antiwar Movement," 19.

47. See Lattin, *The Harvard Psychedelic Club*, 82.

48. Huxley, *The Doors of Perception* and *Heaven and Hell*, 71–2.

49. Elcock, "From Acid Revolution to Entheogenic Evolution," 297, 307.

50. See Metzner's "Introduction" to *Ayahuasca: Hallucinations, Consciousness, and the Spirit of Nature*.

51. Dennis J. McKenna and Terence K. McKenna, *The Invisible Landscape*, 102.

52. Metzner, "Introduction," 3.

Notes to pages 79–84

53. Terence McKenna, *True Hallucinations* and *The Archaic Revival*, 10, 43; Dennis McKenna, *The Brotherhood of the Screaming Abyss*, 130.
54. Ariel Levy, "The Secret Life of Plants," 34.
55. McKenna and McKenna, *The Invisible Landscape*, 12; Charles S. Grob, "The Psychology of Ayahuasca," 214; Elcock, "From Acid Revolution to Entheogenic Evolution," 303.
56. William Burroughs and Allen Ginsberg, *The Yage Letters*, 65; McKenna and McKenna, *The Invisible Landscape*, 24.
57. Terence McKenna, *The Archaic Revival*, 11; Dennis McKenna, *The Brotherhood of the Screaming Abyss*, 285.
58. Terence McKenna, *True Hallucinations*, 49.
59. Metzner, "Hallucinogenic Drugs," 334; Richard Evans Schultes and Albert Hofmann, *Plants of the Gods*, 59; Terence McKenna, *Food of the Gods*, 259, 39.
60. Terence McKenna, *Food of the Gods*, xx.
61. Ursula K. Heise, *Imagining Extinction*, 7.
62. Deloria, *Playing Indian*, 169; Sherry L. Smith, *Hippies, Indians, and the Fight for Red Power*, 8.
63. See Simon Ortiz and Janet McAdams, "A Conversation with Simon Ortiz," 1–2. The phrase "tragic, degraded figures" is from Deloria, *Playing Indian*, 137. Actual Native communities, Deloria adds, were "often unexpectedly socially restrictive" and "did not mesh well with the aggressive individualism of many communes" (159, 137).
64. Gitlin, *The Sixties*, 216.
65. Terence McKenna, *Food of the Gods*, xvi.
66. Brown, *Life Against Death*, 72.
67. Watts, *In My Own Way*, 267.
68. Deloria, *Playing Indian*, 155.
69. Huxley, *The Doors of Perception* and *Heaven and Hell*, 91, 74, 12–4, 99, 23–5, 92. The "reducing valve" metaphor has proven popular in numerous disciplines, from social psychology to cognitive science.
70. Watts, *In My Own Way*, 331.
71. Carl Jung, "Approaching the Unconscious," 56–7 and "The Structure of the Psyche," 152.
72. McKenna and McKenna, *The Invisible Landscape*, 4, 85; Terence McKenna, *True Hallucinations*, 68.
73. Terence McKenna, *True Hallucinations*, 39.
74. See especially Jacques Lacan's "Seminar on 'The Purloined Letter'" and "The Mirror Stage as Formative of the *I* Function as Revealed in Psychoanalytic Experience"; in *Écrits* (W. W. Norton, 2006), pp. 6–46 and 75–81; *The Ego in Freud's Theory and in the Technique of Psychoanalysis* (W. W. Norton, 1988); and *Formations of the Unconscious* (Polity, 2017). Lacan himself found Freud's

218 *Notes to pages 85–100*

theory of infantile narcissism preposterous – any such subjective state of unity comprised a retroactive fantasy.

75. Terence McKenna, *True Hallucinations*, 73–4 and *Food of the Gods*, 98.

76. Krech, *The Ecological Indian*, 27.

77. Simon J. Ortiz, *Woven Stone*, 364–5. *Woven Stone* cited in text for the remainder of Chapter 2.

78. Joni Adamson, *American Indian Literature, Environmental Justice, and Ecocriticism*, 56, xvii, 68.

79. Leslie Marmon Silko, "Interior and Exterior Landscapes," 155.

80. Silko, "Interior and Exterior Landscapes," 167; Robert M. Nelson, *Place and Vision*, 7.

81. Craig S. Womack, *Red on Red*, 16; Snyder, *Turtle Island*, 104.

82. Silko, "Interior and Exterior Landscapes," 159.

83. Ortiz, *Song, Poetry and Language*, 4–6.

84. Ibid., 6.

85. Silko, "Interior and Exterior Landscapes," 158.

86. Krech, *The Ecological Indian*, 216; Adamson, *American Indian Literature*, 66. As Krech points out, diverse tribes have "often favored the extraction of resources, storage of waste, and other developmental projects," but only when they can manage them, toward the goal of economic independence (219). See also Winona LaDuke, *All Our Relations: Native Struggles for Land and Life* (South End Press, 1999).

87. Snyder, *Turtle Island*, 99.

88. Watts, *The Way of Zen*, 147.

89. Watts, *Nature*, 70; *In My Own Way*, 345; and *The Way of Zen*, 42, 145.

90. Watts, *The Way of Zen*, 37.

3 The Universal Wilderness: Race, Cultural Nationalism, and an Identity Politics for the State of Nature

1. Toni Morrison, *Song of Solomon*, 292–3, 278. Cited in text for the remainder of Chapter 3.

2. Albert Schweitzer, *Indian Thought and Its Development*, 262.

3. Donald E. Pease, "National Identities, Postmodern Artifacts, and Postnational Narratives," 3.

4. Bill Devall and George Sessions, *Deep Ecology*, 3.

5. Wilbur L. Thomas, "Black Survival in Our Polluted Cities," 101.

6. Devall and Sessions, *Deep Ecology*, 20, 96.

7. Sarah Jaquette Ray, *The Ecological Other*, 24.

8. Morrison, "The Future of Time," 173–4.

9. Christopher Stone, *Should Trees Have Standing?*, 3–4.

Notes to pages 100–9   219

10. David S. Oderberg, "Natural Law and Rights Theory," 376.
11. Roderick Frazier Nash, *The Rights of Nature*, 11.
12. Pease, "National Identities," 4.
13. Michel Serres, *The Natural Contract*, 46, 39.
14. Ibid., 124.
15. Holmes Rolston, "Is There an Ecological Ethic?", 101.
16. Aldo Leopold, *A Sand County Almanac*, 239. Indigenous depictions of environment, such as N. Scott Momaday's "American Land Ethic" (1970), speak to preexisting models of the enlarged community of nonhuman citizens that Leopold hoped to inspire.
17. Nash, *The Rights of Nature*, 160.
18. John N. Duvall, "*Song of Solomon*, Narrative Identity, and the Faulknerian Intertext," 89; Samuel Allen, "Review of *Song of Solomon*," 31.
19. Thomas LeClair, "'The Language Must Not Sweat.'"
20. Bell Hooks, *Belonging: A Culture of Place*, 117–8.
21. Wes Berry, "Toni Morrison's Revisionary 'Nature Writing,'" 163.
22. Richard D. Ryder, *Victims of Science*, 12; Leopold, *A Sand County Almanac*, 280–95; Edward Abbey, *Desert Solitaire*, 174; Theodore Roszak, *Person/Planet*; Wendell Berry, *The Unsettling of America*, 12. For the Animal Liberation Front quote, see Eric Malni, "Animal Liberation Front."
23. Morrison, "Rediscovering Black History," 46.
24. Paul Outka, *Race and Nature*, 3; Alison H. Deming and Lauret E. Savoy, "Introduction as Conversation," 8; Dorceta Taylor, *Race, Class, Gender, and American Environmentalism*, 40.
25. See especially Bradley G. Shreve, *Red Power Rising*.
26. Paul Chaat Smith and Robert Allen Warrior, *Like a Hurricane*, 18–19.
27. Simon Ortiz, *Woven Stone*, 5.
28. Robert M. Nelson, *Place and Vision*, 39; Craig S. Womack, *Red on Red*, 16.
29. See Shreve, *Red Power Rising*, 175.
30. Bruce J. Schulman, *The Seventies*, 72, 58.
31. See Carol A. Horton, *Race and the Making of American Liberalism*, 40, 122, 128, 130–1.
32. Kwame Ture and Charles V. Hamilton, *Black Power*, 54.
33. Charles Taylor, "The Politics of Recognition," 44. The phrase "pragmatic contradiction" is also Taylor's.
34. Dean E. Robinson, *Black Nationalism in American Politics and Thought*, 85.
35. See Shreve, *Red Power Rising*, 158.
36. See Dean E. Robinson, *Black Nationalism*.
37. Ture and Hamilton, *Black Power*, 44.
38. Robert S. Browne, "The Case for Two Americas—One White, One Black."

39. The phrase "strong racial chauvinism" is from Dean E. Robinson, *Black Nationalism*, 84.
40. Horton, *Race and the Making of American Liberalism*, 181.
41. Doug Rossinow, *The Politics of Authenticity*, 343.
42. Ture and Hamilton, *Black Power*, 34, xvi.
43. Dean E. Robinson, *Black Nationalism*, 73, 72, 71.
44. Amiri Baraka, *Conversations with Amiri Baraka*, 20–1. It's worth noting that Baraka's homogeneous, identitarian idealization of blackness emerged in part through his early engagement with beat writers like Jack Kerouac and Allen Ginsberg, whose own idealization he rejected for its racist undertones, but picked up for the purposes of the Black Aesthetic.
45. Malcolm X, "Organization of Afro-American Unity," 112–3.
46. James T. Stewart, "The Development of the Black Revolutionary Artist," 3.
47. Dean E. Robinson, *Black Nationalism*, 105.
48. Julianne Newmark, *The Pluralist Imagination from East to West in American Literature*, xxiii.
49. Ortiz, "Foreword" to *American Indian Literary Nationalism*, xi.
50. Toni Morrison and Robert Stepto. "'Intimate Things in Place,'" 474; Morrison, "Rediscovering Black History," 50. As numerous Black feminist critics have argued, Morrison participates in a rich tradition of Black women novelists who have contested the totalizing perspective of postwar Black nationalism's Black Aesthetic. See especially Madhu Dubey's *Black Women Novelists and the Nationalist Aesthetic* (Indiana University Press, 1994) and Deborah E. McDowell's *The Changing Same: Black Women's Literature, Criticism, and Theory* (Indiana University Press, 1995).
51. Melanye T. Price, *Dreaming Blackness*, 23; Morrison, "Rediscovering Black History," 42; Carolyn C. Denard, "Introduction" to *What Moves at the Margins*, xviii; Morrison, "Behind the Making of *The Black Book*," 36–7.
52. Kathleen R. Wallace and Karla Armbruster, "The Novels of Toni Morrison," 224. For the phrase "keeping our troubled relics," see Kimberly N. Ruffin, *Black on Earth*, 2.
53. Toni Morrison et al., "Toni Morrison, The Art of Fiction No. 134"; Toni Morrison and Nellie McKay, "An Interview with Toni Morrison," 417.
54. Jennifer Terry, "'Breathing the Air of a World So New,'" 133.
55. Kwame Anthony Appiah, "Identity," 155.
56. Joanna Macy, "Awakening to the Ecological Self," 201.
57. Devall and Sessions, *Deep Ecology*, 66; Nash, *The Rights of Nature*, 151; Appiah, "Identity," 159–60.
58. See Appiah, "Identity," 160.
59. Morrison, *Beloved*, 259.

Notes to pages 117–32   221

60. Morrison, *A Mercy*, 146, 157, 161.
61. Terry, "'Breathing the Air of a World So New,'" 139.
62. Morrison, *Beloved*, 244. Wallace and Armbruster write that Morrison's "portrayals of culturally induced wildness" help her to trouble "the concepts of natural and unnatural, insisting that it is the oppression and hatred that spawn this wildness that are unnatural, rather than the behavior of the person exhibiting it." See "The Novels of Toni Morrison," 217.
63. Claudia Tate, "Interview with Toni Morrison," 164–5.
64. Morrison et al., "Toni Morrison, The Art of Fiction"; Tate, "Interview," 168.
65. Carolyn Finney, *Black Faces, White Spaces*, 47, 8–9, 10. The phrase "clean slate of wilderness" is from Deming and Savoy, "Introduction," 9.
66. Morrison, *Playing in the Dark*, 33 and *A Mercy*, 12.
67. Anthony Hutchison, *Writing the Republic*, 123; Morrison, *Playing in the Dark*, 38, 44.
68. Finney, *Black Faces*, 28.
69. Melvin Dixon, *Ride Out the Wilderness*, 4–5.
70. Terry Gifford, *Pastoral*, 5, 2.
71. Stacy Alaimo, *Undomesticated Ground*, 133–4.
72. Morrison, *A Mercy*, 48–9; Terry, "'Breathing the Air of a World So New,'" 134.
73. Morrison, "Behind the Making of the *Black Book*," 35.
74. Morrison, "Rootedness," 62.
75. Ruffin, *Black on Earth*, 57, 114–5.
76. Dean E. Robinson, *Black Nationalism*, 73.
77. LeClair, "'The Language Must Not Sweat.'"
78. Outka, *Race and Nature*, 5.
79. Finney, *Black Faces*, 9; Robert D. Bullard, "Confronting Environmental Racism in the Twenty-First Century," 91.
80. James H. Cone, *Risks of Faith*, 138.
81. Gurleen Grewal, *Circles of Sorrow, Lines of Struggle*, 63.
82. Ruffin, *Black on Earth*, 2.
83. Luke W. Cole and Sheila R. Foster, *From the Ground Up*, 16.
84. Joni Adamson, *American Indian Literature*, 69.
85. See Cole and Foster, *From the Ground Up*, 19*ff.*
86. "The Principles of Environmental Justice," 181.
87. Thomas, "Black Survival," 101–2.
88. "The Principles of Environmental Justice," 180; Dana Allston, "Moving Beyond the Barriers," 178.
89. Adamson, *American Indian Literature*, 75.
90. Cole and Foster, *From the Ground Up*, 13.

222 *Notes to pages 133–40*

4 The Essential Ecosystem: Reproduction, Network, and Biological Reduction

1. Deborah Slicer, "Wrongs of Passage," 37; Val Plumwood, "The Ecopolitics Debate," 66.
2. Slicer, "Wrongs of Passage," 29.
3. Mary J. Carruthers, "The Re-Vision of the Muse," 304.
4. Diana Fuss's *Essentially Speaking: Feminism, Nature, and Difference* (Routledge, 1989) remains a fabulous resource for thinking through feminism's own sporadic essentialism.
5. See Catherine Roach, "Loving Your Mother: On the Woman-Nature Relation." It's worth noting that Roach's essay is vehemently critical of the perspective it names.
6. Sharon Doubiago, "Mama Cayote Talks to the Boys," 42; Elizabeth Grosz, "Conclusion: A Note on Essentialism and Differences," 334.
7. Kimberlé Crenshaw introduced the idea of intersectionality, now foundational to critical race studies, in "Demarginalizing the Intersection of Race and Sex." For critiques of biologism and other gender essentialisms by women of color at the time of nature feminism's inception, see, for example, the Combahee River Collective Statement (1974) and Cherríe Moraga and Gloria Anzaldúa's *This Bridge Called My Back* (1981).
8. Margaret Atwood, *Surfacing*, 196, 193. Cited in text for the remainder of Chapter 4.
9. Atwood, *Strange Things*, 101; Eleonora Rao, *Strategies for Identity*, 21.
10. See Donna Haraway, "A Cyborg Manifesto." For Haraway, "replication" refers not only to ecological transformations, but also to technoscientific alterations in data.
11. Linda Garber, *Identity Poetics*, 1.
12. Robin Morgan, "Goodbye to All That"; Susan Griffin, *Made from This Earth*, 4.
13. Doubiago, "Mama Cayote Talks to the Boys," 40–1.
14. Gina Wisker, *Margaret Atwood*, 19–20.
15. Jo Brans and Margaret Atwood, "Using What You're Given," 301.
16. Lisa Maria Hogeland, *Feminism and Its Fictions*, 5, 9; Margaret Atwood and Mary Morris, "Margaret Atwood, The Art of Fiction No. 121."
17. Atwood, "A Reply," 340.
18. Catharine R. Stimpson, "Editorial," vi; Atwood, "A Reply," 340.
19. Griffin, *Woman and Nature*, xv, 187, 1; Mary Daly, *Gyn/Ecology*, 10–1.
20. Rosemary Radford Ruether, *Gaia & God*, 143.
21. Plumwood, *Feminism and the Mastery of Nature*, 7, 9.
22. Karla Armbruster, "'Buffalo Gals, Won't You Come Out Tonight,'" 99; Marti Kheel, "Ecofeminism and Deep Ecology," 137; Ariel Kay Salleh, "Deeper than Deep Ecology," 340.

Notes to pages 141–53

23. Ruether, *Gaia*, 171. See also Victoria Davion, "Is Ecofeminism Feminist?"
24. Griffin, *Made from This Earth*, 15.
25. Ann Barr Snitow, "The Front Line," 714; Robert Lecker, "Janus through the Looking Glass."
26. Plumwood, *Feminism and the Mastery of Nature*, 4.
27. Atwood, *The Handmaid's Tale*, 390, 176, 124, 11.
28. Michelle Stanworth, "Reproductive Technologies and the Deconstruction of Motherhood," 16, 14.
29. Brans and Atwood, "Using What You're Given," 302.
30. Atwood, *The Handmaid's Tale*, 285, 159.
31. Victoria Davion, "Is Ecofeminism Feminist?", 17. Catherine Roach points out that, in addition to often (though not always) neglecting the perspectives of women of color, the nature-feminist "all women" platform's "overemphasis on the Goddess as mother" at best discounts and at worst pathologizes women who do not or cannot give birth. See "Loving Your Mother," 58.
32. Atwood, *Strange Things*, 4.
33. Lecker, "Janus through the Looking Glass," 186.
34. Griffin, "Split Culture," 7.
35. Davion, "Is Ecofeminism Feminist?", 22.
36. Armbruster, "Buffalo Gals," 98.
37. Carol Gilligan, *In a Different Voice*, xv, xiii, 17.
38. Nancy Julia Chodorow, "Gender, Relation, and Difference in Psychoanalytic Perspective," 420, 422–34, 431.
39. Ibid., 432.
40. Griffin, *Woman and Nature*, 219, 225–6 and *Made for This Earth*, 7–8.
41. Judith Plant, "Toward a New World," 2, 5; Charlene Spretnak, "Toward an Ecofeminist Spirituality," 128; Ruether, "Toward an Ecological-Feminist Theology of Nature," 146.
42. Griffin, *Woman and Nature*, 224.
43. Griffin, *Made for This Earth*, 8.
44. Naomi Jaffe and Bernardine Dohrn, "The Look Is You," 356.
45. Margaret Atwood and Mary Ellis Gibson, "A Conversation with Margaret Atwood," 108.
46. Karen Newman, *Fetal Positions*, 16.
47. Haraway, *When Species Meet*, 4.
48. Cary Wolfe, *What Is Posthumanism?*, xxv, xxiii, 3.
49. Rosi Braidotti, *The Posthuman*, 4.
50. Joanna Macy, *World as Lover, World as Self*, xi, 12 and "Awakening to the Ecological Self," 205. The phrase "political religion" is from Bruno Latour, "Why Gaia Is Not a God of Totality," 76.

224   *Notes to pages 154–60*

51. See Eli Zaretsky, "From Psychoanalysis to Cybernetics." Zaretsky points out that the role of "feedback"—a concept important to Freud—was especially important in this moment of cross-disciplinary pollination. The cybernetics movement also declined even as psychoanalysis did, largely coming to integrate with New-Age pop psychology.

52. Gilles Deleuze and Félix Guattari, *Anti-Oedipus*, 1.

53. *Anti-Oedipus* is not another attempt at Marx/Freud synthesis, first because it disagrees with the primacy of the Oedipal ego in Freud's schema and second because, unlike the work of Herbert Marcuse, Wilhelm Reich, and other Left Freudians, it does not conceive of political and libidinal economy as separate structures. It's worth mentioning, though, that Deleuze and Guattari greatly admired R. D. Laing, who worked in the same vein as the Freudian Left but specifically pointed to the schizophrenic as the social outcast who best captures an unrepressed psyche. Laing's work was nearly as influential to the New Left and its politics of authenticity as Marcuse's.

54. Deleuze and Guattari, *Anti-Oedipus*, 2–5, 7, 98.

55. Braidotti, *The Posthuman*, 92.

56. Latour, "Why Gaia Is Not a God of Totality," 76.

57. Jane Bennett, *Vibrant Matter*, 20, 2, ix.

58. James Hillman, "A Psyche the Size of the Earth," xix.

59. Bennett, *Vibrant Matter*, xii; Deleuze and Guattari, *A Thousand Plateaus*, 7, 12.

60. Grosz, *The Incorporeal*, 9, 5.

61. Stephanie Clare, "On the Politics of 'New Feminist Materialisms,'" 58.

62. Braidotti, *The Posthuman*, 15; Cary Wolfe, *What Is Posthumanism?*, xv.

63. Diana Coole and Samantha Frost, "Introducing the New Materialisms," 9–10, 7; Clare, "'New Feminist Materialisms,'" 59.

64. Deboleena Roy and Banu Subramaniam, "Matter in the Shadows," 28, 26.

65. Coole and Frost, "Introducing the New Materialisms," 15, 11.

66. For "agent ontologies," as well as a discussion of their history, see Jerry Lee Rosiek and Jimmy Snyder, "Narrative Inquiry and New Materialism."

67. Karla Hammond and Margaret Atwood, "An Interview with Margaret Atwood," 28; Alan Watts, *The Way of Zen*, 5.

68. Grosz, *Becoming Undone*, 98.

69. Karen Barad, "Posthumanist Performativity," 122–3, 139. Drawing inspiration from the work of quantum physicist Niels Bohr, Barad argues that discrete things do not exist independently of their observation. In contrast to a "Cartesian cut," or inherent distinction between subject and object, Barad proposes an "agential cut," a separation effected by intra-action (132–3).

70. Victoria Pitts-Taylor, "Mattering," 16, 4.

Notes to pages 160–75 225

71. Coole and Frost, "Introducing the New Materialisms," 17, 7.
72. Hannes Bergthaller, "Limits of Agency," 38; Grosz, *Becoming Undone*, 88; Melissa A. Orlie, "Impersonal Matter," 132.
73. Braidotti, *The Posthuman*, 47; Susan Hekman, "Constructing the Ballast," 113. Two especially notable revisions by scholars of color are Mel Y. Chen's *Animacies: Biopolitics, Racial Mattering, and Queer Affect* (Duke University Press, 2012) and Alexander Weheliye's *Habeas Viscus: Racializing Assemblages, Biopolitics, and Black Feminist Theories of the Human* (Duke University Press, 2014).
74. Coole and Frost, "Introducing the New Materialisms," 11, 8, 19, 1.
75. Grosz, *Becoming Undone*, 84.
76. Grosz, *Becoming Undone*, 88, 93; Neel Ahuja, "Abu Zubaydah and the Caterpillar," 144–5.
77. Orlie, "Impersonal Matter," 123, 132; Spretnak, "Toward an Ecofeminist Spirituality," 128.
78. Grosz, *Becoming Undone*, 85; Braidotti, *The Posthuman*, 138.
79. Atwood, *The Year of the Flood*, 404. The phrase "merger with the web of non-human forces" is from Braidotti, *The Posthuman*, 138.
80. Braidotti, *The Posthuman*, 136 and "The Politics of 'Life Itself,'" 212–14.
81. Bergthaller, "Limits of Agency," 39–40.
82. Braidotti, *The Posthuman*, 136.
83. Atwood, "Death by Landscape," 110–1; Hammond and Atwood, "An Interview," 28.
84. Atwood, *The Handmaid's Tale*, 367, 251, 95.
85. Ibid., 86.
86. Grosz, *Becoming Undone*, 98.
87. Armbruster, "Buffalo Gals," 101, 99; Plumwood, *Feminism and the Mastery of Nature*, 6.
88. Haraway, *When Species Meet*, 4; Roy and Subramaniam, "Matter in the Shadows," 29.

5 The Death of the Supertramp: Psychoanalytic Narratives and American Wilderness

1. "To stay put is to exist; to travel is to live."
2. Christopher McCandless, *Back to the Wild*, 175; Jon Krakauer, *Into the Wild*, 168. *Into the Wild* cited in text for the remainder of Chapter 5.
3. Peter C. van Wyck, *Primitives in the Wilderness*, 83, 104.
4. Diana Saverin, "The Chris McCandless Obsession Problem."
5. See Marcuse, *One-Dimensional Man* and Saverin, "The Chris McCandless Obsession Problem."
6. *The Call of the Wild*, directed by Ron Lamothe.

7. McCandless, *Back to the Wild*, 147.
8. Bill Devall and George Sessions, *Deep Ecology*, 111.
9. Andrew McLaughlin, "The Heart of Deep Ecology," 86; Devall and Sessions, *Deep Ecology*, 86–9; David Rothenberg, "Introduction: Ecosophy T," 1.
10. Arne Naess, "*Self* Realization," 19–20.
11. Devall and Sessions, *Deep Ecology*, ix, 67; Steven Harper, "The Way of Wilderness," 184, 193, 196.
12. Devall and Sessions, *Deep Ecology*, 66–7.
13. Warwick Fox, *Toward a Transpersonal Ecology*, 231.
14. Naess, *Ecology, Community and Lifestyle*, 9.
15. See McCandless, *Back to the Wild*.
16. *Grizzly Man*, directed by Werner Herzog.
17. See W. L. Rusho, *Everett Ruess*, 178–9, 96.
18. Ibid., 39, 30, 42.
19. Wallace Stegner, *Mormon Country*, 325, 330.
20. Randall Roorda, *Dramas of Solitude*, 151; Geoffrey Galt Harpham, *The Ascetic Imperative in Culture and Criticism*, 26.
21. *Grizzly Man*.
22. Sigmund Freud, *Civilization and Its Discontents*, 24.
23. Ibid., 43–5, 28.
24. Ibid., 48.
25. Ibid., 45.
26. Ibid.
27. Harpham, *The Ascetic Imperative*, xii.
28. Ibid., xiii.
29. McCandless, *Back to the Wild*, 236.
30. *Grizzly Man*.
31. Edward Abbey, *Desert Solitaire*, 146.
32. McCandless, *Back to the Wild*, 21.
33. Krakauer, *Into Thin Air*, 245, 264.
34. Ibid., 270–1.
35. Naess, *Ecology, Community and Lifestyle*, 55.
36. John Seed, "Introduction" to *Thinking Like a Mountain*, 13 and "Beyond Anthropomorphism," 36; Joanna Macy, "Our Life as Gaia," 61.
37. Val Plumwood, *Feminism and the Mastery of Nature*, 177.
38. John Seed and Joanna Macy, "Gaia Meditations," 43.
39. Margaret Atwood, *Surfacing*, 94–5.
40. See Brandon Burk (@brandonburkphotography), "The weekend," Instagram, 26 Aug. 2016.
41. See *FOLK Lifestyle*, www.folklifestyle.com/.
42. Plumwood, "The Ecopolitics Debate," 71.

Notes to pages 199–207

Conclusion: Ecological Consistency

1. Rita Felski, *The Limits of Critique*, 12.
2. Serenella Iovino and Serpil Oppermann. "Introduction" to *Material Ecocriticism*, 1.
3. Felski, *The Limits of Critique*, 12.
4. Richard Rorty, *Achieving Our Country*, 13.
5. Iovino and Oppermann, "Introduction," 6–7.
6. Peter Matthiessen, *The Snow Leopard*, 66; Hanna Meißner, "New Material Feminisms and Historical Materialism," 51.
7. Norman O. Brown, *Life Against Death*, 316; Timothy Morton, "Queer Ecology," 275.
8. Nicole Seymour, *Strange Natures*, 15.
9. Angela Hume and Samila Rahimtoola, "Introduction: Queering Ecopoetics," 140–1.
10. Leo Bersani, *Is the Rectum a Grave?*, 25, 30.
11. Ibid., 100, 57, 86.
12. Greta Gaard, "Toward a Queer Ecofeminism," 115.
13. Catriona Mortimer-Sandilands and Bruce Erickson, "Introduction" to *Queer Ecologies*, 30; Dianne Chisholm, "Biophilia, Creative Involution, and the Ecological Future of Queer Desire," 159.
14. Morton, "Queer Ecology," 275, 277.
15. Bersani, *Is the Rectum a Grave?*, 106; Jon Krakauer, *Into the Wild*, 66.
16. See Vicki Kirby, *Quantum Anthropologies*, 109–10.
17. Jerry Lee Rosiek and Jimmy Snyder, "Narrative Inquiry and New Materialism," 3.
18. See Richard Poirier, *The Renewal of Literature*.
19. Jane Jacobs, *The Death and Life of Great American Cities*, 443.
20. Val Plumwood, *Feminism and the Mastery of Nature*, 177.
21. Bersani, *Is the Rectum a Grave?*, 110.
22. Charles Sanders Peirce, "Some Consequences of Four Incapacities." See also Rosiek and Snyder, "Narrative Inquiry and New Materialism" and Meißner, "New Material Feminisms and Historical Materialism."
23. Donna Haraway, "A Cyborg Manifesto," 1972, 1969.
24. David Schlosberg, *Environmental Justice and the New Pluralism*, 183, 92, 76.
25. Hannes Bergthaller, "Limits of Agency," 46; Haraway, "A Cyborg Manifesto," 1972.

Bibliography

Abbey, Edward. *Desert Solitaire: A Season in the Wilderness.* 1968. Ballantine, 1971.
  Down the River. Dutton, 1982.
  The Journey Home. Clarke, Irwin & Company, 1977.
  One Life at a Time, Please. Holt, 1988.
  Postcards from Ed: Dispatches and Salvos from an American Iconoclast. Edited by
    David Petersen, Milkweed Editions, 2006.
Adamson, Joni. *American Indian Literature, Environmental Justice, and
    Ecocriticism: The Middle Place.* University of Arizona Press, 2001.
Ahuja, Neel. "Abu Zubaydah and the Caterpillar." *Social Text*, vol. 29, no. 1, 2011,
    pp. 127–49.
Alaimo, Stacy. *Bodily Natures: Science, Environment, and the Material Self.* Indiana
    University Press, 2010.
  Undomesticated Ground: Recasting Nature as Feminist Space. Cornell University
    Press, 2000.
Alderman, Harold. "Abbey as Anarchist." *Coyote in the Maze: Tracking Edward
    Abbey in a World of Words*, edited by Peter Quigley, University of Utah Press,
    1998, pp. 137–49.
Allen, Samuel. "Review of *Song of Solomon*." 1978. *Critical Essays on Toni Morrison*,
    edited by Nellie Y. McKay, G. K. Hall & Co., 1988, pp. 30–32.
Allston, Dana. "Moving Beyond the Barriers." 1991. *Environmental Justice in
    Postwar America: A Documentary Reader*, edited by Christopher W. Wells,
    University of Washington Press, 2018, pp. 178–9.
Appiah, Kwame Anthony. "Identity, Authenticity, Survival: Multicultural
    Societies and Social Reproduction." *Multiculturalism: Examining the
    Politics of Recognition*, edited by Amy Gutmann, Princeton University
    Press, 1994, pp. 149–63.
  The Lies that Bind: Rethinking Identity. W. W. Norton & Company, 2018.
Armbruster, Karla. "'Buffalo Gals, Won't You Come Out Tonight': A Call for
    Boundary-Crossing in Ecofeminist Literary Criticism." *Ecofeminist Literary
    Criticism: Theory, Interpretation, Pedagogy*, edited by Greta Gaard and Patrick
    D. Murphy, University of Illinois Press, 1998, pp. 97–122.
Atwood, Margaret. "Death by Landscape." *Wilderness Tips*, edited by
    Margaret Atwood. 1991. McClelland & Stewart, 1999, pp. 97–118.
  The Handmaid's Tale. 1985. Fawcett Crest, 1987.

Bibliography

"A Reply." *Signs*, vol. 2, no. 2, 1976, pp. 340–1.

Strange Things: The Malevolent North in Canadian Literature. Clarendon, 1995.

Surfacing. 1972. Anchor, 1998.

The Year of the Flood. 2009. Anchor, 2010.

Atwood, Margaret and Mary Ellis Gibson. "A Conversation with Margaret Atwood." *Chicago Review*, vol. 27, no. 4, 1976, pp. 105–13.

Atwood, Margaret and Mary Morris. "Margaret Atwood, The Art of Fiction No. 121." *The Paris Review*, no. 117, 1990.

Barad, Karen. "Posthumanist Performativity: Toward an Understanding of How Matter Comes to Matter." *Material Feminisms*, edited by Stacy Alaimo and Susan Hekman, Indiana University Press, 2008, pp. 120–54.

Baraka, Amiri. *Conversations with Amiri Baraka*. Edited by Charlie Reilly, University Press of Mississippi, 1994.

Bennett, Jane. *Vibrant Matter: A Political Ecology of Things*. Duke University Press, 2010.

Bergthaller, Hannes. "Limits of Agency: Notes on the Material Turn from a Systems-Theoretical Perspective." *Material Ecocriticism*, edited by Serenella Iovino and Serpil Oppermann, Indiana University Press, 2014, pp. 37–50.

"Paradox as Bedrock: Social Systems Theory and the Ungrounding of Literary Environmentalism in Edward Abbey's *Desert Solitaire*." *Handbook of Ecocriticism and Cultural Ecology*, edited by Hubert Zapf, De Gruyter, 2016, pp. 105–22.

Berkeley Barb, 13 January 1967.

Berry, Wendell. "A Few Words in Favor of Edward Abbey." *Resist Much, Obey Little: Remembering Ed Abbey*, edited by James R. Hepworth and Gregory McNamee. Sierra Club Books, 1996, pp. 1–14.

The Unsettling of America: Culture & Agriculture. 1977. Counterpoint, 2015.

Berry, Wes. "Toni Morrison's Revisionary 'Nature Writing': *Song of Solomon* and the Blasted Pastoral." *South to a New Place: Region, Literature, Culture*, edited by Suzanne W. Jones and Sharon Monteith, Louisiana State University Press, 2002, pp. 147–64.

Bersani, Leo. *Is the Rectum a Grave? and Other Essays*. University of Chicago Press, 2010.

Biehl, Janet. *Ecology or Catastrophe: The Life of Murray Bookchin*. Oxford University Press, 2015.

Bishop, James. *Epitaph for a Desert Anarchist: The Life and Legacy of Edward Abbey*. Atheneum, 1994.

Bookchin, Murray. *Anarchism, Marxism, and the Future of the Left: Interviews and Essays, 1993–1998*. AK Press, 1999.

"Between the 30s and the 60s." *Social Text*, nos. 9/10, 1984, pp. 247–51.

"The Concept of Ecotechnologies and Ecocommunities." *HABITAT, An International Journal*, vol. 2, no. 1/2, 1977, pp. 73–85.

The Ecology of Freedom: The Emergence and Dissolution of Hierarchy. 1972. AK Press, 2005.

The Modern Crisis. New Society Publishers, 1986.

Post-Scarcity Anarchism. 1970. Working Classics, 2005.

"Social Ecology versus Deep Ecology." *Socialist Review*, vol. 18, no. 3, 1988.

Braidotti, Rosi. "The Politics of 'Life Itself' and New Ways of Dying." *New Materialisms: Ontology, Agency, and Politics*, edited by Diana Coole and Samantha Frost, Duke University Press, 2010, pp. 201–18.

The Posthuman. Polity, 2013.

Brand, Stewart. "Introduction." *The Essential Whole Earth Catalog*, edited by Stewart Brand, Doubleday, 1986.

Brans, Jo and Margaret Atwood. "Using What You're Given: A Conversation with Margaret Atwood." *Southwest Review*, vol. 68, no. 4, 1983, pp. 301–15.

Breton, Gabriel. "The Ideology of the Person." *New University Thought*, vol. 2, no. 2, 1962.

Brown, Norman O. *Life Against Death: The Psychoanalytical Meaning of History*. 1959. Wesleyan University Press, 1985.

Browne, Robert S. "The Case for Two Americas—One White, One Black." The New York Times Magazine, 1 August 1968, p. 50.

Buell, Lawrence. *The Environmental Imagination: Thoreau, Nature Writing, and the Formation of American Culture*. Harvard University Press, 1995.

Bullard, Robert D. "Confronting Environmental Racism in the Twenty-First Century." *The Colors of Nature: Culture, Identity, and the Natural World*, edited by Alison H. Deming and Lauret E. Savoy, Milkweed Editions, 2002, pp. 90–7.

Burroughs, William and Allen Ginsberg. *The Yage Letters*. 1963, 1975. City Lights Books, 2006.

Cahalan, James M. *Edward Abbey: A Life*. University of Arizona Press, 2001.

The Call of the Wild. Directed by Ron Lamothe, Terra Incognita Productions, 2007.

Calvert, Greg. "Participatory Democracy, Collective Leadership and Political Responsibility." *New Left Notes*, 18 December 1967, pp. 1–7.

Calvert, Greg and Carol Neiman. *A Disrupted History: The New Left and the New Capitalism*. Random House, 1971.

Carruthers, Mary J. "The Re-Vision of the Muse: Adrienne Rich, Audre Lorde, Judy Grahn, Olga Broumas." *Hudson Review*, vol. 36, no. 2, 1983, pp. 293–322.

Carson, Rachel. *Silent Spring*. 1962. Houghton Mifflin, 1987.

Chisholm, Dianne. "Biophilia, Creative Involution, and the Ecological Future of Queer Desire." *Queer Ecologies: Sex, Nature, Politics, Desire*, edited by Catriona Mortimer-Sandilands and Bruce Erickson, Indiana University Press, 2010, pp. 359–81.

Chodorow, Nancy Julia. "Gender, Relation, and Difference in Psychoanalytic Perspective." 1980. *Essential Papers on the Psychology of Women*, edited by Claudia Zanardi, New York University Press, 1990, pp. 420–36.

Clare, Stephanie. "On the Politics of 'New Feminist Materialisms.'" *Mattering: Feminism, Science, and Materialism*, edited by Victoria Pitts-Taylor, New York University Press, 2016, pp. 58–72.

Bibliography

Clark, John. "What Is Social Ecology?" *Renewing the Earth: The Promise of Social Ecology*, edited by John Clark, Green Print, 1990, pp. 5–11.

Cole, Luke W. and Sheila R. Foster. *From the Ground Up: Environmental Racism and the Rise of the Environmental Justice Movement*. New York University Press, 2001.

Commoner, Barry. *The Closing Circle: Nature, Man, and Technology*. Alfred A. Knopf, 1971.

Cone, James H. *Risks of Faith: The Emergence of a Black Theology of Liberation, 1968–1998*. Beacon Press, 1999.

Coole, Diana, and Samantha Frost. "Introducing the New Materialisms." *New Materialisms: Ontology, Agency, and Politics*, edited by Diana Coole and Samantha Frost, Duke University Press, 2010, pp. 1–43.

Crenshaw, Kimberlé. "Demarginalizing the Intersection of Race and Sex: A Black Feminist Critique of Antidiscrimination Doctrine, Feminist Theory and Antiracist Politics." *University of Chicago Legal Forum*, 1989, pp. 139–68.

Daly, Mary. *Gyn/Ecology: The Metaethics of Radical Feminism*. Beacon Press, 1978.

Davion, Victoria. "Is Ecofeminism Feminist?" *Ecological Feminism*, edited by Karen J. Warren, Routledge, 1994, pp. 8–28.

Deleuze, Gilles, and Félix Guattari. *Anti-Oedipus: Capitalism and Schizophrenia*. 1972. University of Minnesota Press, 1983.

A Thousand Plateaus: Capitalism and Schizophrenia. 1980. University of Minnesota Press, 1987.

Deloria, Philip J. *Playing Indian*. Yale University Press, 1998.

Deming, Alison H. and Lauret E. Savoy. "Introduction as Conversation." *The Colors of Nature: Culture, Identity, and the Natural World*, edited by Alison H. Deming and Lauret E. Savoy, Milkweed Editions, 2002, pp. 3–15.

Denard, Carolyn C. "Introduction." *What Moves at the Margins*, by Toni Morrison, University Press of Mississippi, 2008, pp. xi–xxvi.

Devall, Bill, and George Sessions. *Deep Ecology: Living as if Nature Mattered*. Gibbs M. Smith, 1985.

Dillard, Annie. *Pilgrim at Tinker Creek*. 1974. Harper & Row, 1988.

Dixon, Melvin. *Ride Out the Wilderness: Geography and Identity in Afro-American Literature*. University of Illinois Press, 1987.

Doubiago, Sharon. "Mama Cayote Talks to the Boys." *Healing the Wounds: The Promise of Ecofeminism*, edited by Judith Plant, New Society Publishers, 1989, pp. 40–4.

Duvall, John N. "*Song of Solomon*, Narrative Identity, and the Faulknerian Intertext." *Bloom's Modern Critical Interpretations: Toni Morrison's* Song of Solomon, edited by Harold Bloom, Infobase, 2009, pp. 87–118.

Ecology Action East. "The Power to Destroy, the Power to Create." *The Ecological Conscience: Values for Survival*, edited by Robert Disch, Prentice-Hall, 1970, pp. 161–9.

Elcock, Chris. "From Acid Revolution to Entheogenic Evolution: Psychedelic Philosophy in the Sixties and Beyond." *Journal of American Culture*, vol. 36, no. 4, 2013, pp.296–311.

Bibliography

Emerson, Ralph Waldo. "Nature." *Selections from Ralph Waldo Emerson*, edited by Stephen E. Wheeler, Houghton Mifflin Company, 1957, pp. 21–56.

Farber, David. "The Counterculture and the Antiwar Movement." *Give Peace a Chance: Exploring the Vietnam Antiwar Movement*, edited by Melvin Small and William D. Hoover, Syracuse University Press, 1992, pp. 7–21.

Felski, Rita. *The Limits of Critique*. University of Chicago Press, 2015.

Finney, Carolyn. *Black Faces, White Spaces: Reimagining the Relationship of African Americans to the Great Outdoors*. University of North Carolina Press, 2014.

Fox, Warwick. *Toward a Transpersonal Ecology*. Green Books, 1995.

Freud, Sigmund. *Civilization and Its Discontents*. 1930. W. W. Norton & Company, 2010.

Fromm, Harold. "Aldo Leopold: Aesthetic 'Anthropocentrist.'" 1993. *The ISLE Reader: Ecocriticism, 1993–2003*, edited by Michael P. Branch and Scott Slovic, University of Georgia Press, 2003, pp. 3–9.

Gaard, Greta. "Toward a Queer Ecofeminism." *Hypatia*, vol. 12, no. 1, 1997, pp. 114–37.

Garber, Linda. *Identity Poetics: Race, Class, and the Lesbian-Feminist Roots of Queer Theory*. Columbia University Press, 2001.

Garrard, Greg. *Ecocriticism*. Routledge, 2012.

Gessner, David. *All the Wild that Remains: Edward Abbey, Wallace Stegner, and the American West*. W. W. Norton & Company, 2015.

Gifford, Terry. *Pastoral*. Routledge, 1999.

Gilligan, Carol. *In a Different Voice: Psychological Theory and Women's Development*. 1982. Harvard University Press, 1993.

Ginsberg, Allen. *Planet News*. 1968. City Lights Books, 1970.

Gitlin, Todd. *The Sixties: Years of Hope, Days of Rage*. Bantam, 1987.

Golley, Frank Benjamin. *A History of the Ecosystem Concept in Ecology: More than the Sum of the Parts*. Yale University Press, 1993.

Gottlieb, Bob, and Marge Piercy. "Movement for a Democratic Society, Beginning to Begin to Begin." 1968. *The New Left: A Documentary History*, edited by Massimo Teodori, Bobbs-Merrill, 1969, pp. 403–10.

Gottlieb, Robert. *Forcing the Spring: The Transformation of the American Environmental Movement*. 1993. Island Press, 2005.

Grewal, Gurleen. *Circles of Sorrow, Lines of Struggle: The Novels of Toni Morrison*. Louisiana State University Press, 1998.

Griffin, Susan. *Made from This Earth: An Anthology of Writings*. Harper & Row, 1982.

    "Split Culture." *Healing the Wounds: The Promise of Ecofeminism*, edited by Judith Plant, New Society Publishers, 1989, pp. 7–17.

    Woman and Nature: The Roaring Inside Her. Harper & Row, 1978.

    Grizzly Man. Directed by Werner Herzog, Lionsgate Films, 2005.

Grob, Charles S. "The Psychology of Ayahuasca." *Ayahuasca: Hallucinations, Consciousness, and the Spirit of Nature*, edited by Ralph Metzner, Running Press, 1999, pp. 214–49.

Bibliography 233

Grosz, Elizabeth. *Becoming Undone: Darwinian Reflections on Life, Politics, and Art*. Duke University Press, 2011.

"Conclusion: A Note on Essentialism and Differences." *Feminist Knowledge: Critique and Construct*, edited by Sneja Marina Gunew, Routledge, 1990, pp. 332–44.

The Incorporeal: Ontology, Ethics, and the Limits of Materialism. Columbia University Press, 2017.

Hammond, Karla, and Margaret Atwood. "An Interview with Margaret Atwood." *The American Poetry Review*, vol. 8, no. 5, 1979, pp. 27–9.

Haraway, Donna. "A Cyborg Manifesto: Science, Technology, and Socialist-Feminism in the Late Twentieth Century." 1985. *The Critical Tradition: Classic Texts and Contemporary Trends*, edited by David H. Richter, Bedford/St. Martin's, 2007, pp. 1966–91.

How Like a Leaf: An Interview with Thyrza Nichols Goodeve. Routledge, 2000.

When Species Meet. University of Minnesota Press, 2007.

Harper, Steven. "The Way of Wilderness." *Ecopsychology: Restoring the Earth, Healing the Mind*, edited by Theodore Roszak, Mary E. Gomes, and Allen D. Kanner, Sierra Club Books, 1995, pp. 183–200.

Harpham, Geoffrey Galt. *The Ascetic Imperative in Culture and Criticism*. University of Chicago Press, 1987.

Hayden, Tom. "The Politics of the Movement." *The Radical Papers*, edited by Irving Howe, Doubleday, 1966.

Trial. Holt, Rinehart and Winston, 1970.

Hedgepath, William. "The Alternative." *Takin' It to the Streets: A Sixties Reader*, edited by Alexander Bloom and Wini Breines, Oxford University Press, 1995, pp. 329–34.

Heise, Ursula K. *Imagining Extinction: The Cultural Meanings of Endangered Species*. University of Chicago Press, 2016.

Sense of Place and Sense of Planet. Oxford University Press, 2008.

Hekman, Susan. "Constructing the Ballast: An Ontology for Feminism." *Material Feminisms*, edited by Stacy Alaimo and Susan Hekman, Indiana University Press, 2008, pp. 85–119.

Hepworth, James. "The Poetry Center Interview." *Resist Much, Obey Little: Remembering Ed Abbey*, edited by James R. Hepworth and Gregory McNamee. Sierra Club Books, 1996, pp. 33–42.

Hillman, James. "A Psyche the Size of the Earth: A Psychological Foreword." *Ecopsychology: Restoring the Earth, Healing the Mind*, edited by Theodore Roszak, Mary E. Gomes, and Allen D. Kanner, Sierra Club Books, 1995, pp. xvii–xxiii.

Himmelman, Jeff. "Peter Matthiessen's Homegoing." *New York Magazine*, 3 April 2014.

Hogeland, Lisa Maria. *Feminism and Its Fictions: The Consciousness-Raising Novel and the Women's Liberation Movement*. University of Pennsylvania Press, 1998.

Hooks, Bell. *Belonging: A Culture of Place*. Routledge, 2009.

234 *Bibliography*

Horton, Carol A. *Race and the Making of American Liberalism*. Oxford University Press, 2005.

Hume, Angela and Samila Rahimtoola. "Introduction: Queering Ecopoetics." *ISLE: Interdisciplinary Studies in Literature and Environment*, vol. 25, no. 1, 2018, pp.134–49.

Hutchison, Anthony. *Writing the Republic: Liberalism and Morality in American Political Fiction*. Columbia University Press, 2007.

Huxley, Aldous. *The Doors of Perception* and *Heaven and Hell*. 1954, 1956. Harper & Row, 1956.

Iovino, Serenella and Serpil Oppermann. "Introduction: Stories Come to Matter." *Material Ecocriticism*, edited by Serenella Iovino and Serpil Oppermann, Indiana University Press, 2014, pp. 1–17.

Jacobs, Jane. *The Death and Life of Great American Cities*. Random House, 1961.

Jaffe, Naomi and Bernardine Dohrn. "The Look Is You." 1968. *The New Left: A Documentary History*, edited by Massimo Teodori, Bobbs-Merrill, 1969, pp. 355–8.

Jung, Carl. "Approaching the Unconscious." *Man and His Symbols*," edited by Carl G. Jung, Dell, 1973, pp. 1–94.

"The Structure of the Psyche." *The Collected Works of C. G. Jung*, edited by Herbert Read et al., Princeton University Press, 1960.

Kaiser, Rudolph. "Chief Seattle's Speech(es): American Origins and European Reception." *Recovering the Word: Essays on Native American Literature*, edited by Brian Swann and Arnold Krupat, University of California Press, 1987.

Kheel, Marti. "Ecofeminism and Deep Ecology: Reflections on Identity and Difference." *Reweaving the World: The Emergence of Ecofeminism*, edited by Irene Diamond and Gloria Orenstein, Sierra Club Books, 1990.

Kirby, Vicki. *Quantum Anthropologies: Life at Large*. Duke University Press, 2011.

Kirk, Andrew G. *Counterculture Green: The* Whole Earth Catalog *and American Environmentalism*. University Press of Kansas, 2007.

Krakauer, Jon. *Into the Wild*. 1996. Anchor Books, 1997.

Into Thin Air. 1997. Anchor Books, 1999.

Krech, Shepard. *The Ecological Indian: Myth and History*. W. W. Norton & Company, 1999.

Laing, R. D. *The Divided Self: An Existential Study in Sanity and Madness*. 1960. Pantheon, 1969.

The Politics of Experience and the Bird of Paradise. Pantheon, 1967.

Latour, Bruno. "Why Gaia Is Not a God of Totality." *Theory, Culture & Society*, vol. 34, no. 2/3, 2017, pp. 61–81.

Lattin, Don. *The Harvard Psychedelic Club: How Timothy Leary, Ram Dass, Huston Smith, and Andrew Weil Killed the Fifties and Ushered in a New Age for America*. HarperOne, 2010.

Leary, Timothy. "Turning on the World." 1968. *The Portable Sixties Reader*, edited by Ann Charters, Penguin, 2003, pp. 331–43.

Bibliography

Lecker, Robert. "Janus through the Looking Glass: Atwood's First Three Novels." *The Art of Margaret Atwood: Essays in Criticism*, edited by Arnold E. Davidson and Cathy N. Davidson, Anansi Press, 1981, pp. 177–204.

LeClair, Thomas. "'The Language Must Not Sweat': A Conversation with Toni Morrison." *The New Republic*, 21 March 1981.

Lee, Martin A., and Bruce Shlain. *Acid Dreams: The Complete Social History of LSD: The CIA, the Sixties, and Beyond.* 1985. Grove Press, 1992.

Leopold, Aldo. *A Sand County Almanac.* 1949. Ballantine, 1966.

Levy, Ariel. "The Secret Life of Plants: The Green-Juice Generation Finds Its Drug of Choice." *The New Yorker*, 12 September 2016, pp. 30–6.

Light, Andrew. "Reconsidering Bookchin and Marcuse as Environmental Materialists: Toward an Evolving Social Ecology." *Social Ecology after Bookchin*, edited by Andrew Light, Guilford Press, 1998, pp. 343–83.

Lopez, Barry. *Arctic Dreams: Imagination and Desire in a Northern Landscape.* 1986. Vintage, 2001.

Crossing Open Ground. 1988. Vintage, 1989.

Love, Glen A. "Revaluing Nature: Toward an Ecological Criticism." *The Ecocriticism Reader*, edited by Cheryll Glotfelty and Harold Fromm, University of Georgia Press, 1996, pp. 225–40.

Lynch, Tom. *Xerophilia: Ecocritical Explorations in Southwestern Literature.* Texas Tech University Press, 2008.

MacIntyre, Alasdair. "After Virtue." 1981. *Justice: A Reader*, edited by Michael J. Sandel, Oxford University Press, 2007, pp. 315–28.

Macy, Joanna. "Awakening to the Ecological Self." *Healing the Wounds: The Promise of Ecofeminism*, edited by Judith Plant, New Society Publishers, 1989, pp. 201–11.

"Our Life as Gaia." *Thinking Like a Mountain: Towards a Council of All Beings*, edited by John Seed, Joanna Macy, Pat Fleming, and Arne Naess, New Society Publishers, 1988, pp. 57–65.

World as Lover, World as Self. Parallax Press, 1991.

Malcolm X. "Organization of Afro-American Unity." 1965. *Modern Black Nationalism: From Marcus Garvey to Louis Farrakhan*, edited by William L. Van Deburg, New York University Press, 1997, pp. 108–15.

Malni, Eric. "Animal Liberation Front: Raids on Medical Laboratories Defended." *Los Angeles Times*, 30 December 1984.

Marcuse, Herbert. "Ecology and Revolution." 1972. *The New Left and the 1960s: Collected Papers of Herbert Marcuse, Volume 3*, edited by Douglas Kellner, Routledge, 2005, pp. 173–6.

Eros and Civilization. 1955. Beacon Press, 1974.

One-Dimensional Man: Studies in the Ideology of Advanced Industrial Society. 1964. Beacon Press, 1991.

Matthiessen, Peter. *In the Spirit of Crazy Horse.* 1980. Viking Press, 1983.

The Snow Leopard. 1978. Penguin, 1996.

Matusow, Allen J. *The Unraveling of America: A History of Liberalism in the 1960s.* Harper & Row, 1984.

McCandless, Christopher. *Back to the Wild: The Photographs and Writings of Christopher McCandless*. Twin Star Press, 2011.

McClintock, James I. "Edwards Abbey's 'Antidotes to Despair.'" *Critique*, vol. 31, no. 1, 1989, pp. 41–54.

McKenna, Dennis. *The Brotherhood of the Screaming Abyss: My Life with Terence McKenna*. North Star Press, 2012.

McKenna, Dennis J., and Terence K. McKenna. *The Invisible Landscape: Mind, Hallucinogens, and the I Ching*. Seabury Press, 1975.

McKenna, Terence. *Food of the Gods: The Search for the Original Tree of Knowledge: A Radical History of Plants, Drugs, and Human Evolution*. Bantam, 1992.

True Hallucinations and *The Archaic Revival*. MJF Books, 1998.

McLaughlin, Andrew. "The Heart of Deep Ecology." *Deep Ecology for the Twenty-First Century*, edited by George Sessions, Shambhala, 1995, pp. 85–93.

Meißner, Hanna. "New Material Feminisms and Historical Materialism: A Diffractive Reading of Two (Ostensibly) Unrelated Perspectives." *Mattering: Feminism, Science, and Materialism*, edited by Victoria Pitts-Taylor, New York University Press, 2016, pp. 43–57.

Metzner, Ralph. "Hallucinogenic Drugs and Plants in Psychotherapy and Shamanism." *Journal of Psychoactive Drugs*, vol. 30, no. 4, 1998, pp. 333–41.

"Introduction: Amazonian Vine of Visions." *Ayahuasca: Hallucinations, Consciousness, and the Spirit of Nature*, edited by Ralph Metzner, Running Press, 1999, pp. 1–45.

Mitchell, Juliet. *Psychoanalysis and Feminism*. Pantheon, 1974.

Morgan, Robin. "Goodbye to All That." *Takin' It to the Streets: A Sixties Reader*, edited by Alexander Bloom and Wini Breines, Oxford University Press, 1995, pp. 499–503.

Morrison, Toni. "Behind the Making of *The Black Book*." 1974. *What Moves at the Margins*, University Press of Mississippi, 2008, pp. 34–8.

Beloved. 1987. Signet, 1991.

"The Future of Time: Literature and Diminished Expectations." 1996. *What Moves at the Margins*, University Press of Mississippi, 2008, pp. 170–86.

A Mercy. Alfred A. Knopf, 2008.

Playing in the Dark: Whiteness and the Literary Imagination. Harvard University Press, 1992.

"Rediscovering Black History." 1974. *What Moves at the Margins*, edited by Toni Morrison, University Press of Mississippi, 2008, pp. 39–55.

"Rootedness: The Ancestor as Foundation." 1984. *What Moves at the Margins*, edited by Toni Morrison, University Press of Mississippi, 2008, pp. 56–64.

Song of Solomon. 1977. Plume, 1987.

Morrison, Toni, and Nellie McKay. "An Interview with Toni Morrison." *Contemporary Literature*, vol. 24, no. 4, 1983, pp. 413–29.

Morrison, Toni, and Robert Stepto. "'Intimate Things in Place': A Conversation with Toni Morrison." *The Massachusetts Review*, vol. 18, no. 3, 1977, pp. 473–89.

Bibliography

Morrison, Toni, et al. "Toni Morrison, The Art of Fiction No. 134." *The Paris Review*, no. 128, Fall 1993.

Mortimer-Sandilands, Catriona, and Bruce Erickson. "Introduction: A Genealogy of Queer Ecologies." *Queer Ecologies: Sex, Nature, Politics, Desire*, edited by Catriona Mortimer-Sandilands and Bruce Erickson, Indiana University Press, 2010, pp. 1–47.

Morton, Timothy. *The Ecological Thought*. Harvard University Press, 2010.

    Ecology without Nature. Harvard University Press, 2007.

    "Queer Ecology." *PMLA*, vol. 125, no. 2, 2010, pp. 273–82.

Naess, Arne. *Ecology, Community and Lifestyle: Outline of an Ecosophy*. Cambridge University Press, 1989.

    "*Self* Realization: An Ecological Approach to Being in the World." *Thinking Like a Mountain: Towards a Council of All Beings*, edited by John Seed, Joanna Macy, Pat Fleming, and Arne Naess, New Society Publishers, 1988, pp. 19–30.

Nash, Roderick Frazier. *The Rights of Nature: A History of Environmental Ethics*. University of Wisconsin Press, 1989.

Nelson, Robert M. *Place and Vision: The Function of Landscape in Native American Fiction*. Peter Lang, 1993.

Newman, Karen. *Fetal Positions: Individualism, Science, Visuality*. Stanford University Press, 1996.

Newmark, Julianne. *The Pluralist Imagination from East to West in American Literature*. University of Nebraska Press, 2014.

Oderberg, David S. "Natural Law and Rights Theory." *The Routledge Companion to Social and Political Philosophy*, edited by Gerald Gaus and Fred D'Agostino, Routledge, 2013, pp. 375–84.

Orlie, Melissa A. "Impersonal Matter." *New Materialisms: Ontology, Agency, and Politics*, edited by Diana Coole and Samantha Frost, Duke University Press, 2010, pp. 116–36.

Ortiz, Simon J. "Foreword." *American Indian Literary Nationalism*, edited by Jace Weaver, Craig S. Womack, and Robert Warrior, University of New Mexico Press, 2005, pp. xii–xiii.

    Song, Poetry and Language: Expression and Perception. Navajo Community College Press, 1977.

    Woven Stone. University of Arizona Press, 1992.

Ortiz, Simon, and Janet McAdams. "A Conversation with Simon Ortiz." *The Kenyon Review*, vol. 32, no. 1, 2010, pp. 1–8.

Outka, Paul. *Race and Nature: From Transcendentalism to the Harlem Renaissance*. Palgrave Macmillan, 2008.

Payne, Daniel G. *Voices in the Wilderness: American Nature Writing and Environmental Politics*. University Press of New England, 1996.

Pease, Donald E. "National Identities, Postmodern Artifacts, and Postnational Narratives." *National Identities and Post-Americanist Narratives*, edited by Donald E. Pease, Duke University Press, 1994, pp. 1–13.

Peirce, Charles Sanders. "Some Consequences of Four Incapacities." *The Essential Peirce*, vol. 1, edited by Nathan Houser and Christian J. W. Kloesel, Indiana University Press, 1992, pp. 28–55.

Petchesky, Rosalind Pollack. "Fetal Images: The Power of Visual Culture in the Politics of Reproduction." *Feminist Studies*, vol. 13, no. 2, 1987, pp. 263–92.

Philippon, Daniel J. *Conserving Words: How American Nature Writers Shaped the Environmental Movement*. The University of Georgia Press, 2005.

Phillips, Dana. *The Truth of Ecology: Nature, Culture, and Literature in America*. Oxford University Press, 2003.

Pitts-Taylor, Victoria. "Mattering: Feminism, Science, and Corporeal Politics." *Mattering: Feminism, Science, and Materialism*, edited by Victoria Pitts-Taylor, New York University Press, 2016, pp. 1–20.

Plant, Judith. "Toward a New World: An Introduction." *Healing the Wounds: The Promise of Ecofeminism*, edited by Judith Plant, New Society Publishers, 1989, pp. 1–6.

Plumwood, Val. "The Ecopolitics Debate and the Politics of Nature." *Ecological Feminism*, edited by Karen J. Warren, Routledge, 1994, pp. 64–87.

Feminism and the Mastery of Nature. Routledge, 1993.

Poirier, Richard. *The Renewal of Literature: Emersonian Reflections*. Yale University Press, 1988.

Price, Melanye T. *Dreaming Blackness: Black Nationalism and African American Public Opinion*. New York University Press, 2009.

"The Principles of Environmental Justice." 2001. *Environmental Justice in Postwar America: A Documentary Reader*, edited by Christopher W. Wells, University of Washington Press, 2018, pp. 180–2.

Quigley, Peter. "Heraclitean Fire, Bakhtinian Laughter, and the Limits of Literary Judgment." *Coyote in the Maze: Tracking Edward Abbey in a World of Words*, edited by Peter Quigley, University of Utah Press, 1998, pp. 1–17.

Rao, Eleonora. *Strategies for Identity: The Fiction of Margaret Atwood*. Peter Lang Publishing, 1993.

Ray, Sarah Jaquette. *The Ecological Other: Environmental Exclusion in American Culture*. University of Arizona Press, 2013.

Roach, Catherine. "Loving Your Mother: On the Woman-Nature Relation." *Ecological Feminist Philosophies*, edited by Karen J. Warren, Indiana University Press, 1996, pp. 52–65.

Robinson, Dean E. *Black Nationalism in American Politics and Thought*. Cambridge University Press, 2001.

Robinson, Paul A. *The Freudian Left: Wilhelm Reich, Géza Roheim, Herbert Marcuse*. Harper Colophon, 1970.

Rolston, Holmes. "Is There an Ecological Ethic?" *Ethics*, vol. 18, no. 2, 1975, pp. 93–109.

Roorda, Randall. *Dramas of Solitude: Narratives of Retreat in American Nature Writing*. State University of New York Press, 1998.

Bibliography

Rorty, Richard. *Achieving Our Country: Leftist Thought in Twentieth-Century America*. Harvard University Press, 1998.

Rosiek, Jerry Lee and Jimmy Snyder. "Narrative Inquiry and New Materialism: Stories as (Not Necessarily Benign) Agents." *Qualitative Inquiry*, vol. 24, no. 8, 2018, pp. 1–12.

Rossinow, Doug. *The Politics of Authenticity: Liberalism, Christianity, and the New Left in America*. Columbia University Press, 1998.

Roszak, Theodore. *The Making of a Counter Culture*. 1968. University of California Press, 1995.

Person/Planet: The Creative Disintegration of Industrial Society. 1977. Anchor, 1978.

The Voice of the Earth. Simon & Schuster, 1992.

"Where Psyche Meets Gaia." *Ecopsychology: Restoring the Earth, Healing the Mind*, edited by Theodore Roszak, Mary E. Gomes, and Allen D. Kanner, Sierra Club Books, 1995, pp. 1–17.

Rothenberg, David. "Introduction: Ecosophy T: From Intuition to System." *Ecology, Community and Lifestyle: Outline of an Ecosophy*, edited by Arne Naess, Cambridge University Press, 1989.

Rothman, Barbara Katz. *The Tentative Pregnancy: Prenatal Diagnosis and the Future of Motherhood*. Viking, 1986.

Roy, Deboleena and Banu Subramaniam. "Matter in the Shadows: Feminist New Materialism and the Practices of Colonialism." *Mattering: Feminism, Science, and Materialism*, edited by Victoria Pitts-Taylor, New York University Press, 2016, pp. 23–42.

Rusho, W. L. *Everett Ruess: A Vagabond for Beauty*. Peregrine Smith Books, 1983.

Ruether, Rosemary Radford. *Gaia & God: An Ecofeminist Theology of Earth Healing*. HarperCollins, 1992.

"Toward an Ecological-Feminist Theology of Nature." *Healing the Wounds: The Promise of Ecofeminism*, edited by Judith Plant, New Society Publishers, 1989, pp. 145–50.

Ruffin, Kimberly N. *Black on Earth: African American Ecoliterary Traditions*. University of Georgia Press, 2010.

Ryder, Richard D. *Victims of Science: The Use of Animals in Research*. Open Gate Press, 1975.

Salleh, Ariel Kay. "Deeper than Deep Ecology: The Eco-Feminist Connection." *Environmental Ethics*, vol. 6, no. 4, 1984, pp. 339–45.

Saverin, Diana. "The Chris McCandless Obsession Problem." *Outside*, 18 December 2013.

Savio, Mario. Speech at Sproul Hall Steps, 2 December 1964. University of California Berkeley Free Speech Movement Archives.

Schlosberg, David. *Environmental Justice and the New Pluralism*. Oxford University Press, 1999.

Schulman, Bruce J. *The Seventies: The Great Shift in American Culture, Society, and Politics*. The Free Press, 2001.

240 *Bibliography*

Schultes, Richard Evans, and Albert Hofmann. *Plants of the Gods: Origins of Hallucinogenic Use.* McGraw-Hill, 1979.

Schweitzer, Albert. *Indian Thought and Its Development.* Beacon Press, 1935.

Searles, Harold F. *The Nonhuman Environment in Normal Development and in Schizophrenia.* International Universities Press, 1960.

Sedgwick, Eve Kosofsky. *Epistemology of the Closet.* University of California Press, 1990.

Seed, John. "Beyond Anthropomorphism." *Thinking Like a Mountain: Towards a Council of All Beings,* edited by John Seed, Joanna Macy, Pat Fleming, and Arne Naess, New Society Publishers, 1988, pp. 35–40.

"Introduction: 'To Hear Within Ourselves the Sound of the Earth Crying.'" *Thinking Like a Mountain: Towards a Council of All Beings,* edited by John Seed, Joanna Macy, Pat Fleming, and Arne Naess, New Society Publishers, 1988, pp. 5–17.

Seed, John, and Joanna Macy. "Gaia Meditations." *Thinking Like a Mountain: Towards a Council of All Beings,* edited by John Seed, Joanna Macy, Pat Fleming, and Arne Naess, New Society Publishers, 1988, pp. 41–3.

Serres, Michel. *The Natural Contract.* 1990. University of Michigan Press, 1995.

Seymour, Nicole. *Strange Natures: Futurity, Empathy, and the Queer Ecological Imagination.* University of Illinois Press, 2013.

Shepard, Paul. "Ecology and Man—A Viewpoint." *The Subversive Science,* edited by Paul Shepard and Daniel McKinley, Houghton Mifflin, 1969, pp. 1–10.

Nature and Madness. 1982. University of Georgia Press, 1998.

"Whatever Happened to Human Ecology?" *BioScience,* vol. 17, no. 12, 1967, pp. 891–4.

Shreve, Bradley G. *Red Power Rising: The National Indian Youth Council and the Origins of Native Activism.* University of Oklahoma Press, 2011.

Sipchen, Bob. "Ecology's Family Feud: Murray Bookchin Turns Up Volume on Noisy Debate." *Los Angeles Times,* 27 March 1989.

Silko, Leslie Marmon. "Interior and Exterior Landscapes: The Pueblo Migration Stories." *Landscape in America,* edited by George F. Thompson, University of Texas Press, 1995, pp. 155–69.

Slicer, Deborah. "Wrongs of Passage: Three Challenges to the Maturing of Ecofeminism." *Ecological Feminism,* edited by Karen J. Warren, Routledge, 1994, pp. 29–41.

Slovic, Scott. *Seeking Awareness in Nature Writing: Henry Thoreau, Annie Dillard, Edward Abbey, Wendell Berry, Barry Lopez.* University of Utah Press, 1992.

Smith, Paul Chaat and Robert Allen Warrior. *Like a Hurricane: The Indian Movement from Alcatraz to Wounded Knee.* W. W. Norton & Company, 1996.

Smith, Sherry L. *Hippies, Indians, and the Fight for Red Power.* Oxford University Press, 2012.

Snitow, Ann Barr. "The Front Line: Notes on Sex in Novels by Women, 1969–1979." *Signs,* vol. 5, no. 4, 1980, pp. 702–18.

Bibliography

Snyder, Gary. "Buddhism and the Coming Revolution." *Takin' It to the Streets: A Sixties Reader*, edited by Alexander Bloom and Wini Breines, Oxford University Press, 2011, pp. 250–2.

The Old Ways: Six Essays. City Lights, 1977.

The Practice of the Wild. North Point Press, 1990.

Turtle Island. 1969. New Directions, 1974.

Spretnak, Charlene. "Toward an Ecofeminist Spirituality." *Healing the Wounds: The Promise of Ecofeminism*, edited by Judith Plant, New Society Publishers, 1989, pp. 127–32.

Stanworth, Michelle. "Reproductive Technologies and the Deconstruction of Motherhood." *Reproductive Technologies: Gender, Motherhood and Medicine*, edited by Michelle Stanworth, University of Minnesota Press, 1987.

Stegner, Wallace. *Mormon Country.* Duell, Sloan, & Pearce, 1942.

Where the Bluebird Sings to the Lemonade Springs: Living and Writing in the West. Penguin, 1992.

Stewart, James T. "The Development of the Black Revolutionary Artist." *Black Fire: An Anthology of Afro-American Writing*, edited by LeRoi Jones and Larry Neal, Morrow, 1968, pp. 3–10.

Stimpson, Catharine R. "Editorial." *Signs*, vol. 2, no. 2, 1976, pp. vi–vii.

Stone, Christopher. *Should Trees Have Standing? Toward Legal Rights for Natural Objects. 1972.* Oxford University Press, 2010.

Students for a Democratic Society. "America and New Era." 1963. *The New Left: A Documentary History*, edited by Massimo Teodori, Bobbs-Merrill, 1969, pp. 172–82.

"Port Huron Statement." 1962. *The New Left: A Documentary History*, edited by Massimo Teodori, Bobbs-Merrill, 1969, pp.163–72.

Tagnani, David. "New Materialism, Ecomysticism, and the Resolution of Paradox in Edward Abbey." *Western American Literature*, vol. 50, no. 4, 2016, pp. 317–46

Tate, Claudia. "Interview with Toni Morrison." 1987. *Conversations with Toni Morrison*, edited by Danielle Taylor-Guthrie, University Press of Mississippi, 1994, pp. 156–70.

Taylor, Charles. "The Politics of Recognition." *Multiculturalism and "The Politics of Recognition"* by Charles Taylor, Princeton University Press, 1992, pp. 25–73.

Taylor, Dorceta. *Race, Class, Gender, and American Environmentalism.* U.S. Department of Agriculture, Forest Service, Pacific Northwest Research Station, 2002.

Teodori, Massimo. "Historical and Critical Notes." *The New Left: A Documentary History*, edited by Massimo Teodori, Bobbs-Merrill, 1969, pp. 3–90.

Terry, Jennifer. "'Breathing the Air of a World So New': Rewriting the Landscape of America in Toni Morrison's *A Mercy.*" *Journal of American Studies*, vol. 48, no. 1, 2014, pp. 127–45.

Bibliography

Thomas, Wilbur L. "Black Survival in Our Polluted Cities." 1970. *Environmental Justice in Postwar America: A Documentary Reader*, edited by Christopher W. Wells, University of Washington Press, 2018, pp. 99–103.

Thoreau, Henry David. *The Journal of Henry David Thoreau, 1837–1861*. Edited by Damion Searls, New York Review of Books Classics, 2009.

Ture, Kwame, and Charles V. Hamilton. *Black Power: The Politics of Liberation*. 1967. Vintage, 1992.

van Wyck, Peter C. *Primitives in the Wilderness: Deep Ecology and the Missing Human Subject*. State University of New York Press, 1997.

Versluis, Arthur. *American Gurus: From Transcendentalism to New Age Religion*. Oxford University Press, 2014.

Wallace, Kathleen R., and Karla Armbruster. "The Novels of Toni Morrison: 'Wild Wilderness Where There Was None.'" *Beyond Nature Writing: Expanding the Boundaries of Ecocriticism*, edited by Karla Armbruster and Kathleen R. Wallace, University Press of Virginia, 2001, pp. 211–30.

Watts, Alan W. *Beat Zen, Square Zen and Zen*. City Lights, 1959.

In My Own Way: An Autobiography 1915–1965. Pantheon, 1972.

Nature, Man and Woman. 1958. Pantheon, 1969.

The Way of Zen. Pantheon, 1957.

Weisberg, Barry. "The Politics of Ecology." *The Ecological Conscience: Values for Survival*, edited by Robert Disc, Prentice Hall, 1970, pp. 154–60.

Wisker, Gina. *Margaret Atwood: An Introduction to Critical Views of Her Fiction*. Palgrave Macmillan, 2012.

Wolfe, Cary. *What Is Posthumanism?* University of Minnesota Press, 2010.

Wolfe, Tom. *The Electric Kool-Aid Acid Test*. 1968. Bantam, 1989.

Womack, Craig S. *Red on Red: Native American Literary Separatism*. University of Minnesota Press, 1999.

Zaretsky, Eli. "From Psychoanalysis to Cybernetics: The Case of Her." *American Imago*, vol. 72, no. 2, 2015, pp. 197–210.

Index

Abbey, Edward:
  Desert Solitaire, 15, 22, 27, 28–31, 35–6, 40–50
  Down the River, 28–31
  Jonathan Troy, 36
  The Monkeywrench Gang
  alternative ecological civilization of, 22, 27, 30,
    31, 36, 43–8
  anarchism of, 28, 30, 31
  conflict with Murray Bookchin, 18, 34–5,
    47
  creative account of self-identity, 40–3
  critique of authenticity's environmentalist
    value, 31, 55–8
  critique of mysticism, 51–2, 68
  critique of psychedelics, 67, 68
  critique of psychoanalysis, 39
  dismissal of ecological science, 35
  dissolution rhetoric of, 14, 15, 49–50, 53, 59
  ideological overlap with the New Left, 28, 29,
    30, 31, 35, 36, 41, 42, 44, 45, 47
  gendered rhetoric of, 44, 48, 56, 123, 188
  perspective on death, 56, 190–1
  racialized rhetoric of, 104
  resistance to environmentalist identity
    politics, 207
abortion, 137, 138, 142, 146, 150, 151
acid, *see* LSD.
Adamson, Joni, 86, 92, 130, 131
agency:
  of human subjects, 25, 127, 200
  of nonhuman animals, matter, or assemblages,
    46, 136, 156, 157, 158, 201, 202
Ahuja, Neel, 131
Alaimo, Stacy, 40, 133, 162
Alcatraz: occupation of, 105, 106, 112
alienation:
  political, 9, 11, 23, 29, 107, 176
  psychic, 9, 10, 13, 29, 37, 52, 75, 77, 103, 113,
    114–15, 177, 179
  from nature, 129, 144
Alpert, Richard, *see* Dass, Ram.

alternative:
  ecology as, 20, 22, 30–1, 36–7, 43–7
  as reference to social organization, 22, 30, 36,
    see also Port Huron Statement.
American Indian Movement (AIM), 112
anarchism:
  and Edward Abbey, 30, 34, 47
  and Murray Bookchin, 30, 32–4, 47, 54,
    176, 178
  and the student movement, 106
Anderson, Elizabeth, 130
Animal Liberation Front, 104
antinuclear movement, 35
antipastoral, 73
antipsychiatry, 80
antisocial thesis, 203–4
antiwar movement, 107, 138
anthropomorphism, 45
Appiah, Kwame Anthony, 20, 21, 115, 116
Armbruster, Karla, 140
asceticism, 184, 188
assemblage, 131, 132, 157, 171, 201
Atwood, Margaret:
  Alias Grace, 153
  The Edible Woman, 153
  The Handmaid's Tale, 141–69
  MaddAddam trilogy, 142, 162
  Oryx and Crake, 142, 162
  Surfacing, 24, 135–9, 141–3, 145–53, 155–6,
    158–9, 161, 164, 196–7
  The Year of the Flood, 162
  anti-essentialism of, 168
  attitude toward abortion and reproductive
    technology, 142
  attitude toward second-wave feminism,
    138, 139
  on Canadian woman protagonists, 135
  in the context of second-wave feminist debate,
    18, 24
  critique of biological reduction in the works
    of, 14, 24, 136, 142, 143

Index

Atwood, Margaret (cont.)
  critique of nature-feminist alignment of
    woman with nature, 133, 141
  illumination of continuity between nature
    feminism and posthumanist thought, 24,
    137, 153
  interpretation of essentialism as a matter of
    matter rather than gender, 147
  perspective on language's relationship to
    ecological consciousness, 159, 163
  resistance to environmentalist identity politics,
    162, 207
  on the role of fiction, 141
authenticity:
  critique of, 20, 25, 26, 200, 201, 202, 207,
    208, 209
  ecological authenticity, *see* ecological
    authenticity
  and feminist politics, 134
  personal authenticity, 3, 6, 13, 39, 57
  politics of authenticity, 2, 7, 8, 9, 12, 29, 30, 45,
    48, 52, 60, 111, 200
  and queer theory, 205
  and racial politics, 23, 97, 98, 109, 111, 112, 113,
    115, 116, 125, 127
  rhetorical nature of, 62, 83, 175, 181, 182, 190,
    195, 205
  as settler-colonial rhetoric, 13, 23, 62, 77, 81, 85,
    86, 98
ayahuasca, 60–1, 66, 68, 78–80, 84

back-to-the-land movement, 22, 33, 43, 76
Barad, Karen, 158–9, 163, 168
Baraka, Amiri, 110, 112, 124, 220
beat generation, 63, 74, 87, 220
Bennett, Jane, 156–7, 201
Bergson, Henri, 83
Bergthaller, Hannes, 35, 163
Berkeley Barb, 63
Berlant, Lauren, 203
Berry, Wendell, 28, 36, 41, 104
Berry, Wes, 104
Bersani, Leo, 203–6
Best, Stephen, 18, 199
biocentrism, 33, 34, 102, 170, 174
biologism, 135, 142, 143, 222
Black Aesthetic, 220
Black liberation theology, 129, 133
Black nationalism, 17, 107, 108, 119
  conflict with postwar liberalism, 96, 108,
    118, 130
  essentialist tendency in *Song of Solomon*, 23,
    110, 111
  rhetorical similarity to environmentalist
    identity politics, 99, 127

sexism within, 109
Black Power, 2, 23, 98, 108, 110–30, 131
Bohr, Niels, 224
Bookchin, Murray:
  Post-Scarcity Anarchism, 34
  and deep ecology, 33, 34, 96, 178, 214
  and Edward Abbey, 34–6, 47, 52
  and the New Left and counterculture, 30,
    31–4, 64
  and psychoanalysis, 10, 37, 53–5, 57
Braidotti, Rosi, 10, 156, 161–4
Brand, Stewart, 43, 76, *see also Whole Earth
  Catalog*
Brown, Norman O., 8, 53–4, 59, 66, 71, 77, 78,
    82, 202
Browne, Robert S.: "The Case for Two
  Americas", 109
Buell, Lawrence, 41
Bundy, Ammon, 208
Burroughs, William, 79

Calvert, Greg, 29, 37, 58
capitalism:
  and environmentalism, 32, 76
  and identity politics, 99
  and radical psychoanalysis, 37, 154, 155, 157
  in *Song of Solomon*, 103
  in *Surfacing*, 138, 149, 155
Carmichael, Stokely, 107–8, 110, 118
Carson, Rachel: *Silent Spring*, 2, 5, 8, 28, 96
Chief Seattle: alleged speech of, 76
Chodorow, Nancy Julia, 134, 144–5, 147
civilization:
  spatially opposed to nature, as facet of
    traditional wilderness narrative, 1, 5, 6, 41
  psychically opposed to nature, as facet of
    environmentalist identity politics, 11, 12, 20,
    131, 132, 146, 172, 173, 200, 205
  counterposed against Indigeneity, 23, 61, 76, 85
  in Left Freudian thought, 10, 37, 38, 66
  in New Left thought, 7, 97
  as patriarchal institution, 117, 134, 143, 144, 145
  as racial institution, 110, 124
  relationship to ego in literary
    environmentalism, 4, 39
  relationship to ego in psychoanalysis, 9, 143,
    186, 187, 188
  in social ecology, 22, 53, 54, 57
  as descriptor for wilderness in *Desert Solitaire*,
    36, 43, 44, 45, 46, 47
  in *The Snow Leopard*, 72
  in *Into the Wild*, 171, 177, 178, 179, 183, 185, 186,
    187, 188, 189, 190, 194
Civil Rights Act, 118
civil rights movement, 11, 100, 104, 105, 106–7

Index

245

and environmental justice, 130, 133
and relationship to Black nationalism, 98, 110, 131
Cleaver, Eldridge, 110, 124
climate change, 6, 98, 128, 193, 201, 205
close reading: relationship to intellectual history, 17, 21
Cody, Iron Eyes, 76
colonialism:
  and authenticity, 13, 23
  of Canada by the United States, 148–9
  and gender, 48, 119, 124, 135
  of Indigenous lands, 62, 86, 91–3, 127
Combahee River Collective, 131, 222
Comment, 33
Commoner, Barry: *The Closing Circle*, 43, 210
commune, 33, 36, 58, 76
communism:
  and environmentalist anarchism, 30, 33, 35
  and postwar liberal consensus, 7
communitarianism, 130
Congress of Racial Equality (CORE), 107
consciousness: expansion of, 22, 51, 59–62, 64–6, 72, 74, 79
Cone, James H., 128–9, 133
Coole, Diana and Samantha Frost: *New Materialisms*, 158, 160–1
Corea, Gena, 133
counterculture, American:
  commitment to authenticity, 2, 3, 44, 63, 209
  decline of, 58, 64, 77
  and environmentalist identity politics, 22, 81, 128
  and Indigenous appropriations, 88, 92, 94
  and psychedelics, 60, 80
  influence on Christopher McCandless, 172
  misogyny among, 138
  psychoanalytic influences, 9, 53, 145, 208
  relationship to New Left, 31, 32, 33, 77, 100
counternarrative, 19, 140
Crenshaw, Kimberlé, 135, 222
cultural nationalism:
  conflict with postwar American liberalism, 106
  in *Song of Solomon*, 96
culture:
  as foil for nature, 1, 5, 11, 41, 44, 94, 143, 160, 164, 171, 175, 180, 186, 205
  as foil for woman as well as nature, 133, 139, 140, 141, 144, 145, 147
cybernetics, 76, 153–4

Daly, Mary: *Gyn/Ecology*, 139–41, 147, 162
Dass, Ram, 65, 70
death drive, 66, 163, 193

deep ecology:
  definition and values of, 33, 102, 178, 179
  commercialization of, 195, 198
  conflict with social ecology, 33, 34, 133, 212
  and dissolution, 12, 172, 181
  feminist critique of, 12, 181, 198
  and psychoanalysis, 77
  and the self, 179
  and *Into the Wild*, 24
Deleuze, Gilles and Félix Guattari: *Anti-Oedipus*, 154–7
Deloria, Philip J., 76, 217
depth:
  in terms of the psyche, 64, 146, 159
  as it illustrates the relationship between psychoanalysis and the network paradigm, 153, 154, 155, 160
Desert Solitaire (Abbey):
  alternative ecological civilization in, 22, 27, 30, 36, 43–8
  dissolution in, 15, 22, 55, 57, 59
  and the environmental movement, 28
  and New Left thought, 29
  psychedelic imagery in, 67
  psychoanalytic undertones of "feeling like a river" in, 47–50
  tension between selfhood and ecosystem in, 31, 35, 40–2, 55–6
Devall, Bill and George Sessions: *Deep Ecology*, 1, 102, 177–9, 181
  and "the minority tradition", 96–7, 113–16
Dewey, John, 19
Dillard, Annie: *Pilgrim at Tinker Creek*, 1, 36, 41, 50–1, 58, 125
Dinnerstein, Dorothy, 134
dissolution:
  as motif, 1, 13–20, 25, 26, 200, 205, 206, 207, 208
  in countercultural discourse, 22, 61, 80
  in deep ecology, 172, 193
  in nature-feminist writing, 146
  in queer ecology, 203
  in *Desert Solitaire*, 15, 22, 55, 57, 59
  in *The Snow Leopard*, 68, 70, 74
  in *Woven Stone*, 62, 91, 92
  in *Song of Solomon*, 23, 95, 96, 99, 102–4, 113, 114, 115, 116, 118, 123, 124, 125, 127, 129, 130, 131
  in the novels of Margaret Atwood, 135, 136, 150, 165, 168
  in *Into the Wild*, 1, 172, 175, 187, 190, 191, 194
Doubiago, Sharon, 135
dualism:
  between man/woman, 8, 138, 140–1, 145

246 Index

dualism (cont.)
  between nature/culture, 41, 133, 140–1, 145, 175,
    180, 185
  between real/artificial, 8, 175, 204
  between self/other, 66, 168

Earth Day, 27–8, 31, 33
Earth First!, 28, 34
ecocriticism, 40
ecofeminism, 19, 25, 138, 152, 172, 202
  definition and values of, 133
  ecofeminist critique of nature feminism, 12, 134
  and *Surfacing*, 143
  see also nature feminism
ecological authenticity:
  definition of, 3, 4, 10, 11, 12, 13
  comparison to similar appeals, 97, 98, 113, 115,
    130, 131
  countercultural appeals to, 22, 61, 62, 63, 92
  deep-ecological appeals to, 181, 193
  feminist appeals to, 135, 140, 143, 144, 146
  New Left appeals to, 22
  political bankruptcy of, 94, 172, 173, 196,
    197, 206
  posthumanist appeals to, 52, 137, 157, 158, 160
  relationship to dissolution, 15, 16, 17, 18, 19,
    20, 21
  social-ecological appeals to, 57
  and *Desert Solitaire*, 29, 30, 31, 42, 50, 55
  and *The Snow Leopard*, 74
  and *Song of Solomon*, 99, 103, 129
  and *Surfacing*, 138, 165
  and *Into the Wild*, 24, 171, 174, 176
ecology:
  and the American counterculture, 60
  and appeals to authenticity, 31, 57
  as holistic unity, 8, 21, 54, 55, 171, 210
  as identity position, 3, 14, 136, 195
  identification with minority populations, 129
  interactions with psychoanalysis, 1, 2, 4, 18, 21,
    23, 38, 39, 53, 61, 154
  and moral outrage, 115
  and New Left politics, 2, 8, 10, 22, 176
  and posthumanist thought, 152, 155, 164
  and representation, 3, 5, 16, 86, 128, 163, 200,
    202, 209
  as science, 2, 3, 4, 5, 99, 134, 210
  and social ecology's dismissal of hierarchy, 31,
    32, 33, 35, 47, 54
  as a subject of repression, 10, 11, 72, 131, 200,
    202, 204
  as system or network, 3, 5, 6, 51, 72, 174, 180,
    197, 200, 206
  in tension with selfhood, 8, 14, 15, 19, 58, 137,
    192, 194, 205, 208

as universal condition, 23, 97, 98, 104, 118,
    135, 170
ecomysticism, 40
ecopsychology, 1, 2, 157
Edelman, Lee, 203
ego:
  in *Civilization and Its Discontents*, 9, 49, 185–9
  in deep ecology, 116, 179, 181
  dissolution of, 11, 13, 70, 74–5, 77, 79, 162, 174,
    177, 181
  in feminist psychoanalysis, 144
  ostensible Indigenous lack of, 74–5, 76, 82
  in Left Freudian thought, 8, 31, 37, 38, 40, 59
  opposed to nature in literary
    environmentalism, 1, 4, 5, 6, 9, 24, 63, 77,
    156, 194
  in posthumanist thought, 154, 162
  and psychedelics, 60, 61, 63, 65, 66, 79, 80, 85
  in queer theory, 203, 204
  relationship to language, 82, 83, 84, 85
  in social ecology, 54, 55
  ostensible weakness in women, 143, 154
  and Zen Buddhism, 67, 69, 70, 71, 74–5, 93
ego psychology, 80, 153
Ehrlich, Paul: *The Population Bomb*, 211
Emerson, Ralph Waldo: *Nature*, 19, 73, 216
Endangered Species Act, 100
environmental consciousness, 198
environmental degradation, 129
environmental humanities, 6, 16, 199
environmentalism:
  as a general movement, 2, 10, 11, 12, 23, 96, 97,
    133, 172, 195, 205
  as a mainstream movement, 80, 96, 98, 130
  as genre, 6
  and authenticity, 31, 52
  and deep ecology, 181, 193
  and Indigenous peoples, 85, 92
  and nature feminism, 143
  and neoliberalism, 197, 198
  New Left attitudes toward, 22, 27, 34, 41, 45
  and spirituality, 76
  white masculine dominance of, 9, 98
  of Edward Abbey, 28, 40, 48
  of Theodore Roszak, 53
environmentalist discourse, 10
environmentalist identity politics, *see* identity
    politics of ecology
environmental justice:
  as a movement, 6, 19, 25, 96–7, 130–3, 207
  antecedents of, 99, 105, 112, 130
  and Simon Ortiz, 62–3, 92–3
environmental movement, 28
environmental policy, 128
environmental politics, 4, 105, 130, 173, 193

Index

247

environmental racism, 18, 86, 128
environmental thinking, 29, 173, 202
environmental thought, 4, 6, 39, 200
environmental writing, 16, 58, 62, 112, 204
epistemology, 140
  conflict with ontology in new-materialist
    thought, 157
Eros, 204, *see also* pleasure principle
essentialism:
  and ecological politics, 21, 24, 133, 136, 202
  and feminist thought, 18, 24, 134, 135, 164
  and new materialism, 136, 137, 162
  and queer ecology, 204
  and race in *Song of Solomon*, 99, 112, 115, 128
ethics:
  and the American counterculture, 63
  and ecofeminism, 134
  and environmentalist identity politics, 13
  and Freud, 188
  and posthumanism, 163
  and the rights-of-nature tradition, 96, 98, 100,
    101, 102
  and social ecology, 52, 57
ethnobotany, 78, 87

fantasy: of merger or self-erasure, 9, 88, 89, 151,
    178, 189, 218
Felski, Rita, 18, 199, 201
feminism:
  in the context of the new social
    movements, 107
  and gender essentialism, 134, 139
  and new materialism, 136
  and psychoanalysis, 134, 144, 145
  and women of color, 139
fetus: as metaphor for psychic prehistory, 146,
    148, 149, 150, 151
Finney, Carolyn, 118
FOLK Lifestyle, 196
Foreman, Dave, 34
Fox, Warwick, 181
Freud, Sigmund
  and the American counterculture, 65–6
  and *Civilization and Its Discontents*, 9, 10, 37,
    39, 71, 180, 185–8, 193, 203
  and feminism, 143
  and new-materialist thought, 160
  and the "oceanic feeling", 9, 49, 79, 185
Freudian Left, 8, 10, 24, 39, 65–77, 155, 172, 188
Fromm, Erich, 30
Fromm, Harold, 39, 170
Fuss, Diana, 222

Gaard, Greta, 204
Gaia hypothesis, 102

as spirituality, 153, 162
Garber, Linda, 136
Gifford, Terry, 73
Gilligan, Carol: *In a Different Voice*, 134, 144–5
Ginsberg, Allen, 59, 63–5, 74, 79, 87, 220
Gitlin, Todd, 63, 66, 77, 81
Goodman, Paul, 153
Google Earth: as critical practice, 16, *See also*
    Heise, Ursula K.
green consumerism, 6, 197
Griffin, Susan: *Woman and Nature*, 133, 138–41,
    143–6, 162
Grob, Charles S., 79
Grosz, Elizabeth, 157, 159, 161–2, 167

Hamilton, Charles V., 107, 108, 110, 118
Haraway, Donna, 21, 136, 152, 199
  and "A Cyborg Manifesto", 152, 207
  and new-materialist method, 160, 163, 168
Hardin, Garrett: "The Tragedy of the
    Commons", 210
Hargrove, Eugene: *Beyond Spaceship Earth*, 102
Harpham, Geoffrey Galt, 184
Hayden, Tom, 37, 58
hallucinogens, *see* psychedelics
Heise, Ursula K., 14, 16, 80
Herzog, Werner: *Grizzly Man*, 182, 185, 190–1
hierarchy: ecology's disruption of, 32–3, 35, 53–4
Hoffman, Abbie, 34
Hogeland, Lisa Marie, 139
holism:
  and ecology, 14, 40, 42, 102, 129, 157, 161,
    162, 193
  and psychology, 38, 145, 161
hooks, bell, 16, 95, 103–4
Human Be-In, 63
humanism, 160
Hume, Angela, 203, 204
Huxley, Aldous:
  on consciousness expansion, 65, 66–7, 68,
    74, 78
  on language as "reducing valve", 83–4

I Ching, 76, 81
id, 58, 63, 66, 71, 154
idealism, 139, 162, 177
identification:
  with animals, 123
  with ecosystem, as a feature of
    environmentalist identity politics, 15, 63
  with ecosystem, in deep ecology, 12, 33, 54, 192
  with ecosystem, in nature feminism, 146, 147
  with ecosystem, in social ecology, 57
  with ecosystem, in *Desert Solitaire*, 31, 55
  with ecosystem, in *Surfacing*, 24

Index

identification (cont.)
with ecosystem, in *The Snow Leopard*, 62
with ecosystem, in *Song of Solomon*, 114, 125, 128
with ecosystem, in *Surfacing*, 137, 143, 148, 151, 164, 166
with ecosystem, in *Into the Wild*, 1, 177, 185, 187, 190
ego-dissolution as expression of, 14
with the Enlightenment subject, 56
as a feature of oral tradition, 88
with matter or energy, 43, 72, 135
with one's mother, 145, 151
with reproductive capacity, 24, 137, 142, 143, 148
with self-image, 90, 151
with victims of American imperialism, 77, 108
identity politics of ecology (IPE), 2, 4, 13, 31, 60, 149
definition of, 3, 10, 116
relationship to the dissertation motif, 14, 18
relationship to ecological authenticity, 11
antecedents of, 20
Christopher McCandless as culmination of, 18, 148, 171, 172, 177, 179, 194, 198
in contrast to environmental justice, 131, 132
as cultural narrative, 12, 168, 208
and deep ecology, 181, 193
indifference to social distinctions, 12, 124
legacy of, 200, 202, 205, 206, 208, 209
literary critique of, 15, 17, 18, 19, 20, 21, 25, 119, 201, 207
and nature feminism, 24, 134, 135, 144, 146
and the New Left, 22
political nihilism of, 25, 148, 172, 173, 198
and posthumanist thought, 136, 137, 154, 155, 156, 157, 161, 162, 163, 164
psychoanalytic framework of, 11, 185, 192
in relation to social movements, 11, 18, 98, 99, 112, 113, 116
revision of the wilderness narrative, 11, 23, 25, 119, 124, 173, 195
universalist scope of, 2, 23, 98, 99, 119, 124, 130
white masculine prejudices of, 13, 23, 99, 124
immediatism, 60
imperialism:
and Canada, 138
countercultural resistance to, 32, 77
and Indigenous Americans, 91, 115
infancy:
and environment, 71–2, 80, 151, 156–7, 180
and gender, 144–5
and Native peoples, 23, 81–2
as psychic state, 9, 10, 37, 38, 49, 66, 84, 90, 154, 185–8, 203

Indians of All Tribes, 105, 112
Instagram: as venue for the wilderness narrative, 3, 196–8
interconnectivity (also interconnection, interconnectedness):
in conflict with the individual, 8, 57, 58, 119, 161
as ecological condition, 11, 17, 25, 104, 125, 152, 206, 207
as environmentalist virtue, 9, 47, 52, 87, 99, 131, 187
in Indigenous storytelling, 88, 91, 92
in psychoanalysis, 79, 144, 145
Interdisciplinary Studies in Literature and Environment, 203
intersubjectivity
as countercultural goal, 59, 69
in *Desert Solitaire*, 49, 52, 59
Into the Wild (Krakauer):
and the "ascetic superhero", 173, 181–5
and *Civilization and Its Discontents*, 185–9
conversational aesthetics of, 173, 178
critical treatment of dissolution and ecological authenticity, 18, 25, 173
dissolution in, 1, 172, 175, 187, 190, 191, 194
psychoanalytic revision of the wilderness narrative represented by, 1, 24, 172, 185–9
references to the New Left and counterculture in, 176–7
relationship between death and ecological authenticity in, 24, 172, 173, 174, 180, 191–5
relationship among nature/culture, real/artificial, and ecology/self dualisms in, 170–1, 175–7, 179, 185–9
representation of sexuality in, 190, 204
speculative characterization of Christopher McCandless in, 173, 174–6, 180
success, cult following, and legacy of, 171, 195
Iovino, Serenella and Serpil Oppermann: *Material Ecocriticism*, 199

Jacobs, Jane, 205
James, William, 19, 73
Jung, Carl, 67, 83–4

Kerouac, Jack: *The Dharma Bums*, 74–5, 220
Kesey, Ken, 59, 64, 66, 69–70, 76, 215
King, Martin Luther, Jr., 106
Krakauer, Jon:
Into the Wild, 1, 18, 24, 25, 170–95, 204
Into Thin Air, 191
resistance to environmentalist identity politics, 207
Krech, Shepard: *The Ecological Indian*, 76, 92

Index

Lacan, Jacques, 84–5, 90
Laing, R. D., 7–8, 65, 80, 224
Lamothe, Ron: *The Call of the Wild*, 174–5
language, symbolic:
  as a generative force for ecological
    consciousness, 23, 62, 86, 87, 89, 90, 92, 93,
    94, 158
  as a limitation to ecological consciousness, 84
  ostensible limitation in Native peoples, 82, 85
  and posthumanist thought, 159, 161
  psychedelic pulverization of, 82, 83, 84, 85
  relationship to ego, 83
  role in Lacanian psychoanalysis, 84, 85
  and Zen Buddhism, 94, 159
  loss of capacity in *Song of Solomon*, 95, 113
Latour, Bruno: "political religion", 153, 156, 162
Leary, Timothy, 60, 64–7, 69, 70, 77–8
Leopold, Aldo: land ethic of, 47, 101–2, 104
Levy, Ariel, 79
liberalism:
  in conflict with cultural nationalisms, 98, 107,
    108, 118, 119, 130, 131
  and environmentalism, 99, 102
  in postwar America, 7, 36, 106
  as universalist ideology, 2, 98, 153
Liberation, 27
libertarianism, 176, 208
  relationship to socialism, 32
Light, Andrew, 212
literary environmentalism, 18, 29
Loeffler, Jack, 29
London, Jack: influence on Christopher
    McCandless, 172, 176, 177
Lopez, Barry: *Arctic Dreams*, 36, 42, 58
Love, Glen A. and Cheryl Glotfelty:
    The Ecocriticism Reader, 39
Lovelock, James, 102
LSD, 59, 64–72
Lynch, Tom, 49

MacIntyre, Alasdair, 95, 130
Macy, Joanna, 59, 64–72, 193
Malcolm X, 108, 110
Marcus, Sharon, 18, 199
Marcuse, Herbert, 3, 10, 30, 44, 49
  Eros and Civilization, 37–9, 40, 54
  One-Dimensional Man, 37
  comparison with other psychoanalytical
    thinkers, 53, 66, 80, 224
  ecological philosophy of, 38–9
  and the New Left, 7, 8, 29, 37
  "repressive desublimation", 172, 198
Marine Mammal Protection Act, 100
Marxism: "first and second nature" of, 33
material ecocriticism, 25, 199, 201–2

matter:
  as essence, 10, 24, 137, 156, 164, 192
  identification with, 42, 43, 98, 135, 136, 151, 153
  vitality of, 5, 156–63, 165, 201–2, *see also* new
    materialism
Matthiessen, Peter:
  The Snow Leopard, 22, 62, 68–74
  and Allen Ginsberg, 79
  and the American counterculture's
    psychoanalytic inspirations, 22, 71
  dissolution rhetoric of, 68–74, 202
  and dissolution's failure, 62, 74, 94
  and the "illusion of the ego", 63
  and Indigenous romanticism, 75–7
  perspective on language's relationship to
    ecological consciousness, 82, 95, 158, 163
  and (the failure of) psychedelic "consciousness
    expansion" as a means to ecological
    consciousness, 62, 68–74
  resistance to environmentalist identity
    politics, 207
  and social justice, 93
  on Zen Buddhism's facilitation of ecological
    consciousness, 68–74
McCandless, Christopher:
  as central figure of *Into the Wild*, *see Into the
    Wild*
  as culmination of environmentalist identity
    politics, 18, 148, 171, 172, 177, 179, 194, 198
  psychoanalytic logic of, 9
  white masculine undertones of, 13
McKenna, Dennis, 78–9, 84, 97
McKenna, Terence, 16, 60, 78–80, 82, 84–5, 97
McKissick, Floyd, 107
Meißner, Hanna, 202
Merchant, Carolyn, 12
merger:
  and death or extinction, 24, 91, 103, 163
  fantasies of, 9, 89, 95, 116, 189
  narrative aspects of, 74, 88, 89, 123, 166, 194
  psychedelic experience of, 15, 66, 82
  in psychoanalysis, 66
  as romantic aesthetics, 40, 93, 96, 162
Metzner, Ralph, 65, 78, 80
Mills, C. Wright: *White Collar*, 3, 30
mimesis, 41
mirror stage, 84, 90
Mitchell, Juliet, 8, 134
Momaday, N. Scott, 89, 219
Moraga, Cherríe and Gloria Anzaldúa: *This
    Bridge Called My Back*, 222
Morgan, Robin: *Sisterhood Is Powerful*, 138
Morrison, Toni:
  Beloved, 116, 117, 120
  A Mercy, 119, 120, 123

250 Index

Morrison, Toni (cont.)
 Song of Solomon, 14, 23, 95–9, 102–4, 108–31
 attitude toward Black nationalism, 99, 111, 113
 attitude toward (liberal) universalism, 98, 118, 119, 120
 attitude toward climate change, 98, 128
 critique of authenticity, 18, 23, 99
 critique of discursive connections between race and nature, 104
 critique of the wilderness concept, 99, 117, 118, 119, 120
 and expectations regarding African-American writing, 104
 maternal boundary-blurring in works by, 116, 117
 perspective on role played by narrative in community self-definition, 113, 124, 126, 158, 163, 168
 resistance to environmentalist identity politics, 207
 skepticism toward romantic Blackness, 124
Morton, Timothy, 12, 21
 on dissolution, 15
 on queer ecology, 204
Movement, *see* New Left
mushrooms, *see* psilocybin

Naess, Arne, 16, 102, 178–81, 192–3
narcissism:
 as collapse between self and other, 122, 124, 126, 129
 as infantile psychic condition, 37, 53, 55, 66, 70, 71, 151, 154, 180, 186, 188, 193, 203, 218
 in queer theory, 204
Nash, Roderick Frazier, 100
National Congress of American Indians (NCAI), 107
National Indian Youth Council (NIYC), 105–8
National Sacrifice Area, 86
Nation of Islam, 107
Native American Church, 78
Native American Renaissance, 89
natural rights tradition, 98, 100
nature: as "real" foil to "artificial" culture, *see* culture *and* civilization
nature feminism, 12, 153
 definition of, 134
 continuity with new materialism, 24, 137, 158, 162
 as environmentalist identity politics, 135, 148
 and identification with reproduction, 140
 and nature/culture dualism, 145
 see also ecofeminism
nature writing, 37, 41, 73
Nelson, Gaylord, 27

Nelson, Robert M., 88
Neo-American Church, 78
neoliberalism: in relation to the wilderness narrative, 173, 198
neoprimitivism, 12, 57
network:
 as critical paradigm, 25, 136, 152, 153, 158, 206
 ecology as, 5, 15, 147, 152, 159, 163, 164, 200
 and essentialism, 24, 153, 161, 168
 and psychoanalysis, 55, 154, 155, 157, 158
 vitality of, 137, 199, 201
New Age, 22, 32, 60–1, 74, 77, 80, 94, 105, 134, 153
New Left:
 collapse of, 58, 63
 in contrast to Old Left, 7, 32
 contributions to radical environmentalism, 10, 22, 33, 45, 53
 distrust of mainstream environmentalism, 27, 34, 197
 effort to reconcile self and ecology, 2, 4, 57
 ideological overlap with Edward Abbey, 28, 29, 30, 31, 35, 36, 41, 42, 44, 45, 47
 influence on Christopher McCandless, 172
 misogyny of, 13, 32, 48, 138
 normative critique of American liberalism, 100
 political legacy of, 208
 and politics of authenticity, 2, 3, 7, 9, 30, 42, 60, 63, 115
 psychoanalytic influences, 7, 8, 9, 37–9, 145
 relationship with Murray Bookchin, 31, 32, 34, 54
 relationship to racial politics, 11, 77, 97
 see also Students for a Democratic Society
New Left Notes, 34
Newman, Karen, 56
Newmark, Julianne, 112
new materialism, 137, 202
 definition and intellectual scope of, 157–60
 continuity with nature feminism, 24, 137, 158, 162
 critique by scholars of color, 158
 rhetorical overlap with environmentalist identity politics, 160–4
new social movements, 2, 9, 42, 97, 106
The New Yorker, 79
New York Federation of Anarchists, 33
Nixon, Richard, 86

Oakes, Richard, 105
Oedipal complex, 154, 203
ontology, 115
 "flat" ontology, 163
 and the network paradigm, 137, 155, 156
 and representation, 157, 160
oral tradition, 89–91, 106

Index

organicism, 102, 204, *see also* Gaia hypothesis
Organization for Afro-American Unity, 108
Orlie, Melissa A., 160, 162
Ortiz, Simon J.:
    Fight Back: For the Sake of the People, For the Sake of the Land, 86
    Going for the Rain, 87
    A Good Journey, 87
    Woven Stone, 23, 86–92
    on Native-American literary nationalism, 106
    on American settler-colonialism, 91, 106
    beat-generation influences on, 87
    environmental justice of, 62, 89–91
    on Indigenous environmentalism, 90–1
    on oral tradition, 89–91, 106
    perspective on narrative's relationship to Native identity and environmentalism, 62, 63, 88–90, 93, 94, 98, 126, 158, 159, 163, 200
    resistance to countercultural projections of authenticity onto Native peoples, 14, 18, 23, 62, 85–6, 89–91, 200
    resistance to environmentalist identity politics, 207
    on romantic stereotypes among Native peoples, 81, 112
Osmond, Humphrey, 65
Outka, Paul, 104
Outside magazine, 171

Pasternak, Boris: influence on Christopher McCandless, 176
pastoral:
    as literary mode, 74, 119
    as characterization, 123
patriarchy: relationship to civilization concept, 134, 140, 143, 144, 146
Pease, Donald E., 96
Peirce, Charles Sanders, 19, 206
People of Color Environmental Leadership Summit, 130
personalism: and the America counterculture, 8, 32, 64, 74
Phillips, Dana, 4
pleasure principle, 10, 66, 186, 187, 188
Plumwood, Val:
    critique of deep ecology, 12, 181, 193, 205
    critique of nature feminism, 133, 140–1
    critique of social ecology, 214
Poirier, Richard, 14, 19, 205
politics of difference, 107
Port Huron Statement, 2, 7, 30, 32, 37
postcritical reading, 199
posthumanism, 152, 154, 158, 162, 163, 200, 201
pragmatism, 19
preservationism, 9, 93, 105

psilocybin, 61, 64, 78, 79, 80
psychedelics:
    and the American counterculture, 22–3, 59–61, 63–8
    and ecology, 68–70, 72–4, 78–81, 156
    entheogenic use of, 60, 65, 78, 94
    and primitivism, 61–2, 80–5, 91
Psychedelic Experience, The, 65
psychoanalysis:
    and deep ecology, 172
    diminishment in influence of, 2, 136, 153, 154, 172, 202
    Edward Abbey's distrust of, 39
    feminist revisions of, 24, 134, 144, 145
    interactions with ecology, 1, 2, 4, 18, 21, 29, 38, 39, 53, 61, 154
    midcentury prominence of, 5
    as narrative structure for environmentalist identity politics, 17, 21, 202, 209
    Left Freudian (Marxist) revisions of, 8, 38–40, 66
    and posthumanist thought, 158
    poststructuralist critique of, 154, 155, 157
    and psychedelics, 65, 84
    in the work of Murray Bookchin, 57
    and Zen Buddhism, 71
Pueblo, 14, 62, 75, 76, 85, 87, 88, 89, 90, 92, 200

quantum mechanics, 160
queer ecology, 202, 204, 205
queer theory, 202, 203

racism, 32, 34, 41, 91, 98, 106, 115, 129, 131, 210
Rahimtoola, Samila, 203, 204
Rat, 34
Ray, Sarah Jaquette, 98
reading: paranoid or suspicious versus generative or reparative, 18, 19, 199, 200, 201
realism, 41, 158, 182
reality principle, 10, 38, 39, 186, 187, 188, 204
Red Power, 108, 112, 130
Regan, Tom: *The Case for Animal Rights*, 100
Reich, Wilhelm, 8, 224
replication: as ecological transformation of matter, 136, 148, 152, 162, 222, *see also* Haraway, Donna
representational strategy, 14
repression:
    and the American counterculture, 63
    in feminist thought, 134
    as a limit on ecological awareness, 11, 72, 75, *see also* identity politics of ecology
    in Marcusan and other Left Freudian philosophy, 8, 38, 53, 66

Index

repression (cont.)
  and the network paradigm, 154, 158, 160, 161, 164, 202
  in New left thought, 2, 30, 31, 58
  as a psychoanalytical aspect of civilization, 36, 179, 186, 188
  in queer ecology, 203, 204
reproduction: identification with, 24, 136, 142, 148, 152, 162, 165
Revolutionary Action Movement (RAM), 107
rhizome, 157, *see also* Deleuze and Guattari
Rich, Adrienne, 133
rights-of-nature philosophy, 102, 106, 130
Roach, Catherine, 12, 134
Rolston, Holmes, 101
romanticism:
  as an American literary movement, 20
  as idealistic tendency, 40, 113, 115, 124
Roorda, Randall, 41, 216
Rorty, Richard, 201
Rossinow, Doug, 7
Roszak, Theodore:
  comparisons between landscape and race, 104
  ecological theory of, 10, 13, 39, 54, 156
  and the Freudian Left, 38, 53
Routley, Richard and Val: "human chauvinism", 100
Ruess, Everett, 183–5
Ruether, Rosemary Radford, 140
Rustin, Bayard, 106
Ryder, Richard: "speciesism", 100

Sandel, Michael J., 130
Santa Barbara oil spill, 5
Saverin, Diana, 171
Savio, Mario, 44–5
Savoy, Lauret, 105
Schaller, George, 68, 72, 74
schizophrenia:
  and Deleuze and Guattari, 155, 224
  and psychedelics, 79, 80
Schultes, Richard Evans and Albert Hofmann: *Plants of the Gods*, 80
Schweitzer, Albert, 96
Searles, Harold F., 10
Sedgwick, Eve Kosofsky, 18
Seed, John, 170, 193
selfhood:
  dismissal of, 3, 58, 181
  dissolution of, *see* dissolution
  erasure of, 18, 19, 20, 53, 62, 73, 116, 119, 124, 166, 173, 183, 184, 185, 198
  expansion of, 17, 52, 53, 191
  inflation of, 124, 173
  as narrative, 42, 56, 93, 94

self-fulfillment, as a Movement value, 8, 9, 14, 22, 31, 35, 37, 43, 53, 54
self-liberation, as a Movement value, 38, 54, 66, 176
  shattering of, in queer theory, 203, 204, 205, 206
  in tension with ecological interconnectivity, 8, 14, 15, 19, 58, 137, 192, 194, 205, 208
Serres, Michel, 101
sexism, 32, 41, 138
Seymour, Nicole, 202
shamanism: and psychedelics, 68, 76, 78, 79, 80
Shepard, Paul, 5
  Nature and Madness, 10
  on ecology's relationship to psychoanalysis, 39–40
Sierra Club, 99, 100
Signs, 139
Silko, Leslie Marmon, 88, 89, 91, 92, 126, 216
slavery: as compared to environmental degradation, 104–5
Smith, Paul Chaat, 105
Snow Leopard, The (Matthiessen):
  and the American counterculture's psychoanalytic inspirations, 22, 71
  antipastoral aesthetics of, 73
  dissolution in, 68, 70, 74
  dissolution's failure in, 74, 94
  facilitation of ecological consciousness by Zen Buddhism in, 68–74
  and Indigenous romanticism, 77
  literary antecedents of, 73
  psychedelic aesthetics of, 72, 73
  (the failure of) psychedelic "consciousness expansion" as a means to ecological consciousness in, 62, 68–74
Snyder, Gary, 6, 60, 63, 82, 84, 87
  The Old Ways, 75
  Turtle Island, 75, 216
  and Indigenous Americans, 75, 76, 89, 93, 216
  and psychoanalysis, 4–5, 6, 11
  and Zen Buddhism, 73, 74, 75
social construction, 3, 5, 167, 205
  and new materialism, 158, 162
  and queer ecology, 203, 204
  relationship to language, 158, 161
social ecology, 10, 22, 30, 31–4
  and the American counterculture, 76
  relationship to deep ecology, 34, 133, 178, 212
  relationship to psychoanalysis, 53–5
  and spontaneity, 70, 111
socialism, 7, 77
  and libertarianism, 8, 32

Index

Song of Solomon (Morrison):
  conflict between liberal universalism and racial authenticity in, 108–9
  dissolution in, 23, 95, 96, 99, 102–4, 113, 114, 115, 116, 118, 123, 124, 125, 127, 129, 130, 131
  and environmental justice, 129–31
  juxtaposition of Black nationalism and environmentalist identity politics, 23, 113–16
  pastoral characterization in, 120–4
  relationship between nature, gender, and misogyny in, 117–20, 121, 124
  representation of Black nationalism in, 109–12
  the role of names in, 126–8
  and the wilderness narrative, 117–24
Spiegel, Marjorie, 133
spirituality, 60, 70, 77, 82, 96
  East Asian, 52, 73, 159
  and the Gaia hypothesis, 153, 162
  Indigenous American, 51, 76, 87
  see also Gaia hypothesis *and* Zen Buddhism
spontaneity:
  and ecological politics, 47, 111, 178
  and language, 82
  and Zen Buddhism, 70
Stanford, Max, 107
state of nature:
  as aspect of the American wilderness narrative, 23, 119
  as aspect of the psyche, 10, 20, 99, 115, 125, 186, 187
  as concept in liberal philosophy, 120
Stegner, Wallace, 37, 59, 184
Stewart, James T., 110
Stone, Christopher, 99–101, 104
Strayed, Cheryl: *Wild*, 195
Student Nonviolent Coordinating Committee (SNCC), 29, 107, 137
Students for a Democratic Society (SDS), 22, 29, 30, 60, 153
  and authenticity, 2, 8, 9, 37, 63
  and Murray Bookchin, 32, 34
  and race, 77, 107, 111
  sexism of, 137
Supertramp, *see Into the Wild*
Surfacing (Atwood):
  agency of the narrator in, 168, 200
  American imperialism in, 138, 148, 149
  anti-essentialism of, 136, 164, 167, 168, 169
  commodification of authenticity in, 196–7
  critique of biological reduction in, 24, 143
  dissolution in, 135, 136, 150, 168
  ecofeminist readings of, 138, 139, 141
  excavation of psychic depth as dismissal of womanhood in, 146, 147
  historical context of, 153

  identification with fetus as expression of essence in, 148, 149, 150, 151
  identification with network in, 24, 135, 136, 137, 148, 151, 152, 155
  identification with reproductive capacity in, 148
  language as limitation on ecological consciousness in, 158, 159, 161
  nature-feminist resonances of, 24, 142, 143
  portrayal of countercultural chauvinism in, 137, 138
  relationship between death and ecological authenticity in, 164–6
  significance of abortion in, 145
Szasz, Thomas, 80

Tagnani, David, 214
Taylor, Charles, 107, 130
Taylor, Dorceta, 105
technology: counterposed against nature, 33, 36, 45, 47, 52
Termination and Relocation, 91, 106
Terry, Jennifer, 117
Thom, Mel, 106, 108
Thoreau, Henry David, 27, 73
  influence on Christopher McCandless, 172, 175, 176, 177
Tolstoy, Leo: influence on Christopher McCandless, 176
Trail of Broken Treaties, 112
transpersonal psychology, 77
Treadwell, Timothy, *see Grizzly Man*
Ture, Kwame, *see* Carmichael, Stokely

Udall, Stewart, 106
unconscious:
  in psychoanalysis, 38, 66, 155
  and psychedelics, 65
  and language, 83, 84
  ostensible relationship to Indigenous peoples, 76
  relationship to nature, 1, 10, 39
  and religion, 71
universalism:
  conflicts with cultural nationalism, 96, 98, 105, 106, 107, 108, 109, 115, 130
  and environmentalism, 57, 101, 112, 113, 119
  as a liberal political value, 2, 23, 100
utopianism, 32, 106

Versluis, Arthur, 60
virtuality, 152
vitality, 14, 137, 156, 174, *see also* matter *and* new materialism

254 Index

Vizenor, Gerald, 112
Vogue magazine, 209

Warren, Karen, 12
Warrior, Clyde, 108
Warrior, Robert Allen, 105
Watts, Alan W., 60, 64
  perspective on language's relationship to
    ecological consciousness, 82, 83, 84, 159, 163
  and psychedelics, 65, 69
  and psychoanalysis, 65, 71, 93–4
  relationship to Timothy Leary, 67
  and Zen Buddhism, 68, 70, 71, 76, 93–4, 96,
    153, 159
Watts riots, 107
Weather Underground, 58, 78
Weisberg, Barry, 27, 28, 30, 44
Whitman, Walt: influence on Peter
  Matthiessen, 73
Whole Earth Catalog, 43, 76, 197
Whyte, William H.: *The Organization Man*, 3
Williams, Terry Tempest: *Refuge*, 132
Wolfe, Cary, 152
Wolfe, Tom: *The Electric Kool-Aid Acid Test*, 59,
  67, 73
Womack, Craig S., 89, 106
womb:
  and psychedelics, 80
  in *Desert Solitaire*, 48, 50, 55, 56
  in *Woven Stone*, 87
  in *Song of Solomon*, 121, 123, 124
  in the novels of Margaret Atwood, 142, 150,
    151, 165
woman:
  biological reduction of, 134, 135, 140, 142,
    151, 165
  as essential identity, 24, 135, 139
  identified with nature, 140, 141, 144, 145

as metaphor for nature, 44, 48, 80, 123
women's liberation, 2, 100, 138
Woven Stone (Ortiz):
  beat-generation influences on, 87
  dissolution (as effect of colonialism) in, 62,
    91, 92
  environmental justice in, 62, 93
  narrative construction of ecological
    relationships in, 23, 88–91
  narrative construction of identity in, 89–90,
    94
  and the Native American renaissance, 89
  resistance to countercultural projections of
    authenticity onto Native peoples in, 85–6
  tension between selfhood and ecosystem in, 88
wilderness narrative:
  traditional, as a spatial distinction between
    nature and culture, 1, 118, 172, 184
  revised by environmentalist identity politics, as
    a psychic distinction between nature and
    culture, 23, 99, 119, 162, 172, 194
  commodification of, 173
  exclusionary aspects of, 23, 99, 118, 119
  persistence in posthumanist thought, 160, 162
Wilderness Act, 100, 118

yajé, *see* ayahuasca
Yippies, 34

Zaretsky, Eli, 224
Zen Buddhism, 60, 70, 82
  apolitical nature of, 93–4
  and the beat generation, 74–5, 87
  and dissolution, 69
  and language, 159
  relationship to ecology, 72, 153
  relationship to psychoanalysis, 71
  in *The Snow Leopard*, 69–72

Recent Books in This Series (*continued from page ii*)

174. STACEY MARGOLIS
Fictions of Mass Democracy in Nineteenth-Century America
173. PAUL DOWNES
Hobbes, Sovereignty, and Early American Literature
172. DAVID BERGMAN
Poetry of Disturbance
171. MARK NOBLE
American Poetic Materialism from Whitman to Stevens
170. JOANNA FREER
Thomas Pynchon and American Counterculture
169. DOMINIC MASTROIANNI
Politics and Skepticism in Antebellum American Literature
168. GAVIN JONES
Failure and the American Writer
167. LENA HILL
Visualizing Blackness and the Creation of the African American Literary Tradition
166. MICHAEL ZISER
Environmental Practice and Early American Literature
165. ANDREW HEBARD
The Poetics of Sovereignty in American Literature, 1885–1910
164. CHRISTOPHER FREEBURG
Melville and the Idea of Blackness
163. TIM ARMSTRONG
The Logic of Slavery
162. JUSTINE MURISON
The Politics of Anxiety in Nineteenth-Century American Literature
161. HSUAN L. HSU
Geography and the Production of Space in Nineteenth-Century American Literature
160. DORRI BEAM
Style, Gender, and Fantasy in Nineteenth Century American Women's Writing
159. YOGITA GOYAL
Romance, Diaspora, and Black Atlantic Literature
158. MICHAEL CLUNE
American Literature and the Free Market, 1945–2000
157. KERRY LARSON
Imagining Equality in Nineteenth-Century American Literature
156. LAWRENCE ROSENWALD
Multilingual America: Language and the Making of American Literature
155. ANITA PATTERSON
Race, American Literature, and Transnational Modernism

154. ELIZABETH RENKER
The Origins of American Literature Studies: An Institutional History

153. THEO DAVIS
Formalism, Experience, and the Making of American Literature in the Nineteenth Century

152. JOAN RICHARDSON
A Natural History of Pragmatism: The Fact of Feeling from Jonathan Edwards to Gertrude Stein

151. EZRA TAWIL
The Making of Racial Sentiment: Slavery and the Birth of the Frontier Romance

150. ARTHUR RISS
Race, Slavery, and Liberalism in Nineteenth-Century American Literature

149. JENNIFER ASHTON
From Modernism to Postmodernism: American Poetry and Theory in the Twentieth Century

148. MAURICE S. LEE
Slavery, Philosophy, and American Literature, 1830–1860

147. CINDY WEINSTEIN
Family, Kinship and Sympathy in Nineteenth-Century American Literature

146. ELIZABETH HEWITT
Correspondence and American Literature, 1770–1865

145. ANNA BRICKHOUSE
Transamerican Literary Relations and the Nineteenth-Century Public Sphere

144. ELIZA RICHARDS
Gender and the Poetics of Reception in Poe's Circle

143. JENNIE A. KASSANOFF
Edith Wharton and the Politics of Race

142. JOHN MCWILLIAMS
New England's Crises and Cultural Memory: Literature, Politics, History, Religion, 1620–1860

141. SUSAN M. GRIFFIN
Anti-Catholicism and Nineteenth-Century Fiction

140. ROBERT E. ABRAMS
Landscape and Ideology in American Renaissance Literature

139. JOHN D. KERKERING
The Poetics of National and Racial Identity in Nineteenth-Century American Literature

138. MICHELE BIRNBAUM
Race, Work and Desire in American Literature, 1860–193

137. RICHARD GRUSIN
Culture, Technology and the Creation of America's National Parks

136. RALPH BAUER
The Cultural Geography of Colonial American Literatures: Empire, Travel, Modernity

135. MARY ESTEVE
The Aesthetics and Politics of the Crowd in American Literature

Lightning Source UK Ltd.
Milton Keynes UK
UKHW010747091220
374873UK00002B/3